CICERO'S CAESARIAN SPEECHES

HAROLD C. GOTOFF

CICERO'S
CAESARIAN SPEECHES

A Stylistic Commentary

The University of North Carolina Press   Chapel Hill & London

© 1993 The University of North Carolina Press
All rights reserved
Manufactured in the United States of America

The paper in this book meets the guidelines for permanence and
durability of the Committee on Production Guidelines for Book
Longevity of the Council on Library Resources.

Library of Congress Cataloging-in-Publication Data

Cicero, Marcus Tullius.
[Orationes. Selections]
Cicero's Caesarian speeches : a stylistic commentary / [edited by]
Harold C. Gotoff.
p.   cm.
Includes bibliographical references and index.
ISBN 0-8078-2075-X (cloth : alk. paper). — ISBN 0-8078-4407-1
(pbk. : alk. paper)
1. Speeches, addresses, etc., Latin.   2. Rome—History—53–44
B.C.—Sources.   3. Cicero, Marcus Tullius—Style.   4. Latin
language—Style.   5. Caesar, Julius.   I. Gotoff, Harold C.
II. Title.
PA6279.A67   1993
875'.01—dc20   92-50816
CIP

97   96   95   94   93   5   4   3   2   1

Harold C. Gotoff, professor of classics at the University of
Cincinnati, is author of *The Transmission of the Text of Lucan in
the Ninth Century* and *Cicero's Elegant Style: An Analysis of the
"Pro Archia."*

FOR LEILA AND DANIEL

multas variasque res in hac vita nobis natura

conciliavit, sed nulla nos magis quam eorum qui

e nobis essent procreati caritate devinxit.

Macrobius *Saturnalia* 1.1

CONTENTS

Acknowledgments   ix

Introduction   xi

Sigla and Abbreviations   xlv

Pro Marcello   3

Commentary   11

Pro Ligario   95

Commentary   105

Pro Rege Deiotaro   185

Commentary   197

Glossary   273

Bibliography   285

Index of Citations   291

General Index   299

ACKNOWLEDGMENTS

I am fortunate in being able to thank two institutions for material help in producing this book. First, I am pleased to express my gratitude to the National Endowment for the Humanities, which awarded me a grant for individual research in 1984–85. It was during this period that I realized the application of the stylistic studies I was developing to an understanding of the presentation of the Ciceronian speech. Further, I am happy to acknowledge the generosity of the Louise Taft Semple Fund of the Department of Classics, University of Cincinnati, in granting support for full-time summer research.

L'Institut de Recherche et d'Histoire des Textes, Paris, expeditiously provided me with microfilms of some of the important manuscripts containing the Caesarian speeches.

Joseph Garnjobst, Elizabeth Miller, and Herman Pontes, graduate students at the University of Cincinnati, helped me make this manuscript presentable and comprehensible; I thank them for having fulfilled their laborious tasks so competently. I was fortunate also to have the acute comments of a splendid Ciceronian, Professor Alan Douglas, on an earlier draft, and the help and encouragement of a friend and colleague, Professor Christopher Craig. Two readers for the University of North Carolina Press made many suggestions that have much improved this final version.

I am especially grateful, in these days when philology in general and commentaries in particular seem not much prized, to Lewis Bateman, Laura Oaks, and the rest of the staff of the University of North Carolina Press for their interest in publishing this kind of book.

1. *Reading Cicero's Oratory*

The unique factor common to Cicero's three Caesarian speeches is that they were delivered before Rome's master by Rome's master orator. Everything hinges on the complex psychological relationship between the two men. Cicero's contemporary letters tell much about his shifting attitude toward the dictator in the years leading up to these works. To a certain extent, however, we must extrapolate from the orations themselves what Cicero thought about Caesar and what he thought Caesar thought about him. I focus on the psychological relationship between the orator of the *Caesarianae* and their singular audience here in the Introduction and, where apposite, in the commentary. The commentary, with a somewhat different philological approach to elucidation, attempts a rhetorical and stylistic analysis focused on the same point, which must be the basis for understanding these speeches.

My work is intended to complement, on a linguistic and stylistic level, that of a number of scholars who in the last fifty years have enhanced the study and appreciation of Cicero's speeches by looking past the traditional subjects of Ciceronian studies and examining the orations as dramatic performances, whether in the courtroom, the Forum, or the Senate. This is practical rhetoric, more vital and more interesting than the mere outlining of speeches and labeling of figures of speech and thought. It is also, finally, the only way to understand and appreciate the brilliance of Cicero and his enormous success. The practice of oratory and its place in Republican politics and society, subjects exciting in themselves, become more meaningful when the work of their only extant exponent is understood, not as set pieces for the edification of later readers, but as the stock in trade of the professional politician, a man who put his competence and authority on the line every time he performed.

The great contribution of Richard Heinze's commentary on *Pro Caelio* and of the more recent works by C. Neumeister, J. C. Classen, and W. Stroh has been to concentrate on the psychology of the oratorical event and examine the ways in which Cicero responds to the demands particular to each case. Every rhetorical stance, every anecdote, every argument, every inflection of a speech, and the manner in which each of these is presented, is calculated to control and direct the attitude of a defined audience in a particular situation. Accuracy, historicity, and logical consequence have no validity except insofar as they contribute to that end. Opinions that Cicero expresses may or not be his own, and need not be consistent between speeches or even within a single work. The arguments Cicero puts forth, whether to elucidate or obfuscate, have the overriding goal of convincing his audience. All is fair in love, war, and oratory. Evidence, facts, and logic are there to be manipulated through the techniques of rhetoric and molded into instruments of persuasion. The voice we hear in the speeches is not that of a teacher or a philosopher. Its goal is not education, but psychological manipulation. Once the votes are counted, judges, senators, the whole Roman people can go back to their usual occasions, just as long as they attended to Cicero's performance and, for whatever reason, were moved to cast their ballots or voice their opinions in accordance with his direction.

To appreciate the art of Cicero, the reader must know something of the artistic conventions that produced the author and within which he worked, especially for an art form as self-consciously traditional as Latin literature. Convention is not all; but without conventions there would be no art. For Cicero, the protocols of the Latin language, of oratorical styles, and of the public channels for oratorical expression created expectations in the minds of listeners—expectations with which the orator could work in controlling his audience.

1.1. Components of Style

The author's control comes partly from the choices he makes in what material he presents (narrative, argument, disquisition, harangue, digression, etc.), the way he presents it (dramatically, didactically, amusingly, intimately, etc.), and where it appears in the work. But the author does not direct his audience by content alone. Every feature of the language he uses—vocabulary, grammar, syntax, composition, rhythm—is calculated to achieve an effect, though never on the basis that for each feature a single corresponding effect is achieved. It is these areas primarily that my commentary addresses. No modern reader of an ancient language can have a reliable intuition of the connotations of its words. Distinctions that would come instinctively to speakers of a modern language do not naturally strike a reader when they occur in Latin or Greek. We supply that loss only by discovering the frequency with which the word is used by classical authors and the range of meanings it has in substantially understood contexts. Such systematic close reading is the basis of philology. The information is often capable of a distressing range of interpretation. Nevertheless, I comment on unusual words and rare usage. Metaphors present a similar problem. We would like to know whether Cicero used a metaphor consciously or not, and if so, how elevated he felt it to be. Generally, the most we know is the frequency with which a particular metaphor is found. Other assumptions depend on context and the level of the surrounding diction.

For both grammar and syntax there is canon and choice; neither, however, is static; and so the choices and the restraints are different for different artists in different genres at different times. Cicero is considered the "norm" of Classical Latin, although I suspect that historical grammars are based at least as much on Caesar. But there is more than one Ciceronian style, even within a single genre; and that is affected by the time at which the text was produced. The modern scholar must therefore try to develop a sense of what the original audience might expect and what might be expected to surprise it. Again, a difficulty arises in determining just what was unusual *for them* and how they responded to the unexpected.

Composition is an especially potent weapon for controlling communication. Latin prose has an expected word order. Adjectives and dependent genitives are normally found near their governing nouns, an adverb should appear close to the word it modifies, even verbs and their subjects, verbs and direct objects, noun clauses and their governing verbs create expectations in the listener; and those expectations may be met, altered, or fully disappointed. The deliberate violation of such expectations, a figure called *hyperbaton,* can be employed for structural embellishment or dramatic purposes. Suspense and surprise, the stuff of drama, are very much a part of oratory; and they are achieved, among other ways, by word order.

In the matter of complex sentences, whether periodic or not, the order in which the constituent parts are presented is often determined by choice and calculation. There is also usually more than one way to express a verbal notion, from simple sentence to dependent clause (under which I include accusative and infinitive) to participial construction to ablative absolute to verbal noun with dependent genitive. Choice is determined partly by the architecture of the complex period. And that is often a function of the presentation of the argument or narrative. But the choice will often also have a dramatic effect. The structural relationship of relative clause to antecedent clause, for example, allows a variety of articulations each of which sets off different impulses in the listener and creates different emphases. In addressing the relationship between clauses and sentences, conjunctions (and their absence) become vital.

In addition to language and composition, in fact intimately related to the latter, is prose rhythm. Cicero speaks of it in various ways in the treatises (see Gotoff 2, 57–65); and he certainly considered it of prime importance. It is, however, a frustrating problem to determine just how Cicero used it and to what effect. Only a limited number of rhythms are used at the ends of periods and of syntactic elements within the period. How to describe, analyze, even count them raises some questions; but they certainly exist. The most common ones are

> 1. the double trochee or dichoraeus: ¯ ˘ ¯ ˘
> 2. the cretic + trochee/spondee: ¯ ˘ ¯ | ¯ ˘, in which either long of the cretic may be resolved into two shorts
> 3. the double cretic: ¯ ˘ ¯ | ¯ ˘ ¯.

In each case the final syllable is anceps (that is, may be short or long), according to Cicero, although Quintilian (9.4.93) claims that his ear hears a difference.

Scholars have counted these final rhythms, or *clausulae,* consciously or unconsciously applying criteria as they went. Eduard Fraenkel spent a large and profitable part of his distinguished career trying to determine Latin phraseology, the rhythm of a Latin sentence. A. Primmer attempted to relate the kind of clausula to the context in which it is used. The imaginative approach taken by both of these scholars is surely valid. All artistic prose is rhythmical; the author appeals to the ear of his audience to punctuate and color what he is saying. Molly Bloom's soliloquy at the end of Joyce's *Ulysses* proves that English prose can be heard without punctuation, if the writer produces rhythms that the reader can hear. But the subtleties of the process in Joyce might defy analysis even for a critic whose native language is English. For Latin the problem is much more difficult. I have commented on prose rhythm frequently, but not consistently throughout the commentary. Since I have no solution to the problem, I do no more than point to the phenomenon, especially insofar as it relates to word order, and encourage the reader to become sensitive to the sounds. Viewed that way, clausulae are perhaps most usefully considered like any other rhetorical technique—something to be noted as a deliberately used device the function and effect of which are determined by the context in which it is found.

1.2. Style and Effect

To cultivate a sensitivity to nuance, the critic must develop his knowledge of the artist's craft. I hope my commentary encourages a more active engagement in the reading of Cicero, an awareness of the choices Cicero had at his disposal in all the areas mentioned above. Our information on the intricacies of the Latin language is always increasing. The elementary student of Latin knows about the ablative absolute but typically will not reflect on the disastrous effect of that construction on the basic and comforting distinction between nouns and verbs. Only the more experienced reader realizes that the same transformational phenomenon is at work, not only in the title of Livy's celebrated work, but frequently enough to be called from that usage the "*ab urbe condita* construction." On a higher level of linguistic sophistication, and less well known, is the way a "weighted noun," that is, a modified noun, can become in feeling more clausal than phrasal, so that the phrasal complex can develop a circumstantial relationship to its predicate. Yet since Cicero knew how to perform such magic, it behooves the reader to notice it, and when it happens to ask why. The response to that question will not always be profound. But often context and the rhetoric of the moment will suggest a convincing answer.

Some of the phenomena mentioned above are found in ancient works on rhetoric under "figures of thought" as a subdivision of *elocutio*. I point out a number of such figures and discuss a number of them, but always in an attempt to show how their use affects the context. The reader should consider the energies of anaphora, the difference between bi- and tripartite construction, the crisp effect of hendiadys. The first job of the critic is to notice these features. Rhetorical studies too often end with mere identification; the critic will try to discern the intended impact. I make aesthetic and rhetorical judgments in the commentary, perhaps too many; but I try in every case to support the judgment with some technical observation. The reader who becomes able to identify the devices Cicero uses, and the choices he makes, will begin to form opinions on the intended effects which, so long as they are tentative, are what careful reading ought to produce.

The effect of a stylistic device depends on how it was heard—one must never forget that the *Caesarianae* were composed to be heard. One observance of a technique will rarely be enough to allow a sure sense of its effect. Hence the need to study parallel passages. I have restricted myself in providing these, first because of limited space and second because deluging the emerging Latinist with additional texts, often out of context in a language still imperfectly grasped, is of limited service. The serious student of Latin literature will get to that soon enough. It is, finally, the only path to the goal of such a reader: to know how the Latin language, especially literary Latin, works, what is conventional and what is exquisite, what a particular word, collocation of words, or syntactic construction would have conveyed to the original audience.

I sometimes supply translations when I subject the reader to parallels; but where I judge the reader will be able to render the Latin without too much difficulty, I try not to preclude the pleasure of recognition. Similarly, although most notes are cut to the bone, very occasionally I have left in a more extensive one as an example of methodology in some area of philology. I have been inexcusably ruthless with the names of scholars whose careful reading of Cicero and Latin in general and whose painstaking collection of material have made the task of a contemporary reader less daunting. They appear in the bibliography. Any student with serious intentions of becoming a reader of Cicero or Latin will have to become conversant with the modern grammarians, the lexicographer (H. Merguet stands alone and supreme), and the school commentators who in their close reading have proven themselves to be the true literary critics of Latin.

The commentary treats the three Caesarian speeches sentence by sentence as texts that demonstrate the psychology of persuasion in the peculiar circumstances that occasioned them. It encourages the reader to be aware of what Cicero is doing and why he is doing it by discerning, insofar as we can, how the original audience would have understood what Cicero was saying, as they heard it. Whether oral or written the communication is linear. Virtually every word, *as it is presented,* creates expectations. Sometimes (and I should have done it more frequently had space permitted) I use diagrams to show the progression of a period. The reader will do well to get in the habit of visualizing this linear movement.

The commentary is comparatively long and sometimes repetitive. Yet attention to details of style, in all its complexity, is necessary for an under-standing of Cicero's art. There is more material for stylistic analysis in a speech of Cicero than most students have been trained to observe. Some of this can be brought out only through a sentence-by-sentence commen-tary. He had more than one style of narrative, logical exposition, praise, or invective; his choice at any point in a speech is a function, not of whim, but of context, pacing, and impact relative to what has gone before and what will follow. Within a section the level of diction, sentence structure, even the choice of addressee are all integral parts of the total effect Cicero is aiming for. Transitions too (or their absence) force the audience to under-stand the progression of arguments in a particular way. As many as possible of these features should be noted and, I think, for pedagogical reasons, not always just once with elaborate, daunting cross-references, and not always at the first occurrence of the feature. To do so would weight the *Pro Mar-cello* inordinately and make it especially slow going, if it did not discourage the reader altogether. The reader should become more engaged as he reads, more receptive to certain kinds of observation. It is as an aid to such en-gagement that this book attempts to serve.

2. The Relationship between Cicero and Caesar

The last generation of the Republic produced the two men who of all Ro-mans have left the strongest impression on posterity, Gaius Julius Caesar and Marcus Tullius Cicero. Born within six years of each other, they died less than two years apart. On the surface they had little in common. In a class-conscious society, they were born to very different stations. Caesar was a Julian, one of the most ancient patrician families; Cicero came from the Italian countryside. Although Arpinum had enjoyed full Roman citi-zenship for some eighty years by 106 B.C. when Cicero was born, forty years later, at the height of his successful career, he could be branded by an aristocrat as an immigrant citizen of Rome—the words are Catiline's (Sall. *Cat.* 31).

Distinction of birth does not exhaust the differences between the two. Nevertheless, striking similarities also come to mind. Both were men of indefatigable energy and almost limitless ambition; both aspired to reach the pinnacle of political power; neither was satisfied to work entirely within the system. Both took great risks. Cicero, by the time he was in his middle twenties, found it advisable to absent himself from Rome after defending a client against agents of Sulla and spent some time in Rhodes in 78, purportedly to study with the rhetorician Molon. Some believe the excuse; but the notion that he would turn his back on a burgeoning career strains credulity. The turmoil of the 80's had already slowed his career.

In 75, after back-to-back prosecutions of two important Sullans, Caesar chose to pursue the same edifying and prudent diversion from City politics—same island, same teacher. This was the decade in which opponents of the senatorial establishment were reducing the effects of the conservative Sullan constitution—parlous, if heady times for an aristocrat married to the daughter of the populist Cinna and himself a nephew of the upstart Marius, or for a provincial orator from Marius' hometown who was building his reputation as the mouthpiece of the opposition to the status quo.

They both backed the right horse, at least for the time being. Cicero was elected quaestor for 75. Caesar, after successful military campaigns in the East conducted without official position, was elected military tribune for 72. In 70 Cicero succeeded in being appointed prosecutor for the trial of Gaius Verres, which would expose the extortionate behavior of a provincial governor and embarrass the Senate that had appointed Verres and was maintaining control of provincial diplomacy. The stakes were high, the political maneuvering vicious. But through diligent research and masterful practical oratory Cicero prevailed and, in the highly competitive field of political advocacy, entered the first rank of public speakers. In 69 Caesar was quaestor; but his speech of that year at the funeral of his aunt, the widow of Marius, stressed his populist associations. When the war against the Pontine king Mithridates, conducted by an optimate general, was floundering, both Cicero and Caesar advocated a special military command for a man who was constitutionally ineligible, Pompey the Great. Cicero spoke in favor of the populist law extending Pompey's command in 66 when he held the office of praetor. In the world of Roman politics neither man could have failed by this time to take notice of the other.

The deviation in the political careers of Cicero and Caesar in the late 60s arose from a shift in Cicero's outlook, occasioned by his winning the consulship in 63. If success turned his head, all but his political enemies and some modern historians will forgive him. Cicero certainly made practical use of the *auctoritas* accruing to his position; but he did not have the chance to enjoy it for long. In one of his first acts as consul he opposed an agrarian reform bill supported by Caesar and Crassus. He prevailed on that front but was soon fending off an attack on the optimates in the form of a prosecution of C. Rabirius, accused of treason in the murder of the populist tribune Saturninus in 100 B.C. Caesar's support of the populist side did not gain Rabirius' conviction (the proceeding was interrupted). It did win him enough favor in populist circles to be elected over two consulars to the august position of pontifex maximus, for which he had no immediately discernible qualifications. Caesar was still pursuing a career on the periphery of the system.

In 65 and 64, when he was not so firmly ensconced in the system and Catiline not so far removed from it, Cicero and Caesar both had dealings with C. Sergius Catilina, scion of an impoverished aristocratic family, who was effectively riding a populist wave to prominence with the financial backing of Crassus. In 66 Cicero had thought of standing for office with Catiline, later of defending him in court. The association went back to 89 and the camp of Pompeius Strabo.

Cicero and Caesar opposed each other openly for the first time on 5 December 63, in the Senate debate over punishment of the Catilinarian conspirators. Cicero urged the death penalty; Caesar spoke for life imprisonment—an early call for leniency. Cicero's position prevailed; but Caesar's had strong popular support. Cicero was honored by the optimates with the title *pater patriae* (*Sest.* 121; *parens patriae* at *Piso.* 6); but his opponents prevented him from delivering a farewell address at the end of his consulship.

As a consular in 62 and *princeps Senatus*, Cicero had reached the top of the political ladder and could not be a candidate for consul again for ten years. What could he do for an encore? He lacked the social and political connections of a Cato. Although rich, he was no match for a Crassus, who could also represent the knights. He had no military ambitions, whether because he failed to realize the political importance of military strength or because he doubted his own competence. When in 51 he was given *imperium* in Cilicia he was reluctant to accept it, as he had eschewed a foreign command in his postconsular year. Perhaps he felt that Rome was his only milieu for exerting influence and gaining power. His strength must be as senior statesman and adviser; but for that role he needed a Pompey or a Cato, a Caesar or an Octavian to advise. The alternative was retirement. Cicero was too resilient, too ambitious, and too optimistic for that.

In a treatise written later Cicero would develop the notion of the orator-statesman in the ideal State as advisor to a great public leader, as Laelius the Wise, he fancied, had guided Scipio Africanus Minor. This must have occurred to Cicero on a practical level much earlier. Pompey was his choice, but may be judged to have been an unfortunate one. The difficulty in part was that Cicero envisioned a leader who would lead within the Republican system. Neither Pompey nor those who represented the system were satisfied with such an arrangement in the late 60s. Although his attempt at a marriage alliance with Cato was rebuffed, Pompey did not with any consistency welcome the gray shadow of Cicero's eminence. Others, he felt, could do him more good. Further, the kind of "friendship" Cicero tried to develop failed because, unlike the typical *amicitiae* that shaped the Roman political system, Cicero's were too "brittle," focusing almost exclusively on ephemeral political expediency, without the reinforcement of common social background and family ties (see Rawson, 6).

Caesar, for his part, continued on the populist path, aggrandizing himself at the expense of the optimates. In 62 he took office as praetor urbanus and, with the Pompeian tribune, Metellus Celer, continued an actively populist program. This may have been a low ebb in the relationship between Cicero and Caesar, especially since Metellus, who had taken office in mid-December 63, had prevented the outgoing consul from making a farewell speech to the people. Caesar was set to support a bill permitting Pompey to stand in absentia for the consulship of 61. Parliamentary irregularities and the threat of senatorial violence forced Caesar to withdraw temporarily, but his willingness to work with Pompey would have been established.

When in 61 the intransigence of the Senate induced Pompey, Crassus, and Caesar to form their political alliance, Cicero's participation was actively enlisted. Pompey made the first overture to Cicero, who before the end of 62 was discovering that his efforts on behalf of the status quo had not earned him any long-term acceptance by the optimates. Cicero was flattered and tempted, although in the end he did not join Pompey against Cato (*Att.* 2.3.4). He claimed (*Prov. Cons.* 41) that Caesar had invited him to join the triumvirate, which invitation he refused in favor of a stance consistent with his Republican ideals. Clearly, though, he was at least sporadically tempted by the attentions of both men and in mid-60 could rationalize his position by contemplating as a service to the state the prospect of improving Caesar (*Att.* 2.1.6). A year later he was disillusioned with Pompey and could report with some glee displays of popular disaffection with both Pompey and Caesar (*Att.* 2.19). Whatever his feelings about

Caesar, Cicero makes clear that his major disappointment was with Pompey (*Att.* 2.21).

The triumvirs abandoned Cicero to his enemy Clodius in 58 and countenanced his exile. They had failed to win his allegiance; and Clodius had become a dangerous force. Cicero later gave Pompey considerable credit for his recall the next year, although there were other influential friends to thank and he enjoyed a broad-based popularity. The general enthusiasm and warmth that met him on his return made Cicero unwilling to weigh in fully with Pompey against the optimates. This seems to be a recurring theme: any possibility of acceptance within the system blinded Cicero to earlier disappointments and persuaded him not to ally himself to the dynasts.

Caesar might in any case have been a better candidate for political courtship. But it was not clear in the late 60s that he would emerge as the force he later became. He may have seemed not much different from Clodius or what Catiline had been in 66, a charismatic populist. When he was elevated to power by Pompey and Crassus, Caesar's consulship in 59 was not one of which the Republican Cicero could approve. Caesar went off to Gaul and Pompey remained in Rome, a growing disappointment to Cicero. Pompey was unwilling to use his personal *auctoritas* consistently; Caesar's power grew with his military success.

Early in 56 a Pompeian tribune advocated reform of Caesar's land settlement of 59. On 5 April Cicero proposed that the question be discussed in the Senate. He referred to his action as "charging the citadel of the triumvirate" (*Fam.* 1.9.8). The proposal was aimed mainly at Caesar and Crassus. But within ten days' time Caesar had summoned Pompey to Luca for a conference that reestablished the alliance of the three dynasts and enhanced their power. This done, Pompey put pressure on Cicero for public support of himself and Caesar, although probably Caesar had persuaded Pompey of the utility of Cicero's contribution. One way or another, Cicero was beginning to see the light: Caesar was a political force to be reckoned with—a patron to whom he could recommend friends and a general to be accommodated, just as he had attached himself to Pompey ten years before. But of the two powerful men Pompey still was Cicero's advisee of choice, for a number of reasons: they had a closer relationship, Pompey was closer to the political system, and Pompey appeared—and would continue to appear until the battle of Pharsalus—as the superior general. Cicero recorded his capitulation in the form of a letter, probably to Pompey, which he referred to as a palinode (*Att.* 4.5.1) and by which he felt himself embarrassed and degraded (*Att.* 4.6.2.)

De Provinciis Consularibus of June or July 56 publicly acknowledged Cicero's accommodation to the triumvirs by its support of Caesar's continued *imperium* in Gaul. He argues, however, that in his reconciliation with Caesar he is merely following the change of heart exhibited by the Senate itself (25). (He also used the opportunity, with great authority, to smear his personal enemies.) By 54 he found himself forced to defend in court friends of the triumvirs he had formerly prosecuted. In so doing he obliged Pompey; but he also took some pleasure in the discomfort he was coincidentally causing his former allies among the optimates who had been so unsupportive of him. In his lost speech defending his former enemy Vatinius, he openly described his action in court as a strategy taken from a lovers' quarrel in Roman comedy, perhaps to draw attention from his own capitulation (*Fam.* 1.1.19). In *Pro Plancio*, of the same year, he repeats the argument that in honoring Caesar he is echoing the opinion of the Roman people and the Senate (93). By 54 Caesar's patronage of Cicero's brother Quintus formed another link. In a letter to Quintus (*Q. Fr.* 2.13.1, February 54) Cicero affirms: "As you know, I have long since been praising your friend Caesar. Believe me, he is dear to my heart and I am sticking close to him."

Successful politics requires the ability to shift allegiance from time to time. The forces with which a politician deals are not static and reliable. By the end of 54, after so many no doubt embarrassing accommodations to Pompey, Cicero's perception of his relationship with the general began to change. In October he complained that "of all men it is only Caesar who loves me as I could wish or even, as others believe, who would want to" (*Q. Fr.* 3.5.4). The year 52 saw Cicero defending Milo against Pompey's interests; but in the final years of the 50s, when the triumvirate dissolved and Pompey was gradually weaned away from Caesar and into the establishment, Cicero remained publicly loyal to and supportive of Pompey.

Cicero was away from Italy as governor of Cilicia between June 51 and November 50, returning for the last stages of the political maneuvering that isolated Caesar. Cicero was mortified by Caesar's crossing of the Rubicon (*o perditum latronem*, *Att.* 7.18.2) and for a time hoped that an opposition, military or popularly political, would develop. He started, once more, to write with warmth about his admiration for, and relationship with, Pompey.

Early in 49, even as Caesar was trying to gain his respect, if not support (*Att.* 8.15A), Cicero described his *clementia* as *insidiosa* (*Att.* 8.16.2). His contempt for Caesar is unremitting in letters of this period to Atticus, in the face of repeated gestures of friendship from Caesar. And as the impasse developed that made civil war inevitable, Cicero never wavered in that disapproval, even as he came to lose respect for Pompey as general and politician and despaired of Cato and his cause. He was outraged by Caesar's impositions, although it became ever clearer that some accommodation must be made to him. His platform was "Pompey and peace" (as it once had been "Pompey and the Senate"), even if Pompey would have to make concessions to preserve the peace. When events and Pompey made such a position impossible, Cicero joined him in Greece in 48, reluctantly, it is true, but in honor of personal commitments and his stated principle: "better to be defeated with Pompey than to win with others"—however much Pompey had disappointed him (*Att.* 8.7, 21 February 49).

On 28 March 49, a crucial and very dangerous time for Rome and Romans, Cicero, even as he wrestled with his conscience over what course he should take, met with Caesar at Formiae (*Att.* 9.18), an interview Caesar had requested and Cicero had anticipated with some trepidation (*Att.* 9.15). Caesar, ever solicitous of the orator (or sensible of his usefulness), urged him to return to Rome and lend credibility to the Senate, which in one form or another had been convening during the crisis. The following exchange took place:

"Come along and work for peace."
"On my own terms?"
"Of course! Would I impose conditions on you?"
"My position will be that the Senate opposes an expedition to Spain and the army being dispatched to Greece. And I shall speak with great sorrow of Pompey."
"But I don't want you to talk that way."
"I assumed that; but that's just why I don't want to be there. I'd have either to say those things or stay away—and say a lot of other things that I wouldn't be able to hold back if I were present." (9.15)

Cicero is clearly pleased with his own display of integrity; whether consciously or not, he also bears witness to Caesar's respect and restraint. And this illustrates at least a facet of their developing relationship.

On 5 March Caesar had written asking to avail himself of Cicero's "advice, influence, standing, and help" (*Att.* 9.6A.1) Cicero responded (*Att.* 9.11A), in courtly terms, citing his own consistent efforts in behalf of peace and his belief that Caesar had been unfairly treated by his political enemies, but also asking respectfully but forcefully to be permitted to intercede for Pompey for his own honor's sake. It is clear from other letters at this time that Cicero was not expressing fully to Caesar a consistently held point of view; he was not, for that reason, necessarily being disingenuous. Cicero still disapproved of Caesar and his followers but was also growing impatient with Pompey and the optimates. Against this, Caesar, directly and through mutual friends, was being solicitous of Cicero; and the possibility of peace remained, along with the more frightening possibility that after Cicero declared against him, Caesar might come to terms with Pompey (*Att.* 10.8.5). Caesar was pressing Cicero not to leave Italy to join Pompey. He would have preferred Cicero in Rome lending legitimacy to the government, but he would settle for neutrality (*Att.* 10.8B).

Yet even as Cicero reiterated his determination to follow Pompey and his devotion to the man, if not entirely to his cause, his esteem was waning. He found Pompey intransigent and excessively vindictive. On leaving Rome on 17 January Pompey had threatened vengeance on towns and senators that did not support him actively (Plut. *Pomp.* 61): "Sulla could do this; shall I not be able to?" (*Att.* 9.10.2). If Caesar was committing a crime (*scelus*) by establishing a tyranny, Pompey would be doing something disgraceful (*flagitium*) by devastating Italy (*Att.* 9.10.3).

Cicero rode out the death throes of the Republic with better grace than many, well aware of the complexities of the problems, cynical about the willingness of any of the power-brokers to make the necessary accommodations. Atticus, with other friends, had been consistently advising Cicero to remain in Rome, unless Pompey should "establish himself securely somewhere." Then might Cicero leave the "underworld" of Rome and prefer being defeated with Pompey in battle to ruling with Caesar "in what would clearly be a sewer" (*Att.* 9.10.7). In spite of his strong, anti-Caesarian language, Atticus could countenance, as Cicero never could, abandoning Pompey and the cause of the optimates in the face of Caesar's "sincerity, restraint, and wisdom"—he does not add: "success" (*Att.* 9.10.9, 18 March 49). A growing number of respectable Romans were demonstrating a similar moral flexibility. So Cicero remained in Italy, agonizing not only about his own position but, and genuinely so, about the safety of his wife and children.

Eventually he did follow Pompey to Greece, with resignation rather than enthusiasm, but was not present at Pharsalus. In the wake of Pompey's defeat and subsequent death, Cicero returned to Brundisium in late 48, believing that the cause had died with its general and feeling no obligation to his successors or conviction about their legitimacy. A year later, in May 46 (*Fam.* 7.3), he would defend that position, singling out as the one unacceptable alternative an alliance with King Juba—precisely the accusation which was later leveled against Ligarius (see below, section 3.2). He was reassured by lieutenants of Caesar that the latter was concerned to protect and enhance Cicero's status (e.g., *Att.* 11.7.5) and received from Caesar a specific exemption from the ban on the return of Pompeians to Italy.

This was a period of justifiable paranoia in Cicero, bred partly of guilt. But there was no evidence that Caesar exhibited anything but goodwill toward him. More difficult for Cicero was a growing fear that the remnants of Pompey's forces, in Africa with Cato, might prevail. Caesar was at this time in Alexandria, besieged and seriously beset. There had been many good reasons to dissociate himself from the Pompeian cause after the loss of its leader, one of which was its impending capitulation. Should circumstances reverse themselves, Cicero could hope for little sympathy (*Att.* 11.16, 3 June 47).

A victorious Caesar arrived at Tarentum in late September 47. Cicero went to greet him; he was warmly met and given permission to return to Rome. According to Plutarch (*Cic.* 39), Cicero was treated with respect and friendship by Caesar from this time forward. Any fears he may have harbored about the sincerity of Caesar's clemency as from a master to his slaves (*Att.* 11.20) failed to materialize. He returned to Rome in October 47 with no intention of practicing politics as usual. Too much had changed. He determined not to speak in the Senate or openly offer his opinion; but he did attend the Senate.

The dictator was wise and unique enough to know that restoring peace was a more delicate task than winning battles and was determined not to employ the solutions that had led to executions and proscriptions in the past. Reconciliation and clemency were a more humane and efficient policy.

Scholars (e.g., Weinstock, Yavetz) now discuss what part Cicero may have played in the formation and publicizing of Caesar's platform. The dictator could have found no more eloquent spokesman than a willing Cicero (see below, section 2). But whether Caesar consciously employed Cicero for this purpose or, if he did, whether he discussed the matter with the orator or just let the rhetoric flow are questions that finally cannot be answered. Posterity has the encomium of *Pro Marcello* and the less ebullient, but still approving *Pro Ligario* and *Pro Rege Deiotaro* as evidence of Caesar's restraint and intelligence. Whether these documents should be considered propaganda pieces by a willingly co-opted Cicero or represent the orator's strategy for continued viability depends largely on the reader's perception, based on other historical evidence and these speeches themselves, of the complex and by no means consistent relationship between the two men.

A change in that relationship can be gleaned from a passage in *Brutus*, written in late 47 and early 46. Cicero's principle in this history of Roman oratory is not to mention the living, but beginning at section 248 an exception is made for two Roman consulars: M. Marcellus, the anti-Caesarian consul of 51, not yet recalled, and Caesar himself. It is significant that in referring to the Civil War in the section on Marcellus (250), Cicero uses the same language, exculpatory for all parties, that is found repeatedly in the *Caesarianae*. In late August 47 he had referred to a *fatali proelio* that would decide the issue of the Civil War (*Fam.* 15.5.2, a letter that twice acknowledges the clemency of Caesar).

The evaluation of Caesar, initiated by "Atticus" (who claims Cicero's concurrence), begins with praise for the purity of Caesar's Latinity. The focus shifts immediately to Caesar's lost grammatical treatise *De Analogia* with its dedicatory encomium to Cicero. A sentence is quoted (and thus preserved for posterity): "and if some have by study and practice achieved the ability to give noble and eloquent utterance to their thoughts—and you as the virtual founder and originator of this fluency (*copia*) we ought to regard as having performed a notable service to the fame and prestige of the Roman people—is acquaintance with this easy and colloquial style to be left on one side?" (253, tr. Douglas, 187). "Founder and originator of this fluency" is an attractive enough phrase; *copia* is a great virtue in eloquence, and that compliment is cited twice more (254 and 255). But the whole protasis serves rhetorically as a foil for Caesar's mention of his own oratorical virtue, mastery of colloquial style.

Responding in his own voice, Cicero accepts the compliment and goes on to compare the public contribution of a great orator favorably with that of a mediocre general. But as the topic is developed, the modifiers disappear as the value to society of the two professions is contrasted. Caesar was introduced as an orator, but as Brutus points out, he has not been heard in more than a decade, during which time his fame has been precisely as a general.

Atticus continues with a general discussion of pure Latinity, which he claims is acquired not so much by scholarly theory as by good usage. He cites as an earlier "corrector of common speech" the historian Sisenna, but immediately tells an anecdote to the man's disadvantage. True, in section 261 he dissociates Caesar from such excesses, but the reader may ask why the anecdote was included. Finally, he credits Caesar with not only exquisite choice of words, but ornamentality in his style and, on the basis of the two qualities, elevates him to the highest rank of orators. The implication is that the "plain" style should not be merely natural Latin, but "naturalism," artistically achieved. Brutus now concurs on the basis of having read Caesar's speeches but ends the *laus Caesaris* by praising his historical writings—a genre irrelevant to a discussion of oratorical excellence. The praise is becoming fainter. (See on *Lig.* 30, *tecum . . . te . . . tuorum*, for a full discussion of this passage and its literary aftermath.)

Beneath the surface here, in part, lies the literary-political debate evident in the 40s between the "Atticists" and "Asianists." The duration, intensity, and terms of the controversy are not clear to us (see Gotoff 2, 45–64); but it may be inferred from the polemical arguments of the *Orator* that Cicero was made to feel defensive. Caesar's antithesis and the comments of Atticus on the naturalness, as opposed to doctrine and techniques, of pure Latin, should be read to some extent in this light, although there is no direct evidence that Caesar took an active part in the debate. But the passage also suggests familiarity and the presumption of equality on intellectual, artistic, and social grounds between Caesar and Cicero, intimate but critical. It bespeaks a confident sense of parity on the part of Cicero and the willingness of Caesar to accept that sense, a willingness that can derive from nothing short of genuine respect.

Later in 46 Cicero seems to have been torn between his enthusiasm for playing some part in rebuilding the state under Caesar ("as a workman, if not an architect") and retiring, with Caesar's blessing, from public service altogether (*Fam.* 9.2.5, 7.33.2). He was being courted by Caesarians (9.16.2) and declaiming for recreation in the company of Caesar's most trusted representatives in Rome (3.33.1). It is at this time that he attributes the cause of the Civil War more to the Pompeians than to Caesar: "I saw that our friends were eager for war, while he was not so much eager as unafraid of it" (9.6.2).

We may assume, then, a gradual shift in Cicero's attitude toward Caesar leading up to a relationship of some intimacy and much mutual respect by the middle of the 40s. The death of Pompey brought an end to his hopes for the old dispensation, but no personal joy to Caesar. The reliability of Caesar's *clementia* and his courtship of Cicero were established beyond question. Besides, his was the only political game in town. After initial reluctance Cicero became a willing participant in Caesar's Rome. He conceived one of his roles to be advocate for the restoration of former Pompeians. In flattering himself that he might serve as advisor to Caesar and the new order, he did not find it too difficult to attribute worthiness to Caesar. At the least, Caesar exhibited the good judgment of appearing to want Cicero in that position.

Caesar's action in pardoning Marcellus won Cicero over completely. In a letter written soon after (*Fam.* 6.6) he praised Caesar's mercifulness, appreciation of artistic talent, openness to persuasion by personal appeals, intelligence and eye for consequence, seriousness, fairness, wisdom, and disposition to extend friendliness and respect to Cicero himself. At this point Cicero could conceive of Caesar as the restorer of the Republic.

Both oratorical and political factors inform the relationship between orator and judge in the two trials portrayed in *Pro Ligario* and *Pro Rege Deiotaro*—a confidence on Cicero's part to be frank and even critical in addressing Caesar and a disposition on Caesar's part to countenance such displays of independence. This is true even of *Pro Marcello,* where, too, Cicero sometimes adopts the role of advisor and critic. What cannot be dismissed, however, is Quintilian's sage observation (9.2.28) that displays of independence can be a form of high flattery. There is a curious statement at *Pro Ligario* 30 to the effect that Cicero had pled many cases with Caesar, back when Caesar's career was associated with the Forum. This assumption of a previous professional relationship not elsewhere attested may be just a rhetorically motivated fantasy. It consists, however, with the attitude of collegiality and mutual respect that Cicero maintains throughout.

Subsequent events convinced him that the dictator's aim was monarchy (see *Marc.* 8, *deo,* and comments there). Still the two could conduct a highly literary exchange on the subject of their opposing works on Cato, Cicero's *Cato* and Caesar's *Anti-Cato.* The very fact that Caesar chose a literary response to Cicero's encomium for the self-martyred champion of republicanism says much about the confidence and pretensions of Caesar. He praised Cicero's piece and Cicero, in turn, praised Caesar's. As late as

December 45 Cicero is credited with having extraordinary influence with the dictator (*Fam.* 5.10A, Vatinius to Cicero); and two weeks later Caesar dined with him (*Att.* 13.52.2). Cicero remembered the occasion as pleasant, if not relaxed. Conversation eschewed politics in favor of literary topics.

Cicero viewed the demise of Caesar with nothing short of glee. It provided an opportunity for public influence and power beyond anything he had known since the year of his consulship. Some think that the short time between the death of Caesar and his own execution by Antony was Cicero's finest hour. Caesar represented political tyranny, whereas Cicero always cherished a Republic which probably looked a good deal more attractive to him as memories of the realities of the 50s faded. But it need not be assumed that Cicero had been insincere in his previous dealings with Caesar. Such a view is neither cogent nor likely. Friends are not under the best conditions perfect; friendships among politicians are less likely to be untinged by serious reservations. There was much in Caesar worthy of Cicero's respect, military prowess aside. He was educated, cultivated, and possessed of substantial charisma. True, he had brought down Pompey; but Pompey was not without his flaws. (It is easier to imagine Cicero at a social affair chatting with Caesar than with Pompey.) Besides, Caesar had been good to Cicero, claiming to value his viewpoint as well as his persuasive skills. All in all, considering his hostility and his apprehensions, Cicero had a very good postbellum experience under Caesar. On 3 May 44, contrasting the government of Antony, Cicero could say of Caesar: "He was for some reason amazingly tolerant of me" (*Att.* 14.17.6). But in a more complex statement on 24 May 24 he admits: "I was so much in his good graces (may the gods confound him, dead as he is!) that at my time of life, since the killing of our master has not set us free, *he* was not a master to run away from" (*Att.* 14.4.3).

3. The Caesarian Speeches

The political circumstances of the Caesarian speeches in 46 and 45 were certainly extraordinary. Caesar had first assumed the dictatorship and given it up, then been honored by the Senate with the title *dictator perpetuus*. The Senate was very different from the one that Cicero had entered in 76 or the body that had found two hundred of its members at Pompey's side at Pharsalus. Nevertheless Caesar allowed it to sit and deliberate, even as he supported, however speciously, other Republican institutions. Cicero still had a platform for public service. The *Caesarianae*, together with his *Philippics* of 43, are the last examples of Republican oratory; but that is not something Cicero would have known. He was plying his trade as best he could under the available circumstances, just as he had done throughout his public career.

The *Caesarianae* have in common their time frame, the person before and to whom, primarily or exclusively, Cicero speaks, and the general subject of clemency for Pompeians in the wake of Caesar's victory. What makes them unique is that they pit Rome's greatest master of the psychology of persuasion against Rome's cleverest and most subtle intellect. Again and again in these speeches Cicero initiates rhetorical strategies contrived to elicit Caesar's collegiality, agreement, and sympathy. But the level of sophistication at which contact is made is extremely difficult to pinpoint. Cicero must assume that specious arguments will be detected, perfunctory flattery will be dismissed, criticism will be taken in good part only if tactfully and acceptably offered. But the orator has ways of making even specious arguments intellectually attractive, flattery seem by turns sincere and ironic, and criticism appear the height of admiration. For a modern reader armed with the historical facts surrounding the circumstances of the speeches and sensitive to the nuances of Cicero's Latin, a good part of the enjoyment of reading the *Caesarianae* will consist of the attempt, however frustrating and imperfect, to understand the levels of communication between orator and judge.

3.1. Pro Marcello

It is difficult to imagine a more exacting test of Caesar's clemency on the political level than the Senate's petition for the recall of M. Claudius Marcellus. The Claudii Marcelli, a plebeian branch of the *gens Claudia,* had been providing the Republic with generals and statesmen for more than two centuries before this Marcellus was elected consul in 51. Born into the establishment, he began his political career in 65 with the quaestorship, which he shared with Cato, who was also a friend. He had also developed a close personal relationship with Cicero, under whom he trained as an orator, and had supported him during the Catilinarian crisis in 63. He had distinguished himself as a judicial orator, defending M. Aemilius Scaurus in 54 together with Cicero, and Milo both in 56 and again in 52, once more with Cicero as his colleague.

By 51 Caesar was on a collision course with the Senate; and Marcellus' opposition to him was a foregone conclusion. The complex question of Caesar's official status hinged on a single constitutional issue. His rise to power had been offensive to the optimates, and he was vulnerable to prosecution that could ruin him politically and personally. But no magistrate with *imperium* could be prosecuted. By the terms of Luca, Caesar's command would end 1 March 49; and he would stand for the consulship of 48. That left a period of ten months in which he might face prosecution, a period Caesar wanted to cover by an extension of his Gallic command.

Marcellus' opposition was comprehensive. He proposed first to terminate Caesar's command altogether on the grounds of his success in pacifying the region and to choose his successor a year in advance. For this extreme position he could not gain the support of Pompey. He also opposed the alternative proposed by Caesar, that he be permitted to stand in absentia for the consulship. Finally, to show his contempt for Caesar's granting of citizens' rights to colonists of Novum Comum in Transpadane Gaul, he had a senator of that region, appointed by Caesar, publicly whipped and in that condition returned to his "patron." By petitioning for the recall of Marcellus, his supporters were asking a great deal of the dictator.

Yet in the crucial meeting of the Senate on 1 January 49 Marcellus appeared less extreme than some of Caesar's enemies. He was disinclined to put the Senate's fate unconditionally in the hands of Pompey and may have entertained, as Cicero suggests (*Marc.* 16), doubts about the fitness of Pompey, should he be victorious, to represent the optimate cause. As one views the period, there is a tendency to envision a simple choice between Pompey and Caesar; conservative optimates would have continued to despise both. In any case Marcellus left Rome, more out of fear of Caesar than enthusiasm for Pompey (*Att.* 9.1.4), whom he nevertheless followed to Pharsalus, where there is no evidence he took part in the fighting. Like Cicero, he considered the cause lost with that battle, and he chose voluntary exile on the island of Mytilene. There, according to Brutus, he led a blameless life of Stoic self-sufficiency and showed no inclination to ask for, or accept, Caesar's pardon.

At a meeting of the Senate in September 46, described by Cicero in *Att.* 4.4, Caesar surprised everyone by announcing his decision to indulge the wishes of the Senate and recall Marcellus. The initial request came from

Caesar's own father-in-law, L. Calpurnius Piso, and was to have been unanimously endorsed. Since the Senate must have been composed largely of men who had supported Caesar earlier or sidled over to him later, it is a little difficult to imagine this spontaneous groundswell of support for an unreconstructed optimate. Still, Cicero was overcome by the gesture (at least he so professes himself at *Att.* 6.6) and delivered *Pro Marcello* as a formal acknowledgment of Caesar's generosity. Marcellus himself appears to have been less enthusiastic about his pardon. He thanked Cicero politely, but did not begin his return journey until May 45. On that trip, at the Peiraeus, he was murdered, apparently for private reasons. Rumors of Caesar's complicity were voiced, but not taken seriously then or now.

There should be recorded, if only as a historical curiosity, the opinion of several scholars, among whom are F. A. Wolf, famous for enunciating the "Homeric question," and the excellent editor of Cicero, Orelli, that *Pro Marcello* is a forgery. The primary impulse, probably, was an inability to believe that Cicero would fawn over Caesar. Linguistic peculiarities and stylistic considerations were enlisted to support this sense, as well as the fact (not unique to *Pro Marcello*) that Quintilian does not cite the speech. But the stylistic innovations are more pronounced in *Pro Ligario,* which Quintilian cites extensively, linguistic peculiarities appear in virtually every speech of Cicero, and a close reading of *Pro Marcello* and the other *Caesarianae* reveals Cicero adopting attitudes that are anything but fawning and abject.

There is no direct evidence that Cicero oversaw publication of this speech. Unlike other *sententiae* which he did circulate, the occasion for this speech came without warning. It was a completely impromptu performance that may have been recorded by a court stenographer at the time. On the other hand, it was his first formal speech since he had left for Cilicia, and it doubtless would have found favor with Caesar; so he may have caused it to be broadcast.

3.2. Pro Ligario

Several months after the successful campaign to recall M. Marcellus, Cicero found himself working in behalf of another former opponent of Caesar. Quintus Ligarius, a member of an equestrian Sabine family that was beginning to distinguish itself at Rome, had gone to Africa as a legate to the provincial governor and been asked to remain when his principal returned to Rome. Thus he happened to be there when war broke out; and he stayed on when a lieutenant of Pompey, P. Attius Varus, usurped control of the province. Ligarius served in Varus' government, was present at the battle of Thapsus, and was captured at Hadrumetum, where, in the first weeks of 46, Caesar secured the province and spared his surviving opponents, among them Ligarius, who was, however, left in exile.

Almost immediately after Caesar's return to Rome, Quintus' brothers, with Cicero as intercessionary, began to petition for Ligarius' recall. Caesar was initially reluctant to extend leniency to Pompeians who had fought in Africa, but finally granted an audience. Although no commitment was immediately forthcoming, Cicero wrote to Ligarius full of hope on the basis of Caesar's reaction. At that point Q. Aelius Tubero requested of Caesar and was granted permission to prosecute Q. Ligarius.

The precise charge and the penalty it entails are not stated. Cicero's impassioned plea (*Lig.* 18) that dead Pompey not be accused of treason may reveal the charge against Ligarius; it may also be hyperbole. The ancient charge of *perduellio* would be heard by a two-man tribunal and carried the death penalty. A trial under this rubric, involving one Rabirius, was a *cause célèbre* in 63, but otherwise there is little historical evidence for its currency. Treason might have come under *maiestas* or *diminutio maiestatis,* with less dramatic consequences for conviction; the trial of a Roman citizen for treason in absentia would have raised larger legal questions. The dictator may certainly have undertaken to decide on such a case alone. Dio says (42.20.1), speaking of the Roman people after Pharsalus, that they empowered Caesar to take whatever action he wished against the followers of Pompey, not that he could not have done so on his own, but to give him the appearance of legal authority: (ἵνα καὶ ἐν νόμῳ δή τινι αὐτὸ ποιεῖν δόξῃ). Even in the absence of sure knowledge of the legal limitations on various Roman judicial proceedings, we may imagine that Caesar had substantial leeway.

In his speech Cicero never mentions that crime, pretending that the principal charge was that Ligarius had been in Africa, which Caesar well knew. But we learn from Quintilian (11.1.78) that Tubero had accused Ligarius of going beyond what was permitted in civil war, which he called a *dignitatis contentio,* and conspired with a foreign monarch, King Juba of Mauritania, against the Roman state. This would be an altogether more serious charge. Cicero himself (see above, section 2) had pronounced such behavior unacceptable, although Cato, whose memory Cicero cherished, would, with others, have been vulnerable to such a charge. Indeed, had Pompey's side won, Juba would have been considered a client of the Roman state. Cicero deflected attention from the actual charges by emphasizing the preternaturally strong Pompeian sympathies of the prosecutor and his father and addressing an incident that gave the Tuberones cause for personal animus against Ligarius. Varus had already seized power in Utica when the Senate ratified Lucius Tubero, father of the prosecutor, to be governor of Africa. When he reached the shores of his province, however, he was denied permission to disembark or to take on provisions—the incident is recorded by Caesar (*BC* 1.31)—in spite of his son's illness. The Tuberones sailed on to Pompey and Pharsalus, blaming Ligarius, who was in charge of coastal defenses, for the insult.

These are the circumstances that gave rise to the prosecution of Ligarius, but the problems raised by that process defy certain interpretation. As dictator, Caesar assumed the judicial prerogative of praetor to decide whether the case should be heard; he also chose to hear it himself, as sole judge, and be exclusively responsible for its disposition. He further exercised the dictator's right to administer justice publicly in the Forum. It seems unimaginable that he would so involve himself in the trial without knowing what his decision would be. But an anecdote in Plutarch (*Caes.* 39.6–7) addresses precisely this issue:

> It is said that when Q. Ligarius was being prosecuted as an enemy of Caesar's and Cicero was defending, Caesar said to his friends, "Why not listen to Cicero pleading after all this time, since in any case, it is established that Ligarius is a criminal and an enemy?" But when Cicero began to speak he affected Caesar powerfully and as the speech progressed with a variety of emotional appeals and spellbinding beauty, it was clear from his change of complexion that Caesar was moved as he registered all the emotions of his soul. Finally, as the orator was describing what took place at Pharsalus, Caesar was emotionally overcome, his body shook, and some documents fell from his hand. And so under compulsion he acquitted Ligarius.

Scholars (see Craig 1, with bibliography) tend to reject this story on the ground that Caesar was not an emotional man. The argument is specious: in a highly rhetorical society like that of Rome, men of wit and discernment must have kept a delicate balance between an intellectual appreciation of the techniques of oratory and a willingness to be moved emotionally by the effects of those techniques. Still, it strains credulity to think that Caesar would have taken time from his busy schedule—it is remarkable how little time the master of the world spent in Rome—just to hear a case concerning a little-known Sabine knight, especially a case brought by the Tuberones. And yet they belonged to an active, if plebeian family, whose participation would lend legitimacy to Caesar's postwar government. They had, however, strongly supported Pompey and had no claims on Caesar. These same scholars maintain that Caesar allowed the proceedings to go forward as a showcase trial for broadcasting political propaganda, expounded by Cicero, in support of his program of reconciliation through *clementia*. Thus the acquittal of Ligarius was a foregone conclusion. They further maintain that Cicero was a party to the charade and that he took the opportunity of producing an ingratiating, encomiastic speech dramatizing the dictator's *clementia*.

Yet given the status of the two men, the pardon of Ligarius could be no more than a pale reflection of that of Marcellus. At *Pro Ligario* 37 Cicero sets up an antithesis between the pardon of Marcellus as a service to the Senate and the recall of Ligarius as a service to the Roman people; but this is pure rhetoric. There is no evidence that Quintus Ligarius or either of his brothers had been popular figures. Besides, it takes two to reconcile; and the pardon of a Pompeian from Africa, where the resistance to Caesar was fiercest and the treatment of Caesarians most brutal, would do nothing to assuage the understandable, but politically inexpedient, desire for vengeance among Caesar's supporters. But by allowing the prosecution and then acquitting Ligarius, Caesar would win no thanks from the Tuberones.

The best evidence against the theory of a rigged trial is Cicero's speech itself. Considering the sophistication of both the judge and the defense lawyer, modern readers may never quite be able to appreciate the subtlety of Cicero's psychological maneuvering vis-à-vis his singular audience. But as a propaganda document the speech should be a clear and unambiguous paean to Caesar and *clementia*, unobscured by (1) extended attacks on the prosecutors for their cruelty, hypocrisy, and interference with Caesar's postwar policy, (2) a thinly veiled, carefully reasoned defense of the client, (3) critical and uncompromising insistence on both the dispassionate wisdom and practical necessity of a policy of reconciliation, and (4) a prominent, extradramatic discussion of the difficulties an orator incurs in defending a case of this sort. All these topics are found in the speech.

While it is difficult to read the speech as anything less than a brilliant

rhetorical instrument, strong, serious, and masterful, calculated to persuade Caesar to recall Ligarius, it is not easy to believe that Caesar was
either disinterested or, as Plutarch suggests, initially hostile but eventually
won over. But Caesar's motive may have been less complicated than modern
critics allege. As dictator he had the right to preside over justice at Rome
in public view; and perhaps the trial of Ligarius provided him with an
opportunity to show himself engaged in dispensing justice, heavily laced
with mercy, with an established crowd-pleaser leading for the defense. The
outcome of the case may have been considered less important than the fact
that it was tried—and seen to be tried—at all. Plutarch's anecdote, then,
may reflect the circumstances, especially if we are willing to entertain the
possibility that Caesar's words and Caesar's reactions may have been calculated for effect.

The speech is typically labeled a *deprecatio,* a plea that makes no attempt
at defense against the charges but lays the defendant's fate upon the mercy
of the court. Quintilian says: "The last expedient is the *deprecatio,* although most say it is never admissible in court" (7.4.17). He then quotes
Pro Ligario 30, where Cicero denies ever having pled in this way before,
and goes on: "In the Senate, however, and before the people and before
the emperor and wherever else clemency is possible in law, the *deprecatio*
has a place."

This raises the question of Caesar's status—a problem of which Cicero
was acutely aware. Was it within Caesar's competence as judge, not as
dictator, to grant clemency, rather than merely interpret the law? The distinction is as artificial as it is nice. Generally speaking, the defense attorney
uses any tactic that he thinks may persuade his judges to vote for acquittal.
Besides, given the special circumstances of the event, with Caesar sitting
as sole judge precisely because he was dictator, this question becomes
moot.

But the label *deprecatio* should not, in any case, blind the reader to the
complex strategy of the speech. Quintilian also comments:

> The *deprecatio,* however, which makes no pretense of being a defense,
> is uncommon and then only before those judges who are not bound
> by any prescribed form of judgment. Yet even those orations delivered
> before C. Caesar and the members of the triumvirate on behalf of their
> opponents, although they use entreaties, contain defense arguments
> nevertheless, unless it is not the action of a powerful defense advocate

to say, *"quid aliud egimus, Tubero, nisi ut quod hic [Caesar] potest nos possemus?"* [*Lig.* 10]. (5.13.5)

In *Pro Ligario* Cicero works hard to exculpate Ligarius, inculpate the Tuberones, and convince Caesar that a pardon would be in his, and Rome's, best interest. For the forensic purpose, a more competent and effective speech would be hard to imagine.

Whether motivated by policy or compassion, Caesar acquitted Q. Ligarius and permitted his return to Rome. In so doing he proved the dictum that no good deed goes unpunished; for on the Ides of March 44, as Plutarch tells us, Ligarius rose from a sickbed at Brutus' behest and took part in the assassination of Caesar, so gaining immortality in the pages of Shakespeare (*Julius Caesar* 2.1.215ff., 3.3.111ff.)

Caesar must have been aware (Cicero alludes to this) that he risked alienating some of his supporters who looked forward to taking vengeance on enemies both public and personal. And this extraordinary man was shrewd enough to know another psychological truth, uttered by Plutarch in regard to Ligarius himself, who "felt less grateful for having received leniency than oppressed by the power that made him need leniency" (Plut. *Brut.* 11).

The speech was delivered in the first of two intercalary months inserted between November and December 46 and copied for publication soon after (*Att.* 13.12.2). Mutual friends sent a copy to Caesar (*Att.* 13.19.2). When a factual error was brought to his attention, Cicero asked Atticus to effect the correction. But the text had been copied and distributed. The error is preserved in all extant manuscripts (see on *Lig.* 33, *videsne*). The speech was much admired in antiquity. Line for line, Quintilian cites it more than any other speech of Cicero.

3.3. Pro Rege Deiotaro

If *Pro Ligario* was unique in having been conducted in the Forum before the dictator acting as sole judge, the circumstances of *Pro Rege Deiotaro* were more extreme. Cicero had pled cases before a single judge, or a limited number, in the past, but only on quite restricted legal matters. Although in *Pro Ligario* he could not exploit the emotional interplay between the jury and the bystanders that he had capitalized on in the past, the case was conducted openly in the Forum. Deiotarus' case was heard in Caesar's home, with a radically reduced audience. Furthermore, since both cases were defenses of Pompeians, the aggrieved party ultimately was Caesar, the judge himself. This is especially true of Deiotarus' trial, in which the king was accused of plotting against Caesar's life.

Galatia, in Anatolia, was named for Celtic invaders who settled the area in the third century B.C. A political organization broken down into king-ships or tetrarchies was imposed in the aftermath of Alexander's conquests. Deiotarus (accented on the -o-) had inherited the tetrarchy of the Tolisto-boli in the western region. Besides increasing his own domain, he was re-warded by Rome for his services in wars against Mithridates VI of Pontus, fought between 88 and 63. In Pompey's settlement, ratified by the Senate in the year of Caesar's consulship (59), he received part of Pontus, including the important city of Trapezus, part of Armenia, and the title of king. He continued to ally himself with Roman interests and wars in the region, supporting, among others, Cicero as proconsul of Cilicia in 52. Both past obligation and diplomatic wisdom persuaded him to side with Pompey when the Civil War broke out. Although by then an old man, he took part in the battle of Pharsalus and only left Pompey after promising that he would raise support for him in the East.

Pompey's death relieved him of that obligation, but he was soon, in any case, preoccupied with a local war. Pharnaces, the son of Pontine Mith-ridates, invaded Lesser Armenia and Cappadocia in the hope of restoring his father's domains. Deiotarus attached himself to Caesar's lieutenant in Asia, Cn. Domitius Calvinus, but to no avail. Pharnaces defeated them jointly.

After his victory in Egypt, Caesar marched around the eastern Mediter-ranean and in Galatia met Deiotarus, who greeted him as a suppliant and begged forgiveness for having supported Pompey. He was reinstated as king, but would have to wait to learn of the final settlement of the territory while Caesar backtracked east and, in a breathtakingly swift victory (hence *veni, vidi, vici*), destroyed Pharnaces at Zela. Returning through Galatia, where he accepted the hospitality of Deiotarus, to Bithynia, Caesar retained Deiotarus on the throne, but of a diminished realm, depriving him of Lesser Armenia among other territories. However much Cicero tries to gloss it over, Caesar had punished Deiotarus for disloyalty.

During Caesar's campaign in Spain, Deiotarus sent an embassy to him at Tarraco asking for the return of his former holdings and/or seeking sup-port in a family struggle for power against Castor, the husband of his daughter and father of the Castor who soon after brought the prosecution against Deiotarus. Apparently this younger Castor was sole prosecutor, relying heavily on the eyewitness account of one of Deiotarus' slaves. Cicero defended the king, whom he had known and with whom he had had cordial and useful dealings in Cilicia in 51.

It is never safe to assume the prosecution charges or strategy from Cicero's defense. Tubero's strongest allegation does not find mention in *Pro Ligario*. In *Pro Rege Deiotaro* the one criminal accusation the defense considers is that Deiotarus had planned the assassination of Caesar when he was a guest of the king during his trip from Zela to Bithynia. With allowances for its highly ironic treatment, the narrative of the allegation may have been substantially as Cicero describes it. To defend against this accusation Cicero uses eight sections, following fourteen sections of general comments on the circumstances of the trial and of Deiotarus' involvement in the Civil War. Before Caesar sitting as sole judge, the prosecution would no doubt have stressed and exaggerated Deiotarus' allegiance to Pompey, at the least as a foundation for the criminal charge. But Cicero devotes a full quarter of his speech to rehearsing and refuting such allegations, centered by a *Castoris vituperatio* accusing the prosecutor of more violent hostility to Caesar. The speech closes with a plea for reconciliation and for clemency.

Once more we are faced with large questions in trying to understand the historical and dramatic situation of a speech. Caesar would have had to give his permission for this case to be heard; its verdict would be solely his. Although there was no audience, the implications of his decision would not be purely judicial. Other client kings whose behavior during the Civil War had been ambiguous would have had a more than passing interest in Caesar's decision. Perhaps that is why Caesar deferred the verdict. He was planning a return to the East the following year and a campaign against the Parthians, to the successful conclusion of which he might have appended a new eastern Settlement. Some moderns believe that it was Caesar's intention to "unite East and West and wipe out the dividing line between victors and vanquished" (Yavetz, 28). This may be the way to understand the trial: as an attempt to get Caesar to take a large view of an eastern potentate and ally of Rome who had, as things turned out, at least for the present, made the wrong commitment. On Caesar's death Deiotarus reconquered Lesser Armenia and, through a bribe, was restored by Antony to his earlier possessions.

One section of the speech is particularly difficult to comprehend. Among other indications of Deiotarus' animus toward Caesar, the prosecution (according to Cicero) had cited a letter to the king from his lieutenant, Ble-samius, reporting some public disenchantment with Caesar at Rome. It is not clear whether the prosecution charges Blesamius with creating these rumors or just passing them along. Cicero maintains that they are just the anonymous scurrilities of city malcontents. He does not say whether the prosecution has the document to quote from in court; physical evidence was, in any case, frequently suspect in antiquity. It is striking that Cicero will enumerate, enlarge upon, and painstakingly refute three different grievances directed at Caesar: that Caesar was behaving like a tyrant, that his statue was placed amidst those of the kings of Rome, and that the people were withholding their applause. It is difficult to imagine that Caesar would have been amused, even in the privacy of his home, to hear them, except perhaps as a display of Cicero's ingenuity at refutation (see my comments ad loc.). This is not the only part of the speech, however, that smacks of the declaimer's preciousness. Asking Caesar, in effect, to supply his own emotional tug (7) is a case in point. Cicero's treatment of the narrative of the assassination attempt, highly effective, is a comic tour de force. The anecdotes on Attalus (19) and Antiochus Magnus (36) seem highly artifi-cial. In a number of ways, much of the speech lacks tension.

Cicero's own critique of his performance survives (*Fam.* 9.12, written in December 45 to Dolabella): "My little speech for Deiotarus, which you asked for, I have with me, though I didn't think I had. And so I've sent it to you. Please read it as a slight and weak defense, not much worthy of publishing. But I wanted to send an old friend and host a little gift, loosely woven of thick wool, as his own gifts usually are." (It must be admitted that the precise meaning of *levidense*, "loosely woven of thick wool," is not known.)

4. Style of the Later Speeches

Erasmus in his *Ciceronianus* casually remarked on a change of style that distinguishes the later oratorical works of Cicero and which he attributed to the orator's maturity. More than three hundred years later, Wilamowitz (332 n. 12) made the same observation but offered another explanation. He attributed the stylistic changes to severe criticism Cicero suffered to-ward the end of his life. The change consists basically of a more restrained use of periodic composition and fewer of the embellishments associated with the more complex syntactic structures. Periodicity is the fashioning of extended, complex sentences in such a way that content and syntax are resolved simultaneously at the end (see Gotoff 2, 66–78). This was never Cicero's sole form of composition; it was not particularly appropriate for plain narrative or for highly charged emotional passages in what he would have called his "high style." (Over the centuries, however, particularly in the Renaissance and beyond, the "high style" became identified with Cicero's most flamboyantly periodic composition.)

Nevertheless, periodicity is the hallmark of Cicero's prose style. No one before or after him in Latin could control so many elements of thought and syntax so smoothly and with such inevitable but interesting progression within the compass of a single syntactic structure. It was this technical mastery that disposed audiences to admire him and sympathize with his arguments, perhaps to take them for granted even when the logic was less than cogent. In an age brought up on expression and composition, his success was stunning.

The periodic style is expository. It is the style, first and foremost, of argumentation and embellished narrative. Since its purpose is to support the orator's own thoughts and to confute his opponents', it must convey logical progression, a sense of coherent discourse. This Cicero does by signaling to his listeners the direction and flow of his thesis. Such anticipatory signals, all of which raise certain expectations in the listener, can be grammatical (an adjective or dependent genitive will be followed by a noun), syntactic (*ita* or *tam* with the verb will be followed by a result clause, or an initial relative clause will be followed by a governing clause with an antecedent pronoun), rhetorical (*non modo* always anticipates *verum/sed etiam*; *non* is frequently followed by *sed*), or lexical (*dico, rogo, impero*).

Expository composition can vary enormously depending on the number and complexity of the constituent members (clauses and phrases) of the period, the diction (including vocabulary and figurative language), and the rhetorical strategy involved. The strategy is supported by the persona of the speaker in any given argument—dispassionate or subjective (amused, outraged, shocked, or skeptical)—and by the stance he takes—conversational, didactic, impatient. Both the persona and stance, in turn, are developed through the devices of periodicity and diction.

It is certainly true that in the speeches delivered after the Civil War, the *Caesarianae* and the *Philippics*, Cicero's style is typically less embellished; the periods are shorter and less complex. Particularly in the *Caesarianae*,

I find that reliance on periodicity for progression and consequence in argumentation is superseded by other, more subtle relationships. I point to a number of places where, although two independent sentences stand in parataxis, the first is made, in sense, to depend on the second. And balances that in earlier speeches would have been achieved through syntax at the level of clauses are produced by collocation, often at the level of simple grammar. The memory lingers, however; see, for example, *Marc.* 13, with sixty-one words between *nam* and *susceptum*.

It is not certain that either Erasmus' explanation of artistic maturity or the more recent one of deliberate correction will account for the change in style. Modern scholars point to a controversy, waged on literary grounds in the 40s, that was fought under the banners of "Attic" and "Asian" styles of composition. (For a good summary see Johnson, 2–4.) It is believed that at this time a reaction developed precisely to the rich flow of full expression that Cicero's periodicity revealed in the Latin language. Adherents of this aesthetic explanation pointed to the plainness and directness of a purer style, one that they identified with prose writers of Athens in the fifth century, Lysias and Thucydides. They argued that as prose style was exported to the rest of Greece, the rhetoricians of the islands and Asia Minor, with a lack of restraint and good taste, embellished the composition until ornamentation became more important than content. These decadent exponents of a less strong, direct, and sincere style were labeled "Asianists."

This description of the controversy is, to be sure, oversimplified. The strictures of the Atticists were not limited to styles of composition. But the emotional overtones of words like "plain," "direct," "decadent," "strong," and "sincere" were present, as they generally are when expression is part of politics, in such controversy. Titling a newspaper *The Plain Dealer* makes a statement: straight and honest talk will be found in its pages. The thesis is that true things come in plain packages; and it may sell newspapers. One is intended to expect simple articulation and literal language. This would not for a moment fool anyone brought up on academic rhetoric. The skillful speaker can obfuscate in any style. What he loses by leanness of ornamentation, he makes up for with the persona of a modest man who speaks from the heart. I have suggested elsewhere that what lay behind the debate between Attic and Asian styles was sociopolitical, a dissatisfaction with the comfortable confidence of a polished speaker representing an entrenched, self-satisfied system (see Gotoff 2, 26–27).

This cannot be proved. But in any case other explanations for the change in Cicero's style occur. Many of the *Philippics* are not full-blown deliberative speeches like *De Lege Manilia* or *De Provinciis Consularibus*. They are brief statements of opinion and suggestions for policy in a continuing crisis, as the Senate met frequently to try to deal with the confusion and imminent civil war that followed Caesar's assassination. There are harangues at hastily called gatherings of the people. And it should be remembered that in the speeches that respond to a crisis that had arisen at the end of Cicero's consulship twenty years earlier, the *Catilinarians,* there is less of the otherwise familiar luxuriousness (see Gotoff 2, 9–18).

The styles of the various Caesarian speeches were also affected by the variety of circumstances under which they were delivered. The first, *Pro Marcello,* was quite possibly delivered extempore and in a genre—a speech of thanksgiving—otherwise unknown to us. The next two lacked the ambience upon which Cicero had always in the past depended for support: the open court and the crowd of spectators. Most important, all three were delivered to a man who, from what we are told, had the talent or the pretension almost to rival Cicero in the profession of political speaker—a single judge, highly intellectual, rhetorically skilled, all-powerful. It would be a mistake to think that, faced with such an audience, the professional speaker would abandon his rhetorical training in his attempt to be persuasive; it would be an equally big mistake to expect him to use the same techniques that were effective under other, more diverse circumstances.

5. A Note on the Text and Commentary

The text of the Caesarian speeches is my own, although I have not collated the manuscripts I report. I have studied them sufficiently to be largely convinced that the manuscripts Clark found in his native England really are some of the best of the known witnesses to these speeches. The α manuscripts are generally the best, the γ manuscripts the most common, though there is evidence that many variants and corrections began in antiquity and contaminated the tradition early. I print an apparatus criticus, because all readers of Latin should get in the habit of checking the evidence on which a text is based. It is not exhaustive; I do not report correcting hands. Variant readings are sometimes discussed in the commentary.

In printing the Latin text I am guilty of some inconsistency. True to scribal conventions and lacking a rubricator, I do not capitalize initial letters of words beginning sentences. On the other hand, I do distinguish *v* from *u*. The punctuation is modern and, for that reason, a bit eclectic; my purpose was to render the Latin easier for modern readers to read.

The genitive singular of nouns in *-ius* and *-ium* are spelled with a single *-i* irrespective of manuscript evidence.

In the commentary, "below" and "above" refer only to features within the same section. Beyond that limit I supply numerical references.

Whenever a proper name appears in quotation marks, the sentiment attributed to him actually comes from a character in a treatise or speech composed by Cicero.

SIGLA AND ABBREVIATIONS

Abbreviations for classical authors and titles and for standard modern reference works are in the general style of the second edition of the *Oxford Classical Dictionary*. Titles of modern journals and series are abbreviated much as in *Année Philologique*.

The Manuscripts of Cicero's Caesarian Speeches

α
{
C — Holkhamicus, olim Cluniacensis 498 saec. ix (continet *Lig.* 18–28, 38–*Deiot.* 6, 16–43)
A — Ambrosianus C. 29 part. inf. saec. x
H — Harleianus 2682 (exemplar posterius) saec. xi
V — Vossianus Lat. O. 2 saec. xi
}

6
{
B — Bruxellensis 5345 saec. xii
D — Dorvillianus 77 saec. xi
E — Erfurtensis (Berolinensis 252) saec. xii
L — Harleianus 2716 saec. xi (deficit ad *Lig.* 6 *oboriatur*)
}

γ
{
a — Harleianus 4927 saec. xii
h — Harleianus 2682 (exemplar prius) saec. xi
m — Mediceus plut. 45 saec. xi (continet *Marc.*, *Lig.* ad 32)
}

σ — Bodleianus auct. Rawl. G. 138 saec. xv (continet *Lig.* 32–38, *Deiot.* 26–42)

g — Gudianus 335 saec. x (continet *Deiot.* 1–26)

Sch. G. — Scholia Gronoviana

Editions Cited in the Apparatus Criticus

Clark (saec. xix–xx = Oxford Classical Texts)
Cratand. (xv = ed. Aldinus)

Eberhard (xix)
Ernestius (xviii–xix)
Garatonus (xix)
Gulielmus (xvi)
R. Klotz (xix–xx = Teubner)
Muretus (xvi)
Reeder (xx)
Victorius (xvi)
Wesenberg (xix)

References Regularly Abbreviated in the Commentary

LH&S   Leumann, Hofmann, and Szantyr, *Lateinische Syntax und
          Stilistic,* vol. 2, part 2.2
K&S   Kühner and Stegman, *Grammatik der lateinischen Sprache*
OLD   *Oxford Latin Dictionary*
R&E   Richter and Eberbard, *Ciceros Reden für M. Marcellus, Q.
          Ligarius, König Deiotarus,* 4th ed.

Modern articles and books are otherwise cited simply by author or editor's
last name. Multiple works by the same author are listed alphabetically in
the Bibliography and assigned a reference number: e.g., Norden 1, 2:99–
100 will lead the reader to Norden's *Antike Kunstprosa,* vol. 2.

PRO MARCELLO

M. Tulli Ciceronis Pro M. Marcello Oratio

1 Diuturni silenti, patres conscripti, quo eram his temporibus usus non 1
timore aliquo, sed partim dolore partim verecundia, finem hodiernus dies
attulit, idemque initium quae vellem quaeque sentirem meo pristino more
dicendi. tantam enim mansuetudinem, tam inusitatam inauditamque clementiam, tantum in summa potestate rerum omnium modum, tam denique 5
incredibilem sapientiam ac paene divinam tacitus praeterire nullo modo
possum. 2 M. enim Marcello vobis, patres conscripti, reique publicae reddito non illius solum sed etiam meam vocem et auctoritatem vobis et rei
publicae conservatam ac restitutam puto. dolebam enim, patres conscripti,
et vehementer angebar, virum talem qui in eadem causa in qua ego fuisset 10
non in eadem esse fortuna, nec mihi persuadere poteram, nec fas esse ducebam, versari me in nostro vetere curriculo, illo aemulo atque imitatore
studiorum ac laborum meorum quasi quodam socio a me et comite distracto. ergo et mihi meae pristinae vitae consuetudinem, C. Caesar, interclusam aperuisti et his omnibus ad bene de omni re publica sperandum 15
quasi signum aliquod sustulisti.

3 Intellectum est enim mihi quidem in multis et maxime in me ipso, sed
paulo ante [in] omnibus cum M. Marcellum senatui reique publicae concessisti, commemoratis praesertim offensionibus, te auctoritatem huius or-
dinis dignitatemque rei publicae tuis vel doloribus vel suspicionibus 20
anteferre. ille quidem fructum omnis ante actae vitae hodierno die maximum cepit, cum summo consensu senatus, tum iudicio tuo gravissimo et
maximo. ex quo profecto intellegis quanta in dato beneficio sit laus, cum
in accepto sit tanta gloria. 4 est vero fortunatus ille cuius ex salute non
minor paene ad omnis quam ad ipsum ventura sit, laetitia pervenerit. quod 25
quidem merito atque optimo iure contigit. quis enim est illo aut nobilitate
aut probitate aut optimarum artium studio aut innocentia aut ullo in laudis
genere praestantior?

1   4 invisitatam *Eberhard*
    6 nullo modo praeterire 6
2   8 meam *ante* voc. *HBDE*, post voc.
      Lγ *om. AV*
    8 vobis: et vobis 6
    9 conservatam ac *om.* α
    10 virum α6: cum viderem virum γ
    10 qui Eγ: qui cum α, cum *BDL*
    10 fuisset α: fuissem (-se *h*) 6γ
    12 vetere Vγ: veteri H6, *om. A*

13 ac (laborum): et *B*
14 meae *ed. Cratand.*: et meae *codd.*
15 omni *om.* α
3 18 in *del. Vict.*
   21 vitae: aetatis *h*
   22 tum praeterea γ
   24 ille 6a: *om.* αhm
4 25 ipsum *Ernesti*: illum *codd.*
   26 ei merito *b*γ
   27 in *om.* 6γ

Nullius tantum flumen est ingeni, nulla dicendi aut scribendi tanta vis
tantaque copia, quae non dicam exornare, sed enarrare, C. Caesar, res tuas
gestas possit. tamen hoc adfirmo et pace dicam tua, nullam in his esse
laudem ampliorem quam eam quam hodierno die consecutus es. **5** soleo
saepe ante oculos ponere idque libenter crebris usurpare sermonibus, omnis
nostrorum imperatorum, omnis exterarum gentium potentissimorumque
populorum omnis regum clarissimorum res gestas cum tuis nec contentionum magnitudine nec numero proeliorum nec varietate regionum nec
celeritate conficiendi nec dissimilitudine bellorum posse conferri, nec vero
disiunctissimas terras citius passibus cuiusquam potuisse peragrari, quam
tuis non dicam cursibus, sed victoriis lustratae sunt. **6** quae quidem ego
nisi ita magna esse fatear, ut ea vix cuiusquam mens aut cogitatio capere
possit, amens sim. sed tamen sunt alia maiora. nam bellicas laudes solent
quidam extenuare verbis easque detrahere ducibus, communicare cum
multis, ne propriae sint imperatorum. et certe in armis militum virtus, lo-
corum opportunitas, auxilia sociorum, classes, commeatus multum iu-
vant, maximam vero partem quasi suo iure Fortuna sibi vindicat et,
quidquid est prospere gestum, id paene omne ducit suum. **7** at vero huius
gloriae, C. Caesar, quam es paulo ante adeptus, socium habes neminem;
totum hoc quantumcumque est, quod certe maximum est, totum est, inquam, tuum. nihil sibi ex ista laude centurio, nihil praefectus, nihil cohors,
nihil turma decerpit. quin etiam illa ipsa rerum humanarum domina Fortuna in istius se societatem gloriae non offert; tibi cedit, tuam esse totam
et propriam fatetur. numquam enim temeritas cum sapientia commiscetur,
neque ad consilium casus admittitur. **8** domuisti gentis immanitate bar-
baras, multitudine innumerabilis, locis infinitas, omni copiarum genere
abundantis. ea tamen vicisti quae et naturam et condicionem ut vinci possent habebant. nulla est enim tanta vis quae non ferro et viribus debilitari
frangique possit. animum vincere, iracundiam cohibere, victo temperare,
adversarium nobilitate ingenio virtute praestantem non modo extollere ia-

1 nulla αBhm: nulli DELa, nullius R.
  Klotz
2 tanta copia 6γ
3 hoc post et 6
5 7 clar. reg. 6
   11 illustratae αγ
6 12 ita αγ: tam 6
   17 sibi 6hm: om. αa

7 18 est post gestum 6
   19 C. om. αa
   23 se ante societatem αγ: ante non 6
   23 tuam se 6a
8 27 ea tamen αγ: sed tamen ea 6
   28 vis, tanta copia γ
   29 victo αD: victum hm, victoriam
      BELa

centem, sed etiam amplificare eius pristinam dignitatem, haec qui faciat   1
non ego eum cum summis viris comparo, sed simillimum deo iudico.
9 itaque, C. Caesar, bellicae tuae laudes celebrabuntur illae quidem non
solum nostris, sed paene omnium gentium litteris atque linguis, neque ulla
umquam aetas de tuis laudibus conticescet. sed tamen eius modi res nes-   5
cioquo modo etiam cum leguntur obstrepi clamore militum videntur et
tubarum sono. at vero cum aliquid clementer mansuete iuste moderate sapienter factum, in iracundia praesertim quae est inimica consilio et in victoria quae natura insolens et superba est, audimus aut legimus, quo studio
incendimur non modo in gestis rebus, sed etiam in fictis, ut eos saepe quos   10
numquam vidimus diligamus! 10 te vero quem praesentem intuemur,
cuius mentem sensusque et os cernimus, ut quidquid belli fortuna reliquum
rei publicae fecerit, id esse salvum velis, quibus laudibus efferemus, quibus
studiis prosequemur, qua benevolentia complectemur? parietes me dius Fidius, ut mihi videtur, huius curiae tibi gratias agere gestiunt, quod brevi   15
tempore futura sit illa auctoritas in his maiorum suorum et suis sedibus.
equidem cum C. Marcelli viri optimi et commemorabili pietate praediti
lacrimas modo vobiscum viderem, omnium Marcellorum meum pectus
memoria obfudit, quibus tu etiam mortuis M. Marcello conservato dignitatem suam reddidisti, nobilissimamque familiam iam ad paucos redac-   20
tam paene ab interitu vindicasti. 11 hunc tu igitur diem tuis maximis et
innumerabilibus gratulationibus iure anteponis. haec enim res unius est
propria C. Caesaris: ceterae duce te gestae magnae illae quidem, sed tamen
multo magnoque comitatu; huius autem rei tu idem dux es et comes. quae
quidem tanta est ut tropaeis et monumentis tuis adlatura finem sit aetas—   25
(nihil est enim opere et manu factum, quod non conficiat et consumat vetustas)—12 at haec tua iustitia et lenitas florescit cotidie magis. ita quantum operibus tuis diuturnitas detrahet, tantum adferet laudibus. et ceteros

	1 facit 6
9	6 obstrepit clamor militum (videntur *add. V*) et tubarum soni *AV*
	9 et insolens α
	9 aut audimus γ
10	12 et os: eos *Faernus*
	15 videntur *HVm*
	19 effudit *Dhm*: in meum pectus se memoria effudit *Madvig*
11	21 igitur *om. αm*

	22 antepones *hm*
	23 C. *om.* α
	24 dux es α: es et dux 6, et dux es γ
	25 ut α*m*: ut nulla 6*ah*
	26 non α *Lact.*: non aliquando 6γ
12	27 lenitas α*a*: lenitas animi 6*hm*
	27 florescet αγ
	27 ita α: ita ut 6γ
	28 adferet (adfert *V*) *AHDLm*: adferat *BEah*

quidem omnis victores bellorum civilium iam ante aequitate et misericor-   1
dia viceras; hodierno vero die te ipse vicisti. vereor ut hoc quod dicam
perinde intellegi possit auditum atque ipse cogitans sentio: ipsam victoriam
vicisse videris cum ea quae illa erat adepta victis remisisti. nam cum ipsius
victoriae condicione iure omnes victi occidissemus, clementiae tuae iudicio   5
conservati sumus. recte igitur unus invictus es, a quo etiam ipsius victoriae
condicio visque devicta est.

   13 Atque hoc C. Caesaris iudicium, patres conscripti, quam late pateat
attendite. omnes enim qui ad illa arma fato sumus nescioquo rei publicae
misero funestoque compulsi, etsi aliqua culpa tenemur erroris humani, at   10
scelere certe liberati sumus. nam cum M. Marcellum deprecantibus vobis
rei publicae conservavit, me et mihi et item rei publicae nullo deprecante,
reliquos amplissimos viros et sibi ipsos et patriae reddidit—quorum et frequentiam et dignitatem hoc ipso in consessu videtis—non ille hostes in-
duxit in curiam, sed iudicavit a plerisque ignoratione potius et falso atque   15
inani metu quam cupiditate aut crudelitate bellum esse susceptum. 14 quo
quidem in bello semper de pace audiendum putavi, semperque dolui non
modo pacem, sed etiam orationem civium pacem flagitantium repudiari.
neque enim ego illa nec ulla umquam secutus sum arma civilia, semperque
mea consilia pacis et togae socia, non belli atque armorum fuerunt. ho-   20
minem sum secutus privato officio, non publico, tantumque apud me grati
animi fidelis memoria valuit, ut nulla non modo cupiditate, sed ne spe
quidem prudens et sciens tam quam ad interitum ruerem voluntarium.
15 quod quidem meum consilium minime obscurum fuit. nam et in hoc
ordine integra re multa de pace dixi et in ipso bello eadem etiam cum ca-   25
pitis mei periculo sensi. ex quo nemo erit tam iniustus rerum existimator,
qui dubitet quae Caesaris de bello voluntas fuerit, cum pacis auctores con-
servandos statim censuerit, ceteris fuerit iratior. atque id minus mirum fortasse tum cum esset incertus exitus et anceps fortuna belli; qui vero victor

1 antea α

2 ipse α: ipsum 6γ

3 auditum *Patricius*: auditu *codd.*

4 illa 6γ: *om.* α

4 erant H *unde* quae erant adempta
   Madvig

5 iure *om.* 6, *post* omnes *m*

5 condicione *del. Clark*

6 es *om.* α6

13 10 at (scelere) R. *Klotz*: ab αγ, *om.* 6

14 17 audiendum α*Em*: agendum
      audiendum *BDL*, agendum
      audiendumque *ah*

15 25 capitis mei: partis meae γ

26 iam erit tam 6

26 existimator rerum 6

28 mir. fort. α*BDL*: fort. mir. *E*, mir.
   videretur fort. (videtur *h*) γ

pacis auctores diligit, is profecto declarat maluisse se non dimicare quam   1
vincere. **16** atque huius quidem rei M. Marcello sum testis. nostri enim
sensus ut in pace semper, sic tum etiam in bello congruebant. quotiens ego
eum et quanto cum dolore vidi cum insolentiam certorum hominum, tum
etiam ipsius victoriae ferocitatem extimescentem! quo gratior tua liberali-   5
tas, C. Caesar, nobis qui illa vidimus debet esse. non enim iam causae sunt
inter se, sed victoriae comparandae. **17** vidimus tuam victoriam proeliorum exitu terminatam, gladium vagina vacuum in urbe non vidimus.
quos amisimus civis, eos Martis vis perculit, non ira victoriae, ut dubitare
debeat nemo, quin multos si posset C. Caesar ab inferis excitaret, quoniam   10
ex eadem acie conservat quos potest. alterius vero partis nihil amplius dico
quam id quod omnes verebamur: nimis iracundam futuram fuisse victoriam. **18** quidam enim non modo armatis, sed interdum etiam otiosis
minabantur; nec quid quisque sensisset, sed ubi fuisset, cogitandum esse
dicebant, ut mihi quidem videantur di immortales, etiam si poenas a populo   15
Romano ob aliquod delictum expetiverunt, qui civile bellum tantum et tam
luctuosum excitaverunt, vel placati iam vel satiati aliquando omnem spem
salutis ad clementiam victoris et sapientiam contulisse.

   19 Quare gaude tuo isto tam excellenti bono, et fruere cum fortuna et
gloria, tum etiam natura et moribus tuis, ex quo quidem maximus est fruc-   20
tus iucunditasque sapienti. cetera cum tua recordabere, etsi persaepe virtuti, tamen plerumque felicitati tuae gratulabere: de nobis quos in re
publica tecum simul esse voluisti, quotiens cogitabis, totiens de maximis
tuis beneficiis, totiens de incredibili liberalitate, totiens de singulari sapientia cogitabis. quae non modo summa bona, sed nimirum audebo vel   25
sola dicere. tantus est enim splendor in laude vera, tanta in magnitudine
animi et consili dignitas, ut haec a Virtute donata, cetera a Fortuna commodata esse videantur. **20** noli igitur in conservandis viris bonis defetigari, non cupiditate praesertim aliqua aut pravitate lapsis, sed opinione
offici stulta fortasse, certe non improba, et specie quadam rei publicae. non   30
enim tua ulla culpa est si te aliqui timuerunt, contraque summa laus quod
minime timendum fuisse senserunt.

---

16   4 certorum *Em*: ceterorum αBDL*ah*
       6 illa: illam δ
       6 iam (tam *m*) αγ: *om.* δ
17   9 vis Martis α*h*
       10 fieri posset δγ
       11 dicam δ
19   23 simul αδ: salvos γ

24 sapientia tua γ
26 est *om.* δγ
   20   28 bonis viris δ
28 defetigari *HBD*: defatigari
       AVEL*ah*
30 specie αδ*a*: facie *hm*
31 culpa ulla γ

21 Nunc venio ad gravissimam querelam et atrocissimam suspicionem tuam, quae non tibi ipsi magis quam cum omnibus civibus, tum maxime nobis qui a te conservati sumus, providenda est. quam etsi spero falsam esse, numquam tamen extenuabo. tua enim cautio nostra cautio est. quod si in alterutro peccandum sit, malim videri nimis timidus quam parum prudens. sed quisnam est iste tam demens? de tuisne—tametsi qui magis sunt tui quam quibus tu salutem insperantibus reddidisti?—an ex eo numero qui una tecum fuerunt? non est credibilis tantus in ullo furor, ut quo duce omnia summa sit adeptus, huius vitam non anteponat suae. an si nihil tui cogitant sceleris, cavendum est ne quid inimici? qui? omnes enim qui fuerunt, aut sua pertinacia vitam amiserunt, aut tua misericordia retinuerunt, ut aut nulli supersint de inimicis, aut qui fuerunt sint amicissimi. **22** sed tamen cum in animis hominum tantae latebrae sint et tanti recessus, augeamus sane suspicionem tuam; simul enim augebimus diligentiam. nam quis est omnium tam ignarus rerum, tam rudis in re publica, tam nihil umquam nec de sua nec de communi salute cogitans, qui non intellegat tua salute contineri suam, et ex unius tua vita pendere omnium? equidem de te dies noctesque ut debeo cogitans, casus dumtaxat humanos et incertos eventus valetudinis et naturae communis fragilitatem extimesco, doleoque cum res publica immortalis esse debeat, eam in unius mortalis anima consistere. **23** si vero ad humanos casus incertosque motus valetudinis sceleris etiam accedit insidiarumque consensio, quem deum, si cupiat, posse opitulari rei publicae credimus?

Omnia sunt excitanda tibi, C. Caesar, uni, quae iacere sentis belli ipsius impetu quod necesse fuit perculsa atque prostrata; constituenda iudicia, revocanda fides, comprimendae libidines, propaganda suboles, omnia quae dilapsa iam diffluxerunt, severis legibus vincienda sunt. **24** non fuit recusandum in tanto civili bello, tanto animorum ardore et armorum, quin quassata res publica, quicumque belli eventus fuisset, multa perderet et

21 4 tamen numquam δ
    4 extenuabo verbis γ
    4 quod si *H, Prisc.*: ut si *cett.*
    7 an ex eo γ: an ex hoc δ,
       axeneone ex *H*, anexeone *V*, an
       ex eone ex *A*, anne ex eo
       Clark
    12 qui superfuerunt *hm*
22 16 communi αδ: omnium *hm*,
       communi omnium *a*

16 qui non *H*δγ: quin *AV*
17 omnium δγ: omnia α, *Sch. Luc. v.*
    686
19 fragilitates *H*
23 22 accedat γ
    23 credimus α: credamus δγ
    27 dilapsa *HV*γ: delapsa *A*δ
    27 diffluxerunt *BDm*: deflux. α*ELa*;
       fluxerunt *h*
24 28 tantoque animorum γ

ornamenta dignitatis et praesidia stabilitatis suae, multaque uterque dux   1
faceret armatus, quae idem togatus fieri prohibuisset. quae quidem tibi
nunc omnia belli volnera sananda sunt, quibus praeter te mederi nemo potest. **25** itaque illam tuam praeclarissimam et sapientissimam vocem invitus audivi: "satis diu vel naturae vixi vel gloriae." satis, si ita vis, fortasse   5
naturae. addo etiam si placet gloriae, at, quod maximum est, patriae, certe
parum. quare omitte, quaeso, istam doctorum hominum in contemnenda
morte prudentiam; noli nostro periculo esse sapiens. saepe enim venit ad
auris meas, te idem istud nimis crebro dicere, satis te tibi vixisse. credo.
sed tum id audirem, si tibi soli viveres aut si tibi etiam soli natus esses.   10
omnium salutem civium cunctamque rem publicam res tuae gestae com-
plexae sunt; tantum abes a perfectione maximorum operum ut fundamenta
nondum quae cogitas ieceris. hic tu modum vitae tuae non salute rei publicae, sed aequitate animi definies? quid si istud ne gloriae quidem satis est?
cuius te esse avidissimum quamvis sis sapiens non negabis. **26** "parumne"   15
inquies "magna relinquemus?" immo vero. aliis quamvis multis satis, tibi
uni parum. quidquid est enim quamvis amplum sit id est parum tum cum
est aliquid amplius. quodsi rerum tuarum immortalium, C. Caesar, hic exitus futurus fuit, ut devictis adversariis rem publicam in eo statu relinqueres
in quo nunc est, vide, quaeso, ne tua divina virtus admirationis plus sit   20
habitura quam gloriae, si quidem gloria est inlustris ac pervagata magnorum vel in suos [civis] vel in patriam vel in omne genus hominum fama
meritorum. **27** haec igitur tibi reliqua pars est; hic restat actus; in hoc
elaborandum est, ut rem publicam constituas, eaque tu in primis summa
tranquillitate et otio perfruare. tum te si voles, cum et patriae quod debes   25
solveris, et naturam ipsam expleveris satietate vivendi, satis diu vixisse dicito. quid enim est omnino hoc ipsum diu, in quo est aliquid extremum?
quod cum venit, omnis voluptas praeterita pro nihilo est, quia postea nulla
est futura. quamquam iste tuus animus numquam his angustiis quas natura

     2 nunc tibi γ
     3 sananda αϐ: curanda γ
25   5 diu . . . vixi: te diu . . . vixisse
      hm
     6 addo ϐγ: addam α
     7 istam quaeso ϐ*m*
     9 auris meas ϐ: meas auris αγ
     9 satis te tibi α: tibi satis te (tibi te
      satis *E*) ϐγ
     11 omnium αϐ: nunc cum omnium γ

     14 quidem *Sch. G.*: quidem tuae αγ,
      tuae quidem ϐ
26   15 parumne α*L*: parumne igitur *BDE* γ
     16 magna: gloriam magnam γ
     22 civis *om.* γ
27   25 et patriae αγ: patriae ϐ
     26 te vixisse *V*
     27 enim est omnino *codd.*: est enim
      Sch. G., Serv. Aen. 10.467
     27 hoc *om.* γ

nobis ad vivendum dedit, contentus fuit, semper immortalitatis amore fla-   1
gravit. **28** nec vero haec tua vita ducenda est, quae corpore et spiritu con-
tinetur; illa, inquam, illa vita est tua quae vigebit memoria saeculorum
omnium, quam posteritas alet, quam ipsa aeternitas semper tuebitur. huic
tu inservias, huic te ostentes oportet, quae quidem quae miretur iam pridem   5
multa habet; nunc etiam quae laudet exspectat. obstupescent posteri certe
imperia, provincias—Rhenum, Oceanum, Nilum—pugnas innumerabilis,
incredibilis victorias, monumenta, munera, triumphos audientes et legentes
tuos. **29** sed nisi haec urbs stabilita tuis consiliis et institutis erit, vagabitur modo tuum nomen longe atque late, sedem stabilem et domicilium   10
certum non habebit. erit inter eos etiam qui nascentur, sicut inter nos fuit,
magna dissensio, cum alii laudibus ad caelum res tuas gestas efferent, alii
fortasse aliquid requirent, idque vel maximum, nisi belli civilis incendium
salute patriae restinxeris, ut illud fati fuisse videatur, hoc consili. servi igitur eis iudicibus qui multis post saeculis de te iudicabunt, et quidem haud   15
scio an incorruptius quam nos. nam et sine amore et sine cupiditate et
rursus sine odio et sine invidia iudicabunt. **30** id autem etiam si tum ad
te, ut quidam falso putant, non pertinebit, nunc certe pertinet esse te talem,
ut tuas laudes obscuratura nulla umquam sit oblivio.

Diversae voluntates civium fuerunt distractaeque sententiae. non enim   20
consiliis solum et studiis, sed armis etiam et castris dissidebamus; erat obscuritas quaedam, erat certamen inter clarissimos duces; multi dubitabant
quid optimum esset, multi quid sibi expediret, multi quid deceret, non nulli
etiam quid liceret. **31** perfuncta res publica est hoc misero fatalique bello;
vicit is qui non fortuna inflammaret odium suum, sed bonitate leniret, ne-   25
que omnis quibus iratus esset, eosdem etiam exsilio aut morte dignos iudicaret. arma ab aliis posita, ab aliis erepta sunt. ingratus est iniustusque
civis qui armorum periculo liberatus, animum tamen retinet armatum, ut
etiam ille sit melior, qui in acie cecidit, qui in causa animam profudit. quae
enim pertinacia quibusdam, eadem aliis constantia videri potest. **32** sed   30
iam omnis fracta dissensio est armis, exstincta aequitate victoris. restat ut

28   2 ducenda *Aϐ*: dicenda *HVγ*
29   10 sedem quidem *γ*
    14 fuisse vid. *ϐhm*: vid. fuisse *α*, vid.
      hoc fuisse *a*
    15 eis *α*: eis etiam *ϐam*, etiam *h*
30   21 erat *αh*: erat enim *ϐ*, erat autem
     am

23 deceret *AVDELa*: diceret *HBhm*
31   24 hoc *om. α*
    25 neque *αγ*: nec qui *ϐ*
    26 omnis *ϐ*: *om. αγ*
    26 etiam *αDEL*: *om.* B*γ*
    29 sit melior *AVγ*: melior sit
     Hϐ

omnes unum velint, qui modo habent aliquid non sapientiae modo, sed   1
etiam sanitatis. nisi te, C. Caesar, salvo et in ista sententia qua cum antea,
tum hodie maxime usus es, manente salvi esse non possumus. quare omnes
te qui haec salva esse volumus et hortamur et obsecramus ut vitae, ut saluti
tuae consulas, omnesque tibi—ut pro aliis etiam loquar quod de me ipso   5
sentio—, quoniam subesse aliquid putas quod cavendum sit, non modo
excubias et custodias, sed etiam laterum nostrorum oppositus et corporum
pollicemur.

33 Sed, ut unde est orsa, in eodem terminetur oratio, maximas tibi
omnes gratias agimus, C. Caesar, maiores etiam habemus. nam omnes   10
idem sentiunt, quod ex omnium precibus et lacrimis sentire potuisti. sed
quia non est omnibus stantibus necesse dicere, a me certe dici volunt, cui
necesse est quodam modo. et quod fieri decet M. Marcello a te huic ordini
populoque Romano et rei publicae reddito, fieri id intellego. nam laetari
omnis non ut de unius solum, sed ut de omnium salute sentio. 34 quod   15
autem summae benivolentiae est quae mea erga illum omnibus nota semper
fuit, ut vix C. Marcello optimo et amantissimo fratri, praeter eum quidem
cederem nemini, cum id sollicitudine cura labore tam diu praestiterim
quam diu est de illius salute dubitatum, certe hoc tempore magnis curis
molestiis doloribus liberatus praestare debeo. itaque, C. Caesar, sic tibi   20
gratias ago ut me omnibus rebus a te non conservato solum, sed etiam
ornato, tamen ad tua in me unum innumerabilia merita, quod fieri iam
posse non arbitrabar, magnus hoc tuo facto cumulus accesserit.

Commentary

Pro Marcello: The title is deceptive, suggesting by the preposition a judicial
speech. This is not a speech in defense of Marcellus, but a *sententia* or

32	1 qui modo hab. 6*ah*: qui hab. α*m*	12 omn. stant. α6: omnibus *om. hm,*
	1 non sap. modo *AVam*: non modo	*post* stant. *a*
	sap. *Hh,* non solum sap. 6	15 solum *om. ahm*
	3 vel maxime 6	15 ut *alt. om.* 6*m*
	4 ut vit. ut sal. t. α: ut vit. t. et sal.	15 omnium *AV*: omni *H,* communi 6γ
	6*a,* ut vit. *hm*	34 16 semper nota 6
	5 ipse 6	17 C. α*D*: M. *BEL, om.* γ
33	9 ut *AVELm: om. BDah*	21 omnibus me 6
	9 oratio mea *hm*	22 unum *om.* αγ
	11 *sed quia* α6: et quoniam γ	23 maximus 6

opinion, formally delivered in the Senate, in which Cicero offers thanks to Caesar for his clemency. See the Introduction, section 3.1. Some grammarians of late antiquity refer to it as *De Marcello*; cf. *De Provinciis Consularibus* or *De Imperio Cn. Pompei,* deliberative speeches.

I

diuturni silenti: Commentators tend to date the beginning of this silence to *Pro Milone* (52 B.C.), the last extant speech before a six-year hiatus. According to the most popular account, Cicero delivered that speech under conditions so adverse that his skills failed him, he abandoned his prepared speech, and had to endure the humiliation of his client's conviction and exile; a full and intelligent account of the evidence can be found in Settle, 237–60. Although he did lose that case, Cicero delivered at least three subsequent speeches in the same year, two in defense of Suffeius and a rare prosecution of T. Munatius Plancus Bursa, all concerned with the slaying of Clodius by Milo on the Via Appia. It is significant that Cicero won all three, even over the opposition of Pompey, at least in the last (see Settle, 256, 260; *Fam.* 7.2.4). There is some dispute as to the date of the last speech, but it appears to have been given later than 9 December 52 (so Shackleton Bailey 1, 2:351, on 7.2). At *Brut.* 157 Brutus laments the fact that Rome has for so long been deprived of Cicero's voice. Cicero refers to his earlier determination not to speak publicly at *Fam.* 4.4.4: "When asked to deliver my opinion I altered my resolve." He attributes this change of heart to Caesar's magnanimity and his duty to the Senate and adds wistfully, but perhaps not with complete introspection, that in doing so he has probably lost the tranquility of his retirement from public life.

diuturni silenti . . . finem: The structure of the opening period closely reflects the conceit Cicero has chosen to lead with. In oratory, as in most literature, little is inevitable. Gentle Caesar or his divine *clementia* might have comprised the first theme, or the noble and valued Marcellus and his imminent return to Rome. Instead Cicero explores the effect of the occasion on himself and claims that Caesar's decision creates a critical moment in his own career and in the life of the Republic. Just so, the sentence pivots on *finem . . . attulit . . . initium.*

Although the period contains a couple of dependent clauses, the suspensions and balances that underlie its movement are structured essentially on words or phrases, e.g., *non . . . sed; partim . . . partim; quae . . . quae-*

que. The opening genitive awaits *finem*, opposed by *initium*, which itself governs a genitive: *dicendi*. Chiastic order, therefore, emphasizes *silenti* and *dicendi*, both separated from their governing nouns by substantial hyperbata. *Adferre initium*, although not a usual Latin phrase, is more natural to the rhetoric than understanding *est* with *initium* and a second predicate in parataxis.

patres conscripti: the normal title of address for Roman Senators. Cicero addresses them here in 2 and in 13; the rest of the speech the addressee is Caesar.

eram . . . usus: The pluperfect signals a subsequent predicate, also in the past (so *Lig.* 1, *paratus veneram*). In *Fam.* 4.4.4 he attributes to a "loss of his former status" his determination "to be silent forever more," using the pluperfect there too (*statueram . . . in perpetuum tacere*) to indicate that his resolve has already been altered.

non . . . sed partim . . . partim: The second half of the major rhetorical balance is broken down into a bipartite balance, marked by anaphora. The *partim*s do not mark polarities, as they usually do (cf. *Lig.* 3), but rather two components of a single response.

timore: perhaps of Caesar's supporters. To claim fear of Caesar would have been indiscreet on Cicero's part and, perhaps, disingenuous. Although he had been close to Pompey, he would be expected to have every confidence in the genuineness of Caesar's gesture and all such gestures since the mid-50s (see the Introduction, section 2). Nevertheless, at *Deiot.* 39 Cicero suggests that general panic might ensue among those pardoned if Deiotarus, who had enjoyed Caesar's *clementia*, should once more to be put in jeopardy; see Caes. *BC* 3.98.2 for the fear with which Caesar might be met ("They threw themselves at me with hands spread") and the efforts he made to allay it.

dolore: a political term for the response to an injustice (*iniuria*) suffered, which can cause either paralysis, as here, or rage, resulting in a vendetta. Cicero does not reveal his grief here; it may include his loss of status during the Civil War (*pristinae dignitatis desiderio*, *Fam.* 4.4.4), the suspension of the Republican constitution, the fate of various friends, and more. For particular reasons see on 2, *dolebam*, and 14, *dolui*.

verecundia: restraint owing to concern or respect resulting from a sense of propriety, rather than fear; cf. *vereor* vs. *timeo.* Again Cicero does not particularize in the initial balance. Part of the reason is given at 2, *nec fas . . . ducebam,* creating a large, echoing, parallel structure:

partim dolore (1):   (2) dolebam . . . et . . . angebar . . .
partim verecundia (1):   (2) nec mihi persuadere poteram nec fas esse ducebam

At *Fam.* 6.6.6, written shortly after *Pro Marcello* and explaining his position in the Civil War, he says: "My sense of shame was stronger than my fear (*pudor quam timor*): I had scruples (*veritus sum*) about not being supportive of Pompey, since he at one time had been supportive of me. And so, overcome by duty or the opinion of good men or shame, just like Amphiaraus in the plays, I approached cognizant and knowingly the plague placed before my eyes." (See 14.)

hodiernus dies: The phrase occurs more times in this (at 1, 3, 4, 12) than in any other speech, emphasizing the occasion as Cicero's rhetorical strategy requires. Cicero stresses the immediacy of the situation: it is *this* day, commemorated by *this* speech, that marks a new start, not only for Marcellus as a citizen but for Rome as a peaceful and orderly Republic. The phrase, which in the ablative is a more immediate and emphatic equivalent of *hodie,* is rarely used in the early speeches. It turns up several times in the *Catilinarians,* and even more in the *Philippics*—moments of intensity. Note the personification accorded to this very special day; compare 3, *fructum . . . maximum ⟨Marcellus⟩ cepit.*

idemque: resumes the subject and introduces the second object of the verb, *initium* in antithesis to *finem.* The pronoun reinforces a parallelism—similarity or, as here, simultaneity—and, with the adverbial force inherent to predicative adjectives, means "likewise"; it may be antithetical, "contrariwise," as at 24.

quae . . . sentirem: indirect questions, the object of *dicendi. Sentirem* refers not merely to Cicero's feelings or perceptions, but to their public expression in the Senate (so 33, *sentiunt*; and see the opening note on *Pro Marcello* above).

enim: Caesar's clemency encourages Cicero to break his silence and perform a Republican political function: participating in and advising on matters of state. At *Fam.* 4.4.4 he also credits his duty to the Senate with having persuaded him to speak.

tantam . . . tam . . . tantam . . . tam: Cicero conveys his enthusiasm with a tetracolon of objects, growing in volume, and alternating anaphora between *tant-* and *tam*. Word order of the phrases shows variety: *inusitatam inauditamque clementiam* (adjective A + adjective B*que* + noun); *tantum in summa potestate omnium rerum modum* (adjective + modified prepositional phrase + [genitive phrase + noun]); *incredibilem . . . ac paene divinam* (adjective A + noun + adjective B).

mansuetudinem: According to Weinstock, 233–43, *clementia* both as a political concept and a term needed developing; hence the search for the right word. So 9, *clementer . . . sapienter.* As an ethical predisposition, Caesar could lay claim to it as long ago as 63 (see the Introduction, section 2). Although the structure is four-part, *denique* sets the final object apart from the first three, all of which are variations on a theme; the last, *sapientia,* treats *clementia* as a rational domestic policy. In provincial administration *mansuetudo* and *clementia* were accustomed virtues (cf. *Verr.* 2.5.115); *mansuetudo* is attributed to Pompey by his defeated enemies (*Pomp.* 42). But it was not something one Roman could properly offer another freeborn citizen. In *Sul.* 72, defending the dictator's son, Cicero reminds his audience of how often his client had interceded in behalf of fellow citizens. He goes on: "but because this is a greater benefit than a citizen ought to be able to grant to another citizen, I ask you to credit to those times that he could do it, to the man himself that he did do it." Caesar explained it as a policy in 49: "Let this be our revolutionary method of conquest: that we arm ourselves with clemency and generosity" (*Att.* 9.7C.1). Cicero was never wholly convinced; writing to Brutus soon after Caesar's death, he argued for a "wholesome severity" as against "a useless show of clemency" (*Brut.* 1.15.10).

inusitatam inauditamque: Perhaps no more than a doublet pointing to a significant deviation from the brutal policies of Marius and Sulla, which Pompey gave every indication he would have pursued; see the Introduction, section 2.

in summa potestate: Caesar was consul, *imperator, princeps Senatus,* pontifex maximus, and dictator for ten years with tribunician power. As *praefectus moribus* he also had censorial powers. Earlier in the year he had celebrated his fourfold triumph over Gaul, Egypt, Pharnaces, and Juba of Africa (but not the Pompeians he simultaneously defeated).

rerum omnium: Latin prefers to balance modifiers evenly between nouns; and *modum*, standing alone after the hyperbaton of *tantum*, is stark. But *rerum modus* in the sense of "moderation" (like *Inv.* 1.5, *moderatrix omnium rerum*; *Leg.* 2.15, *dominos esse omnium rerum ac moderatores deos*), rather than "limit" (cf. *Nat. Deor.* 2.15, *cum videat omnium rerum rationem modum disciplinam*; *Sen.* 85, *habet natura ut aliorum omnium rerum sic vivendi*; *Parad.* 3.25, *rerum modum figere non possumus*), is not Ciceronian. Although *potestate* is already modified, it invites the dependent genitive and governs it.

paene divinam: Cicero uses the word figuratively in impassioned, encomiastic language; so *Verr.* 2.5.41, *o divina senatus admurmuratio*; *Milo.* 91, *vir . . . singulari, divina, incredibili fide*; *Phil.* 10.11, *incredibilis ac divina virtus*. The suggestion of divinity is not, however, to be taken lightly; see on 8, *simillimum deo*, and *Lig.* 38, *ad deos . . . accedunt*.

sapientiam: The attribute Cicero highlights in climax is Caesar's wisdom. He might have left it at Caesar's compassion, but the speech is about policy, not personality. The position of the second, modified adjective (*divinam*) lends it weight.

tacitus praeterire . . . possum: Cicero's opening phrase referred to his determined reticence. But to continue it (*tacitus praeterire*) after the circumstances of *tantam . . . divinam* is out of the question: *nullo modo possum*. The word order with its rhythms supports this movement: *paene divinam* (cretic + trochee), *praeterire* (double trochee), *nullo modo possum* (cretic + trochee). The complex accusative phrase has been awaiting the finite verb which, being infinitive, awaits the governing *possum*.

2

Sentence structure makes the point. Here, with its first mention, the pardon of Marcellus is given larger political import. The Senate and the state are both beneficiaries of the restoration of political processes; thus the phrase *vobis et rei publicae* is articulated repeatedly.

M. enim . . . Marcello: Hyperbaton of the name, when introducing a person, is ornamental (cf. *Lig.* 2, *Q. enim Ligarius*); it calls attention to the phrasing. The ablative phrase, although partially predicative, is clearly instrumental, *illius* showing that it is not an ablative absolute construction. Part of Cicero's rhetorical strategy is to equate the restoration of his own position with the restoration of the Republic. By linking Marcellus' recall with his own renewed political viability and his reactivation with the restoration of the state, Cicero hints at a role for himself in the postbellum government.

non illius solum sed etiam meam: A slight inconcinnity of genitive demonstrative pronoun parallel to possessive adjective is normal in Latin. Roman courts recognized the intercession of a formal advocate (*patronus*), as opposed to the Greek system in which principals pled their own cases, even if the speeches might be composed by professional writers. It is typical for the authority of the advocate to be associated with the status of the client. At *Lig.* 6 Cicero even identifies his client's Civil War position with his own.

vocem et auctoritatem: Hendiadys. Marcellus' authority in the Senate was derived, in part, from his skill as an orator, in part from his social and political position; see the Introduction, section 3.1.

conservatam ac restitutam: two concepts, both subsumed under the frequently used noun *salus*. The first encompasses pardon, the second, permission to return to Rome with full rights. Cicero had to remain in Brundisium after his pardon until Caesar allowed his return to the City. Ligarius had been pardoned but was still in Africa.

restitutam puto: form a favored clausula, the double cretic.

dolebam: echoes, without limiting *dolor*; as *nec fas esse ducebam* takes up *verecundia*.

angebar: intensified by the adverb which weights the predicate and helps form a cretic + trochee clausula; expands "saddened" beyond political associations, (as *nec fas . . . ducebam*, below, adds a dimension to *nec mihi persuadere*); so the doublets are not merely synonymous and, thus, ornamental. The tone, rather, is essentially expository (see on *ergo* below), with a sequence carefully marked out from *in eadem causa* to *non in eadem fortuna* and developed through the moods and tenses of *esse*:

```
virum talem
    qui    in eadem causa
           in qua ego
                                    fuisset
    non    in eadem esse fortuna
```

an intricate, but clearly articulated recognition of the parallelism in position between Marcellus and Cicero and the antithesis between their circumstances which are pointedly not defined.

virum talem: Normal word order would be *talem virum*; this stresses the
adjective; cf. 18, *civile bellum tantum* vs. *tanto civili bello*.

in eadem causa in qua ego: Preposition of antecedent is usually not repeated with the relative when the verb is the same; see on *Lig.* 2, *in ea
parte fuisse.* Here ellipsis, change of person, and balance of *in eadem fortuna* affect the usage and occasion the intensive adjective *eadem* vs. *ea*.

fuisset: The subject is Marcellus, and thus clearly superior here to the possible alternative *fuissem*.

causa . . . fortuna: *Causa* is more general than "the Pompeian cause" as
fortuna is more general than "pardon and restoration"; see on *Lig.* 2, *parte*,
both for sense and difference in structure, and on *Lig.* 6, *in ea voluntate
. . . in qua*. Note how *fortuna* is highlighted in hyperbaton and fortified by
the rhythm produced (cretic + spondee vs. *fortuna esse*).

nec: both loosely connects the previous predication to the one it introduces
and anticipates the next, negative one, preparing for the parallelism between the two predicates.

nec mihi . . . ducebam: a question both of conviction and principle. The
concept of *fas,* moral or religious propriety, is entirely Roman. Caesar's
action has removed Cicero's scruples (*verecundia*) about taking advantage
of his own pardon while Marcellus remained in disgrace. The metaphor in
curriculo is frequent in Cicero, perhaps more strongly felt here as a com-
petition because of *aemulo*. Marcellus was twelve years younger than Cicero, but distinguished as an orator and successful as a politician; see on
vocem et auctoritatem above.

   versari: a slight zeugma; infinitive after *fas esse*. The construction after
persuadere would have been *ut versarer*.

illo . . . distracto: This complex ablative absolute (here the last member of the period) housing a symmetrical rhetorical construction represents a feature of Cicero's later style reminiscent of Caesar's usage; see Gotoff 4, 9–11; for the complex participial phrase enclosing dependent syntax see on 20, *viris bonis*, and 32, *salvo . . . manente*.

aemulo . . . laborum: corresponds complexly to *imitatore . . . studiorum*; civic oratory was a demanding and sometimes dangerous profession. Marcellus had pled for Aemilius Scaurus in 54 and Milo (56 and 52) at the side of Cicero. In a letter to Marcellus from 50 (*Fam.* 15.9), Cicero acknowledges the similarity in the careers and interest of the two men. *Studiorum* refers to scholarly pursuits in philosophy, rhetoric, etc.

quasi . . . a me: After two sets of members paired immediately by *atque* and *ac,* the third set, *socio . . . et comite,* is split by *a me,* which reinforces by position the meaning of *distracto*.

quasi quodam: Cicero deepens the relationship between himself and Marcellus from one of competitors and colleagues to one of intimate friends and traveling companions, whose forced separation is a cause for special pathos. *Quasi* alone would be enough to establish a figurative sense to the whole locution; see *Har. Resp.* 6, *quasi fatali adventu* and *quasi divino munere,* cited at *Lig.* 22, *natam ad bellum . . . gerendum.* The indefinite adjective *quidam* often suggests the figurative use of the noun it modifies, especially after *quasi,* as does *aliquis* (so *quasi signum aliquod,* below). *Aliquis* with *quasi* occurs about half as frequently as *quidam* in the speeches (eleven vs. nineteen times), although both are found in all periods. The essential difference between the two indefinite pronouns probably remains (*quidam* identifiable but undefined; *aliquis* indefinable; see on 26, *cum est aliquid amplius*), but in the vaguer expression of figurative language, the distinction is often blurred. So *Verr.* 2.2.187, *lituras quasi quaedam volnera tabularum recentia,* "erasures like some kind of fresh wounds on the tablets"; *Verr.* 2.5.35, *ut me . . . quasi in aliquo terrarum orbis theatro versari existimarem,* "that I sensed it was as if I were performing in some sort of global or universal theater." See, too, *Verr.* 2.2.8, *nisi C. Marcellus quasi aliquo fato venisset,* "had not C. Marcellus come as if by some sort of fate." When the noun to be taken figuratively is modified by another adjective, the two indefinites behave rather differently; see on *Lig.* 5, *incredibilem quendam.* But why the deliberate marking here of figurative language at all? *Socius* is a normal way of referring to a partnership in business or profession. *Comes* is perhaps somewhat more esoteric; always with the sense of a traveling companion, as in *Furi et Aureli comites Catulli* (Cat. 11), implying the closest bonds of friendship. It is used metaphorically, without qualification, at *Verr.* 2.5.139, cited at *Lig.* 18, *sceleris . . . parricidi. Socius* and *comes* are found together at *Font.* 49, "for then had virtue been the partner of his life and glory the companion of his death," and *Fam.* 1.9.22 (to Lentulus), "You will certainly have me, at least, as a partner and companion of all your proceedings, opinions, etc."; see, too, the passage cited at 14, *socia.* Cicero calls attention with *quasi quodam* precisely to the change in image of Marcellus from rival colleague to intimate companion. Earlier in the same year (46) Cicero recorded his moving farewell to the orator Hortensius, *Brut.* 2: "I was saddened because I had lost not, as many thought, a rival or a detractor of my oratorical reputation, but rather a partner and sharer in our ennobling calling (*consortem gloriosi laboris*)."

distracto: a strong, violent verb; cf. *Deiot.* 15 and *Lig.* 5, *belli discidium.* The hyperbaton of *a me . . . distracto* creates another by separating *socio* from *comite*, the latter drawing pathetic attention to itself by its unanticipated joining. For the interlocking word order see on 16, *quotiens ego eum et quanto cum dolore vidi* and *non . . . causae inter se sed victoriae comparandae*, and on 32, *excubias et . . . laterum oppositus et corporum.*

ergo: more insistent on a logical conclusion than either *igitur*, always postpositive in Cicero, or *quare*, which is semidependent on the previous sentence. As such it appears far more frequently in Cicero's philosophical works than in the speeches.

et mihi . . . et his omnibus: By the explicitly (*et . . . et*) paired datives, a parallelism is subtly suggested between Cicero and the rest of the state and between redress for past hardships and hope for the future.

C. Caesar: Use of the *praenomen* in a vocative is a sign of special respect, its absence a sign of greater intimacy. In the other two Caesarian speeches the *praenomen* is generally found only at the beginning and end; in *Pro Marcello* it is all but invariable (ten of thirteen vocatives); see *Lig.* 37.

consuetudinem . . . aperuisti: It is unclear whether this metaphor, like the next, not otherwise used by Cicero, is from racing, military siege, or economic blockade. Collocation with the following metaphor suggests that it is military, but a racing metaphor has recently occurred.

omni re publica: The phrase is used only once elsewhere in the speeches, at *Verr.* 2.5.175, *tulit haec civitas . . . regiam istam vestram dominationem in iudiciis et in omni re publica,* a context equally expansive.

quasi: This metaphor is strongly qualified (by *quasi* and *aliquod*), although *consuetudinem . . . interclusam aperuisti* was not. See on *quasi quodam socio* above. It is often difficult for the modern reader to know how strongly a Latin metaphor was felt. One should observe when Cicero qualifies a metaphor and when he does not; but that will have more to do with the strength of the figure vis-à-vis the general context than with its intrinsic boldness.

signum: The metaphor is unique in Cicero, perhaps suggested by the judge. A flag was raised from a general's tent as a signal to march out to fight (cf. Livy 22.45 *signum proposuit*; Caes. *BG* 2.20.1). Livy (39.15.11) describes the raising of a flag on the Janiculum, for a muster of armed citizens. Ruch cites *Aen.* 8.1, *ut belli signum Laurenti Turnus ab arce.*

3

intellectum est: The dative, never quite expressing agent in Latin (at least until Tacitus), indicates that the perfect is in effect present. "I have come to learn" or "It is [at this point] known to me"; see Woodcock, 158. Note the position of *enim*; so 19, *tantus est enim,* and at 8, 11, and 26.

quidem: establishes the expectation of another item contrasting with *mihi* and extends the parallelism of the datives. In fact, nothing in the Latin corresponds to *paulo ante,* although the antithesis is felt.

| | mihi quidem | in multis et maxime in me ipso, |
| sed paulo ante | omnibus | cum M. Marcellus . . . concessisti |

The constructions following each dative are neither parallel nor of equal weight. It cannot be too strongly stressed that Cicero's composition is not predominantly symmetrical.

in multis: *Multi* = "many others," as at *Lig.* 15, *quam multi?* and *Deiot.*

7, *pro multis*; see also on *ullo in laudis genere* below. Plin. *Epist.* 6.16 17 has *nox omnibus noctibus nigrior,* "blacker than all other nights."

cum . . . concessisti: As an indicative, temporal clause it merely defines *paulo ante.* Any implication of causality in a subjunctive clause might make the admiration in *te . . . anteferre* appear to be a condition of Caesar's grant of clemency.

commemoratis . . . offensionibus: ablative absolute, pendent to the *cum* clause (see on 2, *illo . . . distracto*), succinctly carries the thrust. Use of *praesertim* in a causal construction other than a *cum* clause is rare in Cicero; see on 20 and *Deiot.* 37.

offensionibus: In pardoning Marcellus, Caesar had referred to his *acerbitas* (*Fam.* 4.4.3), and with good reason; see the Introduction, section 3.1.

dignitatem: of the state, its political power; corresponds to the *auctoritas* of the Senate, its political influence. In an individual it refers to public status or image, the place a man holds in society and what that place entitles him to do for himself and for others.

vel . . . vel: not exclusive, suggests both equally without insisting on either; so *Deiot.* 1, *vel . . . vel.*

suspicionibus: Cicero will address these in 21–23.

ille: Cicero makes Marcellus a natural third beneficiary along with the Republic and the Senate. This *quidem,* described as "contrasting" by Solodow, 30ff., introduces a statement or observation that anticipates another one that is related but not necessarily antithetical. The listener awaits an asseveration, which comes here with *vero*; so too, at 10, *te vero,* and 12, *ceteros quidem . . . ante . . . viceras; hodierno vero die te ipse vicisti.*

fructum . . . maximum: This word order in a hyperbaton (noun . . . adjective) creates surprise, rather than suspense (adjective . . . noun), especially since *maximum* would normally precede its noun (e.g., 6, *maximam vero partem*); see on *Lig.* 30, *causas . . . multas.*

cum . . . tum: on the level of words, correlates but with emphasis, sometimes contrasting, on the second item. Cicero assumes the parallel support of Caesar and the Senate for the recall of Marcellus. Note the placement of *gravissimo et maximo*; the adjectives are attributive, but emphatically placed, achieving a double cretic clausula.

iudicio: The central theme of this part of the speech is that Caesar's judgment, in the sense both of discernment and decisions taken, is his consummate virtue. At 12 it takes precedence over prerogatives of victory itself, and at 13 it establishes that those who are pardoned must be freed of the opprobrium of criminal guilt.

ex quo . . . gloria: The semi-independent relative is a plain, neutral sentence connective, presenting, almost casually here, an explanatory observation on the previous remark. It tends, nonetheless, to break up the progression of thought: "Marcellus, by virtue of his return through your kindness, is an object of admiration; but what makes him really fortunate is that his good fortune elicits such pure general pleasure." Cicero may be having some trouble getting off the ground here, as he tries to intersperse praises of Marcellus with paeans to Caesar. Although the semi-independent relative is practically parenthetical, it is handsomely articulated here as an epigrammatic summation, balancing, through *quanta in dato . . . laus* and *in accepto . . . tanta gloria,* Caesar and Marcellus; see *Lig.* 16, *qua qui . . . utetur,* and *Lig.* 36, *quam . . . cum . . . dederis.* The contrast between the nouns, prominent in final position, is somewhat artificial; elsewhere both *bellicas laudes* (6) and *gloria* (7) for restoring Marcellus, presently referred to as *laus,* are attributed to Caesar. The real distinction is between prepositional phrases, where the participle-noun complexes are of the "*ab urbe condita*" type. That is, the emphasis shifts from the substantive, or phrasal, element to the predicative or clausal force of the participle; see *Lig.* 25, *acceptae iniuriae.* The pairing of *quo numine laeso* and *quidve dolens* at Virg. *Aen.* 1.8–9 makes clear that the emphasis is on *laeso*: "because of what wounding of her divinity or because she was grieved by what?"

profecto: "you must realize." This particle, always subjective, strengthens a predication to the point of expressing a necessity forced upon someone, as *Deiot.* 26.

intellegis: after *intellectum est* gives a resolution to the passage. There is a lesson for Caesar, too, in his grant of clemency.

tanta gloria: By placing *sit* before *tanta,* Cicero sacrifices a dominant, double cretic clausula for a less common one, –⏑–⏑–, labeled by Fraenkel "*Poe-*

nulum tuum" (Fraenkel 4, 16); but see *Deiot.* 43, *clementiae tuae,* the closing clausula of the speech; see also the Introduction, section 1.1. We cannot always tell whether "less common" means "less favored" or "more exquisite."

4

est vero: Initial position of the verb in Latin is infrequent enough to be worth noticing, although the significance of the phenomenon will be various. Here it stresses the reality of the predication, the awaited correction of *ille quidem* above. Elsewhere forms of the verb may emphasize tense or mood (e.g., 29, *erit inter eos,* and 30, *erat*); initial present tenses may dramatize action in narrative; initial past tenses, dispassionate summation of events, as at 31, *perfuncta res publica est . . . ; vicit is.* For contrast through verb position see on 29, *vagabitur. Vero* is an extremely strong assertion.

ille: Acceptance of the pronoun encouraged by 3, *ille,* determines approval of the emendation *ipsum.*

cuius ex salute: a causal relative clause, itself incorporating a comparative clause with paronomasia of *ventura sit* and *pervenerit. Omnes* refers to the Senate. In *Lig.* 37 Cicero asks Caesar to restore Ligarius to the people as he had Marcellus to the Senate. *Salus* will be found to have a number of meanings in these speeches, ranging from health and physical well-being, to personal and political safety, to safe return (from exile), to restoration of civil rights; see *Deiot.* 1, *salutem.*

paene: like *fere,* is used by common Latin idiom to qualify universals, like *omnes.* So at 6; see too 10, *paene ab interitu,* "from virtual extinction." It is not to be taken with *non minor.*

quod quidem: Closely connected with the preceding by the semi-independent relative, this period expresses through *quod* a serious qualification. Cicero's praise of Marcellus is not just perfunctory, and Caesar's pardon of him not just whimsical. He is worthy of the Senate's devotion and Caesar's pardon. For Cicero's insistence on this point in his own case see *Lig.* 19; here it delays his launching his *laus Caesaris. Quidem* is prospective; the qualification will be explained by *enim*; see on 13–14, *bellum. . . . quo quidem in bello.*

merito atque . . . iure: a right that, although Marcellus earned it, is universal and absolute and binding even on Caesar.

aut . . . aut . . . aut . . . aut . . . aut: Here not absolutely exclusive, they indicate that distinction in any one of these qualities would justify admiration; cf. 3, *vel.*

nobilitate: refers to heredity, *probitate* to character, *studio* to education, *innocentia* to lack of partisanship or to troublemaking. The "liberal arts"—philosophy, grammar, poetry, rhetoric—would recommend a man more to Caesar than, say, to a popular forum. Still it is odd to find the virtue, however appropriate to encomia, between moral probity and political disinterestedness.

optimarum artium: The humanistic disciplines, including philosophy, mathematics, music, poetry, and sometimes painting, although worthy of the attention of a freeborn Roman and thus *artes liberales,* took second place, in the Roman public mind, to the arts of warcraft, statescraft, and, Cicero insists (e.g., *De Or.* 1.6, 1.8), public speaking. The canon of the seven liberal arts a postclassical notion.

ullo in laudis genere: One group of manuscripts (α) has the preposition, which predominates in Cicero with the sense "in the matter of, in respect of," especially with the verb "to be"; two others do not. Certainty is impossible: at *Font.* 2 Cicero has *easdem [tabulas] Fonteius instituit et eodem genere pecuniae* but, a few lines later, *[tabulae] . . . ob unam causam et in uno genere sunt institutae,* in both cases "with regard to the same category of money." That the previous ablatives are ungoverned is not a factor, since the last member expands into a phrase. The word order adjective + preposition + noun is always to a degree exquisite. Here, with the noun further modified, it is particularly attractive. *Ullus* has the sense "any [other]," as *multi* can have the sense "many [others]"; see on 3, *in multis.*

nullius . . . flumen ingeni: *Nullius,* responding to *quis praestantior* above (for the tie with the preceding, or juncture, see 10, *praesentem*), is the genitive of *nemo,* not adjective with *ingeni*; see on *Lig.* 11, *Romanus . . . nemo.* When two genitives depend on a single noun, subjective usually precedes objective; see *Lig.* 12, *studia generis . . . virtutis,* for a more awkward case. Although not quite anaphoric, the negatives set up a parallelism between innate talent, and force and amplitude—rhetorical qualities associated, when joined, with the grand style. The metaphor of flowing water is unusual with the concept of talent; *flumen* more commonly governs *orationis, verborum,* or *eloquentiae.* Such a smooth flow is identified with the middle, or periodic, style. While not defining a level of diction, Cicero is certainly thinking about the suitable expression of his gratitude.

vis . . . copia: qualities which have the power to move men's spirits. Amplitude comes from the talent and skill to find words and figures adequate to the occasion (often, to our tastes, more than adequate). The confession of inadequacy to one's task is a rhetorical commonplace that can convey either the modesty of the speaker or the magnitude of his subject. Compare the language at *Verr.* 1.10, *etenim quod est ingenium tantum, quae tanta facultas dicendi aut copia, quae istius vitam . . . aliqua ex parte possit defendere?*

No sentence connective introduces this section; the shift is felt as sudden and nervous. The praise of Marcellus is within the competence of a trained encomiast; Caesar's is a different story. Cicero has to get past the extraordinary task of praising Caesar's military achievements before he can rise to the more difficult one of paying full honor to Caesar's pardon of Marcellus. He makes no attempt to articulate the antithesis between clemency and military genius in a single period. Praise of Caesar's prowess is given a full, extravagantly complimentary period. Only with *tamen affirmo* is the rhetorically critical qualification introduced.

non dicam . . . sed: This is an extension, explicit and precise, of the *non . . . sed* antithesis, a form of *correctio*; both constructions appear at *Clu.* 182, *mulier iam non morbo, sed scelere furiosa . . . nullo adhibito non dicam viro, ne colonum forte adfuisse dicatis, sed bono viro, in fili caput quaestionem habere conata est?* "Did the woman, insane now not with disease but criminality, in the absence of any, I shall not say man, lest you perhaps say her farmer was present, but of any respectable man, try to hold an inquiry against her son's life?" *Dicam* usually is functionally parenthetical, that is, does not affect the grammar, as in 5. Cf. *Deiot.* 2, *ne dicam.*

The two infinitives may correspond generally to the ornate and plain styles of prose or to the difference between *historiae* and *commentarii* (in which case they would constitute a private joke); but the antithesis is rhetorically stronger if the argument taken simply as a fortiori.

tamen hoc adfirmo: The connective *tamen* in initial position is unusual for

Cicero and starkly logical, undercutting the previous assertion; *hoc* explicitly anticipating the statement in the accusative + infinitive is a feature of expository style; see 12, *hoc quod dicam*.

pace dicam tua: The expression is courtly ("by your leave"), the speaker's insistence respectful. The phrase is not frequent in Cicero, although found as early as Plautus; see *Tusc.* 5.12, "But it appears so to Brutus, whose judgment I consider, if I may say (*pace tua dixerim*), far superior to yours" or at *Milo.* 103, "I would say this, my country, with your permission (*pace tua, patria, dixerim*)." The more belligerent sense, "despite your objection," common in academic Latin, is found at *Fam.* 7.17.1 (an extremely formal letter; see Shackleton Bailey 1, 1:334; also *Off.* 3.10.42). The expression is made more robust here by hyperbaton and the clausula thus created (double cretic).

quam eam quam: The awkwardness could have been avoided by using the ablative of comparison *ea quam*. Some see a sign here of extempore performance. But it cannot be said that the Latin is intolerably awkward, and the word order leading up to it, *nullam . . . laudem* intertwined with *esse . . . ampliorem,* is not that of a speaker in trouble.

5

This *laudatio* begins enthusiastically, with *saepe, crebris,* and *usurpare*—the emphatic, pleonastic frequentative of *uti* (see *Milo.* 18 cited at *Lig.* 20, *quibus . . . easdem*). But neither the stative *soleo* nor the artless *idque* introducing the second predicate prepares for the expansive and exuberant embellishments to come: the long hyperbaton of *omnis . . . res gestas,* the *copia* of anaphoric multicola: (*omnis* thrice, *nec* five times, and the ringing genitive plural phrases), and the complimentary conceit with which the period ends.

idque . . . usurpare: *Id* both refers in further anticipation to the object of *ante oculos ponere* and continues it as an explicit and independent part of its own parallel infinitive phrase. The effect of *-que* is "beyond that," "furthermore"; see on 6, *easque,* and *Lig.* 1, *idque*. The observation begins in his mind and is bruited in conversation before being expressed formally and publicly here. *Id* also anticipates the accusative + infinitive, although somewhat less vividly than would deictic *hoc*; see 4, *tamen hoc affirmo,* and 12, *hoc quod dicam.*

omnis nostrorum . . . posse conferri: The accusative + infinitive is elaborate, perhaps somewhat ponderous: a tricolon of weighted genitive plurals introduced anaphorically by *omnis* leads to the beginning of the predicate (*cum tuis*), which is separated from *conferri* by a plethora of conditions in ablative + genitive phrases, all negatived by *nec*.

regum: from Cyrus and Alexander through Pyrrhus, down to Mithridates, a generation ago.

contentionum: general hostilities, as distinct from *proelia*, individual battles.

varietate regionum: During the Civil War alone he had fought in Spain, North Africa, Egypt, Asia Minor, and Greece. Add Gaul and Britain from the 50s.

celeritate conficiendi: a hallmark of Caesar's generalship, stylishly immortalized after his victory at Zela by the slogan *veni, vidi, vici*; see the Introduction, section 3.3.

nec vero . . . lustratae sunt: This second accusative + infinitive unit is expanded by a complex comparative unit with *citius* anticipating a *quam* clause. The first unit was positive, though repeatedly negatived; this is negative in form, though asseveration is more strongly felt through *vero*. The unattainable potential is compared with the experience of all of history by the switch from the present (*posse*) to the perfect (*potuisse*) infinitive.

passibus cuiusquam: unimpeded in any way. The sense of the indefinite general pronoun is extended to the potential phrase and contrasts with *tuis*.

non dicam . . . sed: The balance of *passibus* with *cursibus* is promptly and ostentatiously corrected by parenthetical non *dicam . . . sed*; so 4. The verbs are not synonymous: *peragrare* is used in the sense of military domination at *Prov. Cons.* 33; *lustratae sunt* suggests more leisurely, ceremonial movement—not excluding military review, perhaps less appropriate with *cursibus*. A full clause in the comparative insists on the fact (thus indicative) as opposed to the potentiality.

6

quae quidem: *Quidem* sums up the usual evaluation of Caesar's military achievements and suggests that a new perspective is coming: thus *sed tamen*.

ego nisi ita . . . ut: *Nisi* anticipates the apodosis as *ita* does the *ut* clause— the orderly, syntactically marked progression of logical, expository prose. Normally the commonplace is generalized ("if anyone should fail to admit . . .") and less hyperbolic ("he would be lying").

ita: properly is modal and, as such, expected to qualify a verb rather than an adjective (but see *Lig.* 31, *ita multa*). But it can take on the function of *tam*, which defines quantity. In those cases the concept of quantity is expressed as a special form of the concept of quality, as when *tantus vir* is extended to mean "such a man."

ut ea vix: word order as at 34; more usual is *vix ut*. This order gives *vix* collocation with, and a sense of limitation to, *cuiusquam*.

mens aut cogitatio: personification and abstraction in an almost padded doublet; the first connotes intelligence, the second the exercise of intelligence.

sed tamen: a double, and hence emphatic, adversative to *quidem,* as at 9 and 11; elsewhere used to concede or drop one argument and move to another (so 22 and *Lig.* 2, 16, 20).

maiora: after *magna,* a paronomasia common in Cicero and Latin.

nam . . . et certe . . . at vero: The argument extends to three periods, the logical progression is signaled lexically: theme, justification, countertheme. *Certe* in the first clause marks it as concessive and so anticipates *vero*; see 28.

easque detrahere: *Eas* insists that the conjunction is joining two full and independent predications (the second is compound and antithetical), not just the infinitives; see at 5, *idque*. When connecting two clauses, *-que* implies more than a simple conjunctive "and"; see *Lig.* 1, *idque*.

detrahere: The careful reader of Cicero will often discover places where word order reflects the meaning of the predicate, as here, where the verb separates the object from separative ablative (so 2, *socio a me et comite distracto*; 31, *armorum . . . armatum*; or *Lig.* 3, *nullo . . . negotio*). Repeated infinitive + ablative plurals suggest parallelism. The function of the ablatives varies.

communicare: unusual in literal sense: "to make the common property of." See *Cael.* 13, *cum omnibus communicare quod haberet.*

cum multis: in antithesis with *ducibus*. For *multi* see 3.

ne . . . imperatorum: relentless clarity, but not pleonastic. The unperiodically added *ne* clause implies malevolence, deliberate spitefulness.

et certe . . . maximam vero: Only with *maximam vero partem* does it become clear that this is an antithetical (*multum . . . , maximam vero*), compound sentence. *Multum*, though treated adverbially, is an internal accusative adjective and can be played against *maximam*.

virtus . . . commeatus: A list of more than four items (unless structurally arranged in subunits) conveys abundance, a *congeries* to which items may be added in unpredictable number.

quasi suo iure: a legal metaphor frequently used. Cicero qualifies it here and at *Arch.* 1 (*prope*), in an ornamental passage. Nepos (see just below), using the normal word position of the possessive adjective, does not.

Fortuna: considered a deity and frequently so acknowledged by Caesar himself; see Plut. *Caes.* 38. It was thought of as an enviable, although not necessarily permanent possession of certain people, Caesar among them; see *Deiot.* 21, *eadem tua fortuna.* Nepos makes a very similar point at *Thras.* 1.4, ending *itaque iure suo nonnulla ab imperatore miles plurima vero Fortuna vindicat seque hic plus valuisse quam ducis prudentiam vere potest praedicare.* The personification here is insistent, unlike 10, *belli fortuna.*

quidquid . . . suum: another independent predicate; a restatement, with expository precision (*quidquid . . . id*) of the previous clause. The figure is called *interpretatio*; see on 7, *numquam enim*. For the reverse order of antecedent to relative see on 10, *quidquid belli . . . id*; 14, *qui vero . . . is*; and 17, *quos . . . eos.*

paene: qualifying the universal, *omne*. This is normal Latin idiom and has less force than an English translation of it would; so at 9.

suum: at the end for emphasis and clausula: *omne ducit suum* (double cretic).

7

at vero: strong antithesis. *Vero* is asseverative (so 4, *est vero*; 5, *nec vero*) but recalls the argument from which it parts. *At* introduces something unexpected, usually an objection; so 9, with *vero*.

huius gloriae: vivid, deictic demonstrative: "the glory of what you are doing here." The last time *gloria* appeared (3), it was attached to Marcellus for receiving Caesar's generosity.

quam . . . adeptus: expands on *huius*. For separation of verb and participle in perfect passive see 13, *sumus . . . compulsi*; 11, *adlatura . . . sit*; and 30, *obscuratura . . . sit*. The copula is often found in enclitic position; cf. ἐστι versus ἔστι.

neminem: fully pronominal and predicative with *socium*; see *Lig.* 11, *civis Romanus . . . nemo*. Its position achieves emphasis and a (resolved: ˇˇˇ¯) double cretic with *soci(um) habes*. The intensity of tone begins to rise.

quod . . . maximum est: This appositive noun clause is usually explained as merely specifying *quantumcumque*, which can be large or small. Instead it functions like *quod necesse est, quod caput est*, following an indefinite referent, but preceding and characterizing a clause with particular or identifying descriptive content. In this instance it is precisely parallel to *quantumcumque est*, which is also in apposition both to *hoc* and to *totum est tuum*; thus the particle *certe*. It creates anticipation for the identifying clause; see, more dramatically, 17, *quod . . . verebamur*. The *quod maximum est* at 25 is somewhat different.

totum est . . . tuum: Cicero conveys his insistence with repetition (reinforced, as frequently, by *inquam*; see at 28, *Lig.* 15, and *Deiot.* 8). But his use, for precision, of indefinites and substantived neuter singulars is redolent of logical exposition; see 26, *quidquid . . . amplius*. The possessive adjective is in its normal word position, but stressed in hyperbaton and placement in the period; see 8, *tuam esse totam*.

nihil . . . nihil . . . : four subjects, reinforced by anaphora, also broken down into pairs.

ista: intensified equivalent of *tua* in collocation with *sibi*, creating a tension.

decerpit: a verb used only here in the speeches, a variation on *detrahere* above. The list ends with a double cretic rhythm.

quin etiam: *Quin* introduces a strong corroboration, *etiam* intensifies with enthusiasm or outrage what has preceded and advances a more extreme case. Cicero does not overuse this highly emphatic phrase which gained in dignity in his lifetime; see LH&S, 2:676–77. Of seventeen occurrences in the speeches (only five before 57 B.C.) it appears twice only in *Pro Balbo* (7, 9), *Pro Plancio* (59, 90), and *Pro Milone* (26, 65), and once each in three of the *Philippics*. The content corresponds to the second part (*maximam vero partem*) of the compound sentence in 6.

illa ipsa . . . domina: The appositive is rhetorically expansive and logically concessive. For the substantially modified, or "weighted," nominative concessive to its predicate see below and on *Deiot.* 4, *tua . . . natura.*

se . . . offert: Manuscripts vary on the position of *se*. Fraenkel, trying to determine the boundaries of Latin phraseology, showed that a "weighted" or modified substantive can develop a circumstantial relationship with its predicate (much as does an ablative absolute), and he assumed that the word following the phrase would initiate a new clause (see Fraenkel 2, 129–30). If so, *se* after *istius* would be in the second, or unstressed, position in its clause, where, in inflected languages, unemphatic pronouns often reside (Wackernagel's law).

non offert . . . cedit . . . fatetur: Are the three predicates heard as simple tricolon? Or are *tibi cedit, tuam . . . fatetur* an expansion of the first, marked as bipartite by anaphoric asyndeton? The latter is suggested by the change from negative to positive predication.

cedit: effective personification. For the force of *cedere* (as opposed to *parere*) cf. *Lig.* 22, *cessit . . . paruit*. Fortune, like everyone else from the centurion down, gracefully yields a share of the spotlight.

tuam esse totam: echoes *totum est . . . tuum* above. Because of their constructions and contexts, the possessive adjectives in both clauses are emphatically placed. *Tuam* is anaphoric with *tibi* and stressed by initial position followed by enclitic *esse* (see above on *quam . . . adeptus*).

propriam: with proprietary rights, as Aeolus would have over his wife (Virg. *Aen.* 1.73, *propriamque ⟨Deiopeiam tibi⟩ dicabo*).

numquam enim: epigrammatic coda, itself a doublet in complex restatement (the pattern is parallel and chiastic).

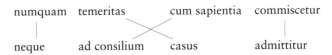

For the *interpretatio* see on 6, *quidquid . . . gestum*. Some refer the remark expressly to Caesar's wisdom and councils; the figure and parallel structures argue for general application.

temeritas: may be rashness resulting from inadvertence, as well as design. Cf. "accident," as at *Div.* 2.85; so, too, Serv. *Aen.* 9.327, *temere passim fortuito, neglegenter*. See *Lig.* 17.

8

domuisti: The section is composed of a single argument, logically presented: statement (*domuisti*), qualification (*ea tamen*), qualification explained (*nulla est enim*), counterstatement in asyndeton ("to conquer emotion"). In the course of the argument the tone becomes more elevated and exuberant.

gentis . . . abundantis: three grand ablative + adjective phrases expand to a weightier fourth.

locis infinitas: Cf. 5, *varietate regionum*; also refers to the difficulty in dealing with tribes having no fixed boundaries.

ea tamen . . . quae: clear, expository locution with antecedent emphatically placed. The inclusion of the *ut* clause in its governing clause is neat, but unusual.

condicionem: From its basic meaning "stipulation," *condicio* extended to connote "property," "character."

nulla est enim: The position of *enim* makes *nulla est* a single entity predicating existence. Cf. 19, *tantus est enim*; 3, *intellectum est enim*; and 26, *quidquid est enim*. Structure echoes preceding.

ferro et viribus: hendiadys, "by the power of the sword."

debilitari frangique: strong verbs; no mere doublet in spite of *-que*. They describe a process in motion.

animum vincere: Infinitive phrases present Caesar's supreme virtues as facts (the infinitive is a noun), rather than actions, before the predication of any examples. Note the progression of attitudes and responses.

iracundiam: may extend past Caesar's personal feelings and refer also to those of his loyal followers, the control of which is essential to the successful execution of political *clementia*.

adversarium: has particular reference to Marcellus and Cicero himself. In the subtle shift from external wars—in which Caesar exercised clemency selectively—to the more delicate domestic situation following the Civil War, Cicero becomes more expansive.

adversarium ... praestantem: handsome honorific phrase bracketing an asyndetic tricolon of qualities. The distinction of the beneficiary adds luster to his benefactor; see on 4, *quod quidem merito,* and *Lig.* 19, where Cicero insists that his own restoration is not to be considered that of a pardoned criminal.

non modo: anticipates a construction extending beyond *extollere* to *amplificare*.

iacentem: The position of the participle, separated by the first of paired infinitives, marks it as adversative and emphatic, as *praestantem*, rounding off the noun phrase, was attributive. The clausula is a favored, resolved cretic + spondee.

amplificare ... dignitatem: Caesar claimed (*Fam.* 4.4.3) to be acceding to the pleas for clemency because of Marcellus' standing (*hominis causa*). Cicero used *pristina dignitas* to describe his own public image before the war; cf. *Fam.* 4.4.4., cited at 1, *dolor.*

haec qui faciat: Infinitives now reveal themselves as a complex, hanging substantive phrase, a list of expressions not grammatically integrated into a predication. *Haec,* pre-positioned, sums them up, perhaps pulling in the reins on rising exuberance, before settling on a construction, itself controlled, in which the relative clause anticipates its antecedent. Before that resolution, a rhetorical antithesis (*non . . . sed*) is begun, with an emphatic variation on the more usual word order (*eum ego non*). *Ego* in enclitic position accents the preceding word and allows stress on the pronoun that follows (cf. 16, *quotiens ego eum . . .*), which would otherwise be weakened in second position (see the glossary s.v. Wackernagel's law). Cicero wanted to make the antithesis work at the level of clauses. Though the comparison is between *cum summis viris* and *simillimum deo,* the construction creates a syntactic opposition between the verbs which call attention to the orator's first-person presence as participant and critic.

deo: The hyperbole is not perfunctory, but suitable to encomium. Cicero already had characterized Caesar's wisdom at 1 as *paene divina*; cf. *Lig.* 38, *ad deos . . . accedunt*. But the language of encomia cannot be translated into political reality. A year after this speech, by order of the Senate, a statue of Caesar was installed in the temple of Quirinus (see on *Deiot.* 33 and 15, *tyrannum*) beside the statues of the kings of Rome. Cicero, among others, interpreted this as a sign of Caesar's political ambition and took umbrage. Dative with *similis* is a later Latin idiom than genitive and is rarer in Cicero, although there seems to be some distinction: genitive depends on a nominal sense of "copy," "image," "likeness," dative on a verbal sense of "approximating," "resembling."

9

Once more Cicero argues the same point in the same logical progression as at 6–7: theme (*itaque*), qualification (*sed tamen*), countertheme (*at vero*).

quidem: marks its compound period as a concession, anticipating *sed tamen*; so at 6 and 11. *Illae* extends the weighted subject of its clause and is in emphatic position, followed by *quidem,* which tends to attach itself to pronouns, without necessarily qualifying them specifically.

sed paene: a variation on *sed etiam,* emphasizing the second member to the virtual dismissal of the first.

litteris atque linguis: Alliterative doublets are a feature of the middle style, ornamental and unhurried; see at 11, *multo magnoque* and *conficiat et* *consumat. Litteris* is not limited to literature but includes inscriptions and monuments.

atque: The choice between *atque* and *ac* is generally determined (as also for *neque* and *nec*) by whether the following word begins with a vowel. The conjunctions were to be limited to the length of a single syllable. If elision with a following word could preserve the *qu-* sound, all well and good; but not at the expense of adding another syllable. An exception to this rule seems to be made *clausulae gratia* here and at 23 (*atque prostrata*); see Gotoff 2, 173; Axelson, 83ff.; and Skutsch, *Ennius, 63*, citing evidence in Livy (*atqu(e)* 1,166 times, *atque* 68, *ac* 1,898).

sed tamen: Cicero introduces the converse forcefully, in an independent period, interrupting the sense of continuation in *conticescet,* a commonplace. But he defines the situation tentatively: *eius modi res* and *nescioquo modo.*

obstrepi: The personal passive of this word is found only here in Cicero; elsewhere it is active with a dative object.

videntur: perhaps pre-positioned, interrupting the ablative phrase, to close the period with the sound of trumpets, in a double cretic. It also treats as a perception (to share) what might otherwise have been offered as fact.

at vero: For the two particles see 7. The apodosis is a surprising exclamation, although the intensity is tempered by what at first appears a pedantic distinction between heroes of life and fiction, with a concentration in the generalizing result clause on fictitious characters. In fact Cicero uses the distinction to build up to his climax.

clementer . . . sapienter: With five adverbs in asyndeton, Cicero still reaches for the right word. Cf. 1, *clementiam . . . sapientiam.*

in iracundia . . . superba est: circumstantial prepositional phrase, symmetrically compound, made exceptionally ornate by governing paired relative clauses. Ciceronian constructions more usually descend in dependence from clauses to phrases.

incendimur: The metaphor, like the personifications in the phrase above, elevates the tone.

audimus aut legimus: correspond to *litteris atque linguis* above. Note the number and variety of paired concepts in this period.

in gestis rebus: normal word order reversed for antithesis with *fictis*, accented by repetition of preposition, as with *in victoria* above. In a less self-conscious locution the preposition would not be repeated in either pair; see 2, *in eadem causa*.

ut eos: Result clauses not anticipated *ita, sic, tam,* etc. provide a general summation of a passage and provide a semi-independent, unperiodic addition; see 17, *ut . . . debeat*; 18, *ut mihi*; and the similar feeling of the semi-independent relative at 3, *ex quo perfecto*. Here, where the exclamatory adjective replaces *tanto*, the clause seems a little less detached from what precedes.

saepe: subtle, perfect placement. It avoids antecedent–relative collocation as well as overly stressing the contrast between *saepe* and *numquam*.

10

vero: breaks off the speculation and introduces the actual example of Caesar, in an *argumentum a minore*. The pronoun in initial position opposes *eos* in the last sentence and begins a long hyperbaton extending to the verbs at the end of the period. The style is embellished.

quem . . . cuius: Asyndeton is usual in Latin for pairs of relative clauses with the same antecedent; see on *Deiot.* 37, *eisque*. *Intuemur* is not synonymous with *cernimus*, having the sense of admiring rather than discerning.

praesentem: contrasts strongly with *quos numquam vidimus* (for the juncture see on 4, *nullius*) and the limitations of fictional characters; it connotes more than a roll-call "present"—perhaps "manifest." Cicero uses the adjective of gods engaged on behalf of the state at *Cat.* 2.19, 2.29, 3.18.

ut . . . velis: epexigetic indirect question, explaining what is revealed by scrutiny of Caesar's thoughts, inclinations, and facial expression. Editors bothered by the lack of an antecedent to the questions accept the emendation *eos* with the *ut* clause characterizing. But *os* has special prominence because *-que* links the first two (hendiadys for "bent of mind" vs. the visible *os*). And of all the objects of scrutiny made possible by Caesar's physical presence, it is most readable.

quidquid . . . id: Within the *ut* clause, the word order relative–antecedent in the indefinite relative clause is a neat expository construction, as at 6, *quidquid . . . gestum*. *Rei publicae* is probably partitive genitive after *quidquid,* though it might be dative.

belli fortuna: a striking phrase found at *Verr.* 2.5.132 and later in this speech (15); perhaps not here personified; cf. *belli calamitas* at *Verr.* 2.2.86, cited just below.

reliquum fecerit: usually described as a colloquial periphrasis for *relinquere.* Cf. Antony in a letter quoted at *Phil.* 13.48 and Cicero at *Att.* 3.8.2. But *Verr.* 2.2.86, *quos civis belli calamitas reliquos fecerat,* or, for that matter, Livy 9.24.13, *quos reliquos fortuna ex nocturna caede fecerat,* puts the phrase in dramatic contexts. It is a stronger variation of the simple verb, enlivening the personification and giving a pathetic characterization to the objects. The language may have come originally from accounting; so Catullus 36.16, *acceptum face redditumque votum.* See on *Lig.* 32, *gratum facere,* which appears to be more common than *gratificari.*

quibus studiis: The apodosis swells to an asyndetic tricolon of exclamatory clauses with virtual anaphora and virtual homoeoteleuton echoing the enthusiasm.

parietes . . . gestiunt: hyperbolic personification, at home in elevated diction, not just encomiastic passages. In *Piso.* 21 temples moan and houses mourn, and at 52 the city walls, houses, and temples seem to rejoice. *In Pisonem* is a speech of vituperation, but the stylistic conventions of such speeches and of encomia are similar. At *Cat.* 2.2, after describing Catiline as sick over his failure to ravage Rome, Cicero goes on, *quae ⟨Roma⟩ quidem mihi laetari videtur, quod tantam pestem evomuerit forasque proiecerit.* See, too, Virg. *Aen.* 4.667, *tecta fremunt,* and 11.38, *maestoque immugit regia luctu.* The frequentative of *gero* is strongly animated, bespeaking energy and intensity.

me dius Fidius: (sc. *iuvet*), an ancient expletive (*divus/dius/deus/*Iu-), in which *Fidius* is an epithet of Jupiter as god of good faith. The first two words are often printed as one, but the personal involvement of *me* is felt, denoting the intense feeling of the speaker. The strong conviction thus expressed is outrage in eight of its twelve occurrences: as at *Sest.* 30, *Piso.* 33, *Dom.* 47, 83, 92, *Phil.* 2.67, *Milo.* 76, 87; others are *Har. Resp.* 50, *Planc.* 9, *Rosc. Am.* 95. The degree of specifically religious intensity of the exclamation is difficult to ascertain.

ut mihi videtur: This expression occurs sixteen times in Cicero: four in the speeches, five in the letters, and seven in the treatises. A late grammarian, M. Sacerdos, says Cicero uses it here to qualify the hyperbole. But its sense elsewhere is invariably modest and low-key: e.g., "I should think," "as far as I can tell," "if I may say." It acts against the force of *me dius fidius* and is therefore suspect. I would prefer the personal *parietes . . . mihi videntur . . . gratias agere gestire.*

illa auctoritas: attribute used by metonomy for its possessor. Cicero's first reference to Marcellus here is oblique—*illa* for *eius hominis* or *sua* (for the reflexive see on *suis sedibus* below) as *iste* for *tuus,* at 7—owing partly to the switch from a general comment on Caesar's attitude to a very special case. Authority is the power, derived from influence, to get a job done, also to support a clientele. It might rest with a political body (like the Senate at 3) or an individual. Great Republican patrons in this respect resembled the romanticized picture of a Mafia "godfather." The Claudii Marcelli, although plebeian, had been senatorial for two hundred years.

suis sedibus: Latin prefers the possessive adjective to the genitive of the pronoun, even at the expense of parallelism; see 2, *non illius . . . sed . . . meam.* The reflexives refer back *ad sensum* to the understood subject: *Marcellus auctoritate praeditus.* At *dignitatem suam* below the referent is *quibus,* a normal Latin usage.

equidem: a reinforced form of *quidem,* it refers only to the first person and now, in initial position (as at 22), highlights Cicero's personal reaction as distinct from that of the Senate.

C. Marcelli: the praenomen of Marcus' younger brother (cos. 49), and of a cousin (cos. 50), whose son by Octavia, Augustus' intended heir, is apostrophized in death by Anchises at the end of *Aen.* 6. This man is referred to at 34 with equal ambiguity as *frater,* which may also refer to a first cousin (*frater patruelis*); see Wilson, and Bush and Cerutti.

commemorabili: the compound, extremely rare in Latin, used here for sheer volume.

pectus memoria obfudit: Is *obfudit* intransitive, in which case *memoria* is ablative ("my heart welled up with the memory")? Or transitive, in which case *memoria* is nominative? No transitive usage meaning "inundated" is found; and parallels exist for neither metaphor. Striving for pathetic effect, Cicero may be stretching usage with a personification, although the only close parallel is *Planc.* 1, *ei temporum meorum memoriam suffragari videbam*, "I realized that the memory of my crisis was casting its vote for this man." Other remarkable metaphors are found in *Marc.*, i.e., 2, *consuetudinem interclusam aperuisti*; 4, *flumen ingeni*; 23, *quae dilapsa . . . diffluxerunt*; and 23, *legibus vincienda sunt.*

quibus tu: not an example of Wackernagel's law (see 7, *se societatem*); *tu* is by no means unemphatic; see 11, *hunc tu,* and Gotoff 1.

etiam mortuis: The adjective is predicative and concessive.

Marcello conservato: The verb *conservare,* found nine times in this speech, entails recovery of position, rights, and prerogatives.

dignitatem suam: indirect reflexive; cf. on *suis sedibus* above.

nobilissimamque: *-Que* is not merely copulative when connecting entire predicates, but sequential or adversative; see 6, *easque.*

nobilissimamque familiam: a second relative clause. Latin does not always require a second relative pronoun; see *Deiot.* 37, *eisque.* The meaning of *familia* extended to household, slaves, retainers, family fortunes. By this time only two brothers and a cousin remained, as far as we know.

iam . . . redactam: The participle may have a somewhat adversative, pathetic nuance after *nobilissimam*, e.g., "most glorious, yet. . . ."

vindicasti: echoes *reddidisti* by position, homoeoteleuton, and clausula.

11

hunc tu igitur: Again (see on 10, *quibus tu*), the pronoun of the addressee should not be considered rhetorically unemphatic. It highlights the contrast of Caesar's experience with that of the Marcelli. In fact *igitur,* omitted by some manuscripts and excluded by some editors, is generally enclitic in Cicero.

hunc . . . diem: logically, *huius gratulationem diei*; such abbreviated expression is called brachylogy.

gratulationibus: like a *supplicatio,* a prayer of public thanks decreed by the Senate to honor a man's military success, in the observance of which the whole population participates. Caesar had been voted an unprecedented fifteen-day *supplicatio* in 57 for victories in Gaul, twenty in 55 for his invasion of Britain, twenty in 52 for victories in Gaul, and forty in 46, his fourfold triumph. The *Pro Marcello* as been referred to as a *gratulatio.*

iure: as at 6, *suo iure*; cf. 13, where *recte* means "correctly."

anteponis: Future, found in some manuscripts, is tempting; it would be a future that pronounces a future fact, not that describes a future action. But the present, conditioned by *iure,* is what Cicero used: "It is right for you to weigh this day and prefer it."

haec . . . res: following *hunc . . . diem*; the deictic pronouns are vivid and immediate.

ceterae . . . huius autem: antithesis to explain and amplify the previous sentence. It is usual in Latin, unlike English, to mention the remaining instances first, before focusing on the particular. *Autem* introduces the proposition contrasted to the *ceterae* clause, not necessarily opposite (here it is a restatement of *haec . . . Caesaris*).

quidem: *Sed tamen* marks a strong adversative, and *autem* introduces a rhetorical contrast.

idem: Cf. at 1, and the propensity in English to translate *idem* as an adverb, e.g., "at the same time, likewise."

quae quidem: Cicero again qualifies *huius rei* in an attempt to characterize it; *quidem* here introduces an amplification (expansion or extension) of what has gone before (= *et ea quidem*); see on 12, *et ceteros quidem,* and Solodow, 110–11. For the force of *et* see also *Lig.* 24, *et prohibiti.* The period begins smoothly: *tanta* (= *tam magna*; cf. *Lig.* 15, *in tanta tua fortuna*) anticipating the *ut* clause which looks as if it will be composed of two parallel predicates in asyndeton, as an alternative to an apodosis with a concessive protasis (so at 28, *quae miretur . . . quae laudet,* and *Deiot.* 27, *multis ille quidem*). *Consumat vetustas* is clearly not the result of *quae . . . tanta est*; see on 12, *florescit.* Instead Cicero interrupts the sequence with a parenthesis (the punctuation is modern, but, since *enim* must be the second element in a sentence, *nihil est enim* must begin an intruded period). The interruption seems to break the speaker's concentration on syntax. He suspends his consideration of destructibility with a dramatic particle (*at* introduces an unexpected and often dramatic, or at least histrionic, twist to the argument) and gives what should have been the second predicate of the *ut* clause now as an independent, hence indicative, clause. Deviation from the expected syntax of a period, an intentional literary device, is called anacoluthon, a metaphor for impromptu delivery.

trophaeis: monuments made up of enemy armor, marking the place where the enemy was stopped and turned. A Greek custom, the Romans adopted it in the late Republic, though Virgil has Aeneas construct one in *Aen.* 11.5–11. *Monumenta* include *tropaea*, but also describe altars, arches, temples, and the like.

monumenta: To give a sense of far-off places and exotic lands Catullus says (11), *Caesaris visens monumenta magni.*

adlatura . . . sit: a periphrastic future subjunctive to insist both on futurity and potentiality; see on 30, *obscuratura . . . sit.* The word order is striking, mostly because of the position of *sit*; cf. 7, *es . . . adeptus.* Cicero may have wanted *aetas* in final position parallel to *vetustas*, for *aetas finem adlatura sit* would give a recognized clausula (molossus + cretic), although less favored than the double trochee of *(fi)nem sit aetas.*

nihil est enim: For position of *enim* see on 8, *nulla est enim.* The parenthesis is ornate and somewhat epigrammatical.

opere et manu: hendiadys for "handiwork."

conficiat et consumat: almost a doublet, but actually sequential; see on 8, *debilitari frangique,* and 23, *perculsa atque prostrata.* The first has the sense "bring to the end of its cycle," and the personification is felt. On alliterative prefixes see 23. The thought is commonplace.

12

florescit: the concept planned for the *ut* clause after *tanta.* The only other occurrence of *florescere* in the speeches is metaphorical and intense in peroration: *Cael.* 79, *nolite, iudices . . . hunc nunc primum florescentem firmata iam stirpe virtutis tamquam turbine aliquo aut subita tempestate pervertere.* Some manuscripts read the future, but the present, marked by "each day," of the inceptive form (*-sc-*) is appropriate. Metonymy (see 10, *auctoritas*) with personification enhances the imagery.

cotidie magis: The word order is remarkable: both adverbs follow verb. *Cotidie* follows verbs at *Prov. Cons.* 24, *quas is egit agitque cotidie,* and elsewhere. Where Cicero stresses process and immediacy together, *cotidie* is permitted an emphatic, if unperiodic place. The postponement of *magis* is more striking.

ita: Initial *ita* marks a summary of what has preceded, in contrast to *-que,* a sentence connective which marks the continuation of a sequence; see *Deiot.* 10.

detrahet . . . adferet: Cicero uses the same antithesis at *Deiot.* 1. The word order of the conceit is intricate: it turns on *quantum . . . tantum* in initial position. *Operibus* corresponds to *laudibus* (both are dative), but they are not in corresponding positions; nor, therefore, are the two verbs. The position of *laudibus* probably owes as much to the clausula it secures, a double cretic, as to any desire for emphasis.

et . . . quidem: expands the proposition with a strong endorsement (see 11, *quae quidem*), although it will presently be qualified in antithesis: *ceteros quidem . . . vero te.* Cicero now treats Caesar's clemency not as a personal virtue, but as a political act. The consequences of past civil disorder were retaliatory bloodbaths, proscriptions (judicial confiscations), and exile. Caesar's policy of forgiveness and restoration was as unique as it was brilliant. Cicero elaborates this point tentatively, comparing times, victors, and, finally, the nature of victory itself.

The parallelism of the period is patent, but far from balanced:

ceteros quidem omnes victores . . . iam antea . . .		viceras.
	hodierno vero die	
te		ipse vicisti.

Quidem introduces the contrast between other leaders and Caesar, realized by *te ipse.* But the second member, marked as asseverative by *vero* (see 12, *et . . . quidem*) rather than merely contrasting (*autem*) or antithetical (*sed*), disappoints the expectation of an antithesis to *ceteros* in first position, giving that place rather to the unique importance of this day (see on 1, *hodiernus dies,* as opposed to "long since").

ceteros . . . victores: Caesar's goal, stated at *BC* 1.32, was "to surpass (*superare*) them in justice and fairness even as he strove to excel (*anteire*) them in his accomplishments."

ipse: The intensive pronoun is found in the manuscripts in both the nominative and accusative. English cannot translate the latter, but Latin can achieve either emphasis. It also has a tendency to dissimilate pronouns; see on 13, *sibi ipsos.* For choice of *ipse* see just below.

vereor: See 1, *verecundia,* a rare admission of inadequacy of expression; so *Tusc.* 1.12, in the mouth of another: *non dico fortasse etiam quod sentio.* At *Harusp. Resp.* 50 Cicero tries to avoid misunderstanding: *velim sic hoc vir [Pompeius] summus atque optime de mea salute meritus accipiat ut a me dicitur. dicam quidem certe quod sentio*; see 13, *at . . . certe.* The conceit turns on meanings of *vincere* in the senses of winning in battle, overcoming, and surpassing. It is not that Caesar has overcome his own inclinations (owing to suspicions or insults) by self-discipline, but that has raised the concept of victory to a higher level by not indulging in the prerogatives of the victor. That is what *ipse* brings out, stressing the achiever, as opposed to *ipsum. Ipse* also makes a better clausula (cretic + trochee). (The point was not crystal clear, as Cicero himself admits and attempts a correction.) *Hoc* provides an explicit antecedent to *quod dicam* in expository diction.

auditum: Read the participle accusative in preference to the ablative supine, although an emendation (and the less exquisite choice); in its passivity it is better suited to *cogitans.*

ipsam victoriam: described in terms of civil war by Cicero, *Fam.* 4.9.3: "All things are horrible in civil wars, but nothing more horrible than victory itself. Even if it goes to the better side, yet it makes the very victors more savage and uncontrolled; so that even if they are not such by nature, they are forced to be so by necessity. The victor is forced even against his will to do many things according to the wish of those through whom he won." When in this frame of mind, at least, Cicero appreciated the uniqueness of Caesar. Cf. *Deiot.* 33, *quae semper in civili victoria sensimus, ea te victore non vidimus.*

victoriam vicisse: paronomasia with alliteration extending to *videris* to make the phrase more memorable. Other examples alliteration occur at 17, *vagina vacuum*, and *Lig.* 1, *fretus fortasse familiaritate*. See, too, Enn. *Ann.* 513 Skutsch, *qui vincit non est victor nisi victus fatetur*.

vicisse videris: produces a dactylic clausula, much avoided in Ciceronian oratory.

adepta: a better reading than *adempta*. The point is that Caesar eschewed the *ius belli*, not merely that he restored what the defeated had lost—as *nam* in the next sentence explains.

victoriae condicione: Cicero uses *victoriae condicio* at *Cat.* 4.22. Otherwise, for victory and war *lex* and *ius* are found. But *iure* here = "rightly."

occidissemus: literally, "been killed"; figuratively, it includes social, financial, or political ruin.

clementiae . . . iudicio: neither whim, nor deeply felt emotion, but deliberately weighing the *ius belli* against other factors and coming to an intelligent decision. This is precisely the *sapientia* of 2 and 7, and of 13, *iudicium* and *iudicavit*. The genitive is appositional. In *De Virtutibus*, Cicero says, "Justice exercised humanely or generously may be called clemency."

recte igitur: Cicero sums up the point and the conceit. *Unus invictus es* harks back to *ceteros quidem omnis*. *Recte* can only modify the predicate if the sense is *diceris esse* or if *invictus* is a title; for the latter see *Deiot.* 33, *tyrannum*. The relative clause is properly not characteristic or causal, but definitional; see on 15, *qui vero*, and Woodcock, 119.

13

atque: introduces a major turn in the argument; cf. *at*, a different and/or antithetical assessment of the argument. As a sentence connective *atque* may clarify, introduce consequences, or augment, either with further points or with another argument, as here and at 15 and 16.

iudicium: See on 3, *iudicio*. An underlying difficulty in evaluating Caesar's action lies in the definition of Caesar's status. Clearly he is in a position to do as he wishes; but is he to be perceived as a dictator issuing a pardon,

or as a judge acquiting defendants? Cicero treats this at the beginning of
Pro Ligario and, for a different purpose, at *Lig.* 30. Here, at least, he puts
Caesar's pardon of Pompeians in a judicial context. *Scelere . . . liberati*
shows that Cicero is interpreting Caesar's action as judicial. The grounds,
strikingly modern, are of diminished responsibility: *fato . . . compulsi*. This
explanation, which Cicero suggests in *Lig.* 17, *Deiot.* 15, and *Brut.* 250,
apparently originates with Caesar, unless the attribution of the phrase "ill-
fated compulsion" to Cacsar at Dio Cassius *Rom. Hist.* 43.17.4 is extrapolated from this passage.

patres conscripti: shifts the point of address from Caesar to the Senate for
the last time.

sumus . . . compulsi: The word order is remarkable for the hyperbaton of
the compound predicate. By removing *sumus* from its expected place directly before *compulsi*, Cicero creates a clausula: cretic + spondee. After
compulsi, *sumus* would have been parallel with *sumus* at the end of the
main clause. But that would stress *sumus* beyond its worth; and the latter
clausula is a double cretic. The placement of *sumus*, a virtual enclitic, also
highlights *fato*; see on 7, *quam . . . adeptus*. On the separation of the constituents of perfect passives see on 7, *es . . . adeptus*; 29, *stabilita . . . erit*;
and 32, *fracta . . . est*.

fato . . . funestoque: a voluminous phrase, interwoven by the position of
sumus and *rei publicae*. Note the word order: *fato* first, before the finite
verb, then the modifiers unfold. *Nescioqui*, like *quidam* (see on *Lig.* 5,
incredibilem quendam), tends to qualify another adjective modifying the
same noun, as eventually it does with *misero funestoque*. It may be argued
that *rei publicae* has to go somewhere and is appropriate where it is. But
still it has the effect of further expanding the ablative phrase. The effect is
one of tentativeness and delicacy in searching for the right expression.

culpa: contrasted with *delictum* at *Lig.* 2.

erroris humani: the fallibility that is part of the human condition; the genitive defines *culpa*. Such distinctions are important after a civil war.

at . . . certe: *At* (an emendation of R. Klotz) has especially strong rhetorical
force when embedded in a sentence. So *Phil.* 2.116, *res bello gesserat,
quamvis rei publicae calamitosas, at tamen magnas*, "He had done things
in war, albeit ruinous to the state, yet beyond all question magnificent."

The objection (of A. Klotz, apparatus criticus ad loc.) that only *tamen* can correlate with *etsi* has not enough evidence for cogency. *At certe* coordinates with negatived conditional (*Quinct.* 97, *Planc.* 29, *Milo.* 93) to mean "yet at least": εἰ μὴ ... ἀλλά. See, too, 25, where the preceding proposition is a concession. *Certe,* like English "surely," runs the gamut from tentative to absolute assurance; but it coaxes, rather than demands, agreement; at *Har. Resp.* 50 (cited at 13, *vereor*) *quidem* contrasts Cicero with Pompey, and *certe* = "in fact," "just," "only," "at any rate."

nam cum: one of the longest periods in the speech; see the Introduction, section 4. The basic structure is:

cum Marcellum	deprecantibus vobis rei publicae	conservavit,
me et	mihi et item rei publicae nullo deprecante,	
reliquos . . . et sibi ipsos et patriae		reddidit . . .
non . . . hostes induxit . . .		
sed	iudicavit . . . bellum esse susceptum	

For all its volume, it is not the progressive or developing kind of period that distinguishes Cicero at his most expansive, but rather is antiphonal in feeling. The verbs in the *cum* clause are synonymous, functioning to distribute three accusatives (*Marcellum . . . me . . . reliquos*) over two predicates, with two objects in the second clause. The two ablatives absolute and two dative phrases correspond to each other chiastically with strong verbal echoes. The longer dative phrase, like the compound direct object, is in the second half. The relative clause provides a loosely fitting appendage to the protasis and gives prominence to Cicero's characterization of their numbers and their social standing, without moving the thought forward. Again the main clause consists essentially of a negative predication and its positive restatement. The sense of antiphonal balance is enhanced by a number of paired items articulated in varying degrees with the suggestion of symmetry. For *cum* + indicative = "at that very moment when," cf. 12, *cum eas . . . remisisti,* and *Lig.* 18, *cum . . . cupiebas*; the same tense of the indicative is used in the main clause.

M. Marcellum . . . me: The two predicates of the *cum* clause are in asyndeton; the two *ets* set the datives in explicit parallelism.

sibi ipsos: Note the dissimilation of cases, as also at *Lig.* 36; see on 12, *te ipse.* For the nonreflexive use of *sibi* see on 9, *suis sedibus.*

quorum ... frequentiam: Cicero uses abstracts (= *quos frequentis*), as with 10, *auctoritas*. The clause is not just honorific. A Senate existed and operated during the Civil War, with fence-straddlers as well as active Caesarians. A substantial number of nobles sided with Caesar; see Shackleton Bailey 2. By this time some former Pompeians must have been present to petition for and welcome Marcellus' pardon—an indication that Caesar's policy was already working. Cicero may well be exaggerating the number (and their *dignitas*).

When a relative clause follows its antecedent at this distance with no demonstrative modifying the antecedent to anticipate the relative (as in *eos viros ... quorum*), the clause may be felt as practically parenthetical (= *et eorum*). Put another way, if it were the last clause of the period, such a relative clause might be taken, and punctuated, as semi-independent; so 33, *quae mea*. For the same phenomenon with a somewhat different sense see on 18, *qui ... excitaverunt*.

non ... sed: antithesis between independent clauses, rhetorically linked. The passive in the accusative + infinitive is not casual, but used to emphasize the contrast with the concept of active enemies.

hostes: vs. *inimicus,* is reserved for external enemies like Juba, or citizens who, like Catiline, were enemies of the state. In January 49 the Senate had declared Caesar a *hostis.*

ignoratione ... crudelitate: The last of the several balances in this period is compound and structured on *potius ... quam*. Cicero is characteristically careful to avoid predictable articulation. Thus *ignoratione* precedes *potius* while its partner, *metu,* follows with elaborate qualification. The balanced pair *cupiditate aut crudelitate* is remarkable for strict brevity and echoing sounds at the beginning and end of the words.

metu: Marcellus went voluntarily into exile in fear of Caesar (*Att.* 9.1.4), playing no role in the fighting. The adjectives suggest the way Cicero now wants that emotion to be interpreted.

cupiditate: As a political term, it is somewhat stronger than *studium,* "partisanship," and implies the hope of personal gain; so at 14.

14

Cicero begins a digression, describing his own motivations at the outset of war. There are similar passages in the other two speeches (*Lig.* 28, *Deiot.* 29). The story is not quite the same each time, and the emphasis varies with the exigencies of context. This apologia conveys a sense of personal obligation rather than of reasoned support (in *Deiot.*) or enthusiasm (in *Lig.*) for Pompey's cause. By presenting himself as a peacemaker, Cicero appears an apt and trustworthy judge of the attitudes of others. In the end he associates Marcellus with his position. But having an ulterior motive and telling a story differently in two places do not by themselves convict a man of disingenuousness. In the closely contemporary *Fam.* 6.6.6 (cited at 1, *verecundia*) he uses similar language to describe his decision as private and personal.

The matter-of-fact diction reflects the sad resignation it describes: four independent predicates to *fuerunt,* three in the first person, connected *semper . . . semperque, nec . . . umquam semperque.*

bellum. . . . [14] **quo quidem in bello:** The repetition of the antecedent in the relative clause is variously considered a feature both of native Italian diction and of the style of documents or reports produced in legal or curial contexts. It is also favored by Caesar in the *Commentarii*. The common denominator appears to be simplicity of style, the desire, furthered through repetition of words, for clarity. Several scholars label this passage "Curia style," the style used in proposing resolutions in the Senate; so Ruch, 58, and R&E, 25. But, first, there are few curial documents with which to compare it; and, second, one feature does not make a style. The repetition of the noun has more in common with 26, *gloriae, si quidem gloria* than with phrases like *dies quo die* or *rem quae res,* which do have a redundant and formulaic ring; see *Lig.* 2, *legatus . . . qua legatione.* Further, in spite of the semi-independent relative, which smooths and tightly binds the transition, there is a strong shift in subject matter; and *quidem* suggests a qualification (in the next sentence with *enim*).

pace . . . pacem . . . pacem: effective repetition.

audiendum: similar impersonal use of the gerundive at *Flac.* 98 (with *de ambitu*); seems to have a specialized meaning, in the language of a *quaes-*

tio, that "a hearing should be afforded on the subject of"; see 18, *cogitandum.*

semperque dolui: a second predicate of equal weight, by the repetition of *semper,* but sequentially associated to the first. For *-que* see on 10, *nobilissimamque.* See, too, 1, *dolebam.*

civium . . . flagitantium: the *pacis auctores* of 15. The genitive phrase, with an active participle governing an object, is neat and concise, but not usual in the speeches; cf. *Lig.* 31, *apud te rogantium.*

neque . . . illa nec ulla: true in the sense that he did not fight at the side of Pompey; see *Fam.* 9.18.2, *in acie non fui.* He certainly did commit himself to Pompey and was with him in Greece. *Lig.* 9, *isdem in armis fui,* is exaggerated to make a rhetorical point. As to Sulla, Cicero admits, *Rosc. Am.* 142, "I took their side, but I took their side unarmed." Cf. 15, *eadem . . . sensi.* For *ulla* see on 3, *in multis.*

semperque: The style is paratactic, with phrasal antithesis. After a negative proposition, a contrasting positive joined with the simple conjunction *-que* becomes "rather."

pacis et togae: a doublet combining a literal and a figurative denomination, the toga being the peacetime garment of Roman citizens; so, too, *belli atque armarum.* This use of doublets has been criticized as "Asian" padding (see the Introduction, section 4, and glossary s.v. "volume"), with overtones of foreign garishness. But the usage is quite natural in prose embellished for dramatic, encomiastic, or merely aesthetic purposes. So at 9 and 11; see notes there. Cicero uses the figure in an epic poem he composed on his consulship (*cedant arma togae*) and glosses the phrase in a sarcastic excess of clarity at *Piso.* 73, *pacis est insigne et oti toga, contra autem arma tumultus atque belli.*

socia: like *amicus,* can be adjective or substantive, masculine or feminine. So *Brut.* 45, *pacis est comes otique socia . . . eloquentia.*

hominem: the most generic description possible, and only slightly stronger than *eum;* see on *Deiot.* 31. Cicero might have used an honorific, *dux,* or even *amicus.*

privato . . . non publico: Observe the difference when a positive proposition precedes a negative, vs. *non . . . sed . . .* Positive–negative completely dismisses the negative proposition in a rhetorical (i.e., antiphonal) anti-thesis. Negative–positive uses the negative to limit or correct the first prop-osition in favor of the second. So 16, *non iam . . . causae, sed victoriae comparandae*. Earlier it might have been useful to compare the validity of the two positions; but this is not the time. Now relative behavior in victory is the point. Cicero had said in a letter to Pompey (*Att.* 8.11D.6), *secutus sum tuum* [sc. *consilium*], *neque id rei publicae causa, de qua desperavi . . . sed te quaerebam, tecum esse cupiebam . . .* In both cases he insists that his motive was personal. He is more interested that Pompey not mis-interpret it as political.

grati . . . memoria: *Fides* is a primary Roman virtue in both public and personal relationships, the foundation of friendships and contracts. Mind-fulness of gratitude owed is an obligation of the debtor. Cf. *Att.* 9.19.2: "bound to him by his favors, I could not be ungrateful."

non modo . . . sed ne . . . quidem: a poignant variation on the usual for-mula.

prudens et sciens: later a legal formula, perhaps, but in Republican times used in context of self-sacrifice; so *Fam.* 6.6.6, where Cicero, quoting a tragedian, compares himself with Amphiaraus, the Argive seer in *Seven against Thebes*, who fights in spite of foreknowledge of his death (cited at 1, *verecundia*). It is also the language of Roman *devotio*, patriotic suicide to appease the gods, exemplified by Decius Mus. See Skutsch, *Ennius*, fr. 191. At *Att.* 10.9A.5, April 49, Caelius used the phrase to urge Cicero against making precisely this commitment. At Ter. *Eun.* 72 a slave embel-lishes histrionically: *prudens sciens vivus vidensque pereo*. On word order see Skutsch, *Ennius*, 356.

ruerem: the most colorful word of the passage; it is violent, as is *interitum*. But violence does not dominate the image that closes the section. *Tam quam* tempers the metaphor; *prudens et sciens* bespeaks abject resignation; and *voluntarium*, a rare word that twice in Cicero modifies *mors*, lingers in final position.

15

quod quidem: like *quo quidem* at the beginning of 14, awaiting explanation, which comes with *nam*. He refers to his advocacy of peace, not his siding with Pompey.

et in . . . et in: The parallelism is explicit, although not symmetrical (*in hoc ordine* is balanced by *in ipso bello*), whereas the logical contrast is the temporal one between *integra re* and *in ipso bello*; the tone is lucidly expository as Cicero establishes his blameless position. He is interpreting Caesar's grant of pardon as an endorsement of his wartime posture.

in hoc ordine: referring perhaps to unpreserved *sententiae* delivered in the frenetic weeks between his return to Rome in late 50 and Caesar's arrival. There is considerable evidence in contemporary letters that he took this position.

integra re: not divided, fragmented, or committed to one or another side; see *Lig.* 1, *integrum*.

eadem . . . sensi: Cf. *Rosc. Am.* 142, *cum eis ⟨Sullanis⟩ sensi, sed inermis sensi*, translated at 14, *neque . . . illa nec ulla*.

capitis mei periculo: Plutarch (*Cic.* 39) claims that after the battle of Pharsalus, Cicero refused Cato's offer of a command and was, in consequence, threatened by a son of Pompey.

rerum existimator: the only occurrence in the speeches of this phrase. *Rerum* is a filler; see *Deiot.* 7, *exercitatione rerum*. *De Rerum Natura* (Lucretius' title) translates Greek Περὶ Φύσεως, "On Nature."

ceteris: usually first in antitheses to prepare for the particular, stressed predicate, often asyndetically, juxtaposed. See on 11, *ceterae . . . huius autem*. In this order, "the rest" are not lightly dismissed as a foil in antithesis; see on 19, *virtute . . . fortuna*.

iratior: "more than a little," rather than a true comparative which would imply Caesar was angry with the peacemakers as well, a possibility precluded by rhetoric and *statim*, which is placed strategically between two words it equally modifies.

atque: here marks the introduction of a new way of looking at an old point (referred to specifically by *id*). This is almost being brought up as an objection.

minus mirum: The tone is brisk, informal: note ellipsis of the verb, for which compare *De Or.* 2.55, *"mimime mirum" inquit Antonius "si ista res adhuc nostra lingua illustrata non est,"* several places in 30, or *Piso.* 68, *nihil ad nos; si ad nos, nihil ad hoc tempus.* At *Lig.* 28, *sed tum sero,* the force of the omission is very different.

fortasse: often expects agreement beyond what logic demands. It is a polite way of forgoing or forestalling argument, as at 25, *"satis"*; *Lig.* 1, *fretus fortasse*; and *Lig.* 19.

tum cum: Correlative pairs can interweave clauses if the first member is embedded in its clause; e.g., 27, *tum te si voles, cum* . . . . Here Cicero favors simplicity; see 26, *cum est aliquid amplius.*

incertus . . . anceps: a doublet in which the second phrase is more figurative than the first; cf. on 14, *pacis et togae.*

qui . . . is: definitional articulation in expository style, relative clause preceding antecedent: "the cherisher is the declarer." It is difficult not to feel an overtone of causality ("by cherishing he declares"), which would expect the subjunctive. For a similar tension see 31, *ingratus . . . civis qui,* and 12, *recte igitur.*

vero: strongly asseverative, dismisses the previous point to insist on this one. Rhetoric dominates pure cogency: logically the previous point was a minor premise to the present one, that is, "While his support of peacemakers was understandable when he might still have had to sue for peace, his continued endorsement of them in victory is really extraordinary."

profecto: so 3.

maluisse se: Cicero makes this point about Caesar in a contemporary letter (*Fam.* 9.6.2). Infinitive in the construction stands for pluperfect subjunctive. Future active participle + *fuisse* is not possible for *malo,* nor it is necessary for verbs of volition or potential.

16

atque huius quidem: The transition is, to put the best construction on it, subtly effected. *Atque* introduces a new direction; see 15. Cicero has just argued that Caesar favored the peacemakers. Now, with an indefinite genitive, deictically spotlighted, and his personal intercession, he includes Marcellus among them. For *quidem . . . enim* see on 14, *bellum. . . . quo quidem in bello.*

sensus: "judgments," like *sententia*; but see also 15, *eadem . . . sensi.*

ut . . . sic: completely explicit correlative, neatly underlining the parity of the two men.

tum etiam: intensive (as in the next sentence, in a different articulation). Cicero here uses the balance to suggest the difficulty of maintaining such a position. Nothing really corresponds to *semper* or to *tum etiam*, but some correlation is felt.

quotiens ego eum et: For the intrusion of *eum* see on 2, *illo . . . distracto*; the collocation of pronouns is common in Latin.

cum . . . tum etiam: is the positive of *non solum . . . sed (verum) etiam*, emphasizing the second member. The echo of *tum etiam* in the sentence before is probably unintentional; Roman writers repeat themselves in ways that we do not allow ourselves.

insolentiam: Many references in the letters attest that Pompey was threatening (and Cicero expecting) Sullan proscription if that side won. See *Att.* 9.10.6, *sullaturit animus eius et proscripturit iam diu*, and, further, *Lig.* 12, *cum . . . qui*. Pompey is probably not among the *certi*; and Cicero elsewhere treats the vengeance of the victors as an abstraction; see at 12, *ipsam victoriam.*

certorum: well-known, though not named, as at *Deiot.* 11. To name who they were (Caes. *BC* 3.82.4 mentions a Pompeian aspirant for praetor; 3.82.3 and 3.83.4, their general confidence) is less important than to establish that they were real and vicious (see *Att.* 8.11.3, 11.6.2) and that Marcellus was not among "them."

extimescentem: The participle (vs. accusative + infinitive) shows that the lead verb is used in its sensory denotation; inceptive *-sc-* also stresses the process, rather than a fact intellectually perceived.

quo: causal, not comparative with *gratior*.

liberalitas: the noblesse oblige of a *liber*, a freeborn Roman citizen.

nobis: The dative should go closely with *debet esse* by grammar, or with *gratior* by diction. Instead it is put virtually at midsentence, separated from both, next to Caesar.

non enim: a parenthetical sentence (the thought flows from "we have seen" to "we saw") passing over the validity of the two sides in favor of perceptions of victory. At *Lig.* 19 Cicero hesitantly begins the comparison with a wariness that does not exclude criticism of Caesar.

non enim iam: *Non iam* means that now is not the time; *iam non* means that a previous negative circumstance has ceased to be operative, so "no longer."

causae ... victoriae: effective word order; *sunt* separated from *comparandae*, dividing *non causae* from *sed victoriae*. (See on 2, *illo ... distracto*.) *Inter se*, which goes grammatically with the verb, is placed between the two objects of comparison, *causae* and *victoriae*.

17

vidimus ... non vidimus: Repetition of the verb, bracketing the whole, in paratactic, asyndetic, antithetical clauses is forceful; for the initial position of verb see 4, *est vero*. The repetition of the verb gives equal value to the second proposition (vs. 14, *privato officio, non publico*).

victoriam ... terminatam: This is a modified direct object, not a noun clause (sc. *esse*). The emphasis remains on experiencing events visually; cf. on 16, *extimescentem*. The point that Caesar did not press his advantage is also made at *Lig.* 19 and *Deiot.* 34. But the argument the observation supports is different each time. Here the emphasis is on Caesar as a reluctant participant, like Cicero and Marcellus (see 16), as opposed to Pompey. In *Pro Ligario* Cicero uses the fact to urge Caesar not to brand his opponents as *hostes*, but in *Pro Rege Deiotaro* Caesar's decency is contrasted with Blesamius' expectation of a tyrant. The point is thus, like so many others, a commonplace to be exploited as needed.

vagina vacuum: The transfer of attributes is called hypallage. The sheath would have been empty, the sword drawn (*strictum*); but desire for alliteration may have occasioned its use in an attractive turn of phrase.

Martis . . . victoriae: "Mars" for war is not highly figurative (Caesar once uses it for "battle," *BG* 7.19). "Victory" for "victor" is probably more so, though the diction is not elevated beyond the normal embellishments of refined expository prose (note the precision of *quos . . . eos*).

perculit: a verb connoting violent and sometimes inhuman action.

ut . . . debeat: For anticipated result clauses that do not continue the periodic flow and are felt as as new sentences see 9, *ut eos,* and 18, *ut mihi.* Although loosely connected by syntax with what precedes, the clause becomes more elaborate, up to the striking image of Caesar wishing to resurrect the dead.

dubitare debeat: rhetorical reinforcement, with alliteration for an emotional argument. The words between *ut* and *si* serve only to pressure the general listener into agreement.

multos: emphatic, placed before protasis of the unreal condition of which it is direct object.

si posset . . . quos potest: a rhetorical correspondence, each clause dependent in its own construction (*excitaret . . . conservat*). Play on *posse,* between past subjunctive and present indicative, reinforces the point. The position of *si posset,* embedded in its apodosis, is remarkable but not awkward. Cicero uses the metaphor of rousing from the dead twice in *Milo.* (79, *ipsum ab inferis excitare*; 91, *excitate, excitate ipsum . . . a mortuis*) and at *Cat.* 2.20; also, in a comic passage, when evoking Appius Claudius Caecus at *Cael.* 33.

quoniam . . . conservat: The hyperbolic conceit of rousing the dead is not the climax of the period in syntax or sense. Caesar's compassion for the salvageable is the nub; it is added in emphatic position, after the requirements of periodicity are met. Plutarch (*Caes.* 46) says that Caesar was distressed by the slaughter of Pompeians and (48) that he wept on hearing of the death of Pompey.

eadem acie: points back to *multos,* specifying the opposing army. For *acie* see 14, *neque . . . illa nec ulla.*

alterius vero partis: i.e., Pompey's. Praise by comparison is a commonplace of encomia. Here the judgment on the Pompeians is especially potent, because of the reserved way Cicero delivers it. The initial genitive, establishing the point of comparison, depends on *victoriam,* the last word of the period. (It cannot go with *nihil;* that would require *de altera parte*). The two clauses that intervene underline Cicero's reticence to say anything (and simultaneously create suspense for what he will say). *Nihil amplius dico,* sometimes used to preempt a statement that may offend, indicates that the expression of the judgment will be restrained. But with *quam id quod . . . verebamur* Cicero characterizes that judgment before pronouncing it in an accusative + infinitive that is the apodosis of an unstated condition ("if they had won"); see on 7, *quod . . . maximum est.* The construction cannot quite be labeled an aposiopesis (in which the sentence is broken off for rhetorical reasons), because *victoriam* does pick up the initial genitive; but it would sound very much like one. The *futuram fuisse* (sc. *si vicisset*) represents a pluperfect subjunctive.

quod . . . verebamur: appositival noun clause describing or characterizing even as it anticipates an ensuing item; see *Lig.* 2, *quod . . . optandum,* or *Brut.* 278, *pedis, quod minimum est, nulla supplosio?* "Was there no—and this would be the minimal response—stamping of the feet?"

18

quidam: The preceding sentence turns out, unsurprisingly, to be a *praeteritio*—the orator's promise not to say something that he has every intention of saying. This indefinite pronoun (vs. *aliquis*) refers to people known but not mentioned.

minabantur . . . dicebant: Imperfects at the end of each clause recall the incessance of the bullying warnings. On the use of coercion by Pompeians see *Lig.* 33.

nec quid . . . sed ubi: The subject of *cogitandum esse,* it sounds like a slogan but is not elsewhere attested. The Pompeians did make this threat (*Att.* 11.6.6). Caesar responded that he would judge those who did not actively oppose him to be on his side; cf. *Lig.* 33; Suet. *Iul.* 75.

cogitandum: For the overtone of a formal inquiry see 14, *audiendum*.

ut mihi: Cicero insists that this summary statement is his own opinion: *mihi quidem*. *Videantur* also signals the construction of the rest of the period.

di immortales: Cicero has already diluted Caesar's responsibility for the Civil War by calling it a *bellum fatale*. He now attributes, if not the victory, at least the wisdom and clemency of the victor, to divine will. He goes further at *Lig*. 19, where he does justify Caesar's victory by reference to the will of the gods. Note the pairs: *tantum/tam, placati/satiati,* and *spem salutis/clementiam victoris,* to which an asymmetrical *et sapientiam* is added.

qui . . . excitaverunt: The relative clause, thus separated from its antecedent, bears a circumstantial, explanatory relationship to the preceding clause despite the fact that it is indicative. For *qui = ii enim* see Woodcock, 188 (6), who does not put it quite correctly. This relative, when used as a connective, may *imply* relationships beyond simple coordination and basic narrative sequence (the so-called καὶ style). But, by using the relative + indicative, the speaker prompts the listener to infer what the logical or rhetorical sequence is; see on 13, *quorum et frequentiam*. The relationship between such relative clauses and the preceding clause is almost paratactic, but not quite.

civile bellum: The usual word order *bellum civile* is reversed for emphasis on the adjective, as at 24 and *Lig*. 28.

bellum tantum et tam luctuosum: For *tam* in such locutions see *Deiot*. 15, *tanti sceleris*; *Deiot*. 37, *quae tanta . . . iniuria*; and *Lig*. 15, *tanta*.

vel placati . . . vel satiati: After a conditional followed by a relative clause these words might suggest to the listener that the main predicate, *ut mihi videantur di immortales,* is being resolved; but *esse* is not forthcoming. Instead participles provide a provisional apodosis for the conditional clause, whereas the phrase *spem . . . contulisse* actually completes the predicate and expresses Cicero's contention, which goes beyond his belief that the gods have been appeased. *Sapientia* added to *clementia* and forming a pair stresses Caesar's conscious decision more than any natural disposition to offer leniency.

19

quare gaude: *Quare,* like *quae cum ita sint,* is a particle of rhetorical sequence leading to a summation rather than, like *ergo* or *igitur* (see 2), of logical sequence leading to a conclusion. The tone of the summation is informed by the imperatives; but cf. 29, *servi igitur.*

tuo isto: The adjectives are redundant; cf. 27, *iste tuus,* and *Lig.* 15, *hac tanta tua.*

bono: *sapientia* and *clementia* as possessions, now defined by antithesis between externally derived and innate qualities. This distinction will be maintained with *virtuti . . . felicitati* and *a virtute donata . . . a Fortuna commodata.* Cicero again balances *fortuna* against *natura* at *Lig.* 38.

cum . . . tum: establishes a variety of relationships between two units, moving from general to particular, lesser to greater; e.g., *Clu.* 138, *commemorationem cum aliorum iudiciorum . . . tum illius ipsius iudici.* Addition of *etiam* emphasizes the greater importance of the second; cf. on 16. Cf. also ἄλλως τε καί = "especially."

sapienti: *Sapiens* is the regular Latin word for "philosopher." Cicero rarely transliterates Greek in the speeches. Stoicism identified wisdom as the philosopher's primary virtue. One criticism of this speech that led Wolf to reject its authenticity (see the Introduction, section 3.1) is what he perceived to be favorable references to Stoicism, although Caesar is identified with Epicureanism. But wisdom is not the exclusive property of the Stoic, and Cicero is not writing a philosophic tract.

cetera: anticipates an antithesis, but in the change of construction the antithetical concepts, *cetera* and *de nobis,* look very unalike. Nevertheless underlying that difference is the bold suggestion that Caesar should consider the returned exiles themselves as symbolic of his greatest achievement. The period is constructed on strong underlying parallelism, but the related parts are diversely presented and disposed. In each half, after the pronoun comes a dependent clause, one temporal, one relative, thus unbalanced. Indeed, *cetera* is part of the *cum* clause; *de nobis* is the antecedent of the relative clause, but constructed in the *quotiens* clause, with its remarkable postponement of the conjunction to assure the prominence of the initial prepositional phrase. Two standard correlatives, *etsi . . . tamen* and *quotiens . . . totiens,* suggest a symmetry they do not achieve. In the first, the verb of the *etsi* clause, which is that of the main clause, is understood; in the second, where the main clause is expanded into an echoing, anahoric tricolon, the *quotiens* clause gets a verb, identical to that in the correlated clause. Balanced datives are inserted into the first correlative and main clause; and the three-syllable homoeoteleuton of the verbs ties that half of the antithesis together. In the second half, the repetition of *cogitabis* performs the same purpose, although not symmetrically. What began as an elaboration on the distinction between the roles of chance and virtue becomes a paean to Caesar's generosity, nobility, and wisdom, each strongly punctuated in the tricolon by anaphora.

non modo . . . sed nimirum: extremely strong affirmation, balanced between an enhancement (*non modo . . . sed etiam*) and a correction (*non . . . sed nimirum*). A listener would sense in the flow of the diction a distinct change of pace following an extensive and complex articulation.

tantus est enim: On *enim* see 8, *nulla est . . . vis.* The hyperbaton of *tanta . . . dignitas* also effectively stresses the predicative force. The use of anaphoric bipartite members in asyndeton almost immediately following an anaphoric (*totiens*), asyndetic tricolon allows a clear sense of the difference in movement and feeling between the two constructions. The bipartite is nervous, suspenseful; the tricolon creates a rhythm of resolution.

a Virtute . . . a Fortuna: part of a symmetrically balanced antithesis creating an ornate but controlled, epigrammatic coda to the argument. *Commodata* is here practically synonymous with *donata,* used to present the antithesis at the level of infinitives, rather than prepositions. For *cetera* see 15. At *Nat. Deor.* 3.88 Cicero says: "It is the judgment of mankind that good fortune must be sought from the gods; wisdom is derived from man himself."

20

noli . . . defetigari: Cicero continues (from *gaude*) in the imperative mode, now advises him on policy. For a similar exhortation on a similar theme see *Lig.* 37, *noli . . . dubitare.*

defetigari: a rare and strong verb only found at *Quinct.* 42, *Cat.* 2.21, *Dom.* 115, and *Planc.* 11.

conservandis: Cf. *Lig.* 32. The gerundive phrase expresses the fact of the action: "in the preservation, restoration."

viris bonis: At the core of the Senate were, in Cicero's political vocabulary, the *boni*. But he frequently extended the term to describe any (to his mind) right-thinking group of individuals. The conditions of periodicity are satisfied with *defetigari*, but what follows is of the greatest importance to his argument. From *non cupiditate* to *rei publicae* all depends on an explanatory participle, *lapsis*, on which pivots the *non . . . sed* antithesis, itself housing a variety of balances:

non	cupiditate . . . aliqua aut pravitate	lapsis,
sed	opinione offici	
	stulta fortasse	
	certe non improba	
et	specie rei publicae.	

The mistake is clearly to be assigned not to *vitia*, but to ideals. Cicero concedes that the ideals may have been deluded.

cupiditate: See at 13.

lapsis: minor indiscretions (see *Lig.* 30, *lapsus est*). So *Phil.* 13.9, *talis vir . . . opinione labi potest; voluntate a re publica dissidere nullo pacto potest,* "A man like that may err in judgment; there is no way he can be at odds with the state."

opinione offici: an unusual phrase. *Opinio* is generally complemented by *de* + ablative or a noun clause. Objective genitive with *opinio*, as opposed to subjective (as in *hominum opinio*), is rare but = accusative + infinitive ("opinion that . . ."); i.e., *Sest.* 82, *si paulo longior opinio mortis Sesti fuisset = mortuum Sestium esse; Cael.* 74, *opinio malefici cogitati = Caelium maleficium cogitavisse; Phil.* 5.32, *opinio ipsa . . . nostrae severitatis = nos severos esse.* Here, uniquely = indirect question or *de officio persolvendo*.

stulta fortasse, certe non improba: *Fortasse* (see at 15) makes an unreserved concession, *certe* (see at 13) hopes to win agreement.

specie quadam: For indefinite adjective see on 13, *fato . . . nescioquo . . . aliqua culpa.* The indefiniteness extends to the choice of the word itself. See *Fam.* 4.4.3: ". . . that I seemed to see some kind of vision (*speciem aliquam*) of a reviving Republic."

non enim: parataxis where hypotaxis might be expected. In sense, the reason (*enim*) for persevering is in the *summa laus* clause, to which *non ulla culpa* is an adversative consideration. See sentences beginning with *itaque* at *Lig.* 29 and 31.

tua ulla culpa: parallel with *summa laus*; so *non . . . ulla,* instead of *nulla,* to negative the clause.

contraque: The *-que* is adversative; cf. 14, *semperque. Contra* is rarely used as here; its insistence on polar antithesis would be noted. It introduces a second clause in conjunction with a sentence connector only five times in the speeches, twice in the same section (26) of *Pro Flacco: quod quidem ego non modo non postulo, sed contra, iudices, vos oro et obtestor ut totam causam . . . contemplemini. nihil religione testatum, nihil veritate fundatum . . . contraque omnia corrupta libidine . . . reperientur.* See the citation from *Dom.* 88 at 22, *omnium,* and from *Piso.* 73, cited at 14, *pacis et togae.*

senserunt: For the perception see *Deiot.* 33, *quae semper in civili victoria sensimus, ea te victore non vidimus;* the theme of *non timendum esse* goes back to the opening of the speech.

21

nunc venio: an explicit, rhetorical transition. The figure by which an orator announces his movement in an argument is called *pro(s)thesis.* The sharpness of the break has persuaded some scholars to assert that the speech is divided into two incompatible parts, others to pronounce the speech a forgery. This section has been labeled a counterargument, or *confutatio,* but it is so only as a strategy: 21–22, an expression of universal support, introduce a strong but intricately related shift from praise of Caesar's past accomplishments to a vigorous enjoinder, beginning at 23, *omnia sunt excitanda tibi,* for Caesar to begin restoring the state—a theme heard at the beginning of the speech. For the transition from 22 to 23 see 22, *doleoque.*

querelam ... suspicionem: so 3, *doloribus vel suspicionibus*. *Querela* is used at *Lig.* 23 to reduce the criminal charges against Ligarius to a matter of Tubero's personal pique. Caesar's *querelae* are not to be taken lightly. It is not clear whether Caesar had specific conspirators in mind. If he did, the danger would likely be coming from his own side, since he clearly did not name his enemy.

atrocissimam: really describes the object of Caesar's suspicion (as with *crimen* at *Deiot.* 2); the parallelism with *gravissimam* is slightly forced. In spite of the frankness with which Cicero takes up the topic, he can hardly bear to mention the subject itself. He talks around it until the first oblique mention in the question: *sed quisnam est iste tam demens?*

non ... magis quam: The construction reflects the nexus of those affected by Caesar's feelings.

non tibi ipsi magis

quam
  cum omnibus civibus
  tum maxime nobis

etsi ... tamen: In the explicit correlation, the calm of reasoned discussion is felt.

spero: + present infinitive, vs. + the future, bespeaks confidence more than hope.

cautio: double sense of caution and safety. It has been pointed out that had Caesar not been assassinated in 44, Cicero would probably not have died in 43.

quisnam est iste: a figment of Caesar's imagination, highly indefinite. The construction reflects in its staccato classification of types of suspects a certain impatience with Caesar's paranoia and a disinclination (short of facetiousness) to entertain the suspicions. But there is some pathos in the challenging questions that keep the passage moving. The basic division is between Caesar's supporters and his enemies: *de tuisne?* ... *an (si nihil tui)* ... *inimici?*. The supporters are divided between (a) newly restored and (b) long-term supporters. Presented in that order, once the first have been categorically dismissed, the second are eliminated a fortiori. Yet Cicero devotes more words to rejecting the possibility of an assassin from among his long-term adherents. Enemies are divided between the dead and the reconciled, who become, like (a) the newly restored, *maximi tui* and thus are given short, epigrammatic shrift.

de tuisne? . . . an . . . qui una tecum fuerunt?: sentence fragments, themselves questions, attempting to answer, by a pressing interrogation, *quisnam . . . ?*

tametsi: a sentence fragment to dismiss abruptly the preceding contention; more commonly *quamquam,* as at 27, and *Lig.* 18.

insperantibus: adjective with adversative function. The placement of the adjective after and separated from its noun gives it added force. For the effect of word order in the hyperbaton of noun . . . adjective see on 3, *fructum . . . maximum.*

an ex eo: *An* suggests the introduction of the group antithetical to (*tuis*) *ne,* but *qui . . . fuerunt* is merely a subdivision of *tuisne.* Clark's *anne* is attractive, allowing the question to be taken rather as dismissively rhetorical than as an alternative to *tuisne.* The reader needs some help not to mistake this *an*; but in performance Cicero kept the distinction as clear as it needed to be. Bell-like clarity is not essential to this universal dismissal of possible candidates.

qui . . . fuerunt: plural because *numero = eorum numero.*

una: often reinforces *cum* with pronouns; see *Lig.* 22. *Simul* is so used at 19.

non est credibilis: predicative; the more usual expression would be neuter adjective + *est* + (accusative + infinitive). The period is a variation on *quis est iste tam demens.*

ullo: supplies the oblique case of *quisquam,* the universal indefinite pronoun after a negative.

quo . . . huius: The point is made neatly and, with the relative preceding its antecedent, in expository fashion and axiomatically.

summa: modifies *omnia.*

huius . . . suae: Possessives bracket the clause; word order gives maximum antithesis to *huius* and a clausula (double cretic). Possessive adjectives often appear in final position for emphasis and because their word shape (in parentheses) can contribute to a cretic foot (. . . ¯) (˘˘); cf. 9, *totum est tuum*.

sceleris: partitive with both *nihil* and *quid*; with *inimici* (nominative) understand *cogitent*.

aut . . . aut: neat, symmetrical, and epigrammatic balance, covering and dismissing the category of *sua* vs. *tua*, and *vitam* is object of both antonymous verbs.

22

sed tamen: returns to the beginning of 21 for a different approach.

latebrae . . . recessus: The first is literally used, but would ordinarily be active, "hiding," not "hidden" places. The ancients were not without an appreciation of psychology. Cicero refers here not to deviousness, as elsewhere when the recesses of the mind are mentioned, but to paranoia. The second noun, found only here in the speeches, is used locally elsewhere to mean a safe haven or retreat. For doublets of literal and figurative sense see on 14, *pacis et togae*. The repetition of the adjective is necessary only for rhetorical purposes and the virtue of amplitude; see on 4, *vis . . . copia*.

sane: concedes or grants for the sake of argument; cf. *Deiot.* 30, *sint sane inimicitiae—quae esse non debebant*.

augeamus . . . augebimus: Paronomasia in use of the same verb in different mood and tense stresses the inevitability of the reaction.

diligentiam: "meticulousness," so here = "vigilance," but more general than *cautio*. A practical Roman virtue, *diligentia* is used sarcastically of Tubero's investigative ability at *Lig.* 1.

omnium: with *quis*, not *rerum*, as anaphora of *tam* shows. *Rerum* is a filler, as at 15. For the partitive see *Dom.* 88, *cum me in iudicium populi Romani nemo omnium vocarit . . . contraque a populo Romano semper sim defensus*.

nihil . . . cogitans: *Phil.* 3.4 is similar in point: *quis enim est tam ignarus rerum, tam nihil de re publica cogitans, qui non intelligat . . . ?* But rhetorically the difference between that bipartite anaphora and the present tricolon is clearly felt: this is fuller and more resolved; see on 19, *tantus est enim*. As frequently with tricola, the third member expands. Despite an accusative object (*nihil*) and a complex prepositional phrase, the participle is used attributively, like *ignarus* and *rudis,* and so is modified by *tam*, not *ita*.

The critical link between Caesar's safety and that of his people is reflected in play on adjectives and pronouns: *tua . . . suam*, and *tua . . . omnium*, as well as *unius . . . omnium*. *unius* is the pronoun; although Latin prefers the possessive adjective to genitive of the personal pronoun, the genitival sense, "of you," prevails. *Vitas*, subject of *pendere* (2nd conj.), must be supplied.

equidem: in initial position, marks a strong imposition of the first person (see at 10) and a strong transition, triggered by the thought of all men's lives depending on Caesar's. Cicero's focus changes abruptly from Caesar's fate to that of the Republic and is none too considerate of Caesar. What follows is a strong, unequivocal demand for the restoration of the constitution and for Caesar's active participation.

cogitans: The active participle, used predicatively (vs. attributively; see on *tam nihil . . . cogitans* above), is most frequently concomitant (= *dum cogito*); see Laughton 2, 31. It may also bear a modal or instrumental sense as at *Lig.* 2, *recusans*, or a motivational sense, especially in the nominative as at *Lig.* 3, *cupiens*. The compound predicate, two verbs placed back-to-back in the middle of the sentence, looks both ways; *extimesco* governs the preceding tricolon and *doleo* the following accusative + infinitive. Note that until the second verb Cicero gives no indication that his subject is shifting from Caesar to the Republic.

casus . . . eventus . . . fragilitatem: redundant tricolon for completeness in reflective or philosophic mode, a restrained form of the expository style. The first introduces a focus more basic than fears of life-threatening plots. The second is perhaps a first allusion to the question, to be addressed later, of Caesar's health. The last is inclusive.

dumtaxat: an adverb frozen from a clause (*dum* + *taxat*, from the stem **tag*, as in *tango, contagio*) with the general meaning "to the extent that it touches"; so "thus far and no further" = "merely," or "at most" or "to no less than this," or "at least"; see at *Deiot.* 1.

immortalis . . . mortalis: rhetorical paronomasia to underline the point; but *unius,* with which a contrast to *publica* may be felt, is of equal importance. *Mortalis* in the singular as a generic word for "man" is rare in Cicero; here it does what *homo* could not.

doleoque: The *-que,* no mere copula, does not explicitly reveal the relationship between the predicates, which may be concomitant or consequential, positive or negative; see on 20, *contraque.* The initial participial phrase, so solicitous of Caesar, now seems like a rhetorical deception.

23

si vero: The movement of the sentence intensifies and the expression heightens as the argument touches back, through virtual repetition in *casus . . . motus,* to Caesar's fears and then rises to a more elevated tone with the first explicit reference to Caesar's preoccupation, immediately tied to the safety of the state.

etiam: in enclitic position, as at 29, *inter eos etiam qui . . .* ; *Cael.* 71, *hoc etiam loco M. Camurti . . . damnatio praedicatur*; *Top.* 76, *huius etiam est generis fama vulgi.* The adverb (a strong connective = *et* + *iam*) more frequently precedes the word it adjoins; e.g., *Lig.* 4, *necessitatem etiam honestam* (where see on *non turpem*), and *Deiot.* 24, *addit etiam illud,* where the pronoun looks forward. See further on 25, *tibi etiam soli*; 29, *erit dissensio*; *Lig.* 7, *ex parte magna*; 10, *etiam . . . sed multo magis*; 19, *melior ea*; and 21, *morbo etiam impediretur.*

insidiarumque consensio: The genitives form a hendiadys "criminal intrigues," defining the crime, but the separation is especially ornamental. The word order, which separates by the verb the two genitives dependent on *consensio,* puts *valetudinis* and *sceleris* in antithetical collocation and achieves two double cretic clausulae: *(mo)tus valetudinis . . . (insidia)rumque consensio.*

consensio: a neutral word, denoting accord; perhaps it reflects only Caesar's state of mind.

si = *etiamsi,* with adversative force; see *Prov. Cons.* 30.

credimus: Latin uses indicative of verb of judging or estimating (so *censeo,* or *arbitror*; *credere* = "to give credence") in rhetorical questions which suggest an implausible supposition. The apodosis of the future-less-vivid condition is in the infinitive. Cicero makes the statement subjective (and includes his audience); see on *sentis* below. The interrogative cast reflects a certain sense of resignation.

omnia: strong asyndetic transition to the main theme of the rest of the speech. It provides an antithesis for *uni,* in a neatly bracketed locution. Dative phrase is weighted by the full vocative (*prae-* and *cognomen*). Suet. *Iul.* 40–44 mentions these reforms as being on Caesar's agenda from 49 and realized by 46.

excitanda . . . quae iacere sentis: Cf. 8, *extollere iacentem.*

sentis: The subjective cast (vs., e.g., *quae iacent*) attributes this assessment to Caesar.

quod necesse fuit: a noun clause, not a relative; see 7, *quod . . . maximum est.* Here without anticipatory referent; see 25, *quod maximum est.* Its effect is to exculpate Caesar and others.

perculsa atque prostrata: Cf. on 17, *perculit.* Cicero uses the same pair of words, not quite synonymous—a sequence of decay is described—as an alliterative doublet along with *iacent* at *Fam.* 4.4.2; see 11, *conficiat et consumat,* also for alliterative prefix.

constituenda: a technical term for restoring to order. Restructuring of the courts was part of Caesar's legislation of 46.

revocanda: in response to a general financial crisis and devaluation following the events of 49; cf. Suet. *Iul.* 41.

comprimendae: lavish consumption by the wealthy, displayed in clothing and feasting, to be controlled by sumptuary laws.

propaganda: To encourage procreation, apparently, Octavian later promulgated a law restricting the time that males between twenty and sixty years of age could be out of the country and generally supported marriage vis-à-vis adultery—at least for the general population; cf. Suet. *Iul.* 42.

dilapsa . . . diffluxerunt: Note the anaphoric prefixes; as with *perculsa atque prostrata* the activities are sequential. The unique metaphor makes little sense; the two verbs are used together of melting ice at *Nat. Deor.* 2.26.

24

non fuit recusandum: impersonal gerundive to exclude human culpability.

tanto ... tanto: The bipartite anaphora intensifies, especially in asyndeton; so 28, *huic ... huic*.

civili bello: For the unusual word order see at 18.

animorum ardor et armorum: Wordplay enhanced by assonance. Note alternating correspondences of the four-word phrase. Cicero refers to passion for fighting again at *Lig.* 28, *omnes ... vincendi studio tenebamur,* where the rhetorical function is entirely different.

quassata: Cicero used this metaphor to describe the Republic in shambles only one other time, a decade earlier, at *Sest.* 73.

fuisset: represents a future perfect in direct speech. The outcome from which one recoils (*recusare*) is generally expressed as a potential with a *quin* or *quominus* clause; so *Deiot.* 43. The indefinite condition of this outcome is, e.g., *quaecumque causa vicerit.*

multa perderet et: The rhetorical flourishes continue: the word order—adjective (of direct object) + verb + *et* + object A + object B—is unusual. It puts *multa* in position to be picked up by another initial *multa* and separates it from the explicit balance of the parallel, qualified objects. The explicitness of the parallelism is striking. The suffering of the Republic should be attributed singularly to neither side, even when its leader is mentioned.

ornmenta: including, but not limited to, taxes and tributes.

stabilitatis suae: resolved double cretic clausula for a strong pause before second *multa*.

armatus ... togatus: See 14, *pacis et togae.*

idem: For contrasting two attitudes in the same entity by *idem* see at 1 and *Deiot.* 16.

fieri prohibuissent: Construction with the infinitive is at home in the speeches, not just at *Lig.* 24 and 25, but as early as *In Verrem*. Woven into the parallelism is a significant, asymmetrically expressed distinction between *facere* and *prohibere*; *fieri* the passive of *facere*.

omnia: with the gerundive, ties this exhortation to the opening of this section, *omnia sunt excitanda*. *Quidem* emphasizes *quae*, making it by position predicative and limiting the predication to it. The word order is intricate: *quae . . . sananda* brackets the clause; *omnia* is separated both from *quae* and *volnera*; *nunc*, separated from the verb, is emphatic; *tibi* is separated from gerundive.

volnera . . . sananda . . . mederi: the only instance of the metaphor "wounds of war." Cicero describes himself as a healer in his earliest speech, *Quinct.* 8. No particle softens the metaphors (see on 2, *quasi quodam socio*); diction of the coda is elevated enough that figurative language need not be qualified.

25

itaque: unexceptional transition to a new theme of considerable rhetorical importance.

illam tuam: See on 19, *tuo isto*, and on 25, *istam*.

praeclarissimam . . . vocem: dispassionate wisdom as an indication of Caesar's equanimity; but some irony may lie behind the paired superlatives.

invitus: key word; its position is stressed because the heavily weighted object clause that precedes must be followed by a pause. It helps to form the cretic + trochee clausula.

satis diu: Caesar's own words in apposition to *vocem*; so 28, *satis diu vixisse dicito*. Caesar, who suffered from epilepsy and other forms of ill health (Suet. *Iul.* 86) and had climbed the highest mountain only to find himself facing the postwar task of reconstruction, had some cause for disenchantment, even depression. His public attitude may also have been in part an act. The language may be earlier than Caesar. In any case, it stuck in Cicero's mind. At the end of *Phil.* 1, referring to his own sacrifice, not retirement, he says: *mihi fere satis est quod vixi vel ad aetatem vel ad gloriam*.

satis: Cicero analyzes Caesar's words one by one in an informal, perhaps impatient (see on 21, *iste*), staccato, low-keyed refutation, in the form of an exchange. Concessions are insistently polite: note the two *si* clauses and *fortasse*; see on 20, *praesertim*.

naturae: referred in 19 to innate qualities, vs. the gifts or impositions of Fortune. Here (at leaast to begin with) = normal span of life with an overtone of personal inclination. Caesar, born around 100, would have been barely fifty-five, not even a *senex*.

addo . . . at: assertion after two concessions, in the same abbreviated style. The present is preferred for simple addition of mitigating or concessive information. So *Deiot.* 24, *addit etiam illud*. For *at* see 13. Cicero will not adhere to this division but will presently urge Caesar's continued engagement on personal grounds as well.

quod maximum est: in apposition (see at 7) to the concept inherent in *at*, i.e., "but here's an objection." So *Phil.* 2.23, *nec tu quidem tota re, sed, quod maximum est, temporibus errasti*, and *Phil.* 5.13, *num Latine scit? num est ex iudicum genere . . . ? num, quod maximum est, leges nostras . . . novit?* "Does he know Latin? Does he come from a juror's background? Does he—and this is most important—know our laws?"

patriae: The notion that a man is responsible to his state is peculiarly Roman (see *Rep.* 1.8; *Fin.* 2.45) despite its Platonic origin (*Off.* 1.22): "as Plato has beautifully expressed it, we are not born for ourselves alone, but our country claims one part of our birth, our friends another." Few Romans would have much credited the Greek character with this noble ideal. Accepting death with equanimity rather than compromising is a private, primarily Stoic virtue, that was amended to civic martyrdom to make Stoicism acceptable to the Roman character.

parum: responding rhetorically to *"satis"* and bracketing the sentence. Cicero rarely operates at the level of adverbs, because in periodic composition they have limited grammatic or structural possibilities; but these are critical and the style is plain. Cf. the list of adverbs at 9. For *parum* = "too little," "very little," see *Lig.* 35; for "insufficient grandeur" see 26.

quare: as at 19, where it sums up before imperative injunction.

omitte, quaeso: Paratactic *quaeso* tones down the imperative, like the English addition of "please"; cf. 26, *vide, quaeso,* and *Deiot.* 20. It is a less syntactic and formal but perhaps more urgent locution than *quaeso ut omittas.*

istam: = *illam tuam,* stronger than *tuam*; the view of learned men as articulated by Caesar. The hyperbaton makes attributive what it brackets, the genitive subjective to *prudentiam*; the prepositional phrase depends on the sense of the word.

noli: reference to public responsibility (see on 25, *patriae*), perhaps less than fully sympathetic; see on *cuius* below, which also calls into question the intensity of Caesar's philosophical beliefs. Cicero, having recently pressed Caesar to treat *clementia* as a philosophical tenet, now urges him to be practical. Only the argument has changed.

enim: not quite logical; explanatory not of *noli* but of *omitte, quaeso,* i.e., "Please abandon this philosophy, for I gather you are pursuing it seriously."

credo: a true, one-word predicate; concedes the principle.

tum: bears considerable weight and provides a quasi-temporal limit for the condition; a variation on *tum . . . cum,* when *cum* is purely causal, as at 27, *tum te.* See, too, 26, *tum cum.* It limits to a stated condition also at *Lig.* 7, *tum denique.*

tibi etiam soli: Not only is Caesar's life inextricably tied to the welfare of the state and its citizens, but it was always fated so to be. That conceit is turned into a contrary-to-fact condition for a concession already logically denied in the pre-positioned apodosis. *Etiam* qualifies *natus esses* and is deliberately misplaced to intensify a progression effected through the repeated dative phrase.

natus esses: For the locution see *Lig.* 22, *natam ad bellum . . . gerendum,* and Hor. *C.* 1.27.1, *natis in usum laetitiae scyphis* [drinking goblets].

omnium: so placed in asyndeton for a strong contrast with repeated *soli,* intensified by *cunctam* ("in its diverse entirety").

omnium . . . res tuae gestae: momentarily encomiastic; but *tantum abes,* added asyndetically, qualifies it as a responsibility, if it does not openly criticize. The adulation inherent in this call to greatness is somewhat diminished by the hint of impatience and scolding.

res tuae gestae: Insertion of *tuae* forbids *res gestae* to be taken as a noun phrase = "achievements," but rather predicatively = *res a te gestae*.

tantum abes: in striking asyndeton. The usual Latin construction is *tantum abest* + *ut* + subjunctive (that is, *ut perfeceris maxima opera*) + a second *ut* + subjunctive. Occasionally *ab* + ablative substitutes for the first *ut* clause. For Cicero's choice see *maximorum operum* below.

perfectione: For the abstract noun see on *Lig.* 1, *ignoratione*, and *Lig.* 3, *legatio*.

maximorum operum: The genitive phrase depends on both *perfectione* and *fundamenta*.

quae cogitas: more pointed than *fundamenta cogitata*, alluding to reforms mentioned above or to projects like the Forum Julium and the temple of Venus Genetrix, still on the drawing board. Perhaps because Cicero is thinking in part of architectural foundations, he does not qualify the metaphor as at *Scaur.* 21, *ut me totius . . . defensionis quasi quaedam iacere fundamenta patiamini*, "that you let me lay down, as it were, certain foundations of my whole defense."

modum . . . definies: a spatial metaphor, to which the deictic adverb *hic* is pointedly, critically (especially with the future) appropriate; the ablative phrases are in apposition with the adverb. The alternatives, now delineated by Cicero, are public honor and Stoic self-sufficiency.

istud: refers to the line of demarcation. Cicero's new point is: if Caesar has miscalculated, he might retire before his place in history is assured. The unspoken assumption is that Caesar contemplates retirement in the confidence that his fame is secure. Cicero returns unapologetically to the theme of glory he had just dismissed for purposes of argumentation with *addo . . . gloriae*.

cuius: moves without pause for breath (semi-independent relative) to this slightly condescending observation, for which see *noli nostro periculo esse sapiens* above. Note asyndeta in the last six sentences; half have been questions. Tone is critical, the rhetoric to a degree pressing.

quamvis sis sapiens: The full clause insists on the substantived meaning "a philosopher."

26

"parumne . . . relinquemus": Cicero imagines Caesar's response though a dramatic figure of thought. The *sermocinatio* is a rhetorical device that creates the fiction of a dialogue. The other speaker may be a straw man or a particular character. Whatever the resemblance to persons living or dead, the respondent, with his words and arguments, is a creation of the orator, who often puts words in the mouths of opponents for the benefit of a third party, i.e., the jury or voters. Now the respondent is also the audience and the deciding judge. The themes touched here may have appeared in Cicero's lost essay *De Gloria*. Whether or not he endorsed the view there, his use here of the thesis, no doubt commonplace, that glory is relative and in the eye of the beholder is determined purely by the strategy he chose to exhort Caesar.

parumne: with *magna,* but set off by hyperbaton, conveys an arch and challenging tone; "Caesar" flings back Cicero's word from 25. Even in the separation there is a hint of scornful litotes: "mere trifles."

immo vero: a spirited denial in a fragmentary sentence; used in animated contradiction or correction (cf. *Cat.* 1.2, *vivit? immo vero in Senatum venit*). *Immo* denies; *vero* insists. The question is whether it responds to "Caesar's" sarcastic question or to the underlying meaning "I have done enough." The next sentence lends weight to the latter interpretation.

quidquid est enim: The nominal defining sentence with a circumstantial modifier for each predication is in the simplest style of philosophical exposition. *Est* predicates existence, rather than equivalence. All the indicatives predicate existence: "Whatever exists, exists as something too small when there exists something grander." In 6 and 10 Cicero picks up *quidquid* with *id,* but there the predicates have some dramatic force; here the abstract phrases makes the diction colorless. Out of the flow comes a definitional point, turned on the sense of the comparative.

id est parum: Cicero turns the mocking words of "Caesar" into an argument on relative meanings of *parum* and *satis*. There is not much syntax in this colloquial exchange. *Tibi* corresponds to *aliis, parum* to *satis.* And the concession in *quamvis multis* strengthens his point.

tum cum: See 25; *tum* is out of periodic order, as at 15, for unadorned precision (vs., e.g., *tum parum est cum* . . .). For *cum* + indicative = "a time when," see 15. Despite the causal overtones in the logic, the argument is limited to the existence in time of *ampliora*; see on 27, *tum te*.

amplius: often has an active sense, as if *amplificans*. The logical movement at 7, where the pardon of Marcellus is characterized only as Caesar's most conspicuous and unshared act, shows the same reluctance to define substantively and the same fairly plain language.

hic: anticipates the *ut* clause. Usual antecedent is a neuter *hoc* or *id*, for the noun clause is neuter. But *hic* is attracted into the case of *exitus*; see on 21, *incredibilis*.

futurus fuit: a state resulting from the completion of action (the original meaning of *tempus perfectum*). "But if the outcome is destined to be that . . ." or "If you are now determined that the result will be thus." So *Lig.* 24, *facturi fuistis*, where, too, note the preference for the indicative future in a highly potential articulation. After a present perfect we might expect primary sequence, but secondary is just as common; cf. Woodcock, 102.

in eo . . . in quo: The diction is still expository.

vide, quaero, ne: is a mild admonition, even without *quaeso*; as at *Lig.* 29.

divina: practically adversative in context.

admirationis . . . gloriae: periphrastic future subjunctive, as at 11. *Admirationis plus habitura* is explained as supplying a passive to *admiror*, as *in suspicionem venire* = "to be suspected," *usui esse* = "to be used." But operative here is the bracketed antithesis of the genitives. Genitive complements to *plus* and other such neuter pronouns are usually in hyperbaton, but almost always follow; here the comparative construction and the desire to bracket the expression with the polarities of *admiratio–gloria* determine word order.

si quidem: (whether it is one word or two) expresses and affirms the truth of a general condition which gives validity to a previous statement.

inlustris . . . meritorum: Eduard Fraenkel was once embarrassed, having pronounced a locution un-Ciceronian, by a schoolmaster who timidly proffered a reference from a Teubner edition. *Parva componere magnis.* I find the interlocking double hyperbaton, here, extraordinary. Adjective A, adjective B . . . noun A, noun B is not a usual pattern in Latin prose for attributing two noun phrases. *Vel in suos* and the phrases which complete that strong, anaphoric unit stand separated from and in anticipation of *meritorum,* on which they depend.

suos: includes friends and dependents as well as family. *Civis* is comprised in *patriam,* and it spoils the expansion of the tricolon. The reflexive is conditioned by *hominum.*

meritorum: substantive, but with sufficient verbal force to govern the doubly anaphoric tricolon of prepositional phrases. The position of *fama* is determined by several considerations: it avoids the confusing collocation of *hominum meritorum*; it assures a favored, resolved cretic + trochee rhythm ($\bar{~}\breve{~}\breve{~}\breve{~}\bar{~}\bar{~}$); it puts an emphatic word in final position, separated from the elaborate (*vel* in tricolon) phrase that requires it. The genitive phrase is massive even for Cicero, but the sentence provides a handsome and very striking coda to its section.

27

haec igitur: begins an extended, optimistic exhortation to Caesar to put aside his apprehensions and, following his natural inclination, to pursue greatness for himself and for the state. The bleak thoughts of the past sections are swept away in a wave of exuberance.

haec . . . hic . . . in hoc: Repetition of the deictic pronoun contributes to the positive energy of this summation; it goes naturally with an expansive gesture; so 32, *haec salva.* Within the tricolon, the syntax and rhetoric change: the first two members establish the metaphor (anaphora conveys urgency; the nouns are practically synonymous), the third shifts to an enjoinder formally articulated (*in hoc . . . ut*). The metaphor comes from the stage and encompasses both the actor and the plot. Life as a dramatic role is a commonplace in Greek literature. Cicero had acknowledged in the past (e.g., at *Arch.* 3, *in eiusmodi persona*) that the orator takes roles. The point here is that Caesar must stay in character to the end of the play.

constituas . . . perfruare: The relationship between the two predicates in the *ut* clause is sequential, but Cicero uses parataxis, giving consecutive force to *-que* (see on 22, *doleoque*); he is already in a result clause. *Constituas* in a technical, political sense, as at 23.

tranquillitate: private repose, absence of personal problems vs. *otium*, as retirement from public and political life, possible for a leader only when the society is well ordered internally and at peace; see André, 182. The distinction may be present at *Arch.* 29, *cum . . . nullum tranquillum atque otiosum spiritum duxerimus.* At *Fam.* 4.4.4 Cicero complains that by coming out of retirement with this speech he has deprived himself of *honestum otium.*

tum: temporal more than circumstantial, as at 26, *tum cum*; the prominent position of *tum* is severely restrictive. This is merely restatement, in a more intricate construction, of what he has just said. The concepts *rem publicam constituas* and *tranquillitate et otio perfruare* correspond to *et patriae* and *et naturam,* which are explicitly balanced, although the syntax changes.

si voles: on the surface respectful, like 25, *si vis . . . si placet,* but perhaps also suggesting some impatience; cf. *Deiot.* 26, *ut volet quisque.*

naturam . . . expleveris: The question of the natural course of life, raised at 25, is now treated as a function of fulfilling one's obligation to the state. With *naturam ipsam,* a distinction is felt from the earlier reference, when the limit appeared more or less up to the individual. The philosophical points are commonplace. Cicero puts Caesar in a logical bind. His attachment to the argument may be judged by the abruptness with which he drops it with *quamquam.*

dicito: Future imperative often has formalistic, legal overtones; here it is used in the apodosis of a future condition.

hoc ipsum: puts in quotation marks a previously used term. Greek could make any word a noun merely by putting a definite article in front of it; Latin lacked that possibility. The antecedent of *quo* is the word cited.

aliquid extremum: "anything final." For the commonplace see *Sen.* 69, *mihi ne diuturnum quidem quicquam videtur in quo est aliquid extremum.* The language in this and the next sentence—so 26, *quidquid est,* etc.—is of definitional logic.

venit: a present perfect in a general temporal clause; cf. *Deiot.* 4, *cum recognovi.* "The aorist-perfect in the subordinate clause denotes an act already completed before the action of the main verb" (Woodcock, 173). The participles *praeterita* and *futura* balance each other, with *postea* further marking the tense distinctions.

voluptas praeterita: The commonplace does not commit Cicero or Caesar to "orthodox" Epicureanism, the Greek philosophy least compatible with Roman attitudes, in spite of the words attributed to him by Sallust (*Cat.* 51.20): "Death resolves every single human woe; afterwards there is scope for neither worry nor joy." Philosophical tenets in speeches are rhetorical tools, not biographical credos. So in *Pro Murena* Cicero attributes to Cato a brand of Stoicism that is devastating in its insensitivity to the human condition.

pro nihilo: occurs with *habere, ducere, putare,* and *esse* for a total of twelve times, six in the *Philippics*. It is more at home in the familiar letters and colloquial dialogues. Though the expression probably derives from accounting, it seems to evaluate things considered trivial or held in contempt, e.g., *Caecil.* 24, [profiteers] *quos . . . contempsit semper ac pro nihilo putavit* or *Verr.* 2.2.40, *ausus es pro nihilo . . . tot res santcissimas ducere?* For the level of diction see *Tusc.* 5.73, [Epicurus] *dicit nullum sapienti esse tempus, etiamsi . . . torqueatur . . . , quin possit exclamare, "quam pro nihilo puto!"* The distribution of this expression in the speeches may exemplify how expressions come into currency.

quamquam: abruptly dismissive of his own argument; cf. 21, *tametsi,* and *Lig.* 24. The philosophic abstraction is taken to be less important to Caesar than an appetite for immortality. This assertion assumes a certain confident familiarity on Cicero's part; cf. 25, *cuius te esse avidissimum.* The language of this sentence fragment is more colorful and vital than that of the sentence it refutes.

iste tuus: stresses the personal drive against the philosophic, but also contrasts that drive with the ambitions of the rest of humanity, when *nobis* appears. The pair of words, in either order, would be less common in more elevated diction.

numquam . . . semper: Lexical opposites mark by position the antithetical, compound predicate.

immortalitatis amore flagravit: The thought is commonplace (so *Arch.* 26); the metaphor very strong, describing intense ambition. Of some eighteen occurrences of *flagro* in the speeches, only two other instances describe the drive for laudable goals: *Piso.* 59, *cupiditate iusti . . . triumphi,* and *Scaur.* c.1.4, *studio laudis.* Elsewhere ablatives like *infamia, amentia,* or *invidia* describe base motivation.

28

nec vero haec: a forceful affirmation of a negative predication, as at 5: "It is most certainly *not . . . .*"

nec haec . . . illa: Caesar's destiny described first negatively, then positively. Symmetry is avoided by variation in the articulation of the demonstratives. In the first part, *haec* is predicative and *tua* attributive; in the second *illa* is attributive, *tua* predicative. Otherwise there is considerable parallelism between the two: position of the demonstratives, repetition of *vita* and the personal pronouns, descriptive relatives following main clauses.

illa, inquam: Normally in such cases Cicero repeats the word or phrase before *inquam,* as at 7, *Lig.* 15, and *Deiot.* 8. Here it is life specified as immortal, not life itself, that is stressed.

alet: Cf. another ornate passage, *Cat.* 3.26, *memoria vestra, Quirites, res nostrae alentur.*

huic . . . huic: Repetition in asyndeton reflects insistence of the tone and excitement of the speaker; see 24, *tanto . . . tanto.*

ostentes: understand "for approval," although no exact parallel can be found.

oportet: far rarer in paratactic construction than with complementary infinitive, keeps the sentence personal. In almost every case *oportet* follows the subjunctive. This reflects a construction from an earlier time when second-person subjunctive could be used for positive commands (as opposed to imperatives, which prose demands) and *oportet* was parenthetical; cf. construction with imperative and 25, *quaeso.*

quae miretur . . . quae laudet: returns to antithesis of 26, *admirationis . . . gloriae.* In an extravagant conceit Caesar's balance sheet with posterity is evaluated and found wanting. The different reactions are fixed in time (see just below), with a bold transferral of the chronology from the judges to the events judged. *Quidem* makes the first of the two independent clauses in sense concessive; see on 15, *vero*. The first *quae* is feminine nominative singular, the second neuter plural accusative—not, perhaps, Cicero at his most elegant.

iam pridem: contrasts with "now," another insistent reminder of Caesar's present duties and obligations; cf. 30, *nunc certe*.

obstupescent: On initial position of verb see 17, *vidimus,* and *vagabitur,* below.

certe: marks a rhetorical concession in parataxis which will be countered at *sed*; cf. 6, *et certe . . . vero.* The list of objects (awaiting a governing verbal element, although they might provisionally be taken as accusatives of respect with the intransitive verb) attains its force more from accretion than rhetorical structuring. Enumerations beyond the tetracolon do not create expectations; see 6, *virtus . . . commeatus.* This list is broken down into more manageable units: a pair of adjective-nouns, a triad (*Rhenum, Oceanum, Nilum,* fluvial allusions to victories over Gaul, Britain, and Egypt), a pair of noun phrases chiastically disposed (note *in-/in-*), and three single nouns (an alliterative pair + *triumphos* with which the adjective *tuos* formally agrees). Only after all these nouns do the paired participles emerge that modify *posteri* and govern all the accusatives. The position of *tuos* is emphatic once the participles resolve the syntax. It also assures a double cretic rhythm, although *et legentes* would have produced a fine double trochee. Caesar had added Farther Gaul and Numidia to the Roman provinces, crossed the Rhine twice (in 55 and 53), reached the Atlantic in 56, and occupied Alexandria in 47.

munera, triumphos: *Munera* refer to public games, shows, and donations a man might offer in his private capacity or as aedile to enhance his public image. *Triumphi,* like supplications, are public holidays at public expense, but redound to the personal credit of the recipient. Caesar's first opportunity to celebrate a triumph in Rome came in 46.

29

sed: strong adversative position; a pretty conceit in which the stability of Rome is a condition for the stability of Caesar's reputation. At 22 the survival of the state was dependent on Caesar's survival. But even here Caesar's effort is necessary for the stability of the state.

stabilita: separated in hyperbaton from and preceding *erit,* is at first syntactically ambiguous (circumstantial participle or compound predicate). For other ornamental hyperbata see 13, *fato sumus . . . funestoque compulsi,* and 16, *causae sunt victoriae comparandae,* where interlocking word order enhances the articulation. The position of *erit* secures a double cretic clausula.

vagabitur: The metaphor is neither qualified (see on 3, *consuetudinem . . . aperuisti*) nor otherwise attested. The initial position of the verb is striking. It makes the length and movement of the predicate uncertain, although *modo,* concessive, indicates that a negative proposition will follow. In the end, with its contrasting notion *domicilium certum non habebit,* it brackets the predicate; see on *Lig.* 22, *vel potius paruit.*

longe atque late: alliterative (so 9, *literis atque linguis*) and leisurely. The two adverbs are paired, in varying order, at *Balb.* 13 and *Pomp.* 35, in both cases connected by *-que.*

sedem . . . domicilium: more than a rhetorical doublet with figurative second member. *Sedes* has civic or public overtones, as in "seat of government." The echo of *stabilita* and the alliteration would both be heard (as at 19, *singulari sapientia*).

erit . . . dissensio: The nominal main clause brackets an unbalanced comparison of present and future judges. Contemporaries are cast into past tense (*sicut inter nos fuit*) respective to the time of the judging. For the strongly predicative position of *erit* cf. 4, *est enim fortunatus. Etiam* qualifies *inter eos* but also looks forward to *sicut inter nos.*

This sentence begins with a main verb and adds clauses unperiodically. The *cum* clause is not anticipated; the second half of the its balance unexpectedly becomes the apodosis of an appended condition. The unpredictable movement of this run-on sentence is not typical of Cicero and may, with the extravagance of the metaphor *salute . . . restinxerit,* indicate extempore composition.

fortasse: mild suggestion of a criticism, since *fortasse* is more insistent than its denotation. *Aliquid* is deliberately vague.

idque: picks up *aliquid* and gives structure and emphasis to *maximum*; see on *et quidem* below. Similarly, at *Phil.* 9.109, *leges Caesaris easque praeclaras . . . evertit*, "he overturned Caesar's laws, and the best ones at that."

salute . . . restinxeris: a bold metaphor, previously unexampled (see, however, on 32, *exstincta aequitate*), in a context not notably elevated.

ut: Purpose or result cannot be readily distinguished in positive articulations. Referents of *illud . . . hoc* are *incendium . . . salute*; the antithesis produced is, for Cicero, notably pointed. The notion that the achievements of war may be attributed to fate, those of peace to a man's innate virtue, has already been raised at 19. But now fate's role is extended to victory in civil war, which is viewed not as glorious, but rather as a conflagration. At 13 and elsewhere Cicero adduces fate specifically to assert that no one was culpable for the war.

servi igitur: By postposition of the sequential particle the exhortation is more strongly felt.

eis . . . qui: for emphatic contrast with flawed, contemporary critics (*nos* below). The notion of posterity as a more impartial judge is found in *Q. Fr.* 1.1.43.

et quidem: creates a framework for a second major adverbial qualifier without repeating *iudicabunt,* which appears again in the next sentence. Cf. *Lig.* 24, *prohibiti estis in provincia vestra pedem ponere et prohibiti summa cum iniuria,* where Cicero insists on the demeaning participle as well as on each modifier.

incorruptius: = *integer*; cf. 4, *innocens.* Cicero may be stretching; hence *haud scio an.*

amore . . . invidia: For the polarities see Tac. *Ann.* 1.1, *sine ira et studio,* or Sall. *Cat.* 51.14, where the speaker is "Caesar"; they were commonplace. *Cupiditas* corresponds to *amor* as *invidia* does to *odium.*

rursus: suggests that present judges might be overly uncritical but that posterity will not be correspondingly critical.

30

id autem: the judgment of posterity; placed outside of the conjunction, *id* appears to be subject of *pertinet* as well, which it is not. Its antithesis is *esse te talem*. Cicero plays with the balances:

id [subject] . . . tum . . . non pertinebit
nunc certe   pertinet   esse te talem [subject]

quidam: the Epicureans, primarily. *Falso* has bothered readers as an unnecessary criticism of a notion Caesar might hold. But the manuscripts are unanimous, the reading is ancient, and attribution to a Christian corrector is unlikely. The notion that one may participate in his future glory is apposite to the argument and therefore entertained. Rhetorically, the rationalistic view is merely a foil for the more inspiring one. Cicero plays the two philosophical positions against each other at *Arch.* 30 and takes modest pleasure in the hope of the latter. Here it is merely a foil for unquestionable public memory. Caesar must assure his future by his present actions.

obscuratura . . . sit: one of five (see also 4, 11, 26, 27) future periphrastics in the speech; a "product of literary precision" (so Woodcock, 137). The verb here is separated from the participle, as at 11, *tuis ablatura finem sit aetas,* for rhythm (here double cretic) and (cf. 31, *functa res publica est*) also with interlocking word order. *Te talem, ut tuas* puts the emphasis just where Cicero wants it.

oblivio: This sentence is one more example of how simple, philosophic exposition can rise to more ornate diction; cf. 27, *quid est enim . . . futura,* or 26, *quidquid est . . . amplius.*

diversae, etc.: another assurance that Caesar need bear no guilt for the Civil War; dispassionate symmetries in nominal and passive sentences. The delicacy and restraint of this section and the next may epitomize *verecundia* in style.

voluntates . . . sententiae: passions and convictions. *Di(s)-* prefixed to both adjectives (and continued in *dissidebamus*) stresses the division; so 31, *ingratus . . . iniustus.*

consiliis . . . studiis: Parallelism is at its neatest and most symmetrical when representing dissension:

non enim	consiliis	solum	et studiis
sed	armis	etiam	et castris

erat obscuritas: Cf. *Lig.* 19, *causa tum dubia*; no subjects, no objects, no agents. By exculpating Caesar in this way, of course, he also excuses Caesar's opposition, leaving the way open for *clementia* less purely benevolent than Caesar may have wanted it understood. For the initial position of *erat* see 29, *erit*.

certamen . . . duces: Tubero used the phrase *dignitatis contentio* to describe, and play down, the cataclysm of the civil war; see the Introduction, section 3.2.

multi dubitabant	quid optimum esset
multi	quid sibi expediret
multi	quid deceret

At this point the demands of tricolon, with anaphora and isocolon, are met. The third member even has a double trochee. All these men made choices based on some kind of advantage or propriety. The structure now becomes a foil: for a fourth group, set in sharp relief by the change of pronoun in a syntactically parallel structure, the choice was a moral one, based on what one was permitted to do—by law, conscience, or personal obligation.

quid liceret: The question of legitimacy might be harder for the Caesarians to answer. This passage should be compared with *Lig.* 19.

31

perfuncta: "played out inevitably"; for separation of *est* see on 29, *stabilita*. The initial position of this and the next verb gives the sense of a dispassionate summation of events. Note the double cretic period formed by the predicate.

fatalique: no blame assigned; cf. 13, *Lig.* 17, *Deiot.* 13; also on 29, *illud . . . hoc*.

vicit is: The contrast between Caesar and Pompey, whose intended brutality in victory is well documented in Cicero's letters, is generalized; the result of the conflict is portrayed as inevitable. The victor is defined—almost determined—by his restraint in victory. Both antagonists are described delicately in characteristic, not attributive clauses that balance each other without being symmetrical. The position of the verb and the lack of connective with the last sentence, which also began with a verb, seem assertive.

fortuna: external agency vs. "goodness," like 29, *consili*, and 32, *aequitate*; not fully personified as at 6, 7, 10, and esp. 19—ablative of means.

inflammaret . . . leniret: The metaphor of a conflagration extinguished by the virtue of Caesar runs throughout the passage from 29, *incendium*, to 32, *exstincta*.

odium suum: The genitival adjective is ambiguous, but probably objective; the strong preference for genitive of personal pronoun for objective genitives is limited to the first and second person, e.g., *pars mei*.

neque . . . iudicaret: as did Pompey. This distinction, made several times in the *Caesarianae*, puts Pompey in a bad light, and perhaps deservedly; see *Lig.* 33. But Pompey had every reason in 50 to consider himself as representing the legitimate government. Lack of positive support particularly in wartime is difficult for governments to accept with equanimity.

neque omnis: The *qui omnis quibus* of 6 can stand (cf. 28, *quae quidem quae*, or 4, *quam eam quam*), but *omnes*, if read, cannot be the antecedent to *eosdem*. The reading of αγ is smoother.

eosdem: The pronoun *idem* providing an antecedent to a relative clause in the order relative–antecedent insists on the complete identity of the two words and a circumstantial relationship between governing and relative clause, even if the relative clause is in the indicative; so *eadem* below, where the connection is slightly different, and *Lig.* 20, *easdem*.

ab aliis . . . ab aliis: deceptive parallelism. The first preposition is of agent, the second, of separation; a similar play on prepositions occurs at *Lig.* 4, *non modo nullum ad bellum, sed ne ad minimam quidem suspicionem belli*.

Twenty thousand troops surrendered voluntarily at Pharsalus, at which point Cicero says he became a *suasor armorum non ponendorum sed abiciendorum* (*Deiot.* 29). Terms at Thapsus required that the opposition be disarmed.

ingratus . . . civis qui: A tension is felt between the indicative in the relative clause, which should denote particularity, and the strong suggestion of a characteristic or generic description; see on 15, *qui vero,* but also on 18, *qui . . . excitaverunt.*

liberatus . . . tamen: The participle is strongly adversative. Observe here the locutions

(1) quibus iratus esset, eosdem . . .   morte dignos
(2) qui . . . liberatus,   . . . tamen retinet
(3) quae . . . pertinacia quibusdam,   eadem aliis constantia

Only the second, by use of *tamen,* makes the precise circumstantial relationship explicit.

armorum . . . animum . . . armatum: Wordplay and word order enhance this singular metaphor; closest parallel is at *Milo.* 2: "to arm with the authority (*auctoritate . . . armare*) of the state the rashness of an aroused mob." *Armatum,* besides bracketing with *armorum,* is reserved for the end to reflect the thought.

in acie cecidit: perhaps a gloss on the next relative clause (and so sometimes omitted by editors); but preceding the more colorful expression as it does, it effects a pathetic intensification. For explanatory *qui* + indicative see on 18, *qui . . . excitaverunt.*

quae enim: Death in battle will seem to some, at least, a proof of true loyalty; the point is delicately put (*videri potest*), for death in Pompey's behalf is by no means a ticket to martyrdom.

eadem: so *eosdem* above.

32

sed iam: a temporal contrast with what has gone before. For *sed* see 29. With a perfect, *iam* = "already."

omnis fracta dissensio est: interlocking word order, with hyperbaton of the weighted subject, of the periphrastic past perfect (see on 29, *stabilita,* and 13, *compulsi*), and of the ablative with the passive participle. The repeated order (participle + ablative) suggests that *victoris* goes with both ablatives. The position of *armis,* then, is not explained by the cretic +

spondee clausula it helps to achieve. At the end of a clause *fracta dissensio* would have made a double cretic clausula; but the overall structure would have suffered.

exstincta aequitate: for the metaphor see on 31.

restat ut: The connection is sequential in a positive sense; the enjoinder of the *ut* clause is the subject of the verb.

omnes unum: Collocation is almost automatic in Latin; so 34, *unum innumerabilia*.

qui modo: For a proviso clause with the indicative see *Deiot.* 16, *qui modo*, and *Flacc.* 64, *quis ignorat, qui modo . . . res istas scire curavit*. For another indicative relative with circumstantial sense see 18, *qui . . . excitaverunt*. Some manuscripts, and all editors, omit *modo* here, and it is not strictly necessary. But it is well to mark the proviso in this infrequent indicative construction.

non . . . modo sed etiam: The second item is always stressed, even if lower on a scale of value than the first; hence "common sense, let alone wisdom"; see on *Deiot.* 15, *non modo perfecto*.

sanitatis: a rare word in Cicero; having one's wits about one, as opposed to having a trained mind of philosophical bent. An abstract noun is needed as a one-word foil for *sapientia*. While the theme of Caesar's safety dominates, Cicero has introduced another concept, alluded to again in Caesar's *sententia*.

salvo . . . salvi: making the safety of Caesar a condition of public safety, but also coupling the former's safety with his (political) wisdom. In the minor balance (*cum antea, tum hodie*) he does not use the fuller form *hoc die* (see on 1), which might sap force from *maxime*. Neither the expanded ablative absolute, encompassing a relative clause referring to Caesar's judgment, nor the use of *nisi* to make it a negative conditional is typical of Cicero; see on 2, *a me . . . distracto*, and *Lig.* 19, *utrisque . . . aberrantibus*.

quare: A spacious construction develops, consisting of two independent clauses each introduced by *omnes*, expanding with exuberance, through the paired predicates *hortamur et obsecramus*—a frequent embellishment of words for "request"—to an anaphorically amplified *ut* clause, to a pair of doublets: *excubias et custodias . . . laterum . . . corporum* at the end.

salva . . . saluti: insistent echoes of the sentence before.

haec salva esse: a rhetorical gesture, deictic, encompassing the sites, the institutions and the personnel within sight of the Forum that make up the Republic; for pronoun see on 27.

omnesque: For *-que* see 14, *doleoque*.

pro aliis: Cicero here and in the next sentence is careful to associate the rest of the Senate with his opinion.

laterum . . . corporum: The first refers to the physical (and vulnerable) body; the second to the life it houses.

oppositus: a noun not otherwise used in the speeches and perhaps strange-sounding. According to Dio Cassius 44.6.1, Caesar refused a bodyguard offered by the Senate.

corporum: *Corpus,* like *caput,* can refer to human life by metonymy.

33

sed: Within an argument, *sed* or *sed tamen* marks a strong adversative, whereas *vero* marks a break and asseveration; so 15. But *sed* has a broader rhetorical function of bringing a whole line of argument to a halt or of resuming after a digression; so *Lig.* 20, *sed ut omittam*; *Lig.* 23, *sed quoquomodo se illud habet*; and *Lig.* 24, *sed iam hoc totum omitto*.

unde: = *a quo,* correlative. Oratorical transition is explicitly marked; see on 21, *prothesis*. Only in a few other places does Cicero use *ordior* to mark the movement of a speech: *Phil.* 2.44 where, with *a principio ordiamur*, he launches into an attack on Antony's early life; *Rosc. Am.* 29, *quid primum querar? aut unde potissimum, iudices, ordiar?* and *Corn.* 1 (frag. 3 Puccioni), *unde igitur ordiar? an ab ipsa lege?* Both of these are examples of *dubitatio* or *aporia*, in which the speaker feigns utter confusion as to how to proceed; so *Lig.* 1, *quo me vertam nescio*.

terminetur oratio: Word order secures a double cretic rhythm (*-netur oratio*), lost if the manuscript variant is accepted.

maximas . . . maiores: The solecism is intentional and excused by rhetoric;

cf. *Cat.* 3.13, *cum illa certissima sunt visa argumenta . . . tum multo certiora illa,* and *Planc.* 5, *id est . . . molestissimum, . . . sed multo illud maius.*

gratias agimus . . . habemus: a slight zeugma; *agere* requires *gratias* (particular words of thanks); with *habere* the idiom demands the singular *gratiam* ("gratitude") unless the subject is plural. The distinction is explained by *nam* and the *sed* clause: "All men have gratitude, not all need to express thanks; I shall." This establishes an antithesis between *omnes* and *me* that carries, not always successfully, to the end of the speech.

quod . . . potuisti: noun clause in apposition to *omnes idem sentiunt*; see 34, *quod . . . arbitrabar.*

precibus et lacrimis: The same phrase appears at *Lig.* 13, recounting a private appeal to Caesar. *Fam.* 4.4.3 describes how senators arose and approached Caesar as suppliants when the question of a pardon for Marcellus was first raised. The context now suggests tears as a response to Caesar's having acceded to the request, no doubt accurately. At 10 Gaius Marcellus wept for joy at Caesar's decision. Perhaps, therefore, not a hendiadys for "tearful supplications."

omnibus stantibus: meaning uncertain. Ideally all senators would offer their opinions on the matter under discussion, beginning with the *princeps senatus,* then the *consulares,* down to junior senators. In practice only a few at the top had the opportunity to speak. Lesser senators would arrange themselves in the proximity of speakers with whose views they wished to be associated; thus the term *pedarii senatores.* Cicero rose to offer his *sententia* because he was senior, because he was particularly close to Marcellus, because he was Cicero; at *Fam.* 5.2.9 he distinguishes between saying his opinion and supporting others' from his seat (*sedens assensi*). This time Cicero did not speak first: see *Fam.* 4.4.4, *cum omnes ante me rogati gratias Caesari egissent.*

quodam modo: sc. *dicere,* which it would be otiose to repeat. Still the ellipsis bespeaks informality, as, for a different reason, at *Lig.* 17, *quod nullo de alio quisquam*; so the indefinite pronoun. In this and the next fairly colorless sentence, Cicero deliberately lingers on the formalities to create a suspense for the emotional explosion everyone knows is coming.

quod fieri decet: Referring just to general thanksgiving and rejoicing by all (in addition to the speeches) at Marcellus' pardon? Or to the perception of

Caesar restoring the Republic as well? The language is deliberately impre-
cise (*quod fieri decet*), in a precise, expository construction: the relative
clause precedes its antecedent. The formula of the datives reasserts the association made at the beginning (e.g., 3) between politics and what might
have been taken as an act of personal generosity. The answer comes in the
next sentence: *de communi salute.*

34

quod autem . . . praestare: a disjointed sentence, perhaps not intentionally
so; Cicero produced an awkward sentence at just this point in *Pro Archia*;
see Gotoff 2, 208–9. The trouble begins because Cicero wants a sentence
to parallel *quod fieri decet* (as *autem* suggests) and to emphasize his appreciation in contrast to the general and ritual thanksgiving. Thus the *quod*
clause comes first, preceding its antecedent *id* in what becomes an intolerable hyperbaton.

summae benevolentiae: Cicero introduces the theme of this sentence—his
own duty, stemming from his affection for Marcellus, to thank Caesar personally—with a predicative genitive, as in *Sest.* 40, *hoc sentire prudentiae
est, facere fortitudinis; et sentire vero et facere perfectae cumulataeque virtutis ⟨est⟩*. Construction usually takes a complementary infinitive: "both
to know and to act is the mark of perfect and complete virtue." What we
have here, for which I find no parallel, approximates *quod ad summam
benevolentiam attinet*. Once on the subject of *benevolentia*, Cicero's *copia*
begins to run wild. He characterizes it: it is his, it is manifest, it is directed
towards Marcellus, it yields to just about no man's. Two clauses describe
the genitive, and there is still no construction for the *quod* clause. Cicero
is chewing on more than he has bitten off.

quae mea: The relative is strictly coordinating (= *et ea*) and almost parenthetical; see 13, *quorum . . . frequentiam.*

omnibus nota: See on 3, *intellectum . . . mihi*. The attraction of the adjective into the relative is an attempt to control *erga eum,* which usually is
attached to a noun and bracketed by an adjective agreeing with that noun,
e.g., *summo erga vos amore*. Prepositional phrases do not typically qualify
nouns in Latin.

ut vix . . . nemini: a characteristic of his goodwill; an antecedent would have been helpful, as at 6, *quae . . . ita magna . . . ut vix,* but this, with *nota,* would make an awkward compound predicate adjective. Cicero had made the same claim to Marcellus a little earlier, in *Fam.* 4.9.4. The position of *nemini* is emphatic and secures a double cretic clausula.

C. Marcello: Marcus' cousin, cos. 50; or truly his brother? See 10.

cum . . . praestiterim: to *praestare,* an a fortiori argument, underlined by *certe.* The pronoun *id* refers not to *benevolentia,* but to *quod . . . est* ("as to the role of absolute devotion." *hoc tempore* picks up *tam diu,* with which *quam diu* is correlated. A slight variation attempts to enliven the paired tricola of ablatives.

C. Caesar: For the *praenomen* see on 3.

sic . . . ut . . . : clearly not resultant: "in this sense, on these terms, namely that . . ."—general circumstance.

unum innumerabilia: paronomasia in collocation taken together with *ad tua in me.*

merita: Cf. on 26, *meritorum.*

quod . . . arbitrabar: in apposition to the entire predicate with no anticipatory referent, as at 33, *quod . . . potuisti,* and *Lig.* 2, *quod optandum.*

magnus . . . cumulus: Hyperbaton stresses the adjective without minimizing the interposed ablative phrase. *Cumulus* is the final measure that brings completion. Thus at *Clu.* 74, with a panel of thirty-two, bribing the seventeen jurors would bring the vote for acquittal over the top (*ad cumulum* = "to the top," "to the crown"). The metaphor begins in the language of accounting and, applied to favors owed and given, is commonplace in Greek and Latin; so *Fam.* 13.17.2, *quam maximus potest mea commendatione cumulus accedat.* "Let the well of your [past] generosity be filled to the very brim by my [present] recommendation."

hoc tuo facto: Deictic *hoc* is rhetorically effective. For the noun *facto* see *Lig.* 29.

PRO LIGARIO

M. Tulli Ciceronis Pro Q. Ligario Oratio

1 Novum crimen, C. Caesar, et ante hunc diem non auditum propinquus 1
meus ad te Q. Tubero detulit, Q. Ligarium in Africa fuisse, idque C. Pansa
praestanti vir ingenio fretus fortasse familiaritate ea quae est ei tecum, ausus est confiteri. itaque quo me vertam nescio. paratus enim veneram, cum
tu id neque per te scires neque audire aliunde potuisses, ut ignoratione tua 5
ad hominis miseri salutem abuterer. sed quoniam diligentia inimici investigatum est quod latebat, confitendum est, opinor, praesertim cum meus
necessarius Pansa fecerit ut id integrum iam non esset, omissaque controversia omnis oratio ad misericordiam tuam conferenda est, qua plurimi
sunt conservati, cum a te non liberationem culpae, sed errati veniam im- 10
petravissent. 2 habes igitur, Tubero, quod est accusatori maxime optandum, confitentem reum; sed tamen hoc confitentem: se in ea parte fuisse
qua te, qua virum omni laude dignum, patrem tuum. itaque prius de vestro
delicto confiteamini necesse est, quam Ligari ullam culpam reprehendatis.

Q. enim Ligarius cum esset nulla belli suspicio, legatus in Africam C. 15
Considio profectus est. qua in legatione et civibus et sociis ita se probavit
ut decedens Considius provincia satis facere hominibus non posset, si
quemquam alium provinciae praefecisset. itaque Ligarius cum diu recusans
nihil profecisset, provinciam accepit invitus; cui sic praefuit in pace ut et
civibus et sociis gratissima esset eius integritas ac fides. 3 bellum subito 20
exarsit, quod qui erant in Africa ante audierunt geri quam parari. quo audito partim cupiditate inconsiderata, partim caeco quodam timore primo
salutis, post etiam studi sui quaerebant aliquem ducem, cum Ligarius domum spectans, ad suos redire cupiens, nullo se implicari negotio passus
est. interim P. Attius Varus qui tum praetor Africam obtinuerat, Uticam 25
venit. ad eum statim concursum est. atque ille non mediocri cupiditate
adripuit imperium, si illud imperium esse potuit, quod ad privatum clamore multitudinis imperitae, nullo publico consilio deferebatur. 4 itaque

---

1　1 non auditum α*BDL*: inauditum *E*γ　　　15 C. α: cum C. ϐ, cum consule γ
　　5 scires ϐ*a*: scire α*hm*　　　　　　　　20 ac ϐ: et αγ
　　7 ut opinor ϐγ　　　　　　　　　　　3　24 et ad γ
2　12 hoc ita γ　　　　　　　　　　　　　25 tum α: *om.* ϐγ
　　13 te Tubero γ　　　　　　　　　　　27 ad privatum αγ: a privato *DEL*, in
　　15 enim αϐ: igitur γ　　　　　　　　　　privato *B*, privato *codd. quidam*
　　15 esset adhuc γ　　　　　　　　　　　*rec.*

Ligarius qui omne tale negotium fugeret, paulum adventu Vari conquievit. 1
adhuc, C. Caesar, Q. Ligarius omni culpa vacat: domo est egressus non
modo nullum ad bellum, sed ne ad minimam quidem suspicionem belli;
legatus in pace profectus in provincia pacatissima ita se gessit ut ei pacem
esse expediret. profectio certe animum tuum non debet offendere. num 5
igitur remansio? multo minus. nam profectio voluntatem habuit non turpem, remansio necessitatem etiam honestam. ergo haec duo tempora carent
crimine, unum cum est legatus profectus, alterum cum efflagitatus a provincia praepositus Africae est. 5 tertium tempus est quod post adventum
Vari in Africa restitit. quod si est criminosum, necesitatis crimen est, non 10
voluntatis. an ille si potuisset illinc ullo modo evadere, Uticae quam Romae,
cum P. Attio quam cum concordissimis fratribus, cum alienis esse quam
cum suis maluisset? cum ipsa legatio plena desideri ac sollicitudinis fuisset
propter incredibilem quendam fratrum amorem, hic aequo animo esse potuit belli discidio distractus a fratribus? 15

  6 Nullum igitur habes, Caesar, adhuc in Q. Ligario signum alienae a te
voluntatis. cuius ego causam animadverte, quaeso, qua fide defendam;
prodo meam. o clementiam admirabilem atque omnium laude praedica-
tione litteris monumentisque decorandam! M. Cicero apud te defendit
alium in ea voluntate non fuisse in qua se ipsum confitetur fuisse, nec tuas 20
tacitas cogitationes extimescit, nec quid tibi de alio audienti de se occurrat
reformidat. vide quam non reformidem, vide quanta lux liberalitatis et sapientiae tuae mihi apud te dicenti oboriatur. quantum potero voce contendam, ut hoc populus Romanus exaudiat: 7 suscepto bello, Caesar, gesto
etiam ex parte magna, nulla vi coactus iudicio ac voluntate ad ea arma 25
profectus sum, quae erant sumpta contra te. apud quem igitur hoc dico?
nempe apud eum qui cum hoc sciret, tamen me antequam vidit rei publicae
reddidit, qui ad me ex Aegypto litteras misit, ut essem idem qui fuissem,
qui me, cum ipse imperator in toto imperio populi Romani unus esset, esse
alterum passus est, a quo hoc ipso C. Pansa mihi hunc nuntium perferente 30

4 1 fugeret α: cuperet effugere δγ
   4 profectus est *B*
5 9 tempus est quod *AVBE*: tempus
     quod *HDL*, est tempus quo γ,
     tempus est quo *A. Klotz*
   10 quod si δγ: si α
   11 potius quam γ
6 19 cum M. δ

21 tacitas *om.* γ
21 de se ipso δ
24 hoc p. R. αδ: hoc R. hoc *m*, p. hoc
   R. *a, Quint. 11.3.166*, p. R. *h*
7 29 qui me . . . esse αγ: qui . . . esse
     me δ
   29 imperio αδ: orbe γ
   30 hunc *om.* δγ

concessos fascis laureatos tenui quoad tenendos putavi, qui mihi tum de- 1
nique salutem se putavit dare, si eam nullis spoliatam ornamentis dedis-
set. 8 vide quaeso, Tubero, ut qui de meo facto non dubitem, de Ligari
audeam dicere. atque haec propterea de me dixi, ut mihi Tubero cum de
se eadem dicerem ignosceret. cuius ego industriae gloriaeque faveo, vel 5
propter propinquam cognationem, vel quod eius ingenio studiisque delec-
tor, vel quod laudem adulescentis propinqui existimo etiam ad meum aliquem fructum redundare. 9 sed hoc quaero: quis putat esse crimen fuisse
in Africa? nempe is qui et ipse in eadem provincia esse voluit, et prohibitum
se a Ligario queritur, et certe contra ipsum Caesarem est congressus ar- 10
matus. quid enim, Tubero, tuus ille destrictus in acie Pharsalica gladius
agebat, cuius latus ille mucro petebat? qui sensus erat armorum tuorum,
quae tua mens, oculi, manus, ardor animi? quid cupiebas, quid optabas?
nimis urgeo. commoveri videtur adulescens. ad me revertar. isdem in armis
fui. 10 quid autem aliud egimus, Tubero, nisi ut quod hic potest, nos pos- 15
semus? quorum igitur impunitas, Caesar, tuae clementiae laus est, eorum
ipsorum ad crudelitatem te acuet oratio? atque in hac causa non nihil equidem, Tubero, etiam tuam, sed multo magis patris tui prudentiam desidero,
quod homo cum ingenio, tum etiam doctrina excellens, genus hoc causae
quod esset non viderit. nam si vidisset, quovis profecto quam isto modo a 20
te agi maluisset. arguis fatentem. non est satis; accusas eum qui causam
habet aut ut ego dico meliorem quam tu, aut ut tu vis parem. 11 haec
admirabilia, sed prodigi simile est quod dicam. non habet eam vim ista
accusatio ut Q. Ligarius condemnetur, sed ut necetur. hoc egit civis Romanus ante te nemo; externi sunt isti mores qui usque ad sanguinem incitari 25
solent odio, aut levium Graecorum aut immanium barbarorum. nam quid
agis aliud? Romae ne sit, ut domo careat, ne cum optimis fratribus, ne cum
hoc T. Broccho avunculo, ne cum eius filio consobrino suo, ne nobiscum

---

2 sal. se put. dare α*am*: se sal. put.
  reddere δ*h*

8 3 dubitem αδ: dubitem dicere γ
    4 aud. dicere α, *Quint. 5.10.93*: aud.
    confiteri γ, non aud. conf. δ

9 8 putet γ
    9 in Africa Ligarium γ
    9 provincia α: Africa δγ

10 17 acuit δ

11 23 admirabilia α: non modo mirabilia

(sunt *add.* γ) δγ

23 similia quae γ
24 sed necetur γ
25 sunt isti *AH*: isti sunt *Va*, isti δ*hm*
25 qui *om.* δ*hm*: qui . . . odio *del.*
  Clark post Sch. G.
25 incitari . . . odio αδ*a*: incitare . . .
  odium *hm*
27 Romae δγ: ut Romae α
28 avunculo suo δ

vivat, ne sit in patria? num est, num potest magis carere his omnibus quam   1
caret? Italia prohibetur, exsulat. non tu hunc ergo patria privare qua caret,
sed vita vis. 12 at istud ne apud eum quidem dictatorem qui omnis quos
oderat morte multabat, quisquam egit isto modo. ipse iubebat occidi nullo
postulante, praemiis invitabat. quae tamen crudelitas ab hoc eodem aliquot   5
annis post, quem tu nunc crudelem esse vis, vindicata est. "ego vero istud
non postulo," inquies. ita me hercule existimo, Tubero. novi enim te, novi
patrem, novi domum nomenque vestrum; studia generis ac familiae vestrae
virtutis humanitatis doctrinae plurimarum artium atque optimarum nota
mihi sunt. 13 itaque certo scio vos non petere sanguinem. sed parum at-   10
tenditis. res enim eo spectat ut ea poena in qua adhuc Q. Ligarius sit, non
videamini esse contenti. quae est igitur alia praeter mortem? si enim est in
exsilio, sicuti est, quid amplius postulatis? an ne ignoscatur? hoc vero
multo acerbius multoque durius. quodne nos domi petimus precibus ac
lacrimis, strati ad pedes, non tam nostrae causae fidentes quam huius hu-   15
manitati, id ne impetremus pugnabis, et in nostrum fletum inrumpes, et
nos iacentis ad pedes supplicum voce prohibebis? 14 si cum hoc domi
faceremus quod et fecimus et ut spero non frustra fecimus, tu repente inruisses et clamare coepisses: "C. Caesar, cave ignoscas, cave te fratrum pro
fratris salute obsecrantium misereat!" nonne omnem humanitatem ex-   20
uisses? quanto hoc durius quod nos domi petimus, id a te in foro oppugnari
et in tali miseria multorum perfugium misericordiae tollere! 15 dicam
plane, Caesar, quod sentio. si in tanta tua fortuna lenitas tanta non esset,
quam tu per te, per te, inquam, obtines—intellego quid loquar—acerbis-
simo luctu redundaret ista victoria. quam multi enim essent de victoribus   25
qui te crudelem esse vellent, cum etiam de victis reperiantur? quam multi

2 hunc ergo α: ergo hunc *DE*γ, hunc
  om. B

12 5 praemiis etiam *E*γ
    5 eodem α6: etiam γ
    8 studia denique γ
    10 sunt omnia 6
13 13 ignoscatur *ed. Junt.*: ignoscat *codd.*
    14 multoque (-que *om. hm*) αγ*E*:
      multoque est *BD*
    14 quodne α*m*, *Sch. G.*: quod 6*a*, si
      quod *h*
    14 domi *del. edd.*
    14 ac α: et γ, *om.* 6

16 oppugnabis 6
14 19 cave credas *ante* cave ign. γ
    21 a te . . . oppugnari et . . . tollere
      codd.: te . . . oppugnare et . . .
      tollere *cod. Lambini*, in tali ⟨te⟩
      miseria . . . tollere *suppl. Schöll*,
      tolli *Clark*
15 23 tanta α*hm*: hac tanta 6*a*
    24 per te per te γ: per te α6, *Quint.*
      (*codd. Ab*), parce per te *Quint.*
      (*cod. M*)
    26 qui *om.* 6
    26 cum etiam 6

qui cum a te ignosci nemini vellent, impedirent clementiam tuam, cum hi,   1
quibus ipse ignovisti, nolint te esse in alios misericordem! **16** quod si pro-
bare Caesari possemus in Africa Ligarium omnino non fuisse, si honesto
et misericordi mendacio saluti civi calamitoso esse vellemus, tamen hominis
non esset in tanto discrimine et periculo civis refellere et coarguere nostrum   5
mendacium, et si esset alicuius, eius certe non esset qui in eadem causa et
fortuna fuisset. sed tamen aliud est errare Caesarem nolle, aliud est nolle
misereri. tum diceres: "Caesar, cave credas. fuit in Africa, tulit arma contra
te!" nunc quid dicis? "cave ignoscas!" haec nec hominis nec ad hominem
vox est. qua qui apud te, C. Caesar, utetur, suam citius abiciet humanitatem   10
quam extorquebit tuam.

    17 Ac primus aditus et postulatio Tuberonis haec ut opinor fuit: velle
se de Q. Ligari scelere dicere. non dubito quin admiratus sis, vel quod nullo
de alio quisquam, vel quod is qui in eadem causa fuisset, vel quidnam novi
sceleris adferret. "scelus" tu illud vocas, Tubero? cur? isto enim nomine   15
illa adhuc causa caruit. alii errorem appellant, alii timorem, qui durius,
spem cupiditatem odium pertinaciam, qui gravissime, temeritatem; scelus
praeter te adhuc nemo. ac mihi quidem si proprium et verum nomen nostri
mali quaeritur, fatalis quaedam calamitas incidisse videtur et improvidas
hominum mentis occupavisse, ut nemo mirari debeat humana consilia di-   20
vina necessitate esse superata. **18** liceat esse miseros—quamquam hoc
victore esse non possumus; sed non loquor de nobis, de illis loquor qui
occiderunt—fuerint cupidi, fuerint irati, fuerint pertinaces; sceleris vero
crimine furoris parricidi liceat Cn. Pompeio mortuo, liceat multis aliis carere. quando hoc ex te quisquam, Caesar, audivit, aut tua quid aliud arma   25
voluerunt nisi a te contumeliam propulsare? quid egit tuus invictus exercitus, nisi uti suum ius tueretur et dignitatem tuam? quid? tu cum pacem
esse cupiebas, idne agebas ut tibi cum sceleratis an ut cum bonis civibus
conveniret? **19** mihi vero, Caesar, tua in me maxima merita tanta certe
non viderentur, si me ut sceleratum a te conservatum putarem. quo modo   30
autem tu de re publica bene meritus esses, cum tot sceleratos incolumi dig-

	2 ipsis *AV*	*Mommsen*	
16	5 redarguere б	15 sceleris *del. Patricius*	
	7 est nolle αб: nolle *a,* non *hm*	19 quaeratur б	
	8 tunc б	**18**	25 quisquam ex te б
	8 Africa Ligarius γ		27 uti Cα; ut бγ
	10 utitur *Ehm*		28 civibus *om.* Cα
17	13 de nullo alio б*hm*	**19**	29 Caesar *om.* αγ
	14 quisquam αбm: quicquam *ah, del.*		31 cum αγ: si б

nitate esse voluisses? secessionem tu illam existimavisti, Caesar, initio, non
bellum, nec hostile odium, sed civile discidium, utrisque cupientibus rem
publicam salvam, sed partim consiliis, partim studiis a communi utilitate
aberrantibus. principum dignitas erat paene par, non par fortasse eorum
qui sequebantur; causa tum dubia, quod erat aliquid in utraque parte quod
probari posset. nunc melior ea iudicanda est quam etiam di adiuverunt.
cognita vero clementia tua quis non eam victoriam probet in qua occiderit
nemo nisi armatus?

20 Sed ut omittam communem causam, veniamus ad nostram. utrum
tandem existimas facilius fuisse, Tubero, Ligario ex Africa exire an vobis
in Africam non venire? "poteramusne" inquies "cum senatus censuisset?"
si me consulis, nullo modo. sed tamen Ligarium senatus idem legaverat.
atque ille eo tempore paruit cum parere senatui necesse erat, vos tum pa-
ruistis cum paruit nemo qui noluit. reprehendo igitur? minime vero. neque
enim licuit aliter vestro generi nomini familiae disciplinae. sed hoc non
concedo: ut quibus rebus gloriemini in vobis, easdem in aliis reprehendatis. **21** Tuberonis sors coniecta est ex senatus consulto, cum ipse non
adesset, morbo etiam impediretur; statuerat excusare. haec ego novi propter omnis necessitudines quae mihi sunt cum L. Tuberone; domi una eru-
diti, militiae contubernales, post adfines, in omni vita familiares; magnum
etiam vinculum quod isdem studiis semper usi sumus. scio Tuberonem
domi manere voluisse. sed ita quidam agebant, ita rei publicae sanctissimum nomen opponebant, ut etiam si aliter sentiret, verborum tamen ipsorum pondus sustinere non posset. **22** cessit auctoritati amplissimi viri,
vel potius paruit: una est profectus cum iis quorum erat una causa. tardius
iter fecit. itaque in Africam venit iam occupatam. hinc in Ligarium crimen
oritur, vel ira potius. nam si crimen est [illum] voluisse, non minus magnum
est vos Africam, arcem omnium provinciarum natam ad bellum contra
hanc urbem gerundum, obtinere voluisse quam aliquem se maluisse. atque
is tamen aliquis Ligarius non fuit. Varus imperium se habere dicebat, fascis
certe habebat. **23** sed quoquo modo se illud habet, haec querela, Tubero,

2 neque 6

3 salvam esse γ

6 melior certe γ

20 10 Ligario Cα: Ligarium 6γ

10 exire . . . Africam *om.* γ

10 vobis *D*: nobis Cα, vos *BED²*,
   om. γ

21 18 excusare *CAV*6γ: excusari *C²H*

19 domo Cα

20 omni denique 6γ

21 scio igitur 6

22 agebat . . . opponebat *BE*

23 verborum 6*hm*, *Sch. G.*: virorum
   C*αα*

22 27 voluisse *sic Baiter*: prohibere illa
   vol. C*αα*, illum vol. 6*hm*

vestra quid valet? "recepti in provinciam non sumus"? quid, si essetis? 1
Caesarine eam tradituri fuistis, an contra Caesarem retenturi? vide quid
licentiae, Caesar, nobis tua liberalitas det vel potius audaciae. si responderit
Tubero Africam quo senatus eum sorsque miserat, tibi patrem suum tra-
diturum fuisse, non dubitabo apud ipsum te cuius id eum facere interfuit, 5
gravissimis verbis eius consilium reprehendere. non enim si tibi ea res grata
fuisset, esset etiam adprobata. **24** sed iam hoc totum omitto, non ultra
offendam tuas patientissimas auris, quam ne Tubero quod numquam cogitavit facturus fuisse videatur. veniebatis igitur in Africam, in provinciam
unam ex omnibus huic victoriae maxime infensam, in qua rex potentissi- 10
mus inimicus huic causae, aliena voluntas conventus firmi atque magni.
quaero: quid facturi fuistis? quamquam quid facturi fueritis dubitem, cum
videam quid feceritis? prohibiti estis in provincia vestra pedem ponere, et
prohibiti summa cum iniuria. **25** quo modo id tulistis? acceptae iniuriae
querelam ad quem detulistis? nempe ad eum cuius auctoritatem secuti in 15
societatem belli veneratis. quod si Caesaris causa in provinciam veniebatis,
ad eum profecto exclusi provincia venissetis. venistis ad Pompeium. quae
est ergo apud Caesarem querela, cum eum accusetis, a quo queramini prohibitos vos contra Caesarem gerere bellum? atque in hoc quidem vel cum
mendacio si voltis gloriemini per me licet, vos provinciam fuisse Caesari 20
tradituros. etiam si a Varo et a quibusdam aliis prohibiti estis, ego tamen
confitebor culpam esse Ligari qui vos tantae laudis occasione priva-
verit. **26** sed vide quaeso, Caesar, constantiam ornatissimi viri L. Tuberonis, quam ego quamvis ipse probarem ut probo, tamen non comme-
morarem nisi a te cognovissem in primis eam virtutem solere laudari. quae 25
fuit igitur umquam in ullo homine tanta constantia? constantiam dico,

23 2 fuistis α: fuissetis ϐγ
    3 Caesar nobis ϐγ: nobis Caesar Cα
    7 adprobata CAVa: eadem probata H,
      probata ϐhm
24 7 non ultra (non tra C¹A¹) Cα: non
      tam ne Dm, non tam ut non ah,
      non tam propter id ne BE
    9 in Afr. in prov. CAV: in pro. in Afr.
      H, in Afr. pro. ϐγ, in Afr. del.
      Clark
   10 infestam ϐγ
   10 rex Cαam: erat rex ϐ, rex erat h

12 fuistis: fuissetis γ
12 dubitem CαD: non dubitem BEγ
25 18 prohibitos vos Cα: pr. esse vos ϐ,
      vos. pr. γ
   20 voltis CαBa: velitis DE, vis hm,
      Prisc.
   20 gloriemini CαBa: gloriari DEhm,
      Prisc.
   21 a alt. om. Cα
   21 estis C: essetis C², cett.
   22 privarit Cα
26 23 L. om. ϐ

nescio an melius patientiam possim dicere. quotus enim istud quisque fe- 1
cisset, ut a quibus partibus in dissensione civili non esset receptus, essetque
etiam cum crudelitate reiectus, ad eas ipsas partis rediret? magni cuiusdam
animi atque eius viri quem de suscepta causa propositaque sententia nulla
contumelia, nulla vis, nullum periculum possit depellere. **27** ut enim ce- 5
tera paria Tuberoni cum Varo fuissent—honos nobilitas splendor ingenium—quae nequaquam fuerunt, hoc certe praecipuum Tuberonis quod
iusto cum imperio ex senatus consulto in provinciam suam venerat. hinc
prohibitus non ad Caesarem ne iratus, non domum ne iners, non aliquam
in regionem ne condemnare causam illam quam secutus esset videretur; in 10
Macedoniam ad Cn. Pompei castra venit in eam ipsam causam a qua erat
reiectus iniuria. **28** quid? cum ista res nihil commovisset eius animum ad
quem veneratis, languidiore credo studio in causa fuistis. tantum modo in
praesidiis eratis, animi vero a causa abhorrebant. an ut fit in civilibus
bellis—nec in vobis magis quam in reliquis? omnes enim vincendi studio 15
tenebamur. pacis equidem semper auctor fui, sed tum sero; erat enim amentis, cum aciem videres, pacem cogitare. omnes, inquam, vincere volebamus,
tu certe qui in eum locum veneras ubi tibi esset pereundum, nisi vicisses.
quamquam ut nunc se res habet, non dubito quin hanc salutem anteponas
illi victoriae. **29** haec ego non dicerem, Tubero, si aut vos constantiae ves- 20
trae aut Caesarem benefici sui paeniteret. nunc quaero utrum vestras iniurias an rei publicae persequamini. si rei publicae, quid de vestra in illa
causa perseverantia respondebitis? si vestras, videte ne erretis qui Caesarem vestris inimicis iratum fore putetis, cum ignoverit suis.

Itaque num tibi videor in causa Ligari esse occupatus, num de eius facto 25
dicere? quidquid dixi, ad unam summam referri volo vel humanitatis vel
clementiae vel misericordiae. **30** causas, Caesar, egi multas equidem
tecum, dum te in foro tenuit ratio honorum tuorum, certe numquam hoc
modo: "ignoscite, iudices: erravit. lapsus est. non putavit. si umquam posthac." ad parentem sic agi solet, ad iudices: "non fecit, non cogitavit. falsi 30

---

	1 istuc Cα		11 in Cn. Cα
	2 esset[que] etiam б		12 cum iniuria γ
	3 eas ipsas partis Cαa: eas ipsas *hm*,	**28**	18 certe praecipue бγ
	eos ipsos б		18 veneras б: venisses αγ
	5 possit бγ: posset Cα		18 tibi *om.* α
27	6 honos *om.* αhm	**29**	27 misericordiae tuae αγ
	9 aliquam in αγ: in aliquam б	**30**	27 equidem *Aah*: et quidem
	10 secutus erat б		*HVбm*

testes, fictum crimen." dic te, Caesar, de facto Ligari iudicem esse, quibus   1
in praesidiis fuerit quaere; taceo, ne haec quidem conligo quae fortasse
valerent etiam apud iudicem: "legatus ante bellum profectus, relictus in
pace, bello oppressus. in eo ipso non acerbus; totus animo et studio tuus."
ad iudicem sic; sed ego apud parentem loquor: "erravit, temere fecit, pae-   5
nitet; ad clementiam tuam confugio, delicti veniam peto, ut ignoscatur
oro." si nemo impetravit, adroganter; si plurimi, tu idem fer opem qui spem
dedisti. 31 an sperandi de Ligario causa non erit, cum mihi apud te locus
sit etiam pro altero deprecandi? quamquam nec in hac oratione spes est
posita causae nec in eorum studiis qui a te pro Ligario petunt tui necessarii.   10
vidi enim et cognovi quid maxime spectares, cum pro alicuius salute multi
laborarent: causas apud te rogantium gratiosiores esse quam voltus, neque
te spectare quam tuus esset necessarius is qui te oraret, sed quam illius pro
quo laboraret. itaque tribuis tu quidem tuis ita multa ut mihi beatiores illi
videantur interdum, qui tua liberalitate fruantur quam tu ipse qui illis tam   15
multa concedas. sed video tamen apud te ut dixi causas valere plus quam
preces, ab iisque te moveri maxime quorum iustissimum videas dolorem in
petendo.

32 In Q. Ligario conservando multis tu quidem gratum facies necessariis tuis, sed hoc, quaeso, considera quod soles. possum fortissimos viros   20
Sabinos tibi probatissimos totumque agrum Sabinum florem Italiae ac
robur rei publicae proponere. nosti optime homines. animadverte horum
omnium maestitiam et dolorem; huius T. Brocchi de quo non dubito quid
existimes, lacrimas squaloremque ipsius et fili vides. 33 quid de fratribus
dicam? noli, Caesar, putare de unius capite nos agere; aut tres tibi Ligarii   25
retinendi in civitate sunt, aut tres ex civitate exterminandi. quodvis exsi-

2 quaerere αam

4 acerbus fuit γ

4 totus animo αa: tametsi totus hm;
   tametsi totus animo 6, iam totus
   animo *Madvig*

4 et: ac 6

5 sic agi solet 6a

5 apud 6: ad αγ

5 erravit . . . fecit γ: erravi . . . feci
   α6

6 ignoscas γ

31 8 de Ligario causa non erit α: Ligario
       causa non sit 6γ

   12 voltus αγ: preces 6

13 quam illius α6a: quae (quam *m*)
   illius causa hmσ

14 tribuis tu α: tribuisti γ, tribuis 6

14 beat. illi α: beat. illi esse *DB*,
   beat. esse illi *E*, esse beat.
   illi γ

15 fruuntur bhm

16 causas ut dixi 6, ut dixi causas
   rogantium γ

32 22 optimos 6

33 25 tibi L. ret. 6: L. ret. tibi α, L. tibi
       ret. γ

   26 ex: e *HDE*

   26 nam quodvis 6

lium his est optatius quam patria, quam domus, quam di penates illo uno 　1
exsulante. si fraterne, si pie, si cum dolore faciunt, moveant te horum lac-
rimae, moveat pietas, moveat germanitas. valeat tua vox illa quae vicit. te
enim dicere audiebamus nos omnis adversarios putare nisi qui nobiscum
essent, te omnis qui contra te non essent tuos. videsne igitur hunc splen- 　5
dorem omnem, hanc Brocchorum domum, hunc L. Marcium, C. Caese-
tium, L. Corfidium, hos omnis equites Romanos qui adsunt veste mutata,
non solum notos tibi verum etiam probatos viros tecum fuisse? atque his
irascebamur, hos requirebamus; his non nulli etiam minabantur. conserva
igitur tuis suos, ut quem ad modum cetera quae dicta sunt a te, sic hoc 　10
verissimum reperiatur. **34** quodsi penitus perspicere posses concordiam
Ligariorum, omnis fratres tecum iudicares fuisse. an potest quisquam dubitare quin si Q. Ligarius in Italia esse potuisset, in eadem sententia futurus
fuerit in qua fratres fuerunt? quis est qui horum consensum conspirantem
et paene conflatum in hac prope aequalitate fraterna [non] noverit, qui hoc 　15
non sentiat: quidvis prius futurum fuisse quam ut hi fratres diversas sen-
tentias fortunasque sequerentur? voluntate igitur omnes tecum fuerunt,
tempestate abreptus est unus qui si consilio id fecisset, esset eorum similis
quos tu tamen salvos esse voluisti. **35** sed ierit ad bellum, dissenserit non
a te solum, verum etiam a fratribus. hi te orant tui. equidem cum tuis om- 　20
nibus negotiis interessem, memoria teneo qualis T. Ligarius quaestor urbanus fuerit erga te et dignitatem tuam. sed parum est me hoc meminisse;
spero etiam te qui oblivisci nihil soles nisi iniurias—quam hoc est animi,
quam etiam ingeni tui!—te aliquid de huius illo quaestorio officio etiam de
aliis quibusdam quaestoribus reminiscentem recordari. **36** hic igitur T. 　25
Ligarius qui tum nihil egit aliud—neque enim haec divinabat—nisi ut tui
eum studiosum et bonum virum iudicares, nunc a te supplex fratris salutem
petit. quam huius admonitus officio cum utrisque his dederis, tris fratres
optimos et integerrimos non solum sibi ipsos neque his tot ac talibus viris
neque nobis necessariis, sed etiam rei publicae condonaveris. **37** fac igitur 　30
quod de homine nobilissimo et clarissimo fecisti nuper in curia, nunc idem

	1 uno illo Ϭγ		tam αα, quoniam . . . quoniam *edd.*,
	5 spl. omnium Ϭ		cum . . . tum *Clark*
	8 tecum fuisse αγ: qui tecum fuerunt	36	26 tui eum *Patricius*: tu eum Ϭγ, eum
	Ϭ, *del. edd.*		tui (tuis H) α, tui se *Clark*
	9 minabamur Ϭ		29 ipsis hσ
34	13 fuisset futurus Ϭ		29 tot ac Eγ: tot αBD
	15 non *del. Hansing*		30 neces. tuis Ϭ
35	23 quam . . . quam Ϭhσ: quam . . .	37	31 clarissimo M. Marcello restituto γ

in foro de optimis et huic omni frequentiae probatissimis fratribus. ut con- 1
cessisti illum senatui, sic da hunc populo cuius voluntatem carissimam semper habuisti. et si ille dies tibi gloriosissimus, populo Romano gratissimus
fuit, noli, obsecro, dubitare, C. Caesar, similem illi gloriae laudem quam
saepissime quaerere. nihil est tam populare quam bonitas, nulla de virtu- 5
tibus tuis plurimis nec admirabilior nec gratior misericordia est. **38** homines
enim ad deos nulla re propius accedunt quam salutem hominibus dando.
nihil habet nec fortuna tua maius quam ut possis, nec natura melius quam
ut velis servare quam plurimos. longiorem orationem causa forsitan postulet, tua certe natura breviorem. qua re cum utilius esse arbitrer te ipsum 10
quam aut me aut quemquam loqui tecum, finem iam faciam. tantum te
admonebo, si illi absenti salutem dederis, praesentibus te his daturum.

Commentary

The introduction to a Ciceronian speech is typically developed around a
commonplace or general theme, of leisurely and somewhat artificial composition and bearing at least some tangential relation to the occasion of
the speech and the speaker's situation. It is highly embellished and aimed
at capturing the interest of the audience and their goodwill toward the
speaker. Some speeches omit a formal exordium, e.g., *Cat.* 1, where indignation propels Cicero immediately into his attack. The rhetorician Grillius (20; Halm 2, 604) notes two other speeches in which Cicero omitted
an exordium, *Phil.* 1 and *Corn.* 1. From the latter he cites *unde igitur ordiar? an de ipsa lege?* as an example of aporia, for which see *Marc.* 33,
unde. The opening of *Pro Ligario* also employs the figure of aporia, as
Cicero confesses—or affects to confess—confusion and despair about
being able to perform at all.

Grillius claims that Cicero's purpose here is to confuse the issue in
order to defend Ligarius against having been in Africa, not against having
been a Pompeian. The strategy, however, of this very theatrical opening
argument is not meant to confuse the highly intelligent and sophisticated
single judge of the case, but to present an appealing travesty of a kind of
oratorical strategy. Cicero's use of this tactic, in some way removing him-

---

38 9 postulet *H*: postulat *cett.*   12 te his dat. α: his te dat. γ, his
 11 aut me αγ: me ϐ   omnibus dat. ϐ

self from the case itself and considering its defense as an abstract problem for lawyers, recurs during the speech, especially at 30; see, too, on 10, *atque*.

I

novum crimen: The irony for which this speech was famous in antiquity establishes itself in the first phrase of this abrupt opening. Quintilian (4.1.39) says that the point of the figure is to dispose Caesar not to take the charge seriously. But in doing that, Cicero also establishes with Caesar a relationship of familiarity in which both advocate and judge may step back from the *res gestae* and criticize the prosecutor's strategy.

In antiquity the word "irony" came close to meaning "derision" or "mockery." Modern critics define it as a figure in which someone says one thing while meaning, or unconsciously evoking, another. It implies only that discourse is taking place at more than one level of understanding and is thus distinguished from sarcasm, a subdivision of irony.

By the end of the section Cicero has also created an opposition between the harshness of Tubero and the leniency of Caesar.

novum: often connotes something out of the ordinary and frightening. Cf. *Verr.* 2.2.158: "It is extraordinary (*novum*), gentlemen, among Sicilians . . . and monstrous behavior (*monstri simile*)." *Novae res* is the regular way of saying "revolution." Quintilian (9.4.92) calls attention to the effective rhythm of these opening words, countenancing *nŏvum*, although, he says, it is usually best to begin with all long syllables.

C. Caesar: The full form of the vocative stresses the weighted, i.e., modified, accusative that precedes it and creates a stronger pause before going on to the second modifier, which is an adjective phrase. For the full vocative see at *Marc.* 2.

non auditum: can be taken literally, but may also have the secondary sense of "unheard of," more usually expressed by *inauditus*, which is avoided here in favor of a double spondee clausula. The latter is found, without negative overtones, at *Marc.* 1 and at *Deiot.* 1 with its literal meaning. Quintilian refers several times to the rhythm of these opening words. At 11.3.108, speaking of "almost unconscious accent (*quaedam latentes sermonis percussiones*), practically feet, to which the delivery of the speaker conforms," he says: "there is one movement (*motus*) at *novum crimen,* another at *C. Caesar,* a third at *et ante hunc diem,* a fourth at *non auditum,* then at *propinquus meus,* and at *ad te,* and at *Quintus Tubero,* and at *detulit.*" Two sections later, on the subject of phrasing for breath-pauses, he goes on: "*novum crimen, C. Caesar,* has, so to say, its own boundary, because a conjunction follows it; then *et ante hunc diem non auditum* are sufficiently self-inclusive." Although Quintilian's remarks raise more questions than they answer, and although Fraenkel was not, with a lifetime of effort, able to solve them (for a summary of his work see Laughton 3), rhythm—and not just at the clausulae—remains a basic factor in the composition of artistic prose; see the Introduction, section 1.1.

propinquus: a blood relation. A *necessarius,* like a *familiaris,* is a close connection, member of the household, or client (or patron). Were he not in the first category, the elder Tubero would have been in the second by virtue of the shared experiences mentioned in 21. The two men remained friends after and in spite of this trial, although some feathers may have been ruffled; see *Att.* 13.20.2. The elder Tubero was probably married to a woman from the *gens Tullia*—a fact useful for Cicero to mention. Usually, when Cicero announces a close relationship with an opponent in a court of law, he at once establishes and exploits the intimacy. Some scholars have remarked, inexplicably to me, on Cicero's politeness to the Tuberones in this speech (e.g., Bowersock, 69: "it is indeed one of the miracles of Cicero's speech in behalf of Ligarius that he succeeded in being so complimentary to the Tuberones while opposing [their case against his client]'").

Q. Ligarium in Africa fuisse: The "charge," so ominously heralded, is expressed in a brief, colorless nominal clause, perhaps echoing the language of that part of the accusation. Yet Cicero could have embellished it, had he wished.

idque: For resumptive pronoun + -*que* see *Marc.* 6, *easque detrahere.* Some complexity is suggested and suspense for further information about the charge.

C. Pansa: Gaius Vibius Pansa, friend and sometime protégé of Cicero and lieutenant of Caesar. He and Aulus Hirtius were consuls in 43. Both joined Octavian against Antony, perhaps persuaded by Cicero, and were killed in 43 at Mutina.

praestanti . . . ingenio: The ablative phrase is predicative to *vir*. The elaborate honorific, a weighted phrase, immediately turns ironic, even adversative, with the qualification in the next words.

fortasse: gives an ironic flavor to this phrase; see *Marc.* 12. Alliteration also contributes to the irony; the figure, used sparingly in developed literary language, like most figures reinforces a tone in association with other literary devices, rather than creating it by itself. See *Marc.* 12, *victoriam vicisse videris*.

ea quae est: Antecedent directly before the relative seems to set the modifier in the highest relief; the periphrasis (vs. *vestra familiaritate*) delays report of Pansa's grievous blunder.

ausus est confiteri: a ponderous, imposing locution, implying a rash stipulation and perhaps, as Caesar is invited to agree, an error in professional judgment. If the charge that Ligarius was in Africa is risible, Pansa's admission of it is clearly harmless. Some scholars maintain that this concession was made earlier at a private audience. Cicero's professed aporia is better explained if Pansa was a *subscriptor*, a colleague in the defense, who had spoken first.

quo me vertam nescio: commonplace in expressing sorrow and calling for compassion. Used figuratively, it is an example of aporia; see opening remarks above. It is found in tragedy: (1) Euripides *Med.* 502–05, νῦν ποῖ τράπωμαι; πότερα πρὸς πατρὸς δόμους / οὕς σοι προδοῦσα καὶ πάτραν ἀφικόμην / ἢ πρὸς ταλαίνας Πελιάδας; ("Now where will I turn? Perhaps to my father's home / which, together with my country I abandoned when I came with you. / Or to the wretched daughters of Pelias?") (2) Enn. 284–85 Vahlen (217–18 Jocelyn), *quo nunc me vortam? quod iter incipiam ingredi? / domum paternamne? anne ad Peliae filias?* cited at *De Or.* 3.217, *aliud vocis genus iracundia sumat, acutum, incitatum, crebro incidens* ("sharp, excited, staccato") . . . *aliud miseratio ac maeror, flexibile plenum interruptum flebile voce.* . . . Remarkably the topos had already been parodied for mock-tragic effect by a grieving Roman matron in Ter. *Hec.* 516, *Perii, quid agam? quo me vortam?* before Catullus (64.177–81) gave it to a histrionic, but unironic Ariadne: *nam quo me referam? quali spe perdita nitor? / Idaeosne petam montes? at gurgite lato / discernens ponti truculentum dividit aequor. / anne patris auxilium sperem? quemne ipsa reliqui / respersum iuvenem fraterna caede secuta?* Even more remarkable, but very important for an understanding of the Roman disposition for melodrama, after 133 B.C. C. Gracchus could use it unashamedly and with effective tragic irony for poignant effect in a real-life situation: *quo me miser conferam? quo vertam? in Capitoliumne? at fratris sanguine madet. an domum? matremne ut miseram lamentantem videam et abiectam?* (Malcovati, 196, from *De Or.* 3.214). Cicero himself had used it dramatically and without embarrassment In *Pro Murena* (88), eight years before *De Oratore* and almost two decades before this burlesque. He does not expect to be convincingly desperate or abject.

paratus . . . veneram: For the pluperfect see on *Marc.* 1, *eram . . . usus*, and *Tull.* 1, *veneram . . . Sed nunc,* "I had come [carefree]. . . . But now. . . ."

cum tu . . . scires: Caesar, who had captured and spared Ligarius at Hadrumetum after Thapsus, is made a character in the travesty, to be gulled by an unscrupulous Cicero. The tense and mood is necessitated by the *cum* clause, but the unrealized potential of the subjunctive is felt; so at 2, *ut . . . posset.*

aliunde: here only in the speeches; at home in more conversational letters.

ut . . . abuterer: depends not on *paratus* alone, which takes an infinitive or *ad* + gerund, but, as a purpose clause, on the whole predicate.

ignoratione: Verbal nouns in -*tio* are generally rare in Cicero, who, in periodic style, prefers the weight of a clause. In particular instances, when the rhetoric demands tighter syntax, they are found; see *Marc.* 25, *perfectione.*

sed quoniam: Although the sentences are brief, the progression of the orator's circumstances and responses is clearly marked by connectives: "and to this. . . . And so. . . . For. . . . But. . . ." This absurd story is told with a very straight face. On initial *sed* see *Marc.* 33.

diligentia: See *Marc.* 22; a Roman virtue in any endeavor from honoring contracts to mastering a discipline; here grudgingly (and ironically) acknowledged.

investigatum: describes the action of tracking dogs, ironic on that level and also because the self-evident and acknowledged fact did not require much ferreting.

confitendum: echo of *confiteri* above. For the impersonal of the gerundive, with formulaic overtones, see on *Marc.* 14, *audiendum*. The impersonal must be maintained here in anticipation of the turn at the end of this section.

opinor: once more, mock resignation. The variant (*ut opinor*) is syntactically more formal and controlled, and therefore perhaps less desperate; cf. *Marc.* 10, *ut mihi videtur.*

necessarius: closer than an *amicus*; see on 1, *propinquus*. Cicero insists on the intimate relationships among the principals.

fecerit ut: producing a noun clause; vs. *ita fecerit ut,* with *ut* clause resultant.

integrum iam non esset: For the secondary sequence see *Marc.* 26, *futurus fuit*. At *Marc.* 15 *integrum* means "whole," "undivided," hence "free of prior commitment, prejudgment, or involvement," as at *Piso.* 58, *non est integrum Pompeio consilio iam uti tuo,* "Pompey no longer has the option of following your advice," and *Phil.* 1.26, *loquor de legibus promulgatis de quibus est integrum vobis.*

omissaque controversia: For -*que* see *Marc.* 14, *semperque*. The compendious ablative absolute curtly dismisses disputes of fact as well as of law.

omnis oratio: not just "entire" (= *tota*), but in every part.

conferenda: gerundive; echoes *confitendum* (*con*- . . . *con*-) and bridges the predicates.

qua . . . cum . . . : The movement of this sentence is not periodic, although it leads to a neat, epigrammatic antithesis at the end. Cicero is deliberately muting the tone to keep it at a conversational level.

non liberationem . . . sed . . . veniam: The construction creates a *correctio* by explicitly denying the wrong interpretation. Here it marks an important distinction between acquittal (*liberatio*), which is within the competence of a judge, and pardon (*venia*), which requires the benevolence of a benign dictator (or a kindly relative; see 30)—though at *Planc.* 52, *quo te liberent aliqua culpa,* the verb has the nonlegal sense "relieve of blame"; similarly *Deiot.* 10, *cum maximis eum rebus liberares.* The distinction is specious;

Cicero made a career of trying to win his cases by enlisting the sympathy of judges.

culpae . . . errati: Connected to the difference between acquittal and pardon is the distinction between their objects. *Culpa,* basically, is the fault for which the accused is held responsible. In private law it is a negligence (often under a contract) and, as such, a blameworthy offense; so at *Deiot.* 10, *perparvam amicitiae culpam.* It is more egregious than an *erratum* or *error,* a mistake, the liability for which may become a legal question (see on *Marc.* 13, *erroris humani,* and 1, *non . . . sed*), but for which one may have to pay (see at *Deiot.* 36, *ille enim furoris multam saustulerat, hic erroris*). The distinction does not always hold; cf. *Marc.* 13, *etsi aliqua culpa tenebamur humani erroris, at scelere certe liberati sumus.* At 17 we hear that the Tuberones called Ligarius' action a *scelus*; but no one else, Cicero says, treats it as anything beyond an error of judgment, and as such capable of forgiveness; see on *Deiot.* 10, *errore communi.* Cicero presents this distinction as Caesar's. See, too, 2, *delicto . . . culpa.*

2

habes igitur: The change in the point of address (from the judge, stressed by the initial position of the second-person verb) is dramatic; the rhetorical figure describing direct address is called apostrophe; see Quint. 4.1.63–67. *Habes* is vivid and direct, like "Ecco!" or "Voila!" (so *Deiot.* 21, *habes crimina*).

quod . . . optandum: Cicero characterizes the object of *habes* in an appositive noun clause, before stating it, thus creating suspense; see *Marc.* 34, *quod . . . arbitrabar,* where no referent anticipates the *quod* clause. The implication, by implied antithesis, is that it will also be least helpful to the defense.

confitentem reum: the basis for a *deprecatio*: the accused will make no effort to defend himself. But the label needs as much qualification as the confession of guilt made here; see the Introduction, section 3.2. There are appeals for mercy in otherwise vigorous defenses, e.g., *Milo.* 100ff., where Cicero describes himself as a *deprecator,* despite having asserted (*Milo.* 6) that he would not ask the judges to waive the charge; and there are rational, if not always convincing, exculpatory arguments throughout *Pro Ligario.*

The normal circumstances and forum for such appeals are described in 30. The irony of the *confitentem reum* becomes apparent in the very next words.

sed tamen hoc: abrupt change in the movement of the sentence; after a strong adversative, the deictic pronoun expects a strong, immediate proviso.

in ea parte fuisse qua: now a smooth run with demonstrative adjective (*ea*) explicitly anticipating the relative. The accusatives *te* and *virum,* where we should expect nominatives in the relative clause, are normal (by attraction) when the verb of the antecedent clause is not repeated. In such circumstances the preposition that introduces the antecedent might have been repeated with the relative; cf. *Marc.* 2, *in eadem causa in qua ego*; its absence was Cicero's choice, allowing the anaphora, forceful in bipartite asyndeton, of *qua . . . qua.*

parte: is not limited to a military side or even a coherent political stance; it need mean no more than "circumstances" or "position," as at 19. See at *Marc.* 2, *causa.* For specific reference to political affiliation see at 16, *voluntatis.*

qua virum: an unexpected addition after *qua te,* which fulfills the needs of periodicity. The honorific appositive creates a small, dramatic pause before the naming of the second person—surprisingly, the father of the prosecutor.

itaque: a colorless narrative conjunction, marking an unceremonious progression to a conclusion that will devastate the prosecution.

prius . . . quam: neat statement (anticipatory *prius* placed well forward) of the accuser's problem and a strong point for the defense; similarly 10, *quorum . . . eorum.* Potential force of subjunctive in the comparative clause is intrinsic to the mood, rather than conventional in syntax, and so felt.

delicto . . . culpam: This polarity does not parallel *culpae . . . errati* in 1. *Delictum* is a wrongdoing prosecuted under private law, deliberate—as opposed to *culpa*—and, if proved, punished by a fine. Damages as well as cost of losses may be assigned the plaintiff. *Delictum* can be forgiven, as at 30 or *Mur.* 62, *eius delicti veniam petit* (with several equally forgivable instances in 62–63), or be requited with punishment, as at *Marc.* 18. It is thus, like *culpa,* differentiated from crime (*scelus*), a public crime which may or may not deserve conviction. But technical language in Classical Latin tends to be less consistent than we should like. Cicero develops the distinctions to serve his purposes.

confiteamini necesse: On paratactic construction see at *Marc.* 28, *ostentes oportet.* As is usual, the subjunctive precedes *necesse est.* As opposed to *necesse* with accusative + infinitive, the focus is sharply on personal obligation. This locution is stronger and more pointed than the impersonal *confitendum est*; and on a different level altogether from Pansa's indiscreet confession (to someone else's wrongdoing).

Q. enim Ligarius: beginning of the *narratio,* the part of the speech in which the *res gestae* are described. It can run the gamut from simple exposition to dramatic presentation or comic (see *Deiot.* 17–22). Cicero often begins narrations with the name of his client, as Quintilian notes (4.2.129). The insertion of the enclitic sentence connective between *cognomen* and *nomen,* a sign of graceful writing, is found also at *Marc.* 2.

cum esset: temporal, but circumstantial beyond that, as the subjunctive suggests. Cicero starts coloring his description of events from the outset, laying down a foundation for Ligarius' innocence of purpose. Cf. *Verr.* 2.5.42, *ex fugitivorum bello aut suspicione belli.*

C. Considius: (sc. Longus), propraetor duly appointed by the Senate as governor in 51–50, returned to Rome to stand for consul.

legatus: a functionary without official power, chosen by the governor of a province. He ranked below the quaestor, an elected financial official.

qua in legatione: In official language and the commentary style of Caesar it is not unusual for an antecedent word to be repeated in the relative clause. This variation occurs here in a straightforward and precise exposition; see *Deiot.* 3, *quaestione.* Although adjectival (not pronominal), the relative is semi-independent and ties the sentence closely to the preceding. Compare on *Marc.* 13–14, *bellum . . . quo quidem in bello. Legatio* refers to the process rather than the group. It is an abstract verbal noun like *Marc.* 25, *perfectio,* and 4, *profectio* and *remansio.*

et civibus et sociis: two constituencies equally pleased by a responsible provincial official: so repeated below. The Roman citizens had substantial

business interests in the province and were motivated by the same considerations by which international businessmen typically are.

ita . . . ut . . . si: The sentence now develops as a complex period into a
minor encomium of Ligarius; see 1, *qua . . . cum*, which also ends more
ornately than it began.

ut decedens: He returned to Rome in 49, without a successor having been
chosen. For present active participle see *Marc.* 22, *cogitans*. It has been
described as representing the conative imperfect, i.e., "as he was preparing
to withdraw," a usage Laughton strongly denies (see Laughton 2, 40–41).
Considius was in the process of departing.

hominibus: somewhat stronger than a pronoun in picking up *civibus et
sociis* from the previous clause; *homines* = "people in general," as at
Deiot. 18.

non posset si: Rhetorically, after a negatived apodosis, *nisi ⟨Ligarium prae-
fecisset⟩* would have been more usual. Here, although the conditional clause
is rhetorically anticipated by the lexical value of *posset* (the mood is necessitated by the result clause), the uniqueness of Ligarius' popularity is
more strongly stressed by the positive locution.

quemquam: general indefinite; completely exclusive after a negative, i.e.,
"no one at all." Quaestor was the logical replacement; hence the preceding
narrative "information."

itaque: narrative sentence connective. *Recusans* and *invitus* are not synonymous. The first connotes action: the participle is still concomitant, but
in context adversative, though there may be an instrumental, gerundival
(= *recusando*) overtone (see Laughton 2, 27). Cf. *Phil.* 1.7, *quae urbs . . .
plus una me nocte cupiens retinere non potuit*. The second, placed strategically for emphasis and cadence (cretic + trochee), connotes resignation; cf. position of *invitus* at *Marc.* 25.

cui sic: semi-independent relative; a frequent connector of sentences in
Caesar's narrative.

in pace: lays the foundation for an antithesis which is not rhetorically structured or anticipated but comes with a bang in the next sentence.

integritas: See on 1, *integrum*; for *fides* see *Marc.* 14, *grati . . . memoria,* and *Lig.* 26, *constantiam.*

3

bellum subito exarsit: Colorful, dramatic language, asyndeton, and construction convey the suddenness and unexpectedness of the outbreak of war, a point reinforced structurally by the tersely phrased *ante . . . geri quam parari.*

quo audito: A semi-independent relative in an ablative absolute is a highly compendious structure, found more frequently in Caesar than Cicero; the implication is of simultaneity, as at *Arch.* 28, *quibus auditis,* "the moment I heard them." Movement into the sentence is swift and tight, but structure develops, becoming more complex as the sentence progresses; so 2, *ita . . . ut . . . si.*

partim . . . partim: may refer to different people; the motivation is stressed; cf. *Marc* 1, where the division is not of exclusive elements. The adverbs here establish an antithesis of modified ablatives in chiastic order.

cupiditate: as at *Marc.* 13, with overtones of personal gain, vs. *studium.* The passive or defensive alternative is fear.

caeco quodam: For the indefinite see 5, *incredibilem quendam.*

primo . . . post: a second antithesis, ambiguous, at least on paper. It is tempting to take the genitives as objective with "fear," but *ducem* governs the genitives.

quaerebant . . . cum: The *cum inversum* construction keeps the sentence moving toward the main point, dramatically suspended.

spectans . . . cupiens: These two subordinate predications in dramatic asyndeton are emotional in themselves and deliberately ambiguous and suspenseful; they do not indicate whether they are causal or adversative. Cicero uses the same dramatic technique at *Verr.* 2.1.74 in a most moving narrative, when a provincial victim of Verres at Lampsacum finds himself on trial before a Roman court. Three extensive *cum* clauses present circumstances that suggest a guilty verdict is forthcoming; they are then summed up and a fourth one added, before a *tamen* is inserted to make clear that, *in spite of* the circumstances mentioned, the defendant was not at that time found guilty. See, too, at *Deiot.* 7, *cum . . . tamen.*

nullo . . . negotio: Hyperbaton emphasizes the negative and perhaps reflects content by word order; see *Marc.* 6, *detrahere. Negotio* as at 4; see *Clu.* 169, *quidquid . . . habuerit sollicitudinis et negoti.*

interim: a sentence connective used in narrative to relate simultaneous actions, thus frequent in Caesar; see 2, *cui sic.*

Varus: previously (*tum* + pluperfect) the duly appointed propraetor in Africa. Now, having lost his cohorts in Italy to Caesar's advancing armies at Auximum, he fled to Africa and was prepared to fill the administrative vacuum de facto. He escaped to Spain after the battle of Thapsus (6 April 46) and died at Munda (17 March 45).

obtinuerat: the regular verb with assignments; his first appointment had been legal; cf. *arripuit* below.

ad eum: Asyndeton, simple syntax, and passive construction convey speedy, inevitable movement.

atque: as opposed to *itaque* (as in the next sentence), connotes consequence more than mere sequence; see on *Marc.* 13. The consequence is usually adversative—as here with the sense "in sharp distinction to what Ligarius did." Hence the emphatic *ille* and the pronounced litotes.

arripuit: a strong, violent verb; this time he had no legal basis.

imperium: a command assigned to an individual by the Senate, usually with limit of time and place, upon ratification by the Comitia Curiata. Cicero therefore corrects his usage in the conditional clause in which *illud* prepares for the *quod* clause that redefines and qualifies; see *Fam.* 11.8.2, *delectus habetur . . . si hic delectus appellandus cum ultro se offerunt omnes,* "A levy is being held . . . if this can be called a levy, when everyone offers himself voluntarily."

The clause is divided into a positive and negative description of the source of Varus' authority, as usual emphasizing the first, where Cicero editorializes: the *privatus* lacks *imperium* (an antithesis with *publico* is heard, but not quite made); the mob lacks *peritia.*

4

qui . . . fugeret: The subjunctive expresses Ligarius' motivation.

paulum: This retirement *was* short-lived, and Ligarius became active in the Pompeian cause; it is not clear why Cicero chose to call attention to the fact here.

adhuc: breaks off the narration (abruptly: no sentence connective) with a direct address to Caesar. Cicero appears to recapitulate, ostensibly for the purpose of determining culpability to this point in the narrative. Quintilian (4.2.51) points to this passage as an example of appending a summary even after a brief narration; he does not analyze Cicero's reason for doing so. The orator establishes a three-part chronology, composed of Ligarius' departure for Africa, his prewar semiofficial tenure in the province, and the period immediately following Varus' arrival. At none of these times, Cicero asserts, did Ligarius evidence hostility towards Caesar. Quintilian also fails to point out that Cicero does not return to his narrative for the crucial period from the outbreak of hostilities in Africa down to Ligarius' capture.

est egressus . . . profectus: Sentences begin simply in asyndeton and develop ornamentation.

nullum ad bellum: a word order (adjective + preposition + noun) often graceful in itself that here, after *non modo, nullum*, negates the phrase (vs. *ne ad minimam quidem*), not just *bellum*. The point put simply and convincingly is hardly contested.

pace . . . pacatissima . . . pacem: Cf. similar insistence at *Marc.* 14. Alliteration with *profectus in provincia* can hardly be casual. The superlative has three parallels in the speeches: *Pro Sest.* 93, *pacatissimis atque opulentissimis Syriae gazis*; *De Dom.* 23, *pacatissimis gentibus*; *De Dom.* 40, *integerrimas pacatissimasque gentis*.

pacem esse: *Esse* is strongly predicative: "that peace was enduring." The dative with the finite verb refers to the province.

profectio . . . remansio: In simplest narrative or expository style Cicero uses abstract nouns for brevity in nominal sentences (cf. *Att.* 8.15.2, *cautior certe est mansio, honestior existimatur traiectio*) or otherwise to reduce number of clauses (e.g., 1, *ignoratione*). *Profectio* is attested before Cicero and may be quasi-technical; *remansio* was likely coined for the present occasion. He sets up the argument with a formal *divisio*; so *Phil.* 1.1, *exponam . . . consilium et profectionis et reversionis meae.*

certe: See at *Marc.* 13; here it seems to ask for at least minimal agreement. The orator sets up a brief and terse elenchus; see on *sermocinatio* at *Marc.* 26. And note the sentence fragments.

voluntatem: conscious choice or allegiance, leading to active commitment. When Ligarius made his commitment, the Senate represented the only choice, although Cicero will claim below that even that choice was for personal reasons reluctantly made; see on 5, *desideri.*

habuit: = *habere in se,* "stemmed from," "involved," "comprised," "entailed"; a rare usage in Cicero, paralleled by *Phil.* 12.30, *mors . . . necessitatem habeat fati,* tr. Shackleton Bailey 2, 319, as "Let my death come by natural necessity."

non turpem: Litotes is lightly felt, because in contrast with the more positive expression *etiam honestam.* The virtual isocolon in asyndeton establishes, with no explanation, an antithesis of terms (*voluntas* vs. *necessitas*) soon to be exploited.

ergo: The argument appears wholly clear and cogent. The point, however irrelevant, is reinforced by summarily echoing *culpa vacat* with *carent crimine* (the change in verbs is mere *variatio*) and a careful redefinition of the two periods, *unum . . . alterum.* But one colorful detail is added: *efflagitatus a provincia,* a strong verb connoting something widespread and vociferous; the personification (note the preposition) is felt.

5

quod . . . restitit: noun clause; accusative of extent of time; cf. *Deiot.* 27, *quidquid . . . vacabat.*

necessitatis: Here the distinction with choice becomes useful, as fate enters the picture; see on *Marc.* 18, *di immortales.* Cicero will not describe Ligarius' activities; rather he elicits sympathy for the circumstances in which those activities took place. This articulation lingers over the rejected alternative; cf. in feeling and emphasis "not of volition, but necessity."

an: introduces the second of alternative questions, the first suppressed. Rhetorically the effect is one of amazement or indignation, by affecting to endorse an intolerable alternative to accepting the speaker's premise: "[Do you agree it was because of necessity], or do you really believe . . . ?"

si potuisset: Cicero gives the impression, through the mood and tense of the verb, that Ligarius would have liked to return to Rome, while omitting to mention the circumstances that seem to have made it absolutely impossible (*ullo modo*) for him to do so.

Uticae . . . Attio . . . alienis: three pairs of compared locatives (or locative ablatives). Cicero deliberately avoids creating the most ornate possible tricolon by not expanding the members. Not only is the second element longer than the third, but it also carries more pathos. The point here is patriotic, not merely personal.

legatio: See on 2, *legatione*.

desideri: not to say that Ligarius did not feel the loss, but it was his advocate's determination that this is the moment to mention Ligarius' homesickness. For a similar instance of strategic choice see 21, *necessitudines*. Previously the *profectio* was described as a political choice, to contrast with a necessity. Now, in order to establish an a fortiori argument in which the initial enterprise is depicted as a sorrowful imposition, but the extension by war of the separation can be treated as something even worse, Cicero introduces a new piece of information. The two genitives probably constitute a hendiadys: "anxious longing." The metaphor comes from augury, from looking to a section of the sky and observing the absence of stars (*sidera*) expected or hoped to be there; so *considerare*. It is not the same as English "desire"; cf. at *Lig.* 35.

incredibilem quendam: With a modified noun *quidam* tends to reinforce the adjective, with a simple noun it attenuates; in both cases it calls attention to figurative or metaphorical usage. For the first see 3, *caeco quodam*, and 17, *fatalis quaedam*; for the second see *Clu.* 73, *quodam odore suspicionis corruptum*, "tainted by a kind of smell of suspicion"; *Arch.* 15, *ratio quaedam conformatioque doctrinae*, "what I might call a science and abstract concept of the discipline"; or *Marc.* 20, *specie quadam rei publicae*. When the indefinite precedes the adjective, it qualifies the phrase; cf. *Arch.* 2, *quoddam commune vinculum*, "a kind of common bond." When it precedes an unmodified noun, it means "a kind of" or "virtual," e.g., *Marc.* 2, *quodam socio,* and *lux quaedam et spes salutis* in the quotation from *Phil.* 10.12 at 6, *lux aboriatur. Aliquis* also attenuates nouns (so, e.g., 8, *ad meum aliquem fructum*), but with modified nouns does not behave in the same way.

incredibilem . . . amorem: effective postponement of noun in hyperbaton.

hic: Vivid use of the deictic pronoun treats Ligarius as if he were in court; cf. *Deiot.* 8.

potuit: Potentiality is in any case marked lexically, but indicative conveys vividness.

belli discidio: separates participle from infinitive, reinforcing the meaning with word order; see on *Marc.* 2, *distracto,* with strong emotional overtones; so *Marc.* 2 and *Deiot.* 15. *Discidium* is an emotional word, used of divorce; see at 19.

6

nullum . . . adhuc: recalls 4, *adhuc, C. Caesar,* in circular fashion at the end of the recapitulation. But Cicero has moved from Ligarius' criminal culpability to his psychological disposition.

voluntatis: neat articulation: prepositional phrase bracketed by adjective-noun phrase. It was not inevitable; cf. *Deiot.* 23, *cum a te animo esset alieno.* Both formulations may suggest their content by word order; see 5, *distractus.*

cuius ego causam . . . defendam: unusual and striking word order; semi-independent relative for close continuity with the previous sentence. That necessitates placing the governing noun, *causam,* in close proximity and separating it from its governing verb by the lead predicate, the imperative.

causam: not specifically the case at law, but his client's circumstances and even, perhaps, the way he directed them—that is, his "cause"; see 26.

fide: i.e., to his client. Advocacy required that the barrister identify with his client in every case; cf. *Clu.* 10, *adductum fide atque officio defensionis,* "forced by loyalty and the duty of defending," and *Deiot.* 1, *fides.* But the stakes here are especially high.

prodo meam: a bold stroke, boldly expressed in a dramatically simple predicate. He might easily have turned it into a clause of result after something like *tanta fide*.

o clementiam: The construction reflects emotion, moving from a two-word predicate to an exclamatory accusative phrase. The word *clementia* now comes easily (see on *mansuetudinem* at *Marc.* 1) and is modified by two adjectives, the second governing an expanding tricolon of ablatives.

litteris monumentisque: The two nouns should be taken together (so *Deiot.* 37) as the third member of a tricolon. The articulation A + B + (C + D) is a favored variation of A + B + C.

M. Cicero: Some manuscripts begin the sentence with the conjunction *cum*, making *nec . . . nec* introduce a compound apodosis. The last two are paired by the negatives and the synonymous verbs in final position, but that does not limit the main clause to them. If that were what Cicero wanted to do, the order *M. Cicero cum* would be more usual. The abrupt, paratactic movement from sentence to sentence is more effective, however. The thought of his own case evokes the expostulation; and he goes on to marvel that he can use the example of his own pardon, which was a greater imposition on the dictator's generosity than that of Ligarius, and that he can do so without any fear.

alium: carefully and explicitly articulated, but a euphemistic periphrasis for his own position. For his client's sake he acknowledges an enthusiasm to which he does not always admit, and which he did not always feel; see on *Marc.* 14. *Alius,* like *alter,* can distinguish anyone or any group from someone explicitly named; see 31, *pro altero.*

in ea voluntate . . . in qua: For the repetition of the preposition cf. on 2, *in ea parte fuisse qua*; here the verb changes.

audienti: a terse dative participial phrase, like *mihi apud te dicenti* below.

de se: i.e., Cicero. The two prepositional phrases with *de* contribute to the suggestion of an identification between Cicero and his client.

vide . . . vide . . . : Anaphoric, asyndetic repetition exudes confidence and enthusiasm; the speaker engages his audience directly with the imperative and intimately with the switch, taking up *reformidat* from the previous sentence, to the first person.

lux . . . oboriatur: metaphor of hope rising with the new dawn. In Ennius 72 Vahlen, Hector's ghost in the *Andromache* was addressed *O lux Trioae*, with tragic irony, because *lux* is used in the sense of "salvation." That sense is not absent here, but is stated more explicitly at *Phil.* 10.12 (of Brutus): "wherever he came, *lux quaedam et spes salutis* would appear." At *Aen.* 2.281 Virgil has: *O lux Dardaniae, spes o fidissima Teucrum*; commentators from Macrobius on cite Ennius. Virgil's debt to Cicero, or at least the tradition of rhetoric common to poetry and prose, has yet to be investigated and appreciated.

sapientiae: Intelligent choice, as often, joins natural nobility as a motive of Caesar's clemency; so at *Marc.* 1 and throughout the three speeches. No man objects to being called intelligent (e.g., *fortis vir sapiensque,* the ancient elogium to L. Cornelius Scipio Barbatus), but generosity and leniency are not often praised as being the result of dispassionate calculation. When Caesar pardoned Marcellus, he claimed that he was indulging the Senate, not pursuing an ingenious plan of reconciliation; see *Fam.* 4.4, cited at *Marc.* 1, *diuturni silenti.*

voce contendam: a phrase unique in Cicero's speeches.

populus Romanus: Although pleading this case before Caesar as sole judge, Cicero would not have been unmindful of the audience in the Forum whose responses he might manipulate to create a sympathetic ambience.

7

suscepto bello: No particle connects this sentence with the last; two participles, in asyndeton, mark the sequence from the start of the war to the moment in question with elegance and dispatch. Compound ablative absolute with temporal movement, followed by a motivational nominative participle, is more typical of historical narrative in Caesar or Livy, but highly effective here. Initial position of the participles, besides being narratively more vivid, stresses the resoluteness of Cicero's decision, which in the letters often sounds more like vacillation. Seven heavy syllables move with deliberation to the pause before the second participle; cf. on 1, *novum*.

Caesar: Vocative engages the addressee and punctuates the compound construction. In ancient rhetorical punctuation an unmodified vocative would not constitute a colon and therefore would not require a pause before and after, but only after.

Vocative is familiar (see on *Marc.* 2), but also something of a challenge. Cicero puts his admission in aggressive terms, rejecting any mitigation but loyalty to Pompey. Quintilian remarks (9.2.28), on bold, fearless utterance (*licentia, parrhesia*): "but often behind this guise lies adulation. For Cicero, when in *Pro Ligario* he says *'suscepto bello,'* not only is considering the advantage of Ligarius, but can in no better way praise the clemency of the victor." There is a contradiction in content, but more so in tone, between this almost defiant admission and that of *Marc.* 14, which is completely abject. Each is perfectly appropriate to the argument that demands it. See, too, *Deiot.* 29. In 28 the lengths to which an advocate will go in adapting circumstances and personality to a rhetorical strategy become extraordinary.

ex parte magna: The position of *magna* is unusual and emphatic; cf. on 3, *multas*. The whole construction would have been much neater as *bello suscepto, Caesar, magnaque ex parte etiam gesto*; but the tension would be lost. But (*pace* Merguet) *etiam* is meant to qualify the ensuing prepositional phrase; see *Lig.* 23, *etiam*. By the time Cicero joined Pompey in June, the war had been going on over five months, and Caesar had gained control of Italy and Sicily.

nulla vi coactus: Statement of circumstances now turns to a nominal participle; the negative, especially in initial position, implies that a positive motivation will follow.

iudicio: Intellectual decision is added to allegiance to Pompey; cf. the fear and ambition for gain that drew others to Pompey (e.g., at 3).

quae erant sumpta: *Ea* periodically anticipates the full clause modifying *arma* (vs. *arma contra te sumpta*); cf. 1, *ea quae est,* where the antecedent is not embebbed in a previous clause. The emphatic position of "against you" explains the construction.

apud quem: not a rhetorical question, which implies its answer, but a vivid introduction to a characterization of someone; so at 19 and 25. The answer is given in sentence fragments, emphasized by *nempe ad eum,* which provides the antecedent for five complex, relative clauses.

qui cum . . . : Note the intricacy of articulation:

```
qui
            cum hoc sciret,
    tamen me
            antequam vidit
    rei publicae        reddidit
```

Two circumstantial clauses are interwoven into a relative clause interrupted in two places.

Cicero heard the news of Pharsalia at Dyrrachium in mid-August 48. He was present for the Pompeian post mortem at Corcyra and removed himself thence to Patrae. Dolabella, his son-in-law and a Caesarian, urged him, presumably with Caesar's blessings, to return to Italy, so he sailed back to Brundisium about 7 October 48. In December 48 Antony announced to Cicero by letter that no Pompeian could remain in Italy. Cicero protested that he had returned by leave of Caesar and was exempted, by name, from the edict.

ex Aegypto litteras: In June 47 Atticus sent Cicero an excerpt of a letter from Caesar, conciliatory but far from effusive (*exigue scripta* at *Att.* 11.16.1). On 12 August Cicero acknowledged receipt from Terentia, his wife, of a more encouraging letter (*satis liberales* at *Fam.* 14.23). Those words suggest that Cicero was not overwhelmed; and if we may extrapolate Caesar's language from *ut essem idem qui fuissem,* we can see why. Cicero waited at Brundisium to pay homage to Caesar on his return from the East either because the same letter told him to expect the dictator there or because its tone was not sufficiently positive to encourage his return to Rome.

imperator: a general with *imperium* who has been proclaimed *imperator* by his troops after a victory. As proconsul in Cilicia in 51 Cicero had defeated some tribesmen and been duly honored by his soldiers. He was given a *supplicatio* over the objection of Cato and awarded six lictors and the *fasces laureati* that went with the title.

a quo . . . concessos: The relative pronoun in Latin, unlike English, can be construed with an element in its clause that is not part of the predicate.

C. Pansa . . . perferente: another ablative absolute with its own predicative construction; see *Marc.* 32, *te . . . manente.*

quoad . . . putavi: Cicero should have relinquished them on his return to

Rome in December 50, but he retained these accoutrements of honor, hoping to parley them into a triumph. Of this he was disappointed.

denique: sums up the series. It is not the same as *tum demum* = "only then."

tum denique: the positive counterpart to *non . . . nisi*; cf. *Marc.* 25, *tum*. It correlates with a condition at *Marc.* 25, *tum . . . si*.

salutem . . . dare: Future more vivid might have been expected, with future infinitive (pluperfect subjunctive representing future perfect indicative). Cicero treats it more like a present general with perfect indicative of the *si* clause represented by the pluperfect subjunctive.

eam nullis spoliatam ornamentis: graceful, interlocking word order.

8

vide, quaeso: This apostrophe, addressed to prosecutor, differs in tone from that at the end of 6 because of *quaeso*, the vocative, and the lack of repetition. It sums up the point begun in 6 with *prodo meam* through a restatement of the argument: if he can speak openly about his own, weaker case and its highly satisfactory result, he can confidently defend Ligarius'.

qui . . . non dubitem: Manuscript variations may obscure Cicero's meaning in this slightly elliptical indirect question. The choice is between *dicere* and *confiteri*. Quintilian (5.10.92), who reads *audeam dicere*, cites this as an *argumentum ex difficiliore*, i.e., Cicero presents himself as a stronger opponent of Caesar's than Ligarius and, thus, more difficult to forgive (see various comments at 31). What preceded suggests that *dicere* is better because more comprehensive; *confiteri* was perhaps occasioned by a memory of 1, *ausus est confiteri*, and *non* later added to improve the sense. Some editors defend *non audeam confiteri* as ironic: "how little reluctant I am to acknowledge"; that would require taking the *qui* clause as adversative. The rhetoric is stronger moving from negative to positive assertion.

atque: marks a new tack (see on 3): the beginning of a digression. Cicero gives an entirely different reason for introducing his own situation. He quickly switches from addressing Tubero, who may well not be convinced by the reason given, to a general narrative exuding sweet reason.

propterea . . . cum: This is the only time *propterea,* inserted in a governing clause, anticipates *ut* + subjunctive. In the philosophical works a *quod* clause (sometimes also *quia*) is now and then separated from anticipatory *propterea,* occasionally even preceding it. For the order, antecedent–relative, in expository style see 2, *prius quam.*

eadem: picks up *haec.* Everything in this sentence contributes to making Cicero's reasoning seem clear, cogent, and dispassionate. *Cum . . . dicerem* is like 6, *mihi apud te dicenti,* but the full clause gives a better setting for *eadem.* The progression—Ligarius' case is like mine, mine is like Tubero's—is strongly felt, and felt to make sense, in part because of the odd placement of *Tubero* next to *mihi* and before the *cum* clause.

cuius . . . industriae: The semi-independent relative, genitive, ties the sentence closely to the preceding; see 6, *cuius . . . causam.* Phrase is a hendiadys; his reputation stems from his work.

vel . . . vel: includes the possibility of all three reasons in a tricolon of causals, the *quod* clauses replacing the causal prepositional phrase. The third member expands to a handsome compliment to the younger Tubero, which *sed hoc quaero* abruptly dashes, returning to the main clause.

ingenio studiisque: the first innate, the second requiring devotion.

propinqui: See 1; intimacy will give way to condescension. *Adolescens* is a vague term; but here and at 9 youthfulness is a ploy for Cicero; he treats the young prosecutor of *Pro Caelio* in the same way. But see too *Deiot.* 17, *isto adulescente.*

aliquem: See 5, *incredibilem quendam.* Cicero had protégés, and his relationship to the family of Quintus Tubero was close. Still, this may be a bit precious; Quintus' career as an advocate was short-lived.

redundare: Figuratively the verb is used in two different senses: places may be overflowing with blood, as at 15, or teeming with people; hatred can redound to one's disadvantage (*Cat.* 1.29), or Tubero's reputation flow back to Cicero's credit.

9

sed hoc quaero: For the abrupt introduction of an inquiry see 29, *nunc.* For *sed* see *Marc.* 33. The niceties are over. Cicero now defends his client by accusing Tubero of hypocrisy, since he too was anti-Caesarian. Quintilian (11.1.78) cites this passage as an example of criticizing opponents for what one has oneself (or what one's client has) done. Tubero charged that Ligarius' behavior was worse: he had stayed in Africa longer and under Juba continued fighting after the struggle between Pompey and Caesar was over. But the difference between Cicero's strategy here and Tubero's (as far as we can recover his argument) was only one of degree. For *hoc* introducing a direct statement (here, question) see 6, *ut hoc populus Romanus exaudiat.*

qui et: three attributes in clear parallel (note anticipatory *et*) in a formula just used in praise of Caesar.

voluit: Cicero will concede the opposite to Tubero at 21, but for now this contrasts with Ligarius' departure (cf. at 5, *plena desideri*). Importance of the second proposition (as favorable to Ligarius) is determined by the third, which makes it appear that Tubero violently opposed Caesar.

prohibitum: This part of the story is never made clear. Ligarius, the Tuberones, and Varus were all Pompeians. One account, by Pomponius in the *Digest* (1.2.2.46), attributes the denial of landfall specifically to Ligarius. At 22 Cicero claims that the decision to bar Tubero was not Ligarius'; Caesar (see at 22, *aliquis*) names Varus. *Queritur* suggests a private complaint; but for Tubero to protest being denied access to Africa as he indicts Ligarius for being there is absurd.

certe: So Cicero says with no corroboration, and a not very assertive particle; see *Marc.* 13.

quid enim: Quintilian cites this splendid passage four times, for apostrophe, as Cicero suddenly switches from talking about Tubero to addressing him (9.2.38); for personification (8.6.12); for climax through accumulation of images (8.4.26–27), and for the rhetorical questions (9.2.6–7, posed "not for information, but for emphasis") which become progressively more excited and staccato, culminating in a sharp and sudden break. Catullus gets the same intensity with the same techniques in a similarly histrionic address at 8.15–18, to his mistress:

scelesta, vae te, quae tibi manet vita?
quis nunc te adibit? cui videberis bella?

quem nunc amabis? cuius esse diceris?
quem basiabis? cui labella mordebis?

("Be gone, wretch! What life remains for you? Who will now approach you? To whom will you seem beautiful? Whom will you love? Whose mistress will you be said to be? Whom will you kiss? On whose sweet lips will you nibble?")

destrictus in acie Pharsalica gladius: a detailed, pictorial phrase neatly rounded in hyperbaton.

agebat: personification, as with the next two predicates. So Quint. 8.6.11: "a bold transference when we attribute to inanimate objects action and motivation." *Ago* means both "doing" and "getting involved with, aiming at."

latus: as a vulnerable part of the body. See at *Marc.* 32.

mucro: figure of synecdoche (naming the part for the whole) and personification.

qui sensus erat armorum?: = *quid senserunt arma?*—another personification. For *sensus* see Virg. *Aen.* 4.406, *quis tibi tum, Dido, cernanti talia, sensus?* The structure practically breaks down here in the excitement.

quae ... animi: This purely nominal sentence, verb omitted, casts four nominatives into the interrogative. Usually translated "On what was your ... bent?"—but without parallels. The force is like that of *quae est* in *Verr.* 2.3.88, *quae est ista praeda, quae vis, quae direptio sociorum.* See *Deiot.* 32, *quae est ista.*

quid cupiebas, quid optabas?: Anaphoric isocolon is still insistent, but the predicates impose some structure and control.

nimis urgeo: Cicero is fond of interpreting the reactions (real or imagined) of his opponents. Tubero may not have showed signs of distress, or if he did, the reason may not have been guilty embarrassment so much as outrage at this prejudicial, perhaps fanciful description. See *Deiot.* 20, *quae trepidatio.* Plutarch says (see the Introduction, section 3.2) that this is when Caesar was overcome by emotion. Quintilian adds: "The speech is cut off as if before its proper end" (9.2.57). We need not assume that Cicero had more to say. Since Caesar was not struck, the description has reached its dramatic climax.

ad me revertar: breaks off the flow of argument again. The break is explicit (for the prothesis see *Marc.* 21, *nunc venio*), but the movement is complicated. At 6 he interrupted the narrative of Ligarius' activities in Africa to appeal to Caesar for leniency because Ligarius had been less devoutly Pompeian than he himself had been. At 8 he announced that he had compared himself with Ligarius in preparation for comparing Tubero to Ligarius. It is to that point that he returns.

isdem in armis fui: The sentence is a double cretic, although Quintilian (9.4.99), omitting the first word, scans a dochmiac (˘ ‾ ‾ ˘ ‾). Cicero will now share his guilt with Tubero, although he was not himself present at Pharsalus. For the expression see the passage from *Sulla* cited at *Marc.* 14, *neque . . . illa nec ulla*.

10

quid autem: For *autem* see 19, *quo modo autem*. The rhetorical progression is far from lucid. This statement mitigates any culpability for having been on the "wrong" side: the aims of the Pompeians (from Cicero to Tubero to Ligarius) were to achieve precisely what Caesar has: absolute power in victory. It is Caesar's exercise of that power to which Cicero is now turning his attention and his potential for influence.

egimus: Cicero's admission is rhetorically binding on Tubero, who could hardly, in any case, deny it, but also on Caesar. Quintilian (5.13.5) cites this period as an example of an aggressive defense within the context of a *deprecatio*; see the Introduction, section 3.2.

quorum . . . eorum: The order is neatly epigrammatic in explicitly structured expository style, especially since the relative pronoun and the demonstrative antecedent each begins its clause; that both are genitive plural is fortuitous. Quintilian (8.5.10) calls this form of argument a *sententia ex contrariis*; i.e., the argument for clemency is precisely the grotesqueness of its opposite; thus the intensive *ipsorum*: it is bad enough that anyone should try to dissuade Caesar's generosity, much less the very men who have been saved by it. He identifies this form of argument, its careful symmetry as described above, closely with what he terms an "enthymeme"—a conceit.

Cicero uses such periods as codas, as Quintilian (8.5.13) observes, citing *Lig.* 2 (where see on *prius . . . quam*). He then complains that the device is too much affected by current writers, who seek to fashion one for every sentence—a succession of cloyingly neat, self-conscious epigrams.

igitur: marks what follows as a logical conclusion, whether or not it is. There are two underlying points: (1) the similarity in aspirations of the two sides argues against excessive punishment of the losers, and (2) whatever the similarity in aspiration, Caesar is distinguished by having extended clemency to the Pompeians. If the very people who enjoy pardon can convince Caesar to refuse it to others, they will be curtailing his distinction.

atque: a new direction; the impudence of recipients of clemency arguing for sternness forms the link. In keeping with the undercurrent that runs through this speech of lawyers' talk about techniques of pleading cases, Cicero now criticizes the opposition on practical forensic grounds. Theirs is an ill-considered strategy.

in hac causa: the theme of the argument, the pleading of a case, in initial position.

equidem: The criticism of professional incompetence is made precisely and directly. In this area Cicero's authority is preeminent. *Equidem* does not dismiss or diminish the litotes, *non nihil,* by contrast with what follows, but rather reserves it while a distinction is made that is fully uncomplimentary to both father and son.

etiam . . . sed multo magis: The second half is clearly stressed; but unlike the usual negative in the first of such expression (*non . . . sed, non modo . . . verum etiam*), *etiam*—which usually intensifies a following item vis-à-vis a preceding one—rivets attention on the first half and the younger Tubero. The father should have known better (a gratuitous insult to the son), but it is the son who is actually mishandling his case.

desidero: See on 5, *desideri.*

quod . . . quod . . . viderit: *Quod*-causal and *quod*-noun clauses are sometimes hard to distinguish, because they are formally and in origin the same. If this were a true causal, the subjunctive should, by a syntactic convention, convey a purported or alleged cause. *Quod*-noun clauses take the indicative, except rarely when they are restrictive, like *quod sciam* (= *quod scire* *possum*) or *quod memineris* (= *quoad memineris* "to the extent that you can . . ."), that is, when the subjunctive has its intrinsic value of potentiality. In those instances the conjunction is usually qualified by *quidem* or *modo*; but see *De Or.* 3.52, *nemo enim umquam est oratorem, quod Latine loqueretur, admiratus,* i.e., "merely in that he could" or "for having the potential to speak Latin"; or *Verr.* 2.5.174, *quod te liberatum existimationis metu consulem cogites, . . . beneficia populi Romani non minore negotio retinentur quam comparantur,* "As to the fact that you may think yourself, because consul, free from worry about reputation, . . . the benefits of the Roman people are as difficult to keep as to acquire."

homo: appositive to predicative ablatives, like 1, *vir,* because Latin does not have a participle (which would here be adversative) for *esse.*

cum ingenio, tum etiam doctrina: The two qualities are often found together; so 8, with *studiis.* But the particles here are crucial: his training should have kept him from making this strategic error, whatever his talent. Innate and acquired powers are discussed at *Marc.* 19.

genus hoc causae: Hermagoras of Temnos (floruit 140 B.C.) was the first to codify four stances, or approaches, for an advocate to consider in pleading a case. The "statis" theory is as obvious and inert as its name suggests. Much more important is the practical consideration of how the case would appear to a jury—*honestum, turpe, dubium, humile* (so *Ad Her.* 1.5)— and how the speaker could best manipulate the jury's initial sense of it. That is what *causae* means here and at *qui causam habeat* below. According to Quintilian (5.13.20), prosecuting an exile and urging Caesar not to pardon him is an inhumane suit (and therefore invidious for the prosecutor). The word order of *genus hoc causae* is unusualy, stressing the deictic adjective.

quovis: "anyone whatsoever," vs. *aliquo* = "someone," although not particularly identifiable, as at 22, *aliquis.* For the locution see 34 and *Piso.* 33, *in tanto . . . odio . . . quaevis fuga quam ulla provincia esset optatior.* Cicero identifies three technical flaws: (1) indicting a man who has confessed, (2) accusing a man who may have a better case than yours, and (3) calling for capital punishment. The focus is still on the case, the subject of the passive infinitive.

nam si vidisset: An analysis by Cicero of the younger Tubero's case will convince him of the incompetence of his strategy, for which the blame is laid squarely on the father's shoulders. This contrary-to-fact structure elegantly and epigramatically convicts the father, not of deliberately sabotaging his son's case, but of failing to anticipate the consequences of the approach he recommends. Cicero then ticks off the mistakes unceremoniously, in that plain style—note the lack of sentence connectives or elaborate syntax—that implies, however speciously, a businesslike sincerity (see the Introduction, section 4). When Cicero again discusses stances an orator can assume (at 30–31), he implies that the competent advocate can discover an apt strategy for every case. Here he stresses how unsympathetically the prosecution is portraying itself. He is not about to make their case convincingly for them.

profecto: See at *Marc.* 3.

arguis fatentem: The bleak oxymoron belittles any sense of accomplishment. Sympathy would be directed towards the accused—the strategy to *deprecatio*. Cicero claimed more than once that he preferred defense to prosecution for this general reason; e.g., *Off.* 2.49ff., *laudabilior est defensio . . . duri enim hominis vel potius vix hominis videtur periculum capitis inferre multis*; it is *sordidum ad famam*. At *Caecil.* 1 he distinguishes "defending many" from "hurting anyone." Quintilian (11.1.57) advises that a prosecutor should always give the impression of reluctance.

aut . . . aut: The careful, symmetrical balance will not fully mask the fact that Cicero attributes to Tubero a position he would never have conceded. It is enough for Caesar to appreciate that the technique is clever and that the argument gains specious weight from the apparent concession. "Equal" is all Cicero needs to establish in order to allege hypocrisy and cruelty.

11

haec admirabilia: a terse predication and a colloquial formula for dismissing one thing in order to stress another. For the plural and omission of the verb in the first half, the singular in the second half, see *Fam.* 12.2.2, *sed haec tolerabilia, illud non ferendum*, and *Phil.* 2.25, *sed haec vetera, illud vero recens. Admirabilia* can cover reactions from "splendid" to (here) "outrageous."

prodigi simili: parallel in citation from *Verr.* 2.2.158 at 1, *novum*.

non habet: strong assertion (verb first, asyndeton) of a balance that holds the affirmative in suspense.

eam: anticipates the result clause; see *Deiot.* 11, *eam partem.*

ista: The emphatic second-person adjective has palpable force, here scorn.

ut necetur: A Roman convicted of a capital crime had the choice of going into exile. But Ligarius was already in that position. From what we can tell, Tubero was arguing for no more than that the sentence of exile not be rescinded.

egit: perhaps purposely indefinite because of an ambiguity in the meaning of *agere*. If "plead a case," the referent of *hoc* is *accusatio*; if "aim for something," *ut necetur.*

civis . . . nemo: It is said that Cicero uses *nemo* as an adjective = *nullus,* but that hardly describes the situation. The only nouns with which it is found more than twice in the speeches are *homo* (where a form of paranomasia is in effect, since *nemo* = *ne* + *homo*), *vir,* and *civis.* In other apparent cases (and some of the above), it is predicative and pronominal, e.g., at *Marc.* 7, *socium habes neminem.* Here it gets particular force, perhaps its very justification, from position; cf. at 17.

externi . . . barbarorum: This sentence is not to be discarded because it appears differently in various manuscripts. Cicero has come to the third flaw in the prosecution's presentation.

levium: for Greeks (like *immanium* for barbarians), a stock Roman epithet, contrasting respectively with Roman *gravitas* and *humanitas.* For the latter see *Deiot.* 32; as to the former, the Romans held in contempt the inability of Greeks to manage a polity responsibly.

quid agis aliud?: *Aliud,* usually placed after *quid,* is here emphatic. Cicero sets up an elenchus (see 4, *certe*) which he pursues with a series of staccato, pathetic questions in the form of ungoverned final clauses. Pathos outweighs logic. It is argued that exile is a fate worse than death. What began as a demonstration of the Tuberones' incompetence to see the consequences of their strategy starts to sound like an aspersion on their humanity. *Romae ne sit* introduces it, but Cicero elaborates on the family relationships (Brocchus was present; so *hoc*) and must return to *ne sit in patria. Nobiscum,* with public overtones, emphatically placed in a new predicate, is slipped into the series of familiars. *Consobrini* originally designated the relation-ship of children of two sisters (**con-sororini*). It became generalized, whence English "cousin."

non: strategically placed and separated from the word it rhetorically qual-ifies (*patria*). Pronouns, as frequently, are in collocation; and *ergo,* well postponed, insists that this sentence be taken as the logical climax of the argument.

hunc: Cicero again, as at 5, dramatically points to his client as if he were present.

vita vis: The Latin phrase is short, alliterative, abrupt; its effect, one of stinging and harsh inevitability, especially after *patria privare.*

12

at: a vigorous response to an unspoken objection. The Roman who Cicero assumes might be adduced is Sulla. His ready response is that Sulla's cruelty did not spread to the judicial system.

istud . . . isto: Second-person possessive adjectives frame the sentence, fo-cusing totally on Tubero's singular and cruel application of justice; cf. sim-ilar order at 16, *suam . . . tuam.*

eum . . . qui: Sulla, senatorial general, dictator in 81–79, and author of vindictive and profitable proscriptions that still could raise shudders in the Roman memory. He had become a rhetorical commonplace, to be exploited even by orators who, like Cicero, might elsewhere praise his conservative republicanism. Indeed, he had become a verb, *sullaturio*; see *Marc.* 16, *insolentiam.*

ipse: sense strongly adversative to ⟨*non*⟩ *quisquam egit* in asyndeton. Plu-tarch (*Sulla* 31) confirms that he offered rewards to those who laid charges if the victims were subsequently executed, to slaves who accused their mas-ters, and to children who implicated their fathers.

occidi: Passive infinitives, usual after *iubeo,* are thought of as facts, not wishes.

postulante: a legal term; see at 17, *aditus et postulatio.*

quae tamen: A relative adjective with a referent in the preceding sentence, like the pronoun, does not permit a sentence connective: *quae = et ea*. *Tamen* therefore has the force of an adverb rather than a conjunction, throwing what it modifies into an adversative light vis-à-vis some other element not otherwise so marked; see *Deiot.* 4, *quod tamen*. A relationship between two notions that usually is expressed between clauses takes place instead on the level of words and phrases and is less precisely spelled out. Here the ellipsis in thought is "You may be adducing this as a precedent, but even this . . .", so *Deiot.* 9, *cui tamen*; *Lig.* 34, *quos . . . salvos*; or *Phil.* 1.7, *quae tamen urbs mihi coniunctissima plus una me nocte cupiens retinere non potuit* ("Although that city [Brundisium] is very special to me, it couldn't keep me for more than one night, however much it wanted to"). See, too, *Deiot.* 11, *in summo tamen timore*. With the play on *crudelitas* and *crudelis*, and the time frame (*aliquot annis post . . . nunc*), the period becomes epigrammatic.

ab hoc eodem . . . : The deictic value of *hoc* is felt, but with *eodem* it also anticipates the relative. As praetor in 64 Caesar allowed proceedings against some of those who had taken part in Sullan proscriptions, although they had been specifically exempted from prosecution by the *lex Cornelia de sicariis*. For his stance in *Pro Rabirio Postumo* see the Introduction, section 2.

aliquot annis post: Note the odd placement of the verbal modifier. Cicero wants the dating of the earlier circumstance to precede that of the present one (*nunc*), while still keeping Caesar's accomplishment as the climax of the sentence.

"ego vero . . . postulo": The orator now establishes a dialogue with Tubero (for the *sermocinatio* see *Marc.* 26), calculated to make his opponent look like a fool rather than a cad. The focus is still on courtroom strategy, not morality.

ita: with the verb; there is no sentence connective.

mehercule: originally *me hercule (adiuvet)* or *me hercule (adiuves)*: vocative, as at *Deiot.* 17. But Cicero says at *Orat.* 157, published in 46, that he prefers saying the latter, his choice being determined by the sound of the phrase. The tone of such expostulations (cf. *Marc.* 10, *me dius fidius*) is sometimes difficult to determine. Paradoxically, they may have stronger religious associations in comedy, although the speaker is being histrionic, than in conversational Latin, where a wide variety of expletive forces can be heard. Here, the irony comes not from the expression itself, but from the effusively conciliatory attitude to which it, along with the anaphoric tricolon, contributes. Tubero's "admission" to which Cicero responds with such warm affirmation (*novi enim . . . novi . . . novi*) is of his own making.

studia . . . virtutis: subjective and objective genitives depending on the same noun; see on *Marc.* 4, *nullius flumen ingeni*, and *Lig.* 14, *multorum perfugium misericordiae*. Genitives with different functions are usually separated by the governing noun. The position here of *vestrae* between two feminine genitives is particularly unfortunate.

generis: P. Aelius Paetus was an eminent jurist at the beginning of the second century, as was his brother Sextus, who also became consul (198) and censor (184). In the mid-second century Q. Aelius Tubero, nephew of Scipio Aemilianus, had been a Stoic philosopher. L. Aelius Stilo distinguished himself as a grammarian and antiquary, a teacher both of Varro and Cicero. The father of the prosecutor was a scholar; the son, after this case, turned from practical oratory to jurisprudence. It is sometimes said that he was impelled to do so by his failure in the present case. But the age of public advocacy had also come to an end.

nota mihi: present perfect, like *Marc.* 3, *intellectum mihi*; variation after tricolon of *novi*.

13

itaque: not a logical deduction, but movement in his patient exposition of the point that Tubero's case is ill considered; so *enim . . . igitur . . . enim . . . an . . . ? . . . vero,* along with *res eo spectat ut, ea . . . in qua, sicuti est*—the last insisting on the reality of the condition even in the indicative (cf. 14, *quod et fecimus*).

certo scio: "Cicero regularly uses this expression of something he assumes to be true, without having actual information; contrast *certum scio* ('I know for certain'), *certe scio* ('I certainly know')": Shackleton Bailey 1, 1:278.

vos: Cicero addresses both son and father.

petere sanguinem: See *Deiot.* 30, *expetere vitam*.

res . . . eo spectat: The anticipatory words *eo* (to *ut*) and *ea* (to *qua*) make the conclusion seem inexorable. The point is not that this case cannot be argued, but that Tubero is arguing it incompetently; see on 10, *quid agis aliud?*

quae est igitur: This and the following sentence repeat insistently and re-inforce the point that Tubero is incompetently leaving the wrong impression.

an: as at 5, implies denial of an unnamed alternative and elevates the emotional tone. Structures are controlled (*quod . . . id*; *ea poena in qua*; *igitur*; *enim*), but the language becomes vivid and pathetic.

vero: is strongly asseverative (cf. 19, *mihi vero*), and the lack of a predicate is felt. Cicero's goal is not merely to portray the continued exile of Ligarius, for which the prosecution argues, as an inhuman punishment, but to suggest that their counsel against clemency will be deleterious to Caesar and the state. The explanation of this assertion takes the form of an elaborate question.

quod ne . . . id: The order relative–antecedent implies a control that soon gives way to indignation.

domi: Most editors reject this, against all manuscripts, as having been added from 14 (see comments there). *Petimus*, present tense, would refer to the present proceeding; but if so, Cicero describes himself—twice within thirty-five words—as behaving in a manner more consonant with a private appeal to Caesar than with anything he has said or done to this point; on *precibus ac lacrimis* see *Marc.* 33. Triple repetition of the word would remind Caesar of the earlier understanding.

The position of the clause treats its content as common knowledge and a fait accompli. The audience with Caesar, described to Ligarius in *Fam.* 6.14 (24 September 46, new calendar), was emotional and resulted in a response from Caesar that was gentle and generous, full of hope. The petition took place in Caesar's home.

fidentes: The participial phrase, weighted by a careful balances in an explicit *non tam . . . quam* framework, suggests the compassion of Caesar as opposed to the belligerence of Tubero. The former is introduced dramatically by the deictic pronoun, the latter characterized unflatteringly in a tricolon of futures, expanding in indignant and emotional questions, although carefully delineated by *ets*. Cicero now addresses the prosecutor alone.

iacentis: The participle is adversative; the present, effective: even as he assumes the suppliant position, he is denied the suppliant's voice. In fact, when Cicero made his plea at Caesar's home, the relatives prostrated themselves; Cicero merely spoke (*Fam.* 6.14.2).

supplicum voce: figurative, pathetic language.

14

si: *argumentum a fortiori,* based on antithesis of *domi* and *in foro*: if it would have been inhumane to interrupt an abject personal plea, how much worse to interfere with this public *deprecatio*? As at 1, Cicero's avowal that he is presenting a *deprecatio* is to a degree outrageous.

cum . . . feceremus: Nontemporal *cum* conventionally requires the subjunctive whether the circumstances are real or hypothetical. In the *quod* clause Cicero at once affirms that the event did take place and reminds Caesar of his disposition at that time.

repente inruisses: an imagined dramatic scene, scripted with an insensitive speech for Tubero.

clamare: of excited speech, whether angry, indignant, or exultant.

cave: a vigorous negative imperative. Usually, with *ne* = "beware of . . ."; this paratactic construction is found in the letters twenty-four times and in the speeches six (thrice in made-up informal speech). It is a feature of colloquial speech, which Cicero is representing here. Some manuscripts begin a tricolon with *cave credas,* but a tricolon here would sacrifice drama for elaboration.

fratrum . . . obsecrantium: For the tight genitive participial phrase (here with a play on words, *fratrum pro fratris*) see *Marc.* 14, *flagitantium,* and *Balb.* 56, *sermones hominum alienis bonis maerentium.*

exuisses: Cicero uses this metaphor elsewhere only at *Att.* 13.2 (May 45), a brief and bitter note. *Humanitas,* specifically attributed to the Aelii Tub-

erones at 12, refers to basic human feelings for other humans, like Caesar's, just above.

quanto hoc durius: Ellipsis of finite verb contributes to heightened pathos.

domi: Expanding on the private audience, Cicero can now concentrate on the emotional scene and pity, rather than on the judicial case and legalities. Note *misereat . . . miseria . . . misericordiae,* the insistence on Tubero's belligerence, and the moving but historically inaccurate description of the Forum as a public sanctuary of compassion.

oppugnari . . . tollere: Manuscripts have passive accusative + infinitive and a complementary infinitive parallel to each other after the neuter adjective predicate. Lambinus (sixteenth century) claimed to have found *te oppugnare* in manuscripts. Editors cannot abide the inconcinnity. I have not found a parallel in Cicero; but that does not mean one does not exist or that Cicero could not have written it as it appears. Concinnity is not an overriding principle of Ciceronian style.

multorum: can depend on *miseria,* even modified by *tali,* or *perfugium.* Genitive goes better with *perfugium* as subjective, *misericordiae* being appositional (cf. *Rosc. Am.* 150, *una spes reliqua est . . . misericordia,* "there is one haven left for Roscius: your pity." Double cretic clausula.

15

dicam plane: transition by changing point of address and by shifting from contrived histrionics relating to the conduct of a case at law to a strongly worded, confident admonition on practical politics; so *intellego quod loquar,* below. *Sentio = sententiam habeo.* See *Marc.* 12, *vereor.*

si in tanta . . . : The sentence has the ingredients of a neat bipartite epigram (*lenitas . . . luctu*), but a correlation is sacrificed to (1) *tanta . . . tanta,* (2) the relative clause with its emphatic, insistent repetition, and (3) the parenthesis that gives the statement a nervous energy and tense immediacy. The position of the nominative *tanta* is predicative; it does not trigger a consecutive or correlative clause (*quam* is purely relative and adjectival). *Lenitas* with *iustitia* is attributed to Caesar at *Marc.* 12.

tanta: is a rhetorically elevated equivalent of *magna*; as at *Marc.* 19, where a result clause does follow, and at *Deiot.* 15, *cuius tanti sceleris,* and *Deiot.* 32, *ista tam impotens.*

inquam: stresses only what is repeated.

intellego quod loquar: Bold insertion prefers intensity to flow and encourages the perception of Cicero as an advisor to Caesar. Cicero's insistence on limiting the spirit of conciliation to Caesar alone implies, as Quintilian (8.3.85) observed, that others in Caesar's camp, to whom Cicero will presently allude, took the more traditional, vengeful view of post–Civil War policy.

redundaret: The metaphor, mild enough in 8, is more frequently used in violent and emotional contexts, as in the speeches *In Verrem* and *In Catilinam,* and found with words like *sanguis* or *invidia.*

ista victoria: ends a handsome clause with a double cretic cadence.

quam multi: substantive, to which the adjective *quot* corresponds. Cicero makes his point in a style that combines the logical cogency of complex periodicity with the heightened excitement of the interrogative mode. Two periods are bound together by the repetition of *quam multi.* The first establishes the antithesis between victors and losers in an a fortiori argument, inverted in the interrogative mode. For *multi* see *Marc.* 3.

essent . . . vellent: Imperfect subjunctive in potential main clauses is rare, since such clauses usually denote an open possibility. After conditional clauses in which past tenses of the subjunctive convey unrealized potential (contrary-to-fact), the imperfect subjunctive in the main clause came to represent unrealized potential in the present; so in independent potential clauses, the imperfect expresses what would be happening, if things were different (as at 16, *diceres*); see Woodcock, 91–92 (section 121 and esp. n. 1). In this sentence the present tense of the subjunctive in the *cum* clauses makes it clear that the potential for such pressure still exists. But Cicero suggests that because of Caesar's policy the potential will not be realized. Understand, e.g., "If you encouraged them." Quintilian (8.3.85) cites this passage as an example of *vox suppressa,* because Cicero does not explicitly acknowledge that proponents of vengeance in fact exist among Caesar's men.

```
quam multi enim essent                de victoribus
        qui te crudelem esse vellent,
                cum etiam             de victis reperiantur?
```

The second argument, expanding the *victores–victi* antithesis, becomes more complex. The echoes of the first sentence are jarring and marked by inconcinnity, although *nolint te esse . . . misericordem* is a purely negative restatement of *te crudelem esse vellent*:

```
quam multi
        qui
                cum a te ignosci nemini vellent,
                                                impedirent clementiam,
        cum hi
                quibus      ignovisti
                        nolint te esse in alios misericordem!
```

cum . . . vellent: causal to *impedirent* and only secondarily characteristic of a group, as was *qui vellent* above. The nuance is that the victors might be universal in their demand for vengeance; Tubero is selective. *Quibus* merely modifies *hi,* and a natural adversative nuance ("although you forgave them") remains unexpressed in the indicative; see on 23, *cuius . . . interfuit. Qui vellent* would have been less asymmetrical, suggesting a parallel with the other *qui* clause, rather than the other *cum* clause (*a te ignosci . . . ignovisti*). *Hi* points the finger of personal vindictiveness directly at the Tuberones.

16

mendacio: Since an unlovely prosecution is also encouraging bad policy, Cicero fancifully introduces the notion of a permissible lie, but with less humor and more point than his preposterous suggestion at the beginning that he had planned to take advantage of Caesar's ignorance. Plato's γενναῖον ψεῦδος (*Rep.* 3.414), often adduced as a parallel, does not endorse the kind of lie Cicero proposes, but advocates rather the creation of a myth. At *Milo.* 10 he asserts as an unwritten law that in dire straits any expedient for saving one's life is *honestum*. As so often in this speech, Cicero appears to lay out forensic strategy openly; see on 30. Horace (*C.* 3.11.35) calls Hypermestra *splendide mendax*; but she had a *periurum parentem,* because

Danaos had made an immoral contract with the sons of Aegyptus. Quintilian (2.17.26–27) endorses efficacious lies for philosophers as well as orators. This is more or less what is granted to writers of rhetorical history (*Brut.* 42). Quintilian (4.2.89–94), instructing his readers in the telling of convincing lies, seems little concerned with morality.

saluti . . . calamitoso . . . discrimine . . . periculo: words all in the vocabulary of judicial oratory; see on *Marc.* 25, *periculo.*

hominis: Cf. *hominis . . . ad hominem* below. This appeals to a basic human contract of humane behavior, not to a policy of reconciliation. The genitive is partitive or predicative (so 26, *magni . . . viri*) and tends to create a universal definition; see the citation from *De Officiis* at 10, *arguis fatentem.*

coarguere: found in some manuscripts; *redarguere* in others. It is difficult to see why any corrector in antiquity or beyond would choose to destroy existing alliteration; the opposite intention may explain the variant. For manuscript corrections introduced to create concinnity see on 33, *minabantur.*

si esset alicuius: The pronoun is indefinite and undefined, but existing. The definitional cast of the predicative genitive is corrected by allowing the slightest possibility of an exception, which does not, however, cover the present case, where hypocrisy would be added to inhumanity.

eadem causa et fortuna: As at *Marc.* 2, the reference here is not just to political affiliation, as it is at *Marc.* 31, *in causa.*

sed tamen: "but beyond that." *Sed* as a sentence connective is strongly adversative to what has gone before; see 20 and, reinforced by *tamen* as at 20, *Deiot* 23 and 31. It does not dismiss the preceding, as *vero* would (so 19), but argues vigorously against it.

aliud est: The distinction is articulated in an antithetical pair of parallel clauses in asyndeton. They fall short of absolute symmetry in the complementary infinitives, the second of which is a resolved cretic-trochaic clausula of the type *esse videatur*, which Quintilian (10.2.17) later complained that self-styled Ciceronians affected to excess.

diceres: that is, if Cicero had employed a permissible lie; unreal potential subjunctive vs. "What are you saying now?" See 15, *essent . . . vellent.*

hominis ... ad hominem: The meaning is not "a real man," but anyone partaking of basic human feeling.

qua qui ... utetur: The passage ends with an epigrammatic expression, directed to Caesar. A continuative relative unassumingly begins a handsomely articulated period.

suam	citius	abiciet	humanitatem
	quam	extorquebit		tuam

suam ... tuam: Possessives neatly bracket the comparative period.

abiciet ... extorquebit: The second verb is much stronger, because Caesar would be resisting.

C. Caesar: For the formal *praenomen* see 37 and *Marc.* 2.

17

ac: opens digression on the genesis of the present litigation, as Cicero reconstructs (*ut opinor*) the events.

aditus et postulatio: technical terms referring to the initiation of a suit; see 4, *profectio ... remansio*. One would go before the praetor and request permission to prosecute; so *Caecil.* 64, *delationem nominis postulare,* and for the demand for punishment, as at 12.

ut opinor: Cicero insists that this is his interpretation of the sequence, as, with *non dubito* in the next sentence, he insists on his interpretation of Caesar's reaction.

nullo de alio quisquam: Caesar would have been surprised by any or all of three things; so *vel*. The first two are given in elliptical *quod* clauses, for which *postularet* or *vellet dicere*—subjunctive as alleged reasons— must be understood. Mommsen removed *quisquam*, making Tubero the subject of all three units. This is neater, but Cicero is not being particularly neat here.

quidnam novi sceleris: The third reason for Caesar's amazement, given in an indirect question. Manuscripts all read *sceleris,* which Patricius (sixteenth century) excised as a gloss from the next sentence. He argued that since the following argument involves defining what the Pompeians did, it makes more sense for the aberrant label *scelus* to come from Tubero's mouth in the next sentence. Caesar then would be surprised because he was well aware what Ligarius had done. But cadence requires the word; and Caesar is surprised precisely because he was well acquainted with Ligarius' situation.

scelus tu illud vocas?: Cicero never acknowledges Tubero's charge that Ligarius had entered a conspiracy against Rome with a foreign prince; see the Introduction, section 3.2. He instead argues against treating partisans of Pompey generally as criminals.

illud: the fact that Ligarius had been in Africa. This sentence can be read either as a question or as an accusatory declarative (i.e., "You and only you . . ."); the weak position of *tu* after initial *scelus* favors the former.

enim: does not give the answer to the rhetorical question, but Cicero's reason for asking it. In the language of reconciliation, participation on either side of the Civil War should not be considered a *scelus*. So *Marc.* 13, 20, 29, 31. *Causa* here = political faction, as at 29; but see 16 and on 19, *dubia*.

alii . . . : an apparently artless list, escalating from the paired *alii* through *qui durius* with four objects, to *qui gravissime*, the top of the ladder, but still falling short of "crime."

error: of judgment, dispassionately made, perhaps like 2, but not *Marc.* 13. *Timor*, less admirable, is still understandable. *Spes*, opportunism, though unworthy, is less strong than political ambition, *cupiditas*, involving active participation, partly for personal gain; see at 3. Hatred of the other side is a strong, negative motivation; *pertinacia* is unreasonable loyalty to the opposition; see 26. Cicero acknowledges at 31 that these terms are subjective. Reckless behavior at the other end of the scale from *error* in the matter of action is not obviously more culpable in terms of intention; see *Marc.* 13, *ignoratione . . . metus . . . cupiditate . . . crudelitate.* For Caesar's publicist or an individual advocate of political reconciliation, these terms have a potential life-and-death value.

nemo: For the position see 11.

et . . . quidem: Cicero introduces an alternative, preferred interpretation of his own.

quaeritur: Passive implies a dispassionate inquiry or *quaestio* for a correct definition.

videtur: as at 12, insists on the subjectivity of the assertion; see on *Marc.* 10.

fatalis quaedam calamitas: the explanation advanced by Caesar (Dio 43.17) and adduced by Cicero at *Marc.* 13 and 31 and *Deiot.* 13. For a good fate see *Har. Resp.* 6, *quasi fatali adventu*, cited at 22, *natam ad bellum . . . gerendum*. For *quaedam* with the figurative language see 5, *incredibilem quendam*, and *Marc.* 13, *fato . . . funestoque*.

improvidas: a loaded attributive, the feeling is one of utter defenselessness, as with the minds of children at Lucr. 4.14, or the emotions of the Trojans confused by the portent of the snakes from Tenedos at Virg. *Aen.* 2.200 (*improvida pectora*). The word, however, is neither particularly poetic nor common.

humana . . . divina: clear antithesis.

18

liceat: introduces a concession, like *fuerint* below. The adjective *miseros* has a variety of senses from derogatory to sympathetic. The reference at first is indefinite with regard to referent and person.

quamquam: sentence fragment impatiently discounting to some extent what precedes; so *Marc.* 27. Utterance begins with a compliment to Caesar, and only distinguishes persons in the grammatical sense with the verb ending. Only then, with much emphasis (*non loquor de nobis; de illis loquor*), does Cicero distinguish between persons, and (in a double trochee) between the living and the dead—whom it would be churlish to demean.

fuerint: Cicero comes back insistently with three more epithets corresponding to the criticisms advanced above with *qui durius*. Returning to *liceat* in a more complex articulution (*carere*, which resolves both content and construction, is suspended to the end), Cicero now asks for a concession, rather than offering one.

sceleris . . . parricidi: first genitive in apposition to next two; the last refers to crimes against the *patria*. On *furor*, the madness that accompanies the

most unspeakable crimes and impels one to commit more, see *Verr.*
2.5.139, *furor enim quidam, sceleris et audaciae comes, istius effrenatum*
animum . . . tanta oppressit amentia ut . . . , "for a kind of mad rage, the
attendant of crime and outrage, afflicted his frenzied mind with such de-
mentia that . . . ."

Pompeio mortuo: The epithet is pure pathos; Caesar was said to have been
much affected by the death of his rival or at least its manner; see on *Marc.*
17, *quoniam . . . conservat.*

hoc . . . audivit: Caesar had made a conscious decision not to brand his
opponents enemies of the state, despite the contempt (*contumelia*) he suffered when a resolution of the people in 52 allowing him to keep his command until 1 January 48, when he could assume the *imperium* of
consulship, was rescinded by his enemies (Caes. *BC* 1.9).

aut tua: At a high level of emotion, Latin puts an untranslatable *aut* between impassioned questions; so Virg. *Aen.* 4.595, *Quid loquor? Aut ubi*
sum? See *Deiot.* 37, *aut quae tanta.* For a similar use of *et* see *Deiot.* 34,
et quem. The repeated formula *quid aliud nisi . . .* is at the core of four
rhetorical questions passionately challenging Caesar to interpret otherwise
Cicero's complementary assessment: *quando . . . quid voluerunt nisi . . .*
quid egit nisi uti . . . idne agebas ut.

tua . . . arma: Caesar's own fighting, as distinct from that of his army in
the next sentence. The position of the adjective before the interrogative is
very striking.

contumeliam: Caesar's word; see at *BC* cited above. In that passage he
affirms that his dignity always came first and was more important to him
than life itself.

tuus invictus exercitus: Caesar wanted it understood that his veterans were
no mercenaries, but Roman citizens fighting for "a just system of government." See Gelzer, 241, quoting from *BC* 3.91, C. Crastinus at Pharsalus:
"This last battle remains; when it is over he will recover his dignity and
we our freedom."

quid: a rhetorical interjection pressing the interlocutor in a cross-examination.

cupiebas: as when he offered to relinquish his Transalpine command in

December 50 or when he agreed to disarm in January 49, if Pompey would do likewise. See *Marc.* 15.

agebas: The mark of the interrogative cast of the sentence is postponed until after the dating clause. *Id,* along with the interrogative form of the sentence, has the force of rejecting the validity of the final clause before it is heard.

boni: See on *Marc.* 20. Although their numbers could be augmented from all segments of society, the *boni* were supporters of Senate-based conservatism and the status quo. Greeks and Romans never had quite our fastidiousness about technical terminology, and *boni* here can also stand in moral opposition to *scelerati* in a nonpolitical sense.

19

mihi vero: In the preceding passage Cicero considered Caesar's view in the inquiry into the proper characterization of the Pompeians. He now comes to his own. *Vero* tends to dismiss one line of argument in favor or another; see 13.

merita maxima: On alliteration see on 1, *fretus fortasse,* and 4, *pace . . . pacatissima . . . pacem.*

certe: marks *tanta* as strongly predicative. Services imply a proportionate debt of gratitude on the part of the recipient.

sceleratum . . . conservatum: a noun phrase, not accusative + infinitive.

autem: a new thought correcting, redefining, or changing the emphasis of the previous one: "more important. . . ." Similarly at 10.

cum . . . voluisses: The *cum* + subjunctive clause is conditional, perhaps used for variety after the previous construction. A similar usage at *Deiot.* 6 is occasioned by a preceding *sic.* For the thought see *Marc.* 13, *hostes.*

incolumi dignitate: The ablative is descriptive.

secessionem . . . aberrantibus: The movement of the sentence strongly supports its emphases with little regard for periodicity. Cicero moves to a positive statement of Caesar's evaluation, in plain language and constructions, essentially paratactic. No sentence connectives mark the progression.

secessionem: passive resistance historically associated with plebeian political struggles; presumably Caesar's word, and the most positive description of what happened. For the position of words see 17, *scelus tu illud vocas*. *Tu* is the fourth second-person form in as many lines. *Illam,* predicative, is feminine by attraction. The qualification, *initio,* is carefully suspended until after the pause of the vocative, and thereby diminished.

discidium: used at 5 in a personal sense of Ligarius' separation from his family.

utrisque . . . aberrantibus: plural *utrisque* because referring to two groups. The new kind of Ciceronian ablative absolute (see on *Marc.* 32, *salvo . . . salvi*) has structural functions: the first participle governs an object, the second controls a minor antithesis. The emphasis is on the verbal aspect: "wanting the safety of the state." This is a gentler statement of conflicting aims than at *Marc.* 30, but Cicero is here dealing with states of mind before the event.

partim . . . partim: different people (as in 3, but unlike *partim . . . partim* at *Marc.* 1), but in both of the groups. See on *Marc.* 30, *consiliis . . . studiis*.

dignitas: In the tentative progression to a definition Cicero uses tentative structures. *Dignitas* refers to the esteem or position in society a man enjoyed, based on background and accomplishments as well as personal or moral worth; it gave one *auctoritas* and demanded respect.

paene: to enhance Caesar's position, which would have seemed to a casual observer (e.g., Deiotarus at *Deiot.* 11) inferior, although Pompey by no means carried the entire Senate with him; see Shackleton Bailey 4. Cicero spoke contemptuously of Caesar's people (*Att.* 7.3.5).

fortasse: The doubt is stronger than the lexical meaning of the word suggests. Cicero ever so delicately insists that Pompey's supporters were superior; see 1, 26, and *Marc.* 20.

tum: rhetorically anticipates *nunc,* forming a rhetorical link between the sentences.

dubia: on both sides. *Causa* in the general, political sense: the set of circumstances or considerations that motivates to an action or point of view, here encompassing the causes of both sides. Cf. 10, *genus hoc causae*. In

20 the general situation of Pompeians in the wake of the Civil War is distinguished from the circumstances of the principals in this litigation.

melior ea: probably *ea causa,* after *causa dubia,* rather than *pars*; a diplomatic, but not for that reason insincere, criterion for settling the problem, although with *etiam* he concedes rather more to Caesar. Quintilian (5.11.42) treats this appeal to divine will as a commonplace. Luc. *Phars.* 1.128, *victrix causa deis placuit, sed victa Catoni,* exploits it altogether differently.

vero: signals an elevation in tone to the epigrammatic conclusion of the argument.

cognita . . . clementia: participle emphatic by position; cf. on 3, *suscepto bello*. Human recognition was slower than that of the gods.

nisi armatus: a strong point in Caesar's favor, used at *Marc.* 17 and *Deiot.* 24.

20

sed: a baldly transitional sentence explaining the movement of the speech, as 24, *sed iam hoc,* and *Marc.* 33.

ut omittam: a formulaic clause, generically of purpose, like *ut ita dicam.*

communem: the situation of all Pompeians; see on 19, *dubia.*

nostram: everything surrounding the present litigation. In fact what follows is much more condemnation of the Tuberones than a defense of Ligarius. The main verb switches to the plural, drawing in Tubero. Just as the earlier narrative extended, by argument and digression, the comparatively short period of time before Ligarius became an active Pompeian (2–5) and omitted the latter period, so the narrative of Tubero lingers (20–28) over the time during which the Tuberones remained loyal to Pompey. It seems to have been a part of Tubero's prosecution that Ligarius remained Pompeian long after he could and should have joined Caesar.

utrum . . . existimas: Interrogative pronouns anticipate the alternative datives. The question begins a brief dialogue in which Cicero informally provides questions, answers, and comments.

tandem: emphatic, impatient of resistance, real or imaginary, perhaps quer- ulous: "now, let us finally get to the main point"—a strong point in Cae- sar's favor, used at *Marc.* 17 and *Deiot.* 34.

nullo modo: ellipsis of *poteratis non venire*. Cicero is being both informal and sympathetic.

sed tamen: a very strong adversative, as at 16, immediately undercuts the sympathetic tone.

atque: raises a new point, going beyond parity to the superiority of Liga- rius' position. Suggestion of strong isocolon and paronomasia of *parere* underline the distinction between Ligarius and the Tuberones.

ille: a use of the demonstrative at home in "plain style" narrative. The best discussion of styles of oratory (or, perhaps, levels of diction) appears, with useful examples, in *Ad Her.* 4.11–16.

paruit: implies absolute obedience; see on 22, *vel potius paruit*.

generi: One of Tubero's ancestors withdrew his support of Ti. Gracchus, a kinsman, when the latter's legislation alienated the Senate.

nomini: in society as reflected in one's family name.

sed hoc non: an abrupt shift in attack after a conciliatory opening; see 9, *sed hoc quaero*. *Hoc* looks forward to the *ut* clause, which is like a jussive (forbidden by the negatived lead verb).

quibus . . . easdem: The relative clause anticipates a chiastically balanced (but not symmetrical) antecedent, significantly reinforced by *idem* for an added nuance here adversative: see at *Marc.* 24, *Marc.* 31, or *Deiot.* 16, and *Milo.* 18, *nunc eiusdem Appiae nomen quantas tragoedias excitat! quae cruentata caede honesti atque innocentis viri silebatur, eadem nunc crebro usurpatur, posteaquam latronis et parricidae sanguine imbuta est,* "Now what tragedies the name of the Appian Way evokes! The place that was ignored in silence when defiled by the slaughter of a good and innocent man is now, even so, constantly on the lips of all, after being stained with the blood of a thief and traitor."

21

Tuberonis: the father. The beginning of a narrative in simple, paratactic style; name of the principal comes first as at 2.

sors: Consuls and praetors decided on postmagisterial appointments for themselves, as provincial governors with *imperium* in the year after holding office. (Occasionally the Senate would recommend a particular appointment.) If the participants could not agree, assignments might be made by lot (*sortitio*). Tubero made no application (*non adesset*; cf. 17, *aditus*), even (*etiam*) pled illness. It is not clear whether and when an excuse of ill health was necessary to explain one's lack of participation at certain functions, or merely courteous. Possibly Cicero's absence (*Att.* 13.13.1) from the inauguration of M. Appuleius to the College of Augurs in early 45 required such an excuse; see Shackleton Bailey 3, 5:310. When C. Aquilius Gallus used ill health as his reason not to stand for consul of 63, Cicero (*Att.* 1.1.1) mocked him (Shackleton Bailey 3, 1:290–91) as a loser whose excuse would be superfluous. *Phil.* 1.28, *nec erit iustior in senatum non veniendi morbi causa quam mortis,* offers problems of interpretation beyond that of whether such an excuse for not attending a Senate meeting is required or expected; see Shackleton Bailey 2 ad loc. In judicial cases the accused could get an adjournment on grounds of illness. This was open to abuse especially in political cases, where postponement could be extended until the accused entered a magistracy and gained immunity. The *lex Tullia de ambitu* (63) may have dealt with this loophole, but the manner in which it did is not clear.

etiam impediretur: *Etiam* generally qualifies the following word, but here seems to qualify the whole clause; so *magnum etiam vinclum,* below.

excusare: "to plead an excuse" used absolutely, perhaps justified by the plain style. The object would be, e.g., "ill health" or "age," not "himself." Passive infinitive not possible.

necessitudines: not limited to kinship by blood or marriage (*affinitas*); see on 1, *propinquus*. The reader may ask why Cicero chose this moment for the further revelation of his intimacy.

domi una: We know something of Cicero's early Roman education; but there is no reference to L. Tubero. *Domi* is mentioned largely for contrast with *militiae*.

contubernales: in the Social War in 89, when Cicero served both under Pompey's father and Sulla, the future dictator. It was precisely in these shared early experiences that adult social and political relationships were formed. They might count for little in a courtroom situation; but even after this speech the friendship of these two men endured; see 1, *propinquus*.

magnum etiam vinclum: main clause, with verb (form of *esse*) omitted in plain exposition (so *Marc.* 15, *id minus mirum*), although *magnum* is emphatically placed. For *etiam* see 21.

studiis: may be educational, professional, or political.

quidam: known by name, but not mentioned. Pompey (see 22) and M. Marcellus have been suggested.

ita . . . ita: Bipartite, asyndetic anaphora reflects the intensity of the pressure brought to bear; see on *Marc.* 24, *tanto . . . tanto*, and *Marc.* 22, *tam . . . tam*.

sanctissimum nomen: In (temporarily) making Tubero's case, Cicero evokes a strong, emotional argument.

etiamsi . . . sentiret: The mood is necessitated by the construction, the tense by the sequence. The result is an ambiguity, artificially resolved in English by the choice between "even if" (potential) and "even though" (conceded fact). Cicero could, if he wished, have insisted upon the reality of a fact; see on 14, *quod et fecimus*. . . .

verborum . . . pondus: The metaphor is used at *De. Or.* 2.73; weight "of authority" and "of a name" at *Verr.* 2.1.144 and *Verr.* 2.4.1, respectively.

22

amplissimi viri: apparently Pompey.

vel potius paruit: a rhetorical *correctio*, as below (cf. on 3, *imperium*, and, for another kind, *Marc.* 26, *immo vero*). It is frequent in the treatises and letters but makes its first appearance in the speeches in 56, found once each at *Sest.* 39, *Balb.* 51, *Cael.* 69; then single appearances at *Planc.* 97 and *Milo.* 30 before these three concentrated usages in *Pro Ligario.* In the *Philippics* Cicero feels comfortable using it no fewer than sixteen times. *Paruit* may entail unwilling submission; *cessit* includes the possibility of becoming persuaded (however reluctantly). Note the position of the two verbs. The less enthusiastic he was at the outset, the more inexplicable his later adherence to Pompey would seem.

una . . . una: Whatever Tubero's reluctance to serve it, the cause was his; i.e., he embarked on his assignment at more or less the same time as other Pompeian senatorial designees. The paronomasia of *una* (ablative, reinforcing *cum* and nominative, modifying *causa*) ties Tubero inextricably to the general situation of pro-Pompeian officials. After the last sentence, *causa* must just be the circumstance of embarking for a province at the outbreak of war.

iam occupatam: i.e., already taken over and being administered (by Varus). Laughton treats the participle as predicative "when it has already been seized" (Laughton 2, 60), although he says that there is a prima facie case that participles modifying objects of prepositions will be attributive. As an attributive, it describes the fait accompli Tubero came upon.

hinc: logical, not local.

vel potius: See above and 23; this correction goes directly to the real motive: the pursuit of a vendetta. *Vel potius* are not usually separated.

voluisse: used absolutely, as an abstract verbal noun: "If you are charging volition, your volition in this matter is no less indictable than anyone else's"; cf. *Phil.* 2.29, *si voluisse interfici Caesarem crimen sit.*

arcem: in the military sense, the most impregnable; not like Rome as *lux orbis terrarum et arx omnium gentium* (*Cat.* 4.11).

natam ad bellum . . . gerendum: a colorful participial phrase. It is only partially correct to gloss *natam* with "suited by nature" and refer to the geography of the province. "Destined at or by birth to . . ." is the sense at *Phil.* 6.9, *Brutum . . . vestraeque libertati natum, non otio suo; Har. Resp.* 6, *ut P. ille Scipio natus mihi videtur ad interitum exitiumque Carthaginis, qui illam . . . quasi fatali adventu solus avertit, sic T. Annius* [sc. Milo] *ad illam pestem* [i.e., *Clodium*] *comprimandam . . . natus esse videtur et quasi* *divino munere donatus rei publicae.* See Marc. 25, *natus esses.* Preceded by an apposition, the phrase interrupts the syntax of the period and for that reason had a strongly circumstantial flavor.

aliquem: highly indefinite; cf. *Marc.* 26, *aliquid amplius, Marc.* 32, *aliquid . . . sapientiae,* and (vs. *quivis*) at 10. This raises a question: why did the Tuberones hold Ligarius responsible, rather than Varus? Cf. Caes. *BC* 1.31.3: "He (Varus) kept Tubero, who was coming to Utica with a fleet, from the port and the town and did not allow his son, who was sick, to set foot on land, but forced him to raise anchor and leave that place." The answer is perhaps that Varus, still actively anti-Caesarian and fighting in Spain, was merely less available for revenge.

atque . . . tamen: a new argument inspired by *aliquis,* now used as if in quotation marks; so *"aliquid"* at *Deiot.* 35.

certe: "at any rate," the minimum concession, even if his *imperium* was not valid and the *fasces,* the emblem of *imperium,* improperly acquired.

23

quoquo . . . habet: Cf. 28, *ut . . . habet. Illud* is in antithesis to *haec.*

querela: The question has become one not of a criminal charge, but of a personal complaint. Except in a judicial context, the importance of a *querela* should not be underestimated; see *Marc.* 21. Unjust or insulting treatment, of which a man may complain, is one of the causes for *dolor* (see at *Marc.* 1) which can start vendettas or wars. See on 25, *acceptae iniuriae,* and the stronger exploitation of Tubero's personal motives at 29.

"recepti . . . sumus": The fact that the complaint is expressed in a direct quotation does not mean that either Tubero so expressed himself.

quid: sc. *facturi fuisti,* as at 24. Periphrastic future apodoses, even of unreal conditions, usually take the indicative (Woodcock, 200), as in the following lines, because the future involves potentiality. "What did you really intend to do, if the opportunity had been given?"

Caesarine . . . Caesarem: Paronomasia underlines the opposition of the future participles.

vide . . . Caesar: abrupt change of addressee (not quite the polite imperative of 6 or 8, nor quite as excited as the repeated *vide* at 6). Having positioned his opponent on the horns of a dilemma, Cicero calls on Caesar to observe. The dilemma is a figure Cicero often uses to demonstrate his own rhetorical cleverness and embarrass his opponent; see Craig 1. Often he goes on to draw the consequences of each (unacceptable) possibility in parallel clauses. For a more embellished instance of the figure see 29; here, no second *si* clause is forthcoming. Although on the surface apparently critical, the rhetorical stance of blaming Caesar for the consequences of his goodness is sufficiently complimentary.

licentiae . . . audaciae: The genitives depend on *quid* and frame the indirect question; *nobis tua* in central collocation. The position of *audaciae*, preceded by *potius,* achieves a resolved double cretic clausula. *Licentia* has a sense of "excessive freedom" appropriate here.

sorsque: See on 21.

ipsum te: Reversal of normal order of pronoun + intensifier stresses the intensifier.

cuius . . . interfuit: relative clause + indicative, with clear, but muted, adversative implications; see 15, *cum . . . vellent.* The illogical construction with the genitive comes about by analogy with *refert,* where *re* is the ablative of *res* and the genitive depends on it or a possessive adjective agrees, e.g., *mea refert.*

non dubitabo: potentially as discomforting to Caesar as is the dilemma to Tubero. *Senatus . . . sorsque* constitute binding authority, and it would ill suit Caesar as imperator or dictator to disapprove. But Cicero is showing off and, in this strategy, wants Caesar to appreciate the fact. A major function of the dilemma is to make a fool of one's opponent. There is no need to demonstrate the weakness of the second alternative. When he gets through exploiting the dilemma, he abruptly invalidates it at 24.

grata . . . probata: a coda handsomely articulated with the strong preposition of *non* and the collocation of the verbs, at the expense of creating a dactylic clausula. On the other hand, the language in this context is insistently neutral and colorless: *cuius id eum . . . eius . . . ea res.*

tibi: For the dative see on *Marc.* 3, *intellectum est.*

24

sed iam hoc: abrupt transition, as at 20; this tactic, used elsewhere (e.g., at *Verr.* 2.5.11), is similar to a *praeteritio* in that he continues to work the possibilities of this alleged excuse through 25. The suggestion that the audience may become offended is also commonplace, e.g., *Cat.* 1.1.

ultra . . . quam: There is no similar usage of the phrase in the speeches, although it does appear in philosophical works, e.g., *Tusc.* 1.16, *ultra enim quo progrediar quam ut veri similia videam non habeo,* "I have no way to get beyond seeing the reflections of truth."

veniebatis: As with the same word in the next section, the imperfect is inceptive and does not assure successful completion of the action (hence *imperfectum*).

igitur: not for logical conclusion, but ostensibly to resume narrative after digression in 22.

provinciam . . . infensam: another extended, ominous epithet for Africa, as in 22. *In Africam,* although not necessary, should not be deleted. Cicero's point is that there was every reason to avoid Africa. In contrast to *natam ad bellum . . . gerendum* above, this phrase seems more purely descriptive.

unam ex omnibus maxime: Cf. *De Or.* 1.99, *unum ex omnibus ad dicendum maxime natum.* When *unus* means "first," or "number one," as Nepos is *unus Italorum (Cat.* 1), it usually takes a partitive genitive; with the cardinal number, the partitive is expressed by *ex* (e.g., *unus ex militibus)* or *de.* As with the parallel, *maxime* may affect the expression.

huic victoriae . . . huic causae: The adjectives are emphatically demonstrative and point to Caesar; by a kind of hypallage = *huius.* If Juba is to be described as an enemy of Rome to whom Ligarius adhered, he will also be portrayed as strongly Pompeian.

in qua: relative clause added on, mentioning two dangers to Caesar, no verb. Juba's father had in 81 been helped to regain his throne by Pompey. Caesar, on the other hand, had supported Juba's enemies and had, according to Suetonius (*Div. Iul.* 71), physically assaulted him in Rome in 61. After the battle of Thapsus Juba was killed by one of his own slaves.

conventus: the community of Roman citizens living in a foreign location. Less formal, perhaps, than a *societas,* a corporation of Romans doing business in a province, they would still look to Roman provincial government for mutual protection and advantage. Although such associations are known to have been operating at Utica, Thapsus, and Hadrumetum, take this as genitive singular depending on *voluntas,* not a third subject, which would leave *voluntas* vaguely abstract. Cf. nontechnical use at *Deiot.* 5.

quaero: asyndeton and parataxis; a formal inquiry is begun; cf. 15, *hoc quaero.* Cicero portrayed the location as hostile to Caesar; now he places Tubero in it.

quid facturui fuistis?: *fuistis* as at 23; the question is direct.

quamquam: For sentence fragment see *Marc.* 27.

et prohibiti: Repetition of the participle is optional, here used to reinforce the insult by not forcing the modal modifier ("in a most insulting manner") to share the same verb that governs the infinitive. For his structural needs he might have used *idque,* as at 1, or *et quidem,* as at *Marc.* 29; cf. 30.

25

tulistis . . . detulistis: conscious paronomasia in parallel position.

acceptae iniuriae: This phrase, an example of the "*ab urbe condita* construction," like the ablative absolute, entails a transformation from nominal and phrasal to verbal and clausal; cf. on *Marc.* 3, *ex quo . . . gloria,* and (here) the quotation from Virgil cited just below.

querelam: See on 23 and Virg. *Aen.* 1.25ff., *causae irarum saevique dolores . . . spretaeque iniuria formae,* "the insult resulting from the fact that her beauty was disprized."

nempe ad eum: In this elenchus Cicero will answer his own obvious, but not rhetorical questions; cf. 7, *apud quem.*

cuius auctoritatem secuti: a logical inference. The identity of *cuius* is revealed only when Tubero makes his move.

veniebatis: *imperfectum* as in 24. Here Cicero is deliberately ambiguous. He uses the indicative to convey their lack of success in a condition that, by the apodosis, is unreal.

venissetis . . . venistis: strong antithesis in collocation of two verbs in chiastic constructions, with asyndeton between the sentences.

quae . . . querela: Note the bracketing of the clause with *quae . . . querela*, and the postponement of *ergo*, which gives force to the question.

a quo queramini: the conflation of two ways of marking an alleged cause. One would be to put it in the mouth of someone other than the speaker, in which case *querimini* would have been enough; the other, to use a subjunctive in the relative clause and give it a causal nuance: *a quo prohibiti sitis*. The latter occurs in *quod*-causal clauses, where the subjunctive means precisely "because, as someone else alleges. . . ." If such a clause actually has a verb of speaking, that verb should be in the indicative; but Cicero often uses *quod diceret*; cf. 25, *possim dicere* vs. *dicam*. Cicero has now defined the charge against Ligarius as preventing the Tuberones from waging war on Caesar.

atque: major shift, returning to the false argument he attributed to Tubero and appeared to dispose of at 23, *non, si tibi grata fuisset, esset adprobata*. There is impatience in Cicero's voice: *quidem* ("at any rate"), *vel* ("for all I care), *si vultis* (cf. *Marc*. 25 and *Marc*. 27), *per me licet* in parataxis with subjunctive; so *Marc*. 28, *oportet*.

26

constantiam: not quite *fides*—the virtue of adherence to contractual obligations (see *Marc*. 14, *grati . . . memoria*, and *Deiot*. 1, *fides*)—but a disposition.

ut probo: to avoid ambiguity created by the need to use the subjunctive in all *quamvis* clauses; so 14, and 21, *etiamsi aliter sentiret*, and 13, *sicuti est*.

virtutem . . . laudari: Cicero made Caesar suffer for his integrity at 23, asserting that the dictator could not have approved Tubero's hypothetical defection to him. By 46 Caesar had apparently lost some patience with the

African opposition; so *Fam.* 6.13.3, written to Ligarius, expressed hope but explained why his intercession had not yet succeeded.

nescio an melius: *correctio;* a term previously used in context is repeated as the object of *dico,* before being replaced by a more appropriate word. A spirited *immo* or *mehercule* may precede the preferred alternative (*die dico? immo hora atque etiam puncto temporis*) or, as here, a more tentative, considered suggestion; but note the force of asyndeton. *Nescio an,* like *Marc.* 29, *haud scio an,* may be thought of as a clause frozen as an adverb, but if so it is always found, as is *forsitan,* with a deliberative subjunctive. All share with *fortasse* the sense of accompanying a tentative assertion that really expects general agreement.

quotus quisque: As *optimus quisque* = "each man who is best" becomes "all the best men," so "each man in what [small] number" becomes "how few men."

ut . . . rediret: The noun clause is in apposition with, or explanatory of, *istud.*

quibus . . . eas ipsas: a very definite identification; cf. 20, *quibus . . . easdem. Partes* refers to a character or role in a play, then a principal, perhaps a "function(ary)"; the preposition *a* treats it as human agency or personification. The absurdity of Tubero's blind loyalty is underlined by the meticulous description (including repetition of antecedent in relative clause) of what he did.

non . . . receptus . . . -que . . . reiectus: similar to the movement of 25, *et prohibiti* (see comments there); but instead of mere repetition of the participle, Cicero varies with a negative restatement in order to make *etiam cum crudelitate* stronger.

magni . . . viri: The partitive genitive (see 28, *erat . . . amentis*), introducing a clause of characteristic, sounds encomiastic as it moves past the paired ablative phrases to an anaphoric tricolon. The sarcasm comes from the contrast of this nobility with the idiocy of what Tubero in fact did. Genitives are predicate, even without *est,* and the expected complementary infinitive is suppressed. For *cuiusdam* see 5, *incredibilem quendam.*

de suscepta causa: See *Deiot.* 42, *causam omnem suscipit.* This and the following participle, as attributives, are a compendious alternative to relatives; cf. 27, *causam . . . quam secutus esset.*

<h1 style="text-align:center">27</h1>

ut . . . cetera: a hypothetical, concessive clause followed by a relative clause denying the premise; for *ut* in unreal conditions see K&S, 2.2:25. *Cetera* awaits *hoc.* The relative is practically parenthetical; see *Marc.* 13, *quorum frequentiam.*

enim: We are led to expect a further explanation of "no danger could deflect"; instead we get a justification for Tubero's determination to serve Pompey in Africa.

honos . . . ingenium: Whenever Cicero trots out praises for L. Tubero, a sharpish blow can be expected; see at 2.

praecipuum: The word and its construction with the genitive is highly unusual in Cicero. Tubero was an optimate; his legitimacy in the post denied him by Varus was beyond question.

iusto cum imperio: not quite accurate; the Comitia Curiata should have ratified the appointments (so Caes. *BC* 1.6). But the greater the legitimacy, the more forbearing of insult Tubero appears.

hinc prohibitus: a paean to obstinacy. Repeated pattern of phrasing enhances the unwavering banality of the code of the Tuberones. The adjectives all refer to his relationship to Pompey and his cause.

non . . . ne: Antithesis is abbreviated, and so intensified, by omission of *venit* in the negative half of the articulation throughout the tricolon.

aliquam: unidentified, "at random"; see on 22, *aliquem.*

in . . . venit . . . iniuria: Three prepositional modifiers are disposed around the one-word predicate, two before it, leaving the twice-modified third and its pathetic relative clause its own space. *(Re)iectus iniuria* gives a double cretic clausula.

28

nihil commovisset: We do not know with what sympathy Pompey welcomed Tubero or how much satisfaction he could have given him, especially since Varus was mastering the threat of Caesar's lieutenant, Curio.

languidiore: Cf. Caes. *BG* 7.27, *languidius in opere versari.* The comparative would have been ironic even without *credo.*

tantum modo: The suggestion of moral withdrawal is made in simple, nominal sentences, encouraging the adoption of this explanation.

in praesidiis: on active duty, but in defensive lines, as at 30.

an: initially, always raises the diction, suggesting a strongly preferred alternative. The construction involves an anacoluthon, since there is no main verb. Some editors assume a lacuna, something lost in all the manuscripts, but the articulation is effective as an aposiopesis, the intentional omission of a thought that is terrible, frightening, or threatening (see *Marc.* 17, *nihil amplius dico*); content of the rhetorical omission can be reconstructed from *vincendi studio tenebamur.*

ut fit: Universal generalization precludes denial; parenthesis further corners Tubero.

nec in vobis magis: as if in the *ut* clause there had been a dative *omnibus.*

enim: explains *reliquis.* Cicero's admission reiterates the universality of the reaction he attributes to his opponent. See on *Marc.* 24, *animorum ardore et armorum.*

equidem: subjective; with the same confidence with which he adduced his own case (6), he describes his motive and experience, but quite differently from there or at *Marc.* 14–15. What was there dutiful resignation and at 6 an unapologetic admission of his allegiance is here presented as a most enthusiastic belligerence (an attitude he extends to the Tuberones).

semper: Between the (objective) genitive and its governing noun, the adverb is in attributive position = "I was a constant advocate of peace," although *auctor* (from *augeo*) is in any case verbal.

sed tum sero: dramatic ellipsis of *fuissem*; "I would have been too late then, if I had continued to be a proponent of peace"; see on *Marc.* 15, *id minus mirum. Tum* sets a limit on his designation as *pacis semper auctor.* For *sero* = "too late" see *Phil.* 2.24, *cum ... Pompeius ... sero ... ea sentire coepisset, quae multo ante provideram.*

erat ... amentis: In constructions with predicative genitive, the indicative is preferred to potential subjunctive even when unfulfillment is implied. Partitive genitive generalizes; see 16.

videres: The force of the second-person is not to single out Tubero, but to generalize the experience (see *Deiot.* 4, *arguare*); but the usage is especially apt here, where Cicero stresses the universality of a response with which he wants Tubero to identify himself. So *omnes* and the first person verbs.

omnes inquam: at first seems to bring the point to a rhetorically circular finish, echoing *omnes enim.* But *tu* is contrasted to *omnes* in stressed position and underlined by *certe,* unexpected because unanticipated, and abrupt in ellipsis. After defining Tubero's position (as fashioned by Cicero) as universal, Cicero singles it out as unique, and uniquely unforgivable.

locum: figurative and used principally to give an explicit antecedent to *ubi.*

veneras: Between the variants *veneras* and *venisses,* the former, in which Cicero challenges the listener to make the valid causal inference from an indicative clause, is more subtle. So at 23, *cuius ... interfuit.* Cicero can and does use indicatives in relative clauses with circumstantial potentiality; see on *Marc.* 31, *ingratus ... civis qui.*

ubi: = *ut ibi* with subjunctive of consequence or result.

pereundum: For the force of the impersonal gerundive see on 1, *confitendum.*

nisi vicisses: An American political conservative, recalling the admonition that if he voted for a certain candidate (later defeated), the war in Vietnam would be escalated, remarked, "I did, and it was." Tubero did not win, nor was he ruined. There is a tacit reminder of the generosity of Caesar and the implication that Tubero, beyond others, had been in need of it.

quamquam: The sentence fragment relegates to the irrelevant past the rationale for belligerence it attributes to Tubero. That unswerving Pompeian is now enjoying Caesar's peace.

se res habet: For this idiom see 23.

non dubito: the subjective cast; the speaker takes the role of a critic or commentator. He represents, in hindsight, Tubero's view—or what Cicero imagines it to be.

hanc . . . illi: The demonstratives, strongly felt, reinforce a temporal antithesis begun with *nunc*. The position of the verb reflects what its meaning conveys: only here in the speeches does *anteponere* separate the accusative from the dative noun; *Marc.* 20 comes closest.

29

non dicerem: Imperfect subjunctive in initial protasis creates the expectation of a condition uncomplimentary to Tubero. Balance of *vos constantiae vestrae* (against *ego*) and *Caesarem benefici sui* sets the charge of ingratitude in high relief. The second alternative is not to be taken seriously.

nunc: after the unreal situation in *non dicerem,* as at 16; cf. 9, *sed hoc quaero.*

utrum . . . an: Cicero exploits his adversary's logical inconsistency, using a dilemma calculated to make himself look clever and his opponent inept; see 23. For maximum effect, he makes his opponent respond. Cicero had earlier (at 23 and 25), with different force, distinguished private complaints from crimes against the state.

videte: urgent, but speciously solicitous; less formal than *nolite* + infinitive; see *Marc.* 26.

vestris . . . suis: The tacit assumption of this neat antithesis is that Ligarius is merely Tubero's enemy. For the bracketing see 16, *suam . . . tuam.*

itaque: With debater's casuistry Cicero dismisses the notion that he is defending Ligarius' case. In the logical movement, the sentence connective links *cum ignoverit suis* to *referri volo.* The underlying thought is: "Tubero got caught on the horns of a dilemma by prosecuting Ligarius; I shall not make the mistake of defending him." The two-part rhetorical question becomes in sense subordinated in this paratactic presentation. *Tibi,* singular, is the only verbal indication that he has shifted his address to Caesar.

de eius facto: See on *Marc.* 34, *hoc tuo facto.*

unam summam: a "main point," as at *Phil.* 2.32, *haec summa est conclusionis meae.* The following genitives are appositional.

vel: as if searching for the right word, or feeling that all three words could be used interchangeably; cf. *Marc.* 1. Caesar rarely used the word *clementia,* although at least one coin was struck with the slogan CLEMENTIA CAESARIS. It may have been raised to the level of a slogan for Caesar's policy by Cicero himself; for Caesar's earlier penchant for leniency see the Introduction, section 2. Skepticism about the sincerity of Caesar's clemency existed in antiquity and has survived until today; see Weinstock, 233–43.

30

causas . . . multas: Cicero begins a discussion, highly theoretical but not ponderous, of strategies possible in the conduct of this defense. He assumes an informal, professional relationship with Caesar, playing to the dictator's competence and experience as an orator. It has been noted that Cicero, defending the case on its merits, would have had either to deny the activities of Ligarius, which he could not do, or to demonstrate their correctness, which, under the circumstances, would not be prudent. But the fact is that Cicero has used arguments both to deny or skirt the worst of Ligarius' anti-Caesarian activities in Africa and to justify at least the early involvement of his client in the Civil War. Whatever the forms of defense abstractly outlined in books on rhetoric, attacking the opposition and its advocates had been a large item in Cicero's practical repertoire from *Pro Roscio Amerino* to *Pro Caelio.*

   Parataxis, often in conspicuously coordinated constructions, dominates this passage. It gives it a sense of unembellished directness and informality; see 31, *preces.*

Caesar: The vocative directly after *causas* creates a pause; see 1, *non auditum.* Cicero insists on a strong antithesis between pleading a defense at law and what he claims to be doing.

multas: stressed by separation and unusual order of adjective and noun. *Multus* typically precedes its noun, as does *magnus*; but see on 7, *ex parte magna,* and *Att.* 7.3.3, *ex parte magna tibi adsentior.* In hyperbaton the separated adjective usually precedes, creating a grammatical suspense for the noun to follow. When the adjective follows the noun, it calls special attention to itself and may have the effect of surprise; see on *Marc.* 3, *fructum . . . maximum*. The best study of the phenomenon is in Norden 3, pp. 391–404.

equidem: a limiting particle virtually always referring in Cicero's speeches to first-person, e.g., *Deiot.* 39, *laboro equidem regis Deiotari causa*. Its placement next to *tecum* insists on the close professional relationship between the speaker and the man he addresses. It prepares for *certe*. As Quintilian (7.4.17–18) says, a *deprecatio* has a limited forum.

causas dicere: of defenses. At *Deiot.* 7, in a similar attempt to create a professional empathy, Cicero reminds Caesar of the many cases he pled in defense of clients. At the very least, these words imply an agreeable memory of earlier times and common causes. A variant reading, *et quidem*, allowing a pause after *multas* and taken closely with *tecum*, "and, in fact, together with you," does not imply the same frequency of joint ventures.

tecum . . . te . . . tuorum: Pronouns keep the presence of Caesar central to this argument. Establishing a bond of collegiality with the judge, never out of place, has a special function here. With Caesar as judge and, in a sense, plaintiff, Cicero's position would be unmanageable (he addresses this problem at *Deiot.* 4). He needs to create for Caesar a nonjudicial persona amenable to a plea for mercy. A straightforward, unironic *deprecatio* might hold little weight with a man of Caesar's forensic sophistication (see on 32), so Cicero highlights his thought process and discusses explicitly, as a problem in strategy, what he is about to do. He compliments Caesar by appearing to share his problem with him.

Caesar's skill as an orator is variously attested; but we know of only a few speeches, none made as a colleague of Cicero. Cicero appears to praise Caesar's abilities at *Brut.* 251ff. (but see the Introduction, section 2) and here, which may in part be responsible for Quintilian's endorsement (10.1.114): *C. vero Caesar, si foro tantum vacasset, non alius ex nostris contra Ciceronem nominaretur*, with a proviso that may have developed entirely from our passage. In Tac. *Dial.* 21.5 Aper, the *laudator temporis acti*, also withholds unqualified praise, attributing the difference between Caesar's potential and achievement to the direction of his career. It was a prosecution in 77 that established Caesar as an orator. The speech was still being read with pleasure in Tacitus' time (*Dial.* 34.7, where the context deals with the young age at which Republican orators began their careers).

Caesar's plea for the lives of the Catilinarian conspirators in 63 is known through the speech reported, but also composed, by Sallust (*Cat.* 51).

ratio honorum: No political office required pleading in the courts, but defense advocacy, if effective, was a way to do favors and make friends, two activities extremely basic to Roman politics. Caesar spoke in behalf of the Achaeans against C. Antonius in 76; and Suetonius (*Div. Iul.* 71) singles out an oration in behalf of a young noble client in 62. On the eve of his departure for Gaul in 58 Caesar made speeches in the Senate defending himself against charges brought by the praetors, C. Memmius and L. Domitius. Then absence from Rome brought a necessary silence. "Brutus" claims at *Brut.* 251 that he never had the opportunity to hear Caesar speak. For the remains of and evidence for Caesar's oratory see Malcovati, 383–97.

certe numquam: contrasts strongly with *multas.* The ellipsis of the verb, *egi,* is an indication of the informality of Cicero's tone here and elsewhere in this passage; see *multas equidem* above and on *ad iudicem* below. Cicero frequently uses *certe* and *fortasse* (see below) with an irony that somewhat reverses their meanings.

ignoscite: language, especially when so tersely stated, redolent of posturing in Roman Comedy, where indulgent fathers and wayward sons are stereotypic characters and professional "intercessors" are available if loyal slaves and friends fail in their appeals to familial authority's better nature. So Ter. *Phorm.* 140, *ad precatorem adeam credo qui mihi sic oret: "nunc amitte quaeso hunc; ceterum posthac si quicquam, nil precor,"* "I'd better go to a *precator,* who can plead for me like this: 'This time let him go, I beg you. But, if ever he should do anything (*posthac si quicquam*), I'll not plead in his behalf.'" (For *precator* see Ter. *Heaut.* 976.) At Ter. *Eun.* 852 the same formula for pleading forgiveness appears in first-person, but in a different context, although the speaker is impersonating another character: *unam hanc noxiam amitte; si aliam admisero, occidito,* "Forgive this one offense; if I ever commit another, kill me."

erravit: Cicero uses the same word in mitigation of Pompeians at *Marc.* 2 and of Deiotarus at *Deiot.* 10, *errore communi lapsus est,* asserting lack of malevolence as he does for Ligarius below: *totus animo et studio tuus.*

non putavit: denial of intent. Aelius Donatus, an ancient commentator on

Terence, citing this passage at *Andr.* 113, says that *putare* refers to one who erred *ex simplicitate pectoris.*

non fecit: phrasing somewhat more formal. Denials are issued in pairs, each set joined by some artifice in parallelism, by anaphora of *non* in the first, and paronomasia of *falsi* and *fictum* in the second. Admission can be artless; defense needs some help.

dic: (like *fac*) followed by accusative + infinitive introduces a supposition or assumption. Whereas *fac* is found in a variety of speeches, *dic* is so used only in *Rosc. Com.,* but there several times in vigorous cross-examinations. In each case there, however, the assumption is immediately repudiated. The tone of that speech is theatrically colloquial, redolent of Roman Comedy. Axer, 17–19, demonstrating that Cicero in his defense of a distinguished actor himself adopted a number of theatrical personae and scenarios from Roman comedy, points to lively dialogues, imperatives, and syntax reflecting everyday speech. This construction is the more idiomatic and pressing equivalent of a protasis of a conditional clause. One effect is to produce parataxis. English idiom allows coordinate construction, "Do that, and you'll be sorry," but always with "and," whereas Latin insists on asyndeton. See *Deiot.* 40, *propone . . . dabis,* and *Phil.* 1.18, *quaere acta Gracchi; leges Semproniae proferentur,* "Ask for the *acta* of Gracchus, and the Sempronian laws will be produced."

iudicem esse: After his opening plea for mercy Cicero has had much to say in mitigation, if not in defense of, his client's activities. But for this "disinterested" discussion on the best conduct of the case, Cicero creates a courtroom scenario in which Caesar is asked, for sake of argument, to play the role of a judge of the facts, as if it were assumed that he will not remain in that role. Cicero fabricates a scene for a hypothetical trial.

quaere: Imperatives bracket the construction; cf. 22, *cessit . . . paruit* and 31, *sperandi . . . deprecandi.* The word order is not casual, although the effect is not the same in all three cases. In the other two, the antitheses are highlighted. In the latter case, the relationship is emphasized by the echo of the first word in the last. Here Cicero enthusiastically urges Caesar's participation in the charade.

in praesidiis: so 28, with emphasis on defense, vs. 10, *isdem in armis fui.*

taceo: almost an aposiopesis. Latin expects a future in what is virtually the apodosis of a supposition, e.g., "Ask on whose side he was, and I shall. . . . But I say nothing." See *dic* above, and K&S, 2.2:164–65.

etiam apud iudicem: that is, acting as a judge (sc. *etiamsi iudex esses*). Cicero pursues the hypothetical nature of this scenario. He also suggests that a real defense was not wholly (note *fortasse*) denied him by the facts of the case. Through a transparent *praeteritio*, he produces, as lines of argument (attenuated by participles, asyndeton, etc.), some of the points he had in fact made earlier at 2–3.

relictus: i.e., by the departure of Considius.

oppressus: The choice of words makes Ligarius a victim.

ad iudicem sic: sc. *loquerer* (not, as some ancients supplied, *agi soleo*)— elliptically abrupt return to the distinction between parent and judge. Cicero sustains the light touch; so *certe numquam* above. Not expecting Caesar to miss the *praeteritio*, he reminds him that this is abstract discourse about a theoretical defense. *Deprecatio* is the announced strategy; and Cicero will plead, like some *precator*, before Caesar as before a parent. Nowhere in the speech is Cicero's language so abject as in this hypothetical, histrionic scene.

confugio . . . peto . . . oro: The Roman advocate puts his own *auctoritas* on the line as an intercessionary; see *Marc.* 2, *non illius solum sed etiam meam vocem*. The tricolon is composed of sample pleas; it is unlikely that they would have been uttered together.

opem . . . spem: a commonplace antithesis. The hope Caesar offers becomes a subtheme in what follows: *sperandi, spes*. Caesar as the hope for the future of Rome (see *Marc.* 2) provides a strong rhetorical pivot: the rationale for the serious employment of a *deprecatio*. Cicero abandons the scenario he has begun of a desperate last resort on the part of a defense lawyer and considers theoretically, with Caesar, its efficacy as strategy. The point is made by sober ellipses; in the second member, where symmetry is suggested, after anaphoric *si*, by *plurimi* in antithesis to *nemo*, we expect something like *licet etiam mihi hoc modo dicere*. Instead Cicero shifts the burden to Caesar and moves from general circumstances to the particular.

31

an: openly aggressive and indignant; for *an* see on 5. Cicero has got caught up in his own fiction and is reacting; but which persona of Cicero is it? And how is he being controlled by the speaker?

sperandi . . . deprecandi: Gerunds emphasize the antithetical cast of the sentence by bracketing position. Quintilian (5.10.92) cites this as an *argumentum ex difficiliore,* with the sense that it should not be more difficult for Ligarius to expect pardon than it was for Cicero. But the argument is more complex with the text of α, an *argumentum ex genere ad speciem.* Quintilian adds: "if everybody is eligible" (see on *altero,* below), "so is Ligarius."

de Ligario: Some manuscripts and Quintilian read the dative, but the contrast is between the two gerundives as they apply to and concern the advocate.

causa non erit: In this expression with *an,* the supposition being questioned is put vividly in the indicative—though not always; Quintilian (see just above), with most manuscripts, reads the deliberative subjunctive when citing our passage.

mihi apud te: Collocation of references to the advocate and the judge is crucial, as in 30, *egi . . . equidem tecum.* See, too, 6, *quanta lux . . . mihi apud te dicenti oboriatur.*

altero: often contrasts one person with all others taken as a class. So Plaut. *Amphit.* 1046, *quis me Thebis alter vivit miserior; Off.* 1.4, *nulla . . . vitae pars, . . . neque si tecum agas quid, neque si cum altero* (that is, anyone but yourself) *contrahas, vacare officio potest.* If Caesar's position as judge and injured party is complex, so is that of Cicero, recipient of Caesar's clemency and now seeking the same consideration for Ligarius. *Etiam,* qualifying *pro altero,* emphasizes the absurdity of Ligarius' singular exclusion.

quamquam: The speed and ease with which Cicero drops lines of reasoning should be noted; see at 24 and *Marc.* 27. No argument is worth more than the effect it achieves; once that effect is gained, Cicero has no further use for it. After all his posturing about the appropriate oratorical technique, Cicero shifts to an extrarhetorical consideration.

causae: a valid, argued defense, the "case" he might logically make; see on 10 and what follows here.

in eorum studiis: not limited to formal oratory, but covering other efforts, petitions and intercessions, by men close to Caesar, such as Pansa. The unique character of the present engagement, in which the sole judge of the case is also the only man in Rome who can grant the pardon requested, as well as the victorious leader of the side against which Ligarius fought, comes close to surfacing here. (A discreet reproach to Caesar on this ground has been noticed in Cicero's earlier words (30, *dic te . . . iudicem esse*); see R&E ad loc. and on *etiam pro altero* above.) Almost every decision Caesar made in this period would have political and social implications and therefore be subject to extrajudicial advice and special pleading by those around him.

tui necessarii: refers back to *eorum,* antecedent of *qui.* A genitive plural phrase, after *eorum* or anywhere else, would have been cumbersome. The nominative phrase, in final position and apposition to *qui,* may seem awkward, but it has the effect of impressing upon Caesar (partly by position and double cretic clausula) that Ligarius' supporters include Caesar's intimates. We do not know whether any insider besides Pansa intervened in behalf of Ligarius.

vidi: subjective, and speaking to their relationship. Cicero can analyze Caesar as judge (and "parent"). But he holds in suspense what he will assert to be crucial to Caesar's decision. *Nec . . . nec* above, having already created the anticipation of a positive assertion, are not resolved until *causas.* Cf. the suspense achieved at *Deiot.* 4, a statement of Cicero's resolved fears.

spectares: The indirect question with its dependent *cum* clause is the first object of the predicate; *causas . . . gratiosiores esse,* to which the indirect question is a descriptive appositive, finally names the criterion Cicero attributes to Caesar's good judgment, the expected object of *vidi.* Cicero acknowledges this quality in Caesar also at *Fam.* 6.6.8, *cedit multorum iustis et officio incensis, non inanibus aut invidiosis voluntatibus.*

cum . . . laborarent: a purely temporal clause, attracted into subjunctive. The verb regularly describes oratorical exertions.

alicuius: No one special is in mind, as at 27, *aliquam.*

causas: the circumstances or considerations that motivate. Having referred, hyperbolically, to important supporters of Ligarius, Cicero dismisses their importance, however familiar they may be to Caesar; on *necessarius* see 1. The underlying principle is blameless, even noble; but also necessary. Unlike Marcellus, Ligarius was not well connected; so *quam tuus esset* below.

apud te rogantium: The use of the active participle genitive substantivized (i.e., not modifying a noun) with a verbal construction is exceedingly rare; cf. *Marc.* 14, *civium pacem flagitantium.*

itaque: unemotional, expository transition which connects the preceding not with the following sentence, which is, so to say, subordinated in parataxis, but the one after that: "You are not influenced by the petitioner's relation to you. And so, although you are generous to your intimates, you are affected by the petitioner's relationship to his subject"; as at 29. See, too, on *Marc.* 20, *non enim.*

quidem: anticipating a contrast, as at 32, indicates that its predicate is concessive, and, in sense, subordinate to the next; see *Marc.* 28, *quae miretur . . . quae laudet*; so *Deiot.* 18, *Iovis . . . numquam . . . homines fortasse.* Owing to paratactic composition, *itaque* really introduces *video* in the next sentence, which after interruption, has the nuance of a *sed . . . tamen* movement. For *sed* after *quidem* see at 32.

ita (multa): modal adverb with *tribuis,* setting up the result clause; not quantitative with *multa,* as at *tam multa* below.

illi . . . qui tua; tu . . . qui illis: a compliment handsomely articulated.

video: subjective cast, as on *vidi* and *videantur* above, stressing the personal relationship, finally transferred to Caesar: *videas.*

preces: now instead of *voltus* (above), as less important than the *causa.* Cicero speaks shamelessly about the degree of sincerity in the professional advocate (*precator*)—presumably including himself.

Parataxis suggests straightforward, plain talk, reflected by lack of complexity in the syntax. Cicero develops an antithesis between Caesar's generosity to his friends and his sympathy for Ligarius' petitioners, predicting that Ligarius' advocates, even if they are not those intimates whom a man would naturally favor, will prevail because Caesar appreciates their sincerity. (See *Fam.* 6.12.2, *valent apud Caesarem non tam ambitiosae ro-gationes quam necessariae*). But Cicero slips in a second point: depth of emotion outweighs competence in expression. *Gratia*, influence with Caesar, will come from the personal interest of the undistinguished supporters of his undistinguished client, only because their cause is just.

ab iisque: *Iis* anticipates the relative. *-Que* is a strong connective of predicates; see *Marc.* 6, *easque detrahere*. It is still considered enclitic, although regularly not attached to prepositions.

iustissimum: predicative in hyperbaton. Cf. for effect 33, *hoc verissimum reperiatur*.

dolorem in petendo: remarkable word order for *iustissimum in petendo dolorem*. The rhythm, in this unadorned phrasing, is double trochee, as at *in dolorem,* below. The position of the gerund parallels the gerundive at 32, *in Ligario conservando*.

32

in ... conservando: *In* + ablative of gerundive or gerund = "in the process of . . ."; so 31, *Marc.* 20; cf. 38, *dando*.

quidem: contrasting, and in sense subordinating in the manner of an adversative clause. The number of Caesar's friends who support Ligarius is exaggerated by the use and placement of *multis* (*quidem* attaches itself to the pronoun but qualifies *multis*). Cicero hints that indulging Ligarius' supporters will have a broader political effect.

gratum facies: periphrasis as at *Phil.* 11.31, *regem Deiotarum patrem et regem Deiotarum filium . . . senatui populoque Romano gratum esse facturos.* The form *gratificari* is found five times in the speeches, twice in the fragmentary *Corn.* 1 (fr. 38 and 62 Puccioni). For another periphrasis with *facere* see *Marc.* 10, *reliquum facere*.

necessariis tuis: predicative with *multis*; phrase in final position as at 31.

quaeso, considera: both polite and, with anticipatory *hoc*, formally expository. *Quaeso* is more frequently postpositive to the imperative. In this position it is more strongly felt.

quod soles: comments on the enjoinder, *considera,* as at 2, *quod . . . op-*

tandum, and *Marc.* 23, *quod necesse fuit,* rather than standing in opposition to *hoc,* which anticipates the contents of the next sentence.

possum . . . proponere: Position shows that the verb is not merely the conditional auxiliary. This group exists and Cicero can, he claims, muster them to be added to Caesar's supporters.

Sabinos: The origins of the *gens Ligaria* were in Sabine country, where Caesar sought refuge after his marriage to a daughter of the populist Cinna incurred the anger of Sulla. The laudatory epithets of the Sabine population therefore serve two functions. In the previous section it was argued that emotional petitions, finally, will not move Caesar. Cicero now presents a highly emotional picture (so *maestitia* and *squalorem*) of the intimates of Ligarius. Caesar is urged to consider that their grief is traditional and real. Their political value, in any case, is immediate and also real. At *Clu.* 196 Cicero embellishes the character of municipal character witnesses.

probatissimos: See 33, *probatos.*

animadverte . . . vides: Caesar is drawn into the group of Ligarius' supporters, as encompassed by Caesar's stated view of allies and enemies. The construction, like 30, *dic . . . taceo,* is a vivid variant on paired imperative and future indicative. Note *horum . . . huius*; *maestitiam et dolorem*; and *lacrimas squaloremque.* The plain style allows effective and affecting articulation.

T. Brocchi: Ligarius' uncle.

non dubito: litotes: "I know very well." Relative is semi-independent in this tightly woven clause, but virtually parenthetical (*de quo* = *et de eo*); see *Marc.* 13, *quorum . . . frequentiam.*

33

quid . . . dicam: abrupt transition. He knows just what to say, and says it without undue politeness (note the absence of a polite verb in parataxis with the imperative, like 37, *obsecro* with *noli*); cf. *Marc.* 25, *omitte, quaeso.*

capite: highly figurative argument. *Caput* refers to Ligarius' existence as a Roman citizen with civil rights. The punishment of *capitis diminutio* (loss of civil rights) is effected by exile, as well as by death. For the brothers, no more is meant than a lifetime of deprivation. The argument of indissoluble brotherhood, adduced at 5, is expressed in a terse, explicitly balanced period, reinforced by the numbers: *unius . . . tres . . . tres . . . uno.*

exterminandi: an antonym to *retinere* but much stronger and more emotional. The chiastic balance suggests polarities more absolute than they need or are likely to be.

quam . . . si . . . moveant . . . moveat . . . moveat: Three sets of tricola, all anaphoric, lift the emotional tone of the argument, the thesis of which is clearly exaggerated: "any sort of exile is preferable." (The construction effects similar exaggeration at 10 and 34.)

illo . . . exsulante: another trailing ablative absolute (*Marc.* 2, *illo . . . distracto*), for a conditional protasis, in a syntactically suppressed style.

moveant . . . : This tricolon of initially placed verbs, asyndetically repeated in descending length of period, conveys (appropriately) more force than polish. It repeats the elements of the previous tricolon in reverse order.

germanitas: an uncommon, abstract noun for sake of brevity; see on 2, *legatione.*

valeat . . . vox . . . vicit: Cicero has been exhorting Caesar since 32, *animadverte.* The first approach was emotional; he now turns to advice on policy. Alliteration reinforces the elegance of the expression; see on *Marc.* 12.

audiebamus: subjective introduction to a quotation; at issue is not just Caesar's slogan but the expectations it has raised. The antithesis was doubtless neatly put by Caesar, as a politically brilliant riposte to Pompey's threat (alluded to at *Marc.* 18). Avoidance of absolute symmetry in the antithesis may be Cicero's. Here the words will have the convenient effect of tying Ligarius' supporters to Caesar by definition.

videsne . . . tecum fuisse: Editors all reject the final two words (absent in one family of manuscripts). *Videsne,* then, is like *vides* in 32. But if Caesar stands by his slogan, then all noncombatants are Caesarians, his men. A fortiori, these men, the friends and relatives of Ligarius, there present, known to Caesar and proved loyal, were on his side. If they are not that, they have little distinction. In fact one person named, L. Corfidius, had died unknown to Cicero. The gaffe was pointed out by T. Ligarius, and Cicero asked Atticus to have the name erased from all copies of the speech (so *Att.* 13.44.3). It remains in all manuscripts. A similar phenomenon occurs at *Phil.* 2.86. Cicero approved Atticus' suggestion that he change *quid indignius quam vivere eum* to *indignissimum est hunc vivere*. The manuscripts do not reflect the change.

-*Ne* with forms of *videre* tends, like *nonne,* to expect a positive response.

splendorem omnem: abstract nouns for the people described, as with the Sabines, above, and at *Marc.* 10, *auctoritas. Splendidus* describes their status as knights, with white togas and gold rings, not their present appearance.

adsunt: for the purpose of bearing witness in court; as at *Arch.* 8.

veste mutata: Dressing in *squalor* as a symbol of mourning in national crises real or imagined is an indication of ancient Roman histrionics. For other Ciceronian occurrences see *Sest.* 26, *Planc.* 21, 29, 87. In the higher orders it included replacing characteristic dress with plain clothes or turning the toga to conceal the purple stripe of senatorial office; see Dio 38.14, 56.31. Ordinary citizens might also stain their togas with ashes; hence *squalor* above.

probatos: Beyond the historically proven Sabines at the beginning of this section, the friends and relatives of Ligarius are now validated by Caesar's principle.

atque: an emphatic new consideration (see on *Marc.* 13)—actually an old one adduced to remind Caesar that neutrality had been dangerous (so *Marc.* 18). The sequence would be clearer if the subject had continued with these men, that is, "They were on your side and yet they endured our anger."

his . . . hos . . . his: repetition of the deictic demonstrative pronoun for emotional emphasis. See *Marc.* 27, *haec . . . hic . . . hoc.*

non nulli . . . minabantur: Manuscripts divide between first- and third-person. Either is possible with *non nulli. Minabamur* is probably a correction for the sake of concinnity and the anaphoric tricolon; see on 16, *coarguare.* The argument against treating *minabantur* as a later attempt to exculpate Cicero is that he gains no rhetorical advantage by including himself here. *Non nulli minabamur* would put him among the extremists to no purpose.

tuis suos: the most extreme liberty I have found with the reflexive. *Suos* is reflexive to *tuis,* which does not offend in third-person predications like *cuique sua fata sunt. Suos* is generalized from the case of Q. Ligarius alone.

quem ad modum cetera ... sic hoc: explicit balances in a coda; see on *Marc.* 11.

34

penitus perspicere posses: Alliteration in the Latin calls attention to itself, almost insisting on (with *penitus*), not just acknowledging, the unfathomable depths of their fraternal love. In rhetoric as in logic, an argument beginning with an unreal condition can assert anything in the apodosis. In this argument from probability, Cicero must first establish the premise of fraternal unity, as urged in 5. Although it is acknowledged that Caesar cannot confirm this of the Ligarii, three words clearly marked as second-person leave Caesar little doubt as to where he would stand.

an: This lively suggestion of an alternative does not encourage a considered response. The argument from probability is extended; the judge is now universal humanity. In the interrogative cast, *quisquam* stands for *non ... quisquam* in declarative.

futurus fuerit: For the tense see on 24. Mood is determined by syntax after *dubitare quin.*

in qua: i.e., for political neutrality. On the repetition of the preposition see on 2 and *Marc.* 2.

quis est: The syntax is involved enough to have confused the ancient reader who added *non* before *noverit.* The articulation might have been have been simply put *qui novit ..., sentit ...* ; but Cicero makes the relative clauses characteristic after *quis est* and casts the sentence in the interrogative and negative mode (in the same vein as *potest quisquam dubitare quin*). The first relative limits, the second universalizes. *Qui non sentiat* is parallel to *qui noverit* in asyndeton.

conspirantem ... conflatum: For the paired prefixes see 5, *discidio dis-*

tractus; *Marc.* 1, *conficiat et consumat*; but also 16, *refellere et coarguere*. The metaphor, felt as such (hence *paene*), comes from the ancient equivalent of welding bronze. The temperature of the fire is raised by means of bellows, and the pieces are melded together with flux.

aequalitate: *aequali aetate* or *aequali animo*? Probably the first; in Roman family life it should not be assumed that any three (surviving) brothers would be close in age; if the second, *in* + accusative would be better with *conflatum*. For the abstract noun see on 33, *germanitas*.

prius: = *potius*.

ut . . . sequerentur: This potential or result clause is compared with *quidvis*, the accusative subject of *futurum fuisse*, which represents the apodosis of an unreal condition.

voluntate . . . tempestate: Cf. Virgil *Aen.* 1.108, *tres* [sc. *navis*] *Notus abreptas in saxa latentia torquet*, a forceful metaphor not merely for the calamity of war or civil unrest (see *Planc.* 11, *qui in hac tempestate populi iactemur et fluctibus*, or *Att.* 10.4.5, *ea ipsa tempestate eversam esse rem publicam*) but for helplessness in the face of an act of god in contrast with *voluntas*. Although Cicero plays on the antithesis of *omnes–unus*, he does not allow those words to compete by emphatic position with *voluntate–tempestate*.

igitur: may not be justified by the logic of what preceded.

quos . . . tamen: not adversative to the protasis, but to an implied concessive protasis; see 12, *quae tamen*.

35

sed ierit: a new hypothesis; concessive subjunctive, for the sake of argument. Cf. 18, *fuerint cupidi*. For the rhetorical force of *sed* see 20 and *Marc.* 33.

hi . . . tui: strong assertion after concession, *tui* vigorously predicative: "These are the people who implore you; and they are your people." A *deprecatio*, with no irony.

interessem: Cicero's interest in Caesar's affairs was not always friendly, although especially in the years between Luca (55) and Cicero's departure for Cilicia (51), Caesar was assiduous in his political courtship, and Cicero was not unresponsive. In adjusting to the politics of the triumvirs, he was obliging Pompey more than Caesar; see the Introduction, section 2.

quaestor urbanus: dispenser of state funds in Rome. In 56 he may have expedited release of funds for Caesar's Gallic legions, an expenditure Cicero had supported in spite of a shortage in the treasury. Cicero seems to have a particular service in mind; so 36, *huius admonitus officio.* The period ends with an impressive double cretic.

spero: a period more encomiastic than logically cogent. Caesar's memory was famous (so *Deiot.* 42, *qua plurimum vales*). Cicero compliments it charmingly with the commonplace that affects to treat a virtue as a fault. See 31 for a similar conceit on Caesar's generosity. *Spero* + present infinitive = "I trust," "I expect," rather than "I hope"; see *Marc.* 21.

etiam te: vs. *me* above; the expectation of the infinitive after *spero* awaits the relative clause and a parenthetical clause. After the interruption, its accusative subject, *te,* is repeated before the infinitive is expressed. *Recordari* is not, as *reminiscentem,* synonymous with *meminisse,* but implies conscious effort at recall.

nihil: Quintilian (6.3.108) quotes this clause as *qui nihil soles oblivisci nisi iniurias,* with a somewhat different emphasis; Cicero puts more stress on *oblivisci* to balance *recordari.* For *solere* in complimentary expressions see *Deiot.* 9.

quam . . . ingeni tui: *Animus* is spirit, motivated by a combination of intellect and feeling; so *Deiot.* 7, *quid animi.* It is often an energy, manifested externally: one's temper. *Ingenium* is essential character, the inner resources brought to bear in any situation. In criticizing Lucretius (*Q. Fr.* 2.9.3), Cicero contrasts *ingenium* as "natural talent" with *ars,* "acquired skills." At *Brut.* 278 he says to the plain stylist, M. Calidius: *ubi dolor? ubi ardor animi, qui etiam ex infantium ingeniis elicere vocem et querelas?* "Where is the outrage? Where is that passion of the spirit that can elicit speech and protest from the inner resources even of the inarticulate?" At *Off.* 1.80–81, *fortis vero animi et constantis est non perturbari in rebus asperis . . . , sed praesenti animo uti et consilio nec a ratione discedere. quamquam hoc animi, illud ingeni magni, praecipere cogitatione futura et aliquanto ante constituere quid accidere possit in utraque parte,* he suggests that integrity, steadfastness, and rational response are attributable to *animus,* whereas forethought and the ability to weigh future possibilities so as never to be taken by surprise are in the realm of *ingenium.* Unfortunately, having made this comprehensible distinction, he goes on: *haec* (what he has just attributed to *ingenium*) *sunt opera magni animi et excelsi et prudentia consilioque fidentis,* virtually equating *magnum ingenium* and *magnus animus.* This is not to say that Cicero does not have any distinction in mind; there may be a similar distinction in the paired nouns at *Deiot.* 37, *in animo et virtute*; cf. *Deiot.* 20, *regio et animo et more.* For Seneca (*Epist.* 114) the distinction is local between mind and heart: *non potest alius esse ingenio, alius animo color.*

The manuscripts give the rhetorical structure for the two predicate genitives variously as correlative (*quam . . . tam*), which requires a distinction, or parallel (*quam . . . quam*), which may make a distinction or treat the two nouns as virtually synonymous. I read repeated *quam* as an intensification and am not convinced that Cicero is striving here for an important distinction between *animus* and *ingenium.*

aliquid . . . recordari: Verbs of remembering usually take a genitive. Here the object is an internal accusative pronoun (as *nihil* was of *oblivisci;*); the prepositional phrases with *de* are partitive with *aliquid*; see on 37, *nulla de. . . .*

quibusdam quaestoribus: particular people, unnamed. Caesar will be able to supply the names of quaestors who were less obliging.

reminiscentem: active participle = *dum* clause.

36

haec: his brother's difficulties and trials; see on *Marc.* 32. The parenthesis is not frivolous: many families did keep a foot in both camps.

nisi ut: a noun clause, purposive, in apposition to *aliud,* or more precisely, a pronoun to be supplied after *nisi* = e.g., *nihil egit maius quam id, ut. . . .*

tui: genitive of pronoun, objective with *studiosum.*

quam . . . cum . . . dederis: intricate word order in a very confident statement: semi-independent relative separated from *dederis,* to which it is object; *huius* separated from *officio* by participle governing phrase; conjunction *cum* postponed.

utrisque: The plural (distributive = "each of two") is not so easily explained as at 19, where both of the two entities are plural. Also *horum,* not *his,* is expected with it. The progression moves from Titus (the compliant quaestor) to Titus and his brother still in Rome, to all three brothers.

sibi ipsos: intensive and reflexive pronoun referring to the same people in different cases; see on *Marc.* 12, *te ipse,* and *Marc.* 13, *sibi ipsos.*

condonaveris: excuse someone for the sake (in response to the petition) of someone else. The tense, same as *dederis,* shows simultaneous action. Cicero expands the recipients of Caesar's leniency from the brothers Ligarius to the Roman state in four quick moves. At 11, detailing what Ligarius in exile would lose, he included *nobis.* Cicero reminds Caesar that this is a political trial.

37

fac . . . quod . . . fecisti; nuper . . . nunc idem: recalls the precedent of Marcellus' pardon. Parallelism implies that Ligarius is as popular with the Forum as was Marcellus with the Senate. While *nuper* and *nunc, curia* and *foro* clearly correspond, what picks up *de homine* is not *de Q. Ligario* but *de fratribus.* Rhetorically this is consistent, for the pardon of Ligarius is not conceived of as an act of generosity solely for Quintus.

concessisti illum: A predictable antithesis leads to a surprising conclusion. After *ut . . . illum senatui and sic . . . hunc populo,* one might expect *ille dies* to be met with *hic dies.* The exhortation to Caesar to make a habit of pardoning former Pompeians is unexpected, although a new thread has been introduced: *gloriosissimus. . . . illi gloriae.*

si . . . quaerere: period including a pair of superlative adjectives that set Caesar and the Roman people in parallel ends in a crescendo with a double cretic clausula.

populo . . . gratissimus: The word *popularis* was identified with antisenatorial political groups because of their tendency to appeal to the people at large. As such, it was not in the best tradition of Roman statesmanship: so *nimium gaudens popularibus auris* (Virg. *Aen.* 6.816). The optimates considered Caesar a *popularis,* a role of which Cicero disapproved as rabble-rousing when he was not in sympathy with the cause; see *Har. Resp.* 42, on Clodius as a *homo popularis,* and *Clu.* 31. For rhetorical purposes Cicero could arrogate to himself some popular sentiments (e.g., *Rabir. Perd.* 11: "Which of us is a *popularis?*"); and he certainly took advantage of his popular support when he returned from exile.

C. Caesar: fuller name used in vocative, as at the beginning of the speech (1, 4; *Deiot.* 1, 4, 6), so at end (*Deiot.* 40, 43); the shorter form between *Lig.* 6 and 33, thirteen times; between *Deiot.* 7 and 36, twelve times. In *Marc.,* not a judicial speech, C. Caesar in ten of thirteen addresses. For fuller form of vocative see 16 (in an enthymeme), *Deiot.* 34 (a pretty, encomiastic *sententia*), and *Deiot.* 16.

nihil est tam populare . . . : The predicative form of this compound sentence in asyndeton with essentially parallel structures is definitional. Level of diction is diminished from the previous sentence; it does not rise again. The remaining sentences seem fairly discrete and are composed around simple or complex verbal antitheses in comparisons. The peroration is serious and solemn, but stylistically decidedly low-key.

bonitas: the same word used at *Marc.* 31. There the single abstract word was chosen for balance, here for definitional simplicity.

nulla . . . misericordia est: forms a companion to *nihil est tam populare,* similar but not symmetrical. The prepositional phrase is partitive with *nulla* (sc. *virtus*), as 35, *aliquid de . . . officio,* and *Marc.* 21, *nulli de inimicis.*

38

homines . . . hominibus: an extravagantly encomiastic conceit, prettily rather than lavishly articulated. Neither language nor syntax elevates the sentence. This kind of compliment is commonplace in encomiastic oratory, not to be taken literally by the recipient; see on *Marc.* 8, *deo.*

dando: The gerund with an object (as opposed to *salute danda*) is very rare, except when the object is a substantived adjective or, sometimes, to avoid a plural genitive gerundive phrase, when Cicero wants to avoid the prominent echo. It occurs, however, at *Phil.* 2.10, *addendo diem,* and at

Verr. 2.5.113, in a made-up speech: *testes interficiendo*. After *quam*-comparative, *dando* is parallel to *nulla re*. Any kind of full clause here would have made for a smoother, more elaborate period.

fortuna . . . natura: a motif exploited more fully at *Marc.* 7. The antithesis is almost symmetrically expressed and the period ends with a double cretic.

longiorem . . . breviorem: a pretty epigram, bracketed by its key words, restrained in keeping with the theme articulated in the next sentence. Clausula: resolved cretic + spondee.

utilius . . . te . . . quam . . . me . . . loqui: a point similar to the one here made out of deference to Caesar, partly as orator, partly as dictator, is found in different circumstances at *Deiot.* 7, *tuum est . . . ad te ipsum referre*. Here may be the reason for the subdued tone. As at 31, Caesar is not to be moved by rhetoric to a merciful decision. There will be no histrionics. To deny the efficacy of rhetoric and to encourage, instead, a considered judgment may be an effective rhetorical ploy. This may also explain the generally less flamboyant style of the *Caesarianae*—a deference to the oratorical abilities Cicero has ceded to the distinguished single judge.

tantum: pronominal, not adverbial; the verb takes a double accusative.

illi absenti . . . dederis, praesentibus te his daturum: terse, chiastic balance. A last oblique reference to his absent client is outweighed by a reference to the present audience, Caesar's supporters old and new, the Romans of his future state.

PRO REGE DEIOTARO

M. Tulli Ciceronis Pro Rege Deiotaro Orationis

1 Cum in omnibus causis gravioribus, C. Caesar, initio dicendi commoveri 1
soleam vehementius quam videtur vel usus vel aetas mea postulare, tum in
hac causa ita multa me perturbant ut quantum mea fides studi mihi adferat
ad salutem regis Deiotari defendendam, tantum facultatis timor detrahat.
primum dico pro capite fortunisque regis. quod ipsum etsi non iniquum 5
est in tuo dumtaxat periculo, tamen est ita inusitatum regem reum capitis
esse ut ante hoc tempus non sit auditum. 2 deinde eum regem quem ornare antea cuncto cum senatu solebam pro perpetuis eius in nostram rem
publicam meritis, nunc contra atrocissimum crimen cogor defendere. accedit ut accusatorum alterius crudelitate, alterius indignitate conturber. 10
crudelem Castorem, ne dicam sceleratum et impium qui nepos avum in
capitis discrimen adduxerit, adulescentiaeque suae terrorem intulerit ei
cuius senectutem tueri et tegere debebat, commendationemque ineuntis
aetatis ab impietate et ab scelere duxerit, avi servum corruptum praemiis
ad accusandum dominum impulerit, a legatorum pedibus abduxerit. 3 fu- 15
gitivi autem dominum accusantis, et dominum absentem et dominum amicissimum nostrae rei publicae, cum os videbam, cum verba audiebam, non
tam adflictam regiam condicionem dolebam quam de fortunis communibus
extimescebam. nam cum more maiorum de servo in dominum ne tormentis
quidem quaeri liceat, in qua quaestione dolor elicere veram vocem possit 20
etiam ab invito, exortus est servus qui quem in eculeo appellare non posset,
eum accuset solutus. 4 perturbat me, C. Caesar, etiam illud interdum,
quod tamen cum te penitus recognovi, timere desino: re enim iniquum est,
sed tua sapientia fit aequissimum. nam dicere apud eum de facinore contra
cuius vitam consilium facinoris inisse arguare, cum per se ipsum consi- 25
deres, grave est; nemo enim fere est qui sui periculi iudex non sibi se ae-
quiorem quam reo praebeat. sed tua Caesar praestans singularisque natura
hunc mihi metum minuit. non enim tam timeo quid tu de rege Deiotaro,
quam intellego quid de te ceteros velis iudicare. 5 moveor etiam loci ipsius

---

1   3 multa me α, *Prisc.*: me multa δγ   C²AH
      5 etsi αδa: si gh   12 disc. cap. γ
2   8 ante CAVB   13 debeat γ
      8 solebamus δ   14 ab scelere αγ: scelere δ
      10 perturber γ   3   17 cum verba audiebam *om. DE*
      11 crudelem Castorem γ: crudelis   21 possit CAV
         Castor CVδ, crudelis Castor est   4   22 C. *om. Cα*

insolentia, quod tantam causam quanta nulla umquam in disceptatione
versata est dico intra parietes, dico extra conventum et eam frequentiam
in qua oratorum studia niti solent: in tuis oculis, in tuo ore vultuque adquiesco, te unum intueor, ad te unum omnis spectat oratio; quae mihi ad
spem obtinendae veritatis gravissima sunt, ad motum animi et ad omnem
impetum dicendi contentionemque leviora. 6 hanc enim, C. Caesar, causam si in foro dicerem eodem audiente et disceptante te, quantam mihi
alacritatem populi Romani concursus adferret! quis enim civis ei regi non
faveret cuius omnem aetatem in populi Romani bellis consumptam esse
meminisset? spectarem Curiam, intuerer forum, caelum denique testarer
ipsum. sic cum et deorum immortalium et populi Romani et senatus beneficia in regem Deiotarum recordarer, nullo modo mihi deesse posset oratio. 7 quae quoniam angustiora parietes faciunt, actioque maximae causae
debilitatur loco, tuum est, Caesar, qui pro multis saepe dixisti, quid mihi
nunc animi sit ad te ipsum referre, quo facilius cum aequitas tua, tum au-
diendi diligentia minuat hanc perturbationem meam.

Sed ante quam de accusatione ipsa dico, de accusatorum spe pauca dicam. qui cum videantur neque ingenio neque usu atque exercitatione rerum
valere, tamen ad hanc causam non sine aliqua spe et cogitatione venerunt. 8 iratum te regi Deiotaro fuisse non erant nescii; adfectum illum
quibusdam incommodis et detrimentis propter offensionem animi tui
meminerant; teque cum huic iratum, tum sibi amicum esse cognoverant;
quodque apud ipsum te de tuo periculo dicerent, fore putabant ut in exulcerato animo facile fictum crimen insideret. quam ob rem hoc nos primum
metu, Caesar, per fidem et constantiam et clementiam tuam libera, ne residere in te ullam partem iracundiae suspicemur. per dexteram istam te oro
quam regi Deiotaro hospes hospiti porrexisti, istam, inquam, dexteram
non tam in bellis neque in proeliis quam in promissis et fide firmiorem. tu
illius domum inire, tu vetus hospitium renovare voluisti; te eius di penates
acceperunt, te amicum et placatum Deiotari regis arae focique viderunt. 9 cum facile orari Caesar, tum semel exorari soles. nemo umquam

5   2 domesticos parietes ба
    4 omnis αγ: omnis mea б
6   6 causam, C. Caesar б
    8 ei *om.* б
    8 regi: rei *gh*
    12 in rege Deiotaro *hg*
7   18 nec . . . nec б

8   20 adfectum *Hγ*: afflictum *Aб*
    23 quodque αγ: cumque б
    25 et per clementiam б
    28 tam *del. Manutius: hab. codd.,*
        Prisc.
    28 in proeliis: in *om.* б
9   31 exorari γ

te placavit inimicus, qui ullas resedisse in te simultatis reliquias senserit. 1
quamquam cui sunt inauditae cum Deiotaro querelae tuae? numquam tu
illum accusavisti ut hostem, sed ut amicum officio parum functum, quod
propensior in Cn. Pompei amicitiam fuisset quam in tuam. cui tamen ipsi
rei veniam te daturum fuisse dicebas, si tum auxilia Pompeio vel si etiam 5
filium misisset, ipse aetatis excusatione usus esset. 10 ita cum maximis
eum rebus liberares, perparvam amicitiae culpam relinquebas. itaque non
solum in eum non animadvertisti, sed omni metu liberavisti, hospitem agnovisti, regem reliquisti. neque enim ille odio tui progressus, sed errore
communi lapsus est. is rex quem senatus hoc nomine saepe honorifi- 10
centissimis decretis appellavisset, quique illum ordinem ab adulescentia
gravissimum sanctissimumque duxisset, isdem rebus est perturbatus homo
longinquus et alienigena quibus nos in media re publica nati semperque
versati. 11 cum audiret senatus consentientis auctoritate arma sumpta,
consulibus praetoribus tribunis plebis nobis imperatoribus rem publicam 15
defendendam datam, movebatur animo et vir huic imperio amicissimus de
salute populi Romani extimescebat, in qua etiam suam esse inclusam videbat. in summo tamen timore, quiescendum esse arbitrabatur. maxime
vero perturbatus est, ut audivit consules ex Italia profugisse, omnis con-
sularis (sic enim ei nuntiabatur) cunctum senatum, totam Italiam effusam. 20
talibus enim nuntiis et rumoribus patebat ad orientem via, nec ulli veri
subsequebantur. nihil ille de condicionibus tuis, nihil de studio concordiae
et pacis, nihil de conspiratione audiebat certorum hominum contra dignitatem tuam. quae cum ita essent, tamen usque eo se tenuit quoad a Cn.
Pompeio legati ad eum litteraeque venerunt. 12 ignosce, ignosce, Caesar, 25
si eius viri auctoritati rex Deiotarus cessit, quem nos omnes secuti sumus.
ad quem cum di atque homines omnia ornamenta congessissent, tum tu
ipse plurima et maxima. neque enim si tuae res gestae ceterorum laudibus
obscuritatem adtulerunt, idcirco Cn. Pompei memoriam amisimus. quan-

5 tum *codd. aliquot recent.*: cum
  αβ*ag*, tantum *h*
6 ipse tamen δ
10 6 ita cum α*ah*: itaque cum δ, ita si
  cum *g*
  7 amicitiae δ: in amicitia α,
    inimicitiae γ
  9 progressus est γ
  11 quique cum δ
11 14 sumpta esse γ

15 novis *BE*γ
18 esse αδ: ut sibi esset (esse *g*) γ
19 omnis α*g*: omnisque δ*a*, omnis et *h*
20 ei nunt.: enunt. δ
20 esse effusam δ
21 nec ulli: nulli . . . nuntii γ
23 certorum *HBDE*: ceterorum *AV*γ
25 ad eum legati δγ
12 27 ad quem αδ: in quem γ
  28 nec αγ

tum nomen illius fuerit, quantae opes, quanta in omni genere bellorum
gloria, quanti honores populi Romani, quanti senatus, quanti tui quis ignorat? tanto ille superiores vicerat gloria, quanto tu omnibus praestitisti.
itaque Cn. Pompei bella victorias triumphos consulatus admirantes numerabamus, tuos enumerare non possumus. **13** ad eum igitur rex Deiotarus venit hoc misero fatalique bello, quem antea iustis hostilibusque bellis
adiuverat, quocum erat non hospitio solum, verum etiam familiaritate coniunctus, et venit vel rogatus ut amicus, vel arcersitus ut socius, vel evocatus
ut is qui senatui parere didicisset; postremo venit [ut] ad fugientem, non
ad insequentem, id est ad periculi, non ad victoriae societatem. itaque Phar-
salico proelio facto a Pompeio discessit; spem infinitam persequi noluit;
vel officio si quid debuerat, vel errori si quid nescierat, satis factum esse
duxit; domum se contulit teque Alexandrinum bellum gerente utilitatibus
tuis paruit. **14** ille exercitum Cn. Domiti, amplissimi viri, suis tectis et
copiis sustentavit, ille Ephesum ad eum quem tu ex tuis fidelissimum et
probatissimum omnibus delegisti, pecuniam misit, ille iterum, ille tertio
auctionibus factis pecuniam dedit qua ad bellum uterere; ille corpus suum
periculo obiecit, tecumque in acie contra Pharnacem fuit, tuumque hostem
esse duxit suum. quae quidem a te in eam partem accepta sunt, Caesar, ut
eum amplissimo regis honore et nomine adfeceris.

 15 Is igitur non modo a te periculo liberatus, sed etiam honore amplissimo ornatus arguitur domi te suae interficere voluisse. quod tu nisi eum
furiosissimum iudicas, suspicari profecto non potes. ut enim omittam cuius
tanti sceleris fuerit in conspectu deorum penatium necare hospitem, cuius
tantae importunitatis omnium gentium atque omnis memoriae clarissimum lumen exstinguere, cuius ferocitatis victorem orbis terrae non exti-
mescere, cuius tam inhumani et ingrati animi, a quo rex appellatus esset,
in eo tyrannum inveniri—ut haec omittam, cuius tanti furoris fuit omnis
reges, quorum multi erant finitimi, omnis liberos populos, omnis socios,

 1 illius αγ: eius δ
 3 tanto . . . quanto αγ, *Serv. Aen.*
  11.438: quanto . . . tanto δ
 3 omnibus Aδ: in omnibus Vγ, omnia
  H
13 8 evocatus γ: vocatus αδ
 9 ut *del. R. Klotz*
 9 non ad ins. δh: non ut ad αa, non
  ut g
 10 periculum Egh

14 15 tuis: civibus γ
 15 et prob. *om.* γ
 17 uterere αDE: -ris B, -remini γ
15 22 domi te suae αδ: te domi suae γ,
  domi suae te *Mart. Cap. et al.*
 23 iudices δ
 23 profecto suspicari γ
 26 cuius tantae a
 26 terrae α: terrarum δγ
 29 omnis socios omnis liberos populos γ

omnis provincias, omnia denique omnium arma contra se unum excitare? 1
quonam ille modo cum regno, cum domo, cum coniuge, cum carissimo
filio distractus esset tanto scelere non modo perfecto, sed etiam cogitato? 16 at, credo, haec homo inconsultus et temerarius non videbat. quis
consideratior illo, quis tectior, quis prudentior? quamquam hoc loco Deio- 5
tarum non tam ingenio et prudentia quam fide et religione vitae defenden-
dum puto. nota tibi est hominis probitas, C. Caesar, noti mores, nota
constantia. cui porro qui modo populi Romani nomen audivit, Deiotari
integritas gravitas virtus fides non audita est? quod igitur facinus nec in
hominem imprudentem caderet propter metum praesentis exiti, nec in fa- 10
cinerosum, nisi esset idem amentissimus, id vos et a viro optimo et ab homine minime stulto cogitatum esse confingitis? 17 at quam non modo
non credibiliter, sed ne suspiciose quidem! "cum" inquit "in castellum Blucium venisses et domum regis hospitis tui devertisses, locus erat quidam
in quo erant ea composita quibus te rex munerari constituerat. huc te e 15
balneo priusquam accumberes, ducere volebat. erant enim armati qui te
interficerent, in eo ipso loco conlocati." en crimen, en causa, cur regem
fugitivus, dominum servus accuset! ego mehercules, Caesar, initio cum est
ad me ita causa delata, Phidippum medicum, servum regium, qui cum le-
gatis missus esset, ab isto adulescente esse corruptum, hac sum suspicione 20
percussus: "medicum indicem subornavit; finget videlicet aliquod crimen
veneni." etsi a veritate longe, tamen a consuetudine criminandi non multum res abhorrebat. 18 quid ait medicus? nihil de veneno. at id fieri potuit
primum occultius, in potione, in cibo; deinde etiam impunius fit quod, cum
est factum, negari potest. si palam te interemisset, omnium in se gentium 25
non solum odia, sed etiam arma convertisset; si veneno, Iovis illius quidem
hospitalis numen numquam celare potuisset, homines fortasse celasset.

2 quonam *BDg*: quoniam *Cαah*, quomodo *E*	15 munerare 6γ
2 cum domo *om.* γ	16 balineo *CA*
2 clarissimo *B*γ	16 erant enim αγ: ibi enim erant 6
16 5 tectior *CαD*: rectior *BEγ*	16 qui 6: ut αγ
9 audita est αγ: sit audita 6	19 ita *Müller, edd.*: ista *codd.*
10 prudentem *Cα*	19 Phidippum 6: philippum *Cαγ*
10 caderet *CHVγ*: cadere *A*, cadere posset 6	20 ab ipso 6
	21 perculsus *Aa*
17 12 at quam: atque γ	18 24 primo 6
13 in castellum *om. Cα*	24 vel in cibo γ
13 Blucium *Garatonus*: luceium *codd.*	24 quod: quidquid *Cα*
	26 illius quidem (quidem *om. a*) *codd.*: ille quidem *Ernestius*

quod igitur et conari occultius et efficere cautius potuit, id tibi et medico   1
callido et servo, ut putabat, fideli non credidit; de armis, de ferro, de insidiis
celare te noluit? **19** at quam festive crimen contexitur! "tua te" inquit
"eadem quae semper fortuna servavit; negavisti tum te inspicere velle."
quid postea? an Deiotarus re illo tempore non perfecta continuo dimisit   5
exercitum? nullus erat alius insidiandi locus? at eodem te cum cenavisses
rediturum dixeras, itaque fecisti. horam unam aut duas eodem loco ar-
matos ut conlocati fuerant retinere magnum fuit? cum in convivio comiter
et iucunde fuisses, tum illuc isti ut dixeras; quo in loco Deiotarum talem
erga te cognovisti, qualis rex Attalus in P. Africanum fuit, cui magnificen-   10
tissima dona ut scriptum legimus, usque ad Numantiam misit ex Asia, quae
Africanus inspectante exercitu accepit. quod cum praesens Deiotarus regio
et animo et more fecisset, tu in cubiculum discessisti. **20** obsecro, Caesar,
repete illius temporis memoriam, pone ante oculos illum diem, voltus hominum te intuentium atque admirantium recordare: num quae trepidatio,   15
num qui tumultus, quid nisi modeste, nisi quiete, nisi ex hominis gravissimi
et sanctissimi disciplina? quid igitur causae excogitari potest cur te lautum
voluerit, cenatum noluerit occidere? **21** "in posterum" inquit "diem dis-
tulit, ut cum in castellum Blucium ventum esset, ibi cogitata perficeret."
non video causam loci mutandi; sed tamen acta res criminose est. "cum"   20
inquit "vomere post cenam te velle dixisses, in balneum te ducere coepe-
runt; ibi enim erant insidiae. at te eadem tua fortuna servavit; in cubiculo
malle dixisti." di te perduint, fugitive! ita non modo nequam et improbus,
sed fatuus et amens es. quid? ille signa aenea in insidiis posuerat quae e
balneo in cubiculum transire non possent? habes crimina insidiarum; nihil   25

19   4 semper б: saepe αγ
    5 re . . . non perfecta CαBD: rex . . .
      non perfecta re Eγ
    8 retineri CA, retine H
    12 regio et б: et Cα, et regio a, regio
      gh
20   14 illum ante oculos б
    15 quae CHб: qua a, quid AVg, ei
      quam h
    16 qui CHбa: quid AVgh
    16 modeste б: moderate γ, modo
      Cα
21   17 lotum E
    19 Blucium *Garatonus*: luceium *mss,*
      del. Clark

20 mutandi loci б
22 eadem tua Cαб: eadem tua illa *ah,*
  illa tua g
22 in cubiculum (-o D) te ire бa
23 perduint BD: perdunt (-ent A)
  CαE, perdant γ
23 non ita Cα
23 nequam et γ: nihili et *Clark,* nihil
  sed D, *om.* αBE
24 sed fatuus et αγ: et fatuus sed
  etiam б
24 in (in *add.* B²E² insidiis BEDγ: in
  balneo Cα
25 transire (-ent AV) Cαgh: transferri
  бa

enim dixit amplius. "horum" inquit "eram conscius." quid tum? ita ille 1
demens erat ut eum quem conscium tanti sceleris habebat, ab se dimitteret,
Romam etiam mitteret, ubi et inimicissimum sciret esse nepotem suum et
C. Caesarem cui fecisset insidias, praesertim cum is unus esset qui posset
de absente se indicare? **22** "et fratres meos" inquit "quod erant conscii, 5
in vincla coniecit." cum igitur eos vinciret quos secum habebat, te solutum
Romam mittebat qui eadem scires quae illos scire dicis?

Reliqua pars accusationis duplex fuit, una regem in speculis semper
fuisse, cum a te animo esset alieno, altera exercitum eum contra te magnum
comparasse. de exercitu dicam breviter ut cetera. numquam eas copias rex 10
Deiotarus habuit quibus inferre bellum populo Romano posset, sed quibus
finis suos ab excursionibus et latrociniis tueretur et imperatoribus nostris
auxilia mitteret. atque antea quidem maiores copias alere poterat, nunc
exiguas vix tueri potest. **23** at misit ad nescio quem Caecilium; sed eos
quos misit, quod ire noluerunt, in vincla coniecit. non quaero quam veri 15
simile sit aut non habuisse regem quos mitteret, aut eos qui missi essent
non paruisse, aut qui dicto audientes in tanta re non fuissent, eos vinctos
potius quam necatos. sed tamen cum ad Caecilium mittebat, utrum causam
illam victam esse nesciebat an Caecilium istum magnum hominem putabat? quem profecto is qui optime nostros homines novit, vel quia non nos- 20
set, vel si nosset, contemneret. **24** addit etiam illud: equites non optimos
misisse. veteres, credo, Caesar, nihil ad tuum equitatum: sed misit ex eis
quos habuit electos. ait etiam nescio quem ex eo numero servum iudicatum.
non arbitror, non audivi; sed in eo etiam si accidisset, culpam regis nullam
fuisse arbitrarer. 25

"Alieno autem a te animo." quomodo? speravit, credo, difficiles tibi Alexandreae fore exitus propter regionum naturam et fluminis. at eo tempore
ipso pecuniam dedit, exercitum aluit; ei quem Asiae praefeceras nulla in
re defuit, tibi victori non solum ad hospitium, sed ad periculum etiam atque

2 haberet γ

5 indicare *Victorius*: iudicare *CAV*,
diudicare *H*, vindicare δ*ah*

22 6 coegit *Cα*

8 in spec. semp. fu. *Cah*: semp. in
spec. fu. δ, in spec. fu. semp. *ag*

12 latrociniis hostium γ

23 14 Caec. nesc. *quem* δ

15 non sit γ

16 qui missi essent α γ: quos misisset δ

17 audientes *CαDag*: obedientes *BE*,
obaudientes *h*

24 22 veteres credo *Cαδa*: credo *gh*

23 etiam *om. hδg*

26 animo fuit γ

28 ei *om.* δ

28 in *om.* δ

29 etiam *om.* δ

aciem praesto fuit. **25** secutum bellum est Africanum. graves de te ru- 1
mores qui etiam furiosum illum Caecilium excitaverunt. quo tum rex
animo fuit qui auctionatus sit seseque spoliare maluerit quam tibi pecuniam non subministrare? "at eo" inquit "tempore ipso Nicaeam Ephes-
umque mittebat, qui rumores Africanos exciperent et celeriter ad se 5
referrent. itaque cum esset ei nuntiatum Domitium naufragio perisse, te in
castello circumsederi, de Domitio dixit versum Graecum eadem sententia
qua etiam nos habemus Latinum: "pereant amici dum inimici una intercidant.'" quod ille si esset tibi inimicissimus, numquam tamen dixisset;
ipse enim mansuetus, versus immanis. qui autem Domitio poterat esse ami- 10
cus qui tibi esset inimicus? tibi porro inimicus cur esset, a quo cum vel
interfici belli lege potuisset, regem et se et filium suum constitutos esse
meminisset? **26** quid deinde? furcifer quo progreditur? ait hac laetitia
Deiotarum elatum vino se obruisse in convivioque nudum saltavisse. quae
crux huic fugitivo potest satis supplici adferre? Deiotarum saltantem quis- 15
quam aut ebrium vidit umquam? omnes sunt in illo rege virtutes, quod te,
Caesar, ignorare non arbitror, sed praecipue singularis et admiranda frugalitas. etsi hoc verbo scio laudari regem non solere. frugi hominem dici
non multum habet laudis in rege; fortem iustum severum gravem magni
animi largum beneficum liberalem—hae sunt regiae laudes, illa privata est. 20
ut volet quisque, accipiat. ego tamen frugalitatem id est modestiam et temperantiam, virtutem maximam iudico. haec in illo est ab ineunte aetate cum
a cuncta Asia, cum a magistratibus legatisque nostris, tum ab equitibus
Romanis qui in Asia negotiati sunt, perspecta et cognita. **27** multis quidem ille gradibus officiorum erga rem publicam nostram ad hoc regium 25
nomen ascendit. sed tamen quidquid a bellis populi Romani vacabat, cum
hominibus nostris consuetudines amicitias res rationesque iungebat, ut non
solum tetrarches nobilis, sed optimus pater familias et diligentissimus agri-
cola et pecuarius haberetur. qui igitur adulescens nondum tanta gloria
praeditus nihil umquam nisi severissime et gravissime fecerit, is ea existi- 30

---

1 aciem *V6h*: etiam *A*, ad aciem *Hag*
25 1 rumores sparsi γ
3 animo fuit 6: animo erga te fuit γ,
   animo *Cα*
3 exspoliare *AVa*
3 tibi esset *Cα*
12 et potuisset *H*, et inposuisset *C*
26 14 in convivio nudumque *CV*
16 in illo sunt 6

16 reges *CHVγ*
19 magni animi *CαBD*: m. animum σ,
   magnanimum *Eh*
20 hae *CAV6h*: haec *Hag*
27 24 quidem ille *AV6a*: ille quidem
   CHσ
27 amicitias . . . rationes *om. Cα*
28 sed etiam *6a*
28 et dilig.: et *om. Cα*

matione eaque aetate saltavit? **28** imitari, Castor, potius avi mores dis- 1
ciplinamque debebas, quam optimo et clarissimo viro fugitivi ore male dicere. quodsi saltatorem avum habuisses neque eum virum unde pudoris
pudicitiaeque exempla peterentur, tamen hoc maledictum minime in illam
aetatem conveniret. quibus ille studiis ab ineunte aetate se imbuerat—non 5
saltandi, sed bene ut armis, optime ut equis uteretur—ea tamen illum exacta iam aetate defecerant. itaque Deiotarum cum plures in equum sus-
tulissent, quod haerere in eo senex posset, admirari solebamus. hic vero
adulescens qui meus in Cilicia miles, in Graecia commilito fuit, cum in illo
nostro exercitu equitaret cum suis delectis equitibus quos una cum eo ad 10
Pompeium pater miserat, quos concursus facere solebat, quam se iactare,
quam ostentare, quam nemini in illa causa studio et cupiditate conced-
ere! **29** tum vero exercitu amisso ego qui pacis semper auctor, post Phar-
salicum autem proelium suasor fuissem armorum non ponendorum sed
abiciendorum, hunc ad meam auctoritatem non potui adducere, quod et 15
ipse ardebat studio illius belli et patri satis faciendum arbitrabatur. felix
ista domus quae non impunitatem solum adepta sit, sed accusandi etiam
licentiam; calamitosus Deiotarus qui et ab eo qui in isdem castris fuerit, et
non modo apud te, sed etiam a suis accusetur! vos vestra secunda fortuna
Castor non potestis sine propinquorum calamitate esse contenti? 20

30 Sint sane inimicitiae quae esse non debebant—rex enim Deiotarus
vestram familiam abiectam et obscuram e tenebris in lucem evocavit; quis
tuum patrem ante quis esset quam cuius gener esset audivit?—sed quamvis
ingrate et impie necessitudinis nomen repudiaretis, tamen inimicitias hominum more gerere poteratis, non ficto crimine insectari, non expetere vi- 25
tam, non capitis arcessere. esto, concedatur haec quoque acerbitatis et odi
magnitudo; adeone ut omnia vitae salutisque communis atque etiam humanitatis iura violentur? servum sollicitare verbis, spe promissisque cor-
rumpere, abducere domum, contra dominum armare, hoc est non uni
propinquo, sed omnibus familiis nefarium bellum indicere. nam ista cor- 30
ruptela servi si non modo impunita fuerit, sed etiam a tanta auctoritate

---

28 6 exacta iam aetate *Reeder:* iam   16 faciendum esse δσ
    aetate Cα, cuncta iam exacta aetate   17 etiam accusandi αγ
    (aetate *om.* E) δγ   20 Castor *om.* AV
29 13 tum *Clark:* cum *codd.*   **30** 23 antea δσ
    13 auctor Cασ: auctor fui BDa   23 genere CHδ
    14 autem *om.* BE   24 repudiaretis BE: repudiaritis CαDγ
    14 deponendorum δσ   26 acerbitas Aσ
    16 ipsius δ   29 abducere Cαα; adducere δσ

adprobata, nulli parietes nostram salutem, nullae leges, nulla iura custo-   1
dient. ubi enim id, quod intus est atque nostrum, impune evolare potest
contraque nos pugnare, fit in dominatu servitus, in servitute dominatus. **31** o tempora, o mores! Cn. Domitius ille quem nos pueri consulem
censorem pontificem maximum vidimus, cum tribunus pl. M. Scaurum   5
principem civitatis in iudicium populi vocavisset, Scaurique servus ad eum
clam domum venisset et crimina in dominum delaturum se esse dixisset,
prendi hominem iussit ad Scaurumque deduci. vide quid intersit—etsi
inique Castorem cum Domitio comparo—sed tamen ille inimico servum
remisit, tu ab avo abduxisti; ille incorruptum audire noluit, tu corrupisti;   10
ille adiutorem servum contra dominum repudiavit, tu etiam accusatorem
adhibuisti. **32** at semel iste est corruptus a vobis. nonne cum esset perductus et cum tecum fuisset, refugit ad legatos? nonne ad hunc Cn. Domitium venit? nonne audiente hoc Ser. Sulpicio clarissimo viro qui tum
casu apud Domitium cenabat, et hoc T. Torquato optimo adulescente se a   15
te corruptum, tuis promissis in fraudem impulsum esse confessus est? quae
est ista tam impotens, tam crudelis, tam immoderata inhumanitas? idcirco
in hanc urbem venisti ut huius urbis iura et exempla corrumperes, domesticaque inmanitate nostrae civitatis humanitatem inquinares?

33 At quam acute conlecta crimina! "Blesamius" inquit—eius enim   20
nomine optimi viri nec tibi ignoti male dicebat tibi—"ad regem" inquit
"scribere solebat te in invidia esse, tyrannum existimari, statua inter reges
posita animos hominum vehementer offensos, plaudi tibi non solere."
nonne intellegis, Caesar, ex urbanis malevolorum sermunculis haec ab istis
esse conlecta? Blesamius tyrannum Caesarem scriberet? multorum enim   25
capita civium viderat, multos iussu Caesaris vexatos verberatos necatos,
multas adflictas et eversas domos, armatis militibus refertum forum. quae
semper in civili victoria sensimus, ea te victore non vidimus. **34** solus inquam es, C. Caesar, cuius in victoria ceciderit nemo nisi armatus. et quem
nos liberi in summa populi Romani libertate nati non modo non tyrannum,   30

---

	3 et in serv. *Cαa*		18 domestica inhumanitate *BE*
31	8 apprehendi 6σ	**33**	21 nom. opt. viri *H, Prisc.*: hominis
	9 confero *Cαa*		nom. opt. viri *CAV*, nom. opt.
32	12 iste est corruptus *CH*6σ: est corr.		hominis 6, nom viri opt. γ
	iste *AVa*		22 in (*om. AD*) invidia esse *CαDa*:
	12 productus *BE*		invidiose *BE*
	17 impotens αγ*D*: inpudens *BE*	**34**	30 liberi *om. H*

sed etiam clementissimum in victoria vidimus, is Blesamio qui vivit in   1
regno, tyrannus videri potest? nam de statua quis queritur, una praesertim,
cum tam multas videat? valde enim invidendum est eius statuis, cuius tropaeis non invidemus. nam si locus adfert invidiam, nullus est ad statuam
quidem rostris clarior. de plausu autem quid respondeam? qui nec desi-   5
deratus umquam in te est, et non numquam obstupefactis hominibus ipsa
admiratione compressus est, et fortasse eo praetermissus quia nihil volgare
te dignum videri potest.

35 Nihil a me arbitror praeteritum, sed aliquid ad extremam partem
causae reservatum. id autem aliquid est, te ut plane Deiotaro reconciliet   10
oratio mea. non enim iam metuo ne illi tu suscenseas, illud vereor ne tibi
illum suscensere aliquid suspicere. quod abest longissime, mihi crede, Caesar. quid enim retineat per te, meminit, non quid amiserit, neque se a te
multatum arbitratur, sed cum existimaret multis tibi multa esse tribu-
enda, quo minus a se qui in altera parte fuisset ea sumeres, non recu-   15
savit. **36** etenim si Antiochus Magnus ille, rex Asiae, cum postea quam a
L. Scipione devictus Tauro tenus regnare iussus est, omnem[que] hanc
Asiam quae est nunc nostra provincia amisisset, dicere est solitus benigne
sibi a populo Romano esse factum, quod nimis magna procuratione liberatus modicis regni terminis uteretur, potest multo facilius hoc se Deio-   20
tarus consolari. ille enim furoris multam sustulerat, hic erroris. omnia tu
Deiotaro, Caesar, tribuisti, cum et ipsi et filio nomen regium concessisti.
hoc nomine retento atque servato, nullum beneficium populi Romani, nullum iudicium de se senatus imminutum putat. magno animo et erecto est,
nec umquam succumbet inimicis, ne fortunae quidem. **37** multa se ar-   25
bitratur et peperisse ante factis et habere in animo atque virtute, quae nullo
modo possit amittere. quae enim fortuna aut quis casus aut quae tanta
possit iniuria omnium imperatorum de Deiotaro decreta delere? ab om-

---

1 vidimus cod. Lob: ducimus Cαγ,
  ducem vidimus *E*, vidimus ducem
  BD
4 invidimus δ
6 in te Cα: a te δγ
35   9 praeteritum Cαa: praetermissum δσ
9 extremam partem causae *CH*:
  extremam (-um σ) causae partem
  δσ, extremum causae *AVa*
10 conciliet *CH*

14 existimaret *CH*: existimarer *A*,
  existimares δγ
15 a se qui *H*: assequi *cett.*
36   16 qui postquam σ
17 est CαDγ: esset *BE*
17 -que *del. Garatonus*
20 hoc *om.* δσ
21 sustulerat *CH*: distulerat *AV*,
  sustinuerat δa, subierat σ
37   26 reperisse δ

nibus est enim is ornatus qui postea quam in castris esse potuit per aetatem, 1
in Asia Cappadocia Ponto Cilicia Syria bella gesserunt. senatus vero iudicia
de illo tam multa tamque honorifica quae publicis populi Romani litteris
monumentisque consignata sunt, quae umquam vetustas obruet aut quae
tanta delebit oblivio? quid de virtute eius dicam, de magnitudine animi 5
gravitate constantia? quae omnes docti atque sapientes summa, quidam
etiam bona sola esse dixerunt, eisque non modo ad bene, sed etiam ad
beate vivendum contentam esse virtutem. 38 haec ille reputans et dies
noctesque cogitans non modo tibi non suscenset—esset enim non solum
ingratus, sed etiam amens—verum omnem tranquillitatem et quietem se- 10
nectutis refert acceptam clementiae tuae. quo quidem animo cum antea
fuit, tum non dubito quin tuis litteris quarum exemplum legi quas ad eum
Tarracone huic Blesamio dedisti, se magis etiam erexerit ab omnique sollicitudine abstraxerit. iubes enim eum bene sperare et bono esse animo,
quod scio te non frustra scribere solere. memini enim isdem fere verbis ad 15
me te scribere meque tuis litteris bene sperare non frustra esse iussum. 39 laboro equidem regis Deiotari causa, quocum mihi amicitiam res
publica conciliavit, hospitium voluntas utriusque coniunxit, familiaritatem
consuetudo attulit, summam vero necessitudinem magna eius officia in me
et in exercitum meum effecerunt. sed cum de illo laboro, tum de multis 20
amplissimis viris quibus semel ignotum a te esse oportet, nec tuum beneficium in dubium vocari, nec haerere in animis hominum sollicitudinem
sempiternam, nec accidere ut quisquam te timere incipiat eorum qui sint
semel a te liberati timore. 40 non debeo, C. Caesar, quod fieri solet in
tantis periculis, temptare ecquonam modo dicendo misericordiam tuam 25
commovere possim. nihil opus est. occurrere solet ipsa supplicibus et ca-
lamitosis nullius oratione evocata. propone tibi duos reges et id animo
contemplare quod oculis non potes: dabis profecto id misericordiae quod
iracundiae denegasti. multa sunt monumenta clementiae tuae, sed maxima
eorum incolumitates quibus salutem dedisti. quae si in privatis gloriosa 30
sunt, multo magis commemorabuntur in regibus. semper regium nomen in
hac civitate sanctum fuit, sociorum vero regum et amicorum sanctissimum. 41 quod nomen hi reges ne amitterent te victore timuerunt, reten-

1 est enim is ornatus *Cαa*: enim his
ornatus est σ, enim est ornatus ϐ
7 bona sola *Cαa*: sola bona ϐσ
7 eisque *Nohl*: isque *vel* hisque *codd.*
38 11 acceptam refert ϐ

39 21 beneficium tuum ϐ
40 24 C. *om. Cαa*
25 ecquonam *Gulielmus*: et quonam
CH, quonam *AVϐγ*
29 maxima *Wesenberg*: maxime *codd.*

tum vero et a te confirmatum posteris etiam suis tradituros se esse 1
confidunt. corpora sua pro salute regum suorum hi legati regii tradunt,
Hieras et Blesamius, et Antigonus, tibi nobisque omnibus iam diu noti,
eademque fide et virtute praeditus Dorylaus qui nuper cum Hiera legatus
est ad te missus, cum regum amicissimi, tum tibi etiam ut spero pro- 5
bati. **42** exquire de Blesamio num quid ad regem contra dignitatem tuam
scripserit. Hieras quidem causam omnem suscipit et criminibus illis pro
rege se supponit reum. memoriam tuam implorat qua vales plurimum. negat umquam se a te in Deiotari tetrarchia pedem discessisse, in primis finibus tibi praesto se fuisse dicit, usque ad ultimos prosecutum; cum e 10
balneo exisses, tecum se fuisse, cum illa munera inspexisses cenatus, cum
in cubiculo recubuisses, eandemque adsiduitatem tibi se praebuisse pos-
tridie. **43** quam ob rem si quid eorum quae obiecta sunt cogitatum sit,
non recusat quin id suum facinus iudices. quocirca, C. Caesar, velim existimes hodierno die sententiam tuam aut cum summo dedecore miserrimam 15
pestem inportaturam esse regibus, aut incolumem famam cum salute. quorum alterum optare illorum crudelitatis est, alterum conservare clementiae
tuae.

Commentary

I

The opening sentence of this speech—forty-five words, five dependent
clauses, with interwoven periodicity—is more typical of a Ciceronian *exordium* than that either of *Pro Marcello* or *Pro Ligario* or any of the *Philippics*. The construction is remarkably complex. Concerns and complaints
about the difficulties of proceeding with a case are commonplace in the
exordium. Yet, the difficulties Cicero faces are not negligible; the mise-en-
scène is unique, the venue being the home of Julius Caesar and the audience
limited to the dictator, presumably his *consilium* of close advisors, and a
few others; see on 32, *Cn. Domitius*.

---

41   1 se esse confidunt *Caa*: esse (*om. E*)   artignus *Cα*, antigronus *a*
      confido 6σ   **42**   6 suam *CAVa*
      2 regii *Caa*: tibi regii *B*, regii tibi σ   10 se praesto 6σ
      3 antigonus *Bσ*: antigenus *DE*,   11 munera *om. CH*

```
         cum in omnibus causis . . .
  tum       in hac causa      ita multa me perturbant
                              ut quantum mea fides studi . . .      adferat . . .
                                  tantum          facultatis timor detrahat.
```

cum . . . tum: The pattern *cum* + subjunctive (occasionally indicative; see *Mur.* 56, *quae cum sunt gravia, tum illud acerbissimum est*; *Sest.* 2, *in quo cum multa sunt indigna, tum nihil minus est ferendum,* and on 38, *cum antea fuit*) followed by a main clause introduced by *tum* describes a general situation circumstantial to a main predicate that is a special instance of that situation, rather than, as is much more common, with *tamen* in the main clause, an exception to it. For *cum . . . tum* in general see on *Marc.* 19.

According to "Crassus" at *De Orat.* 1.120, the competent orator, preparing to plead, should feel butterflies in his stomach. Whether he will declare those feelings to his audience is a different matter—a function of rhetorical strategy, intended simultaneously to characterize the case and to win sympathy; cf. *Clu.* 51 (66 B.C.), *semper equidem magno cum metu incipio dicere,* and the different treatment at *Caecil.* 41 (70 B.C.), where he claims that the present case upsets and frightens him in spite of his large and varied courtroom experience.

in omnibus causis: to be picked up by *in hac causa.*

C. Caesar: For this fuller vocative at the beginning of the speech see on *Lig.* 37.

vehementius: generates a comparative clause; different word order would have made an interwoven clause (*vehementius commoveri soleam quam*) and given greater value to the awaited *quam* clause. But choices are not made purely for flow; see 2, *ei cuius.*

vel . . . vel: Nonexclusive alternatives, they differ little here from *et . . . et*; cf. at *Marc.* 4.

usus: practical experience stemming from 7, *exercitatio dicendi.* For all his treatises on rhetoric, Cicero knew that the orator was trained in the Forum.

aetas: Cicero was now sixty-two, having delivered his first public speech, *Pro Quinctio,* in 81, at the age of twenty-five. Twenty-five years earlier, in the *Divinatio Caecilium* (cited above), he suggested that the fear he was feeling was particular to the case and exceptional.

ita: modifies the verb, not *multa,* and is antecedent to a result clause characterizing the predicate. But see *Lig.* 31, *ita (multa),* and on *Marc.* 6, *ita magna.*

quantum . . . tantum: Cicero avoids isocolon between the correlative clauses by altering the position of the second genitive. *Studi* depends on *quantum,* not *fides*; separation of the partitive genitive from its governing neuter pronoun is unexceptional.

adferat . . . detrahat: The same words are found in antithesis at *Marc.* 12. also with *quantum . . . tantum* correlative, but with paired datives, rather than genitives.

fides: practically a contractual obligation, owed to the client by his advocate; as at *Lig.* 6.

salutem: Throughout these speeches *salus* has a number of meanings, from well-being, to safety, to safe return, to protection of safety, whether personal or civil. Cf. at *Marc.* 4, 18, 21, 22*bis,* 25*bis,* 29, 32, 33, and 34, with similar range at *Lig.* 31, 36, 38, and 39; *Deiot.* 40; and *Marc.* 32, *salvo, salva. Salus* has an even more basic meaning at *Lig.* 3, where in antithesis to *studium*; *Deiot.* 11, *salute populi Romani*; and 30, *vitae salutisque communis . . . iura.* It has an almost technically judicial sense at *Lig.* 1 and *Deiot.* 1 and 41.

timor: commonplace for establishing relationship with the judge. Cicero's present apprehensions take some forty-seven lines to enumerate (1) the trial of a king (three lines), (2) the seriousness of the charges (two and one-half), (3) the viciousness and baseness of the accusers (fifteen), (4) a *iudex in sua causa* (eight and one-half), and (5) the venue of the case (more than eighteen). The second and third have counterparts in earlier speeches. It would take courage, or the affectation of courage, to complain to Caesar about the particular problems he created by judging this case as an interested party and hearing it in private. To impeach the judge would be folly. Instead he deals with these problems in such a way as to flatter and amuse Caesar. He would not have expected Caesar to fail to notice either intention.

primum: establishes rhetorical control with the illusion of systematic organization, anticipating *deinde, accedit ut,* etc.

dico: Cicero brings up a delicate issue delicately, beginning with a disclaimer of any concern about being at a disadvantage, but immediately adds a proviso.

capite: as in "capital punishment," but, with *fortunisque,* more than that. For the legal term *diminutio capitis* see *Lig.* 33. *Pro capite et fortunis* appear as a formula at *Rosc. Am.* 5, where the latter refers to goods and assets that would be lost by confiscation to the man convicted and to his family. Such resources were essential to a political career. Thus, losing in such a case is a *calamitas;* see on 40, *periculis.*

regis: His local title is tetrarch. The Latin title would issue from the Senate, by statute or usage. Caesar had already recognized the authority of Deiotarus and son; see 36.

quod . . . etsi: refers back to the antecedent clause taken as a fact, i.e, "pleading for the life. . . ." *Quod = et hoc* and is subject only of the *etsi* clause; cf. the formula *quae cum ita sint;* where the semi-independent relative and the subordinating conjunction compete for first position, the former prevails. Clark goes through tortuous but unnecessary punctuation to make the accusative + infinitive an appositive to *quod* as subject of *inusitatum est.* Presumably the awkwardness or ambiguity we notice would be resolved in presentation. Apart from other considerations, the plain diction of the context (nominal, definitional sentences) suggests a simpler structure.

ipsum: "taken by itself," like 4, *per se ipsum.*

iniquum: not "unjust," but "intolerable," "unfair to demand of someone," like having to plead before a judge who is an interested party, in 4.

in tuo . . . periculo: *In* + ablative expresses a circumstance mitigating the predicate; see on 15, *in eo.*

periculo: stemming from the charge of attempted assassination. There is an ambiguity: *periculum* can refer to the hazards (so ⟨ex⟩*peri-or*) of a case at law (so 4, *sui periculi*). *Iudex,* may mean "a judge who is an interested party" or "who has something to lose," e.g., *Verr.* 1.158, *iudicem quaestionis suae.*

dumtaxat: "insofar as," as opposed to "merely" at *Marc.* 22. The preposition of the possessive *tuo* has already accented Caesar "particularly in a case where *periculum* is involved, and especially your very own."

regem reum ... esse: Infinitives are nouns that present actions as facts. The fact now described is not Cicero's defense of a king, but the prosecution of a king, a situation so rare as to be awesome. The collocation of *regem reum*, alliteration playing against dissimilation of endings, would sound as striking as the situation it describes.

non ... auditum: For the ambiguity see on *Lig.* 1.

2

deinde: The singularity of the case is enhanced by contrast to the standing of the accused.

eum regem: placed long before its governing verb, separated by an impressive relative clause, explicitly heralded by *eum* to distinguish him from other kings; cf. *ei cuius* below.

ornare: follows directly on the relative to great effect. It will be answered by *defendere* at the end of the period. With the verbs they complement, the infinitives create chiasmus.

antea: qualifies the infinitive it follows (as well as *solebam*) and prepares for antithetical *nunc*. Construction now becomes more complex. *Pro ... meritis* corresponds to *contra ... crimen*; the first follows, the second precedes its predicate.

cuncto cum senatu: See *Har. Resp.* 29, *Deiotarum saepe a senatu regali nomine dignum existimatum ... sed alter [Deiotarus] est rex iudicio senatus ... appellatus*; the year was 56. At *Phil.* 11.34 (trying to get the Senate to enlist the king's aid) Cicero says that Pompey considered Deiotarus to be, beyond any other man on the face of the earth, friendly, well-disposed, and loyal to the Roman people.

pro ... meritis: encompassing not just *in rem publicam* but the stressed possessives *eius in nostram*; for an even more elaborate phrasing see *Marc.* 26, *inlustris ... meritorum.* Deiotarus is established as a valuable and acknowledged friend of Rome. Services done for someone are expressed with *in* or *erga* + accusative; to have served the state well is *bene de republica* *mereri. Merita* are limited to services rendered in the course of duty; *beneficia* include voluntary acts of kindness and favors.

contra: with special antithetical force after *cum* and particularly *pro*.

atrocissimum: As at *Marc.* 21, the adjective describes the object of the noun, not the noun itself. That is, it is not the charge but the crime charged that is *atrocissimum*.

cogor: Clearly antithetical elements, described above, in the two clauses create a vivid contrast between *solebam* (imperfect of habituation), flanked by two asymmetric prepositional phrases, and *cogor,* which is also accentuated by its stressed position beginning a colon after the weighted prepositional phrase.

accedit ut . . . conturber: The next three preoccupations are introduced more subjectively: *conturber* . . . ; 4, *perturbat* . . . ; 5, *moveor.* Of these, only the first is substantive and part of the defense. The problems of Caesar's status and the venue of the trial are otherwise exploited. *Accedit* is constructed with *ut* + subjunctive when a narrative fact is added; with *quod* + indicative when a logical reason is added.

alterius . . . alterius: a terse rhetorical *divisio,* explained at greater leisure in the following sentences.

indignitate: of the household slave. Roman law did not permit persons in a relationship of dependence to bring charges or even to be questioned in trials against their principals (see at 3 and 31): i.e., children against fathers, freedmen against patrons, slaves against masters—hence the enormity of Sulla's having solicited such people's testimony, at *Lig.* 12. Exceptions were made for incest and treason.

crudelem Castorem: The first member of the *divisio* is attached to his epithet in a terse, abrupt accusative phrase (see next note), either continuing from the previous predication or, more likely, exclamatory, that becomes the main clause of a forty-eight-word period. Structure of the period is both parallel and interwoven. The predicate is explained by a relative clause with five perfect subjunctive verbs. The intended effect is cumulative. The last two charges, linking Castor to the second accuser, are in asyndeton; the first three verbs are connected by -*ques.* The more vulgar manuscripts offer *crudelem Castorem,* an accusative of exclamation; the accusative appears to be necessitated by the next expression.

ne dicam: is a kind of rhetorical *correctio,* suggesting a stronger epithet by explicitly refusing to insist on it. It is quite different from *non dicam X, sed Y,* a form of meiosis that raises a stronger assertion but insists only on a lesser or more restricted one; as at *Marc.* 4 and 5. This is the earliest appearance of the expression in the speeches; it is found three times in the *Philippics:* 12.9, *Gallia D. Bruti nutum, ne dicam imperium, secuta* . . . ; 12.24, *ipsi, ne dicam mihi, rei publicae poenas dederunt*; and 13.12, *satis inconsiderati fuit, ne dicam audacis, rem ullam ex iis attingere.* In the last two instances *ne dicam* is parenthetical and definitely does not affect the grammar; *Phil.* 12.9 is not certain. It is rare in the treatises (*Off.* 2.67, *Fin.* 5.22, *Nat. Deor.* 1.59, *Amic.* 82) and letters (*Fam.* 9.16.3, 12.30.3, and 4.7.3, *a plerisque, vel dicam ab omnibus*). Cf. *Lig.* 22bis, *vel potius,* introducing a preferred alternative as if conceived on the spur of the moment.

In the present instance, unless the whole clause is parenthetical, the evidence argues for *crudelem Castorem.* So Madvig 2, 648–49.

sceleratum et impium: distinct epithets, explained below.

nepos avum: Effective collocation of relatives, frequent in Latin, can stress the perversity of a relationship—e.g., Cat. 64.117, *linquens genitoris filia vultum*—but need not: Virg. *Aen.* 1.590, *nato genetrix,* and 10.800, *genitor nati parma protectus.*

adulescentiae . . . terrorem: a grotesque concept in contrast to the normal functions of youth presently alluded to.

ei cuius: Collocation stresses Castor's outrage as perpetrator; see *Lig.* 1, *ea quae est.* Had *ei* been embedded in its clause (so *Lig.* 7), the introduction of the pronoun would have been stressed, as opposed to precise identification; cf. *eum regem* above; 6, *civis . . . regi*; 13, *is qui*; and on 1, *vehementius.*

tueri et tegere: alliterative doublet; so *Lig.* 16 and 36; *Marc.* 23; the effect is pathetic. Cicero is at pains throughout this speech to portray Deiotarus as past his prime and vulnerable. In his power struggles with his family he was capable still of exquisite brutality.

commendationemque: "claim to good reputation"; *Off.* 2.46, *prima igitur* *commendatio* (= *Off.* 2.44, *causa celebritatis et nominis,* speaking of young men) *profiscitur a modestia cum pietate in parentis, in suos benevolentia.*

ineuntis aetatis: "coming of age," as at 26. The phrase emphasizes predication in the participle; an example of the "*ab urbe condita* construction."

impietate . . . scelere: The first is directed against family, the second against society at large.

avi servum: rather than *regis servum,* adds a pathetic overtone to impiety.

corruptum: Cicero chose a passive participle modifying the object and bipartite asyndeton in preference to a tricolon of active verbs. For *praemiis,* "bounties," cf. *Lig.* 12.

pedibus: A *pedisequus* is a personal servant: cf. English "*hand*maid." Phidippus is described as being in a menial position to the delegation Deiotarus sent to Rome, from which Castor wooed him away. Cf. with this purely nominal use of *legatio* the predicative use at *Lig.* 2.

3

fugitivi: continues the structure of the *divisio,* introducing the second accuser at the head of a period, but in a different case and not by name. He is by name Phidippus and by trade a physician, but only one thing about him now concerns Cicero. Besides its literal meaning (relevant here), *fugitivus* is also a pejorative applied to slaves generally; so found in Roman comedy (Plaut. *Ps.* 1.3.131).

fugitivi . . . os: The listener waits for the noun on which the genitive depends, and for the syntax governing the period (thirty words), until the slave's master is in various and appealing ways mentioned and described. The very phrase *fugitivi . . . dominum accusantis* would appall the freeborn Roman; treachery is added to baseness by *absentem*; the fact that Deiotarus is a political ally of the Roman state is an appeal for further sympathy.

et dominum: *Repetitio* (cf. *Lig.* 24, *et prohibiti*) has several functions, one of which is to develop a climax. Nothing interferes with the tight opening genitival phrase. The next points to Phidippus' treachery, the third to Deiotarus' relationship to Rome. Each is sympathetic to Deiotarus, each adjective is given more attention than if both had modified a single noun.

amicissimum . . . rei publicae: apparently true, of him and most petty despots, when there was one Rome to serve. See *Fam.* 15.4.5 for Cicero's good opinion of him when campaigning in Cilicia in 51.

cum . . . videbam: The long postponement of the conjunction is striking. Indicative in the *cum* clauses for a strictly contemporaneous temporal relationship; so at *Lig.* 18.

regiam: the adjective, rather than *regis*, to balance *communibus*.

condicionem: *Condiciones* were terms offered, at *Marc.* 12, or conditions associated with X and his/its position, including X's "nature," or "the human condition"; so *Milo.* 92, *generis hominum condicione*.

more maiorum: The highest authority for precedent to which a speaker could appeal, particularly if it was in his interest.

de servo in dominum: Language is formal for a *quaestio de servo in dominum*; see 42, *exquire de Blesamio*, and *Rosc. Am.* 120, *in dominos quaeri de servis iniquum est*. Evidence from slaves for or against their masters could be extracted only under torture and with permission of the masters. A master who prevented his slaves from being interrogated was viewed with suspicion; he was under pressure to "offer his slaves." If they did not implicate him, even under torture, it was taken as a strong indication of innocence. To avoid offering them, Milo freed his slaves when Clodius' heir demanded their interrogation. The ancient commentator Asconius claims that the presiding officer of the court ordered the (former) slaves handed over for questioning, but *Milo.* 58 shows that they were never tortured: "Had he not freed them, men would have been consigned to torture who had saved their master. . . . There is nothing that so pleases this man in his adversity as that, whatever may happen to him, they have received their proper reward"—a clever counter to the rebuke of not "offering one's slaves."

quaestione: As with the introductory *cum* clause, the sense of this is adversative, pointing to the outlandishness of the main clause *exortus est servus*. For the repetition of the antecedent in the semi-independent relative see *Lig.* 2, *legatus . . . qua in legatione*.

etiam ab invito: suggests by position the formal antithesis that follows. The point is made with expository precision: the relative clause (adversative) preceding its expressed antecedent provides a neat coda. *In eculeo* and *solutus*, representing polarities, though not symmetrical, bracket the construction.

eculeuo: or *equuleo* (a diminutive of *equus*), a rack over which the victim was stretched.

4

perturbat: Note the position of the verb. This concern is, like the first one (see at 1, *primum dico*), characterized and dismissed before being mentioned. The matter is a delicate one, but Cicero arouses considerable suspense for it.

etiam illud: *Illud* both looks forward to an explanation of the fear at *nam* below and extends the main predicate past the substantial punctuation of the modified vocative to provide a structure for the further modifiers *etiam* and *interdum*.

quod tamen: This is a relative, rather than a noun *quod* clause, although it might be argued that since *timeo* is stative (= *timidus sum*), *quod* represents not a direct object, but an accusative of respect. *Tamen* does not correlate with an explicit adversative marker (like *cum* or *etiamsi*), but indicates presence of an adversative nuance; so *Lig.* 12, *quae tamen*.

cum . . . recognovi: perfect because anterior to *desino*.

re . . . sapientia: The usual antithesis is *re . . . verbo*, in which the word generally is not consonant with reality. Here Caesar's wisdom overrides the peril of the situation. Cicero began praising Caesar's wisdom in *Marc.* 1.

dicere: present circumstances abstracted into a general situation by infinitive phrase; it complements the neuter predication (*grave est*) which usually precedes the infinitive: word order and hyperbaton here are momentous. The subject is delicate, the construction intricate; so *arguare* below.

arguare: A subjunctive may appear by convention in a relative clause dependent on a noun clause; here clearly marked as hypothetical by a generalized second-person verb.

cum ... consideres: like *arguare,* a generalized second-person, although perhaps not quite so general. See on *Lig.* 28, *videres.*

fere: Latin tends to qualify universals like *nemo* or *omnis* in a way different from English, and at times translation is too explicit. But in this case there is an actual exception.

sui periculi: See on 1.

iudex: predicative and circumstantial: "being a judge."

tua ... natura: *Sed,* a strong adversative, shifts from the hypothetical to the exceptional particular judge. *Tua,* separated from its noun by the vocative and a pair of adjectives, creates in hyperbaton a heavily weighted nominative. Fraenkel 2, 129, showed that such a phrase, as a "Kolon" (Latin *membrum,* "clause"), can bear a circumstantial relationship to its predicate. Here the sense is causal: "being so distinguished and special, your nature diminishes my fear." See *Marc.* 7, *illa ipsa ... domina,* and 11, *vir ... amicissimus.*

non ... tam timeo ... quam intellego: Strikingly (because it is rarely so articulated), the negative correlation takes place on the level of parallel governing verbs with subsidiary balance in the anaphoric *quid tu de rege Deiotaro ... quid de te ceteros.*

quid ... velis: Cicero evaluates Caesar's decision as policy rather than piety.

5

insolentia: At *Rosc. Am.* 88 Cicero attributes his client's nervousness to his "*insolentia* with the forum and law courts"; see 1, *cum ... tum,* for Cicero's own acknowledged fears.

causam ... dico: Hyperbaton bracketing the correlative clause highlights the singularity of the case.

nulla: ablative. *Disceptatio* is a generic term encompassing any kind of argument or disquisition. For the *actor,* the man arguing, it always implies an audience to impress; see 6.

dico ... dico: *repetitio* to stress each of the novel and (potentially) daunting circumstances, enumerated unperiodically for emphasis; similar repetition at *Lig.* 24, *et prohibiti.*

parietes: walls of a private house (cf. *murus,* of a city), vs. *in foro* below.

conventum: the gathered public, Cicero's beloved *corona* (although when it serves his purpose he can refer to them as "a bunch of hayseeds" (*conventus agrestium, Mur.* 61). Not quite the same as *frequentia,* a large, milling crowd. The two nouns form a hendiadys "a packed audience," as at *Arch.* 3, *tanto conventu hominum ac frequentia,* although the adjective and following relative modify only the second. Cf. Tacitus *Dial.* 39.4 (written about a century and a half after Cicero's death): "The orator needs the clamor and applause and something like a theater audience. Such were available on a daily basis for the older orators, when large numbers and nobles packed the Forum, when clients and delegations from tribes and towns and a substantial part of Italy stood at the side of accused defendants in their peril."

in tuis oculis: Cicero will go back to comparing venues, but first he treats with some passion the unusual circumstance of this single and singular presiding judge. Repeated forms of the second-person pronoun and adjective intensify.

adquiesco: "I comfort myself"; admittedly a somewhat cold comfort. The preferable alternative is expressed in *spectarem . . . intuerer . . . testarer,* below. Some find here and in other references to the circumstances of the trial criticism of Caesar for allowing himself to be *suae causae iudex.* Clearly this sentence is not entirely encomiastic; Cicero would have preferred a more traditional situation. But he should be credited with enough tact not to offend Caesar beyond the limit that the dictator's ego would put on such criticism.

unum omnis: especially effective in collocation and as the second instance of *unum.* The last two words form a double cretic clausula.

quae . . . leviora: The period turns on the antithesis of *gravissima* and *leviora* (note the slight inconcinnity between superlative and comparative), balancing *ad spem* + gerundive phrase in genitive vs. *ad motum* + genitive and *ad impetum* + two genitives (a larger inconcinnity). In this locution the initial *quae* is not taken up by an *ea* but becomes the subject of ⟨*sunt*⟩ *leviora.* With a backhanded compliment to himself, Cicero asserts that he will convince Caesar with logic but would prefer those stronger, emotional appeals with which he so successfully moves his larger audiences. He is clearly being ironic, but at what level of irony he is operating is less clear.

leviora: For the comparative see 7, *angustiora,* and on *Marc.* 15, *iratior.*

ad motum animi: probably refers to the audience, although Cicero acknowledges elsewhere that he was not unaffected by his own rhetoric (Winston Churchill too believed that his own tears were a valid criterion for the emotional power of his oratory). The next two phrases refer to the speaker. They probably comprise a hendiadys: *impetus* has to do with drive or energy, *contentio* with combativeness and raised adrenalin.

6

hanc . . . causam: demonstrative in strong position, separated from its noun by the weighted vocative, and causing postponement of the clausal conjunction. On formal vocative for rhetorical purposes see *Lig.* 16; for postponement of conjunction see 3, *cum videbam.*

disceptante: The word denotes investigation by rigorous analysis, the taking apart and examination of an argument. Note the less usual and therefore emphatic position of *te* in the ablative absolute.

alacritatem: energy and ardor. The symbiotic relationship of orator and audience is not to be dismissed or suspected just because Cicero refers to it openly. His task is to establish it, *mutatis mutandis,* with Caesar. That may account, more than any extrinsic consideration, for the style of the Caesarian speeches; see the Introduction, section 4, and *Lig.* 37, *utilius . . . te . . . quam . . . me . . . loqui.*

civis . . . regi: not merely because of the orator's skill; considerations like the *auctoritas* and *gratia* of the principals as well as their advocates played a part in public trials in the Republic. The antecedent demonstrative embedded in the clause antecedent to the relative focuses on Deiotarus before describing him; cf. on 2, *eum regem,* and 13, *is qui.*

consumptam: not necessarily a strong metaphor. At *Marc.* 11 it is strengthened in the apparent doublet: *conficiat et consumat.* Generally, when used with such objects as *vim, tempus,* or (here only) *aetatem,* the adjective *omnem/omne* gives it special all-inclusive force.

meminisset: The subjective cast makes the perception stronger than the fact itself; the subjunctive is causal = *cum is meminisset.*

spectarem: as opposed to focusing on Caesar alone, as at 5. These are orators' tricks precluded by present circumstances. Note the change in word order after two verb-first clauses.

Curiam: called *Hostilia* because its origins were with King Tullus Hostilius. Rebuilt by Sulla, it was seriously damaged in the riots following the death of Clodius in 52. Its replacement, for inclusion in the Forum of Julius, was part of Caesar's program. Since it was still closed in 44, the Senate met at the theater of Pompey on the Ides of March.

intuerer: inspiring; see on 20.

ipsum: emphatic position, and a dichoraeus in the clausula.

cum . . . recordarer: absorbs the sense of an unreal condition when correlated with subjunctive in secondary tense in the governing clause, as at *Lig.* 19, *cum . . . voluisses.*

beneficia: accusative, with *recordor,* of what is being actively recalled (so *Marc.* 19); cf. *de* + ablative with reminiscences (*Lig.* 35). Acts of generosity from the sources mentioned add substantially to Deiotarus' status.

7

quae: the rhetorical techniques described above. *Angustiora* is predicative.

parietes: used figuratively, suggesting the metaphor.

actioque . . . loco: the stronger point (*-que*) in remarkable order. Genitive is objective with *actio,* but also depends on *loco,* oddly placed to avoid one clausula (dactylic) and secure another ($\bar{}\breve{}\breve{}\bar{}\bar{}\breve{}\bar{}$).

actio: Beyond the other four responsibilities of the competent orator— invention, disposition, elocution, and memory—performance is critical. At *De Or.* 3.213 and *Orat.* 56 Cicero cites Demosthenes' dictum that the three most important skills for the orator are *actio, actio, actio.*

tuum est: This is the equivalent of the predicative genitive + infinitive, Latin here as always preferring the genitival adjective to the genitive. Given Cicero's present limitations, the burden falls on Caesar by virtue of his expertise to measure by his own standard the emotions Cicero might have conveyed in the right circumstances—*and,* as a matter of equity and kindness, to adopt towards the defendant a disposition that would naturally result from such emotional appeals. The argument is as farfetched as it sounds.

pro multis saepe: Cicero might have used *et quidem, idque,* or even repetition of the verb to give equal weight to the adverb and prepositional phrase, and to each greater weight than it receives in this locution; cf. *Lig.* 30. For similar collocations see *Cat.* 3.23, *multi saepe honores . . . iusti habiti sunt,* and *Marc.* 34, *omnibus semper.* On Caesar's oratorical career see on *Lig.* 30, *tecum . . . te . . . tuorum.*

quid . . . animi: partitive, = "what my disposition is"; see *Lig.* 37, *quam animi.* Pronouns underlie the transfer of responsibility for the proper emotional response from Cicero to Caesar.

quo facilius . . . minuat: a more forceful and, therefore, more memorable alternative to *et aequitate diligentiaque minuere . . . perturbationem.*

aequitas . . . diligentia: the two virtues of a judge, appealed to endlessly by orators. The request to alleviate an advocate's concerns is also commonplace.

ante quam . . . dico: future expected, but see *Milo.* 7, *antequam ad eam orationem venio, . . . videntur ea esse refutanda.* On *prothesis* see *Marc.* 33; the device establishes a rapport with listeners and gives an impression of reasoned organization.

cum . . . tamen: The nuance of *cum* is not established until *tamen* is heard: see *Lig.* 3, *spectans . . . cupiens.*

usu atque exercitatione: hendiadys; see on 1, *usus. Rerum* is mostly a filler; see *Marc.* 15 and 22. There is no evidence of a professional *patronus* pleading the prosecution in this case.

aliqua spe et cogitatione: almost a hendiadys, "with reasoned expectation." *Non sine* makes the expression strongly positive through litotes.

8

Sections 8–14 are a plea for reconciliation between Cicero's client and the judge. Establishing the existence of an extrajudicial bias before pleading the *res gestae* is a ploy adopted by Socrates in the *Apology*. Cicero will return to the theme at the end.

te . . . fuisse: The infinitive, representing a pluperfect, suggests that Caesar's anger was assuaged by the time of the main predication; cf. *Lig.* 1, *veneram*.

non erant nescii: litotes. The pattern of narrative in the accusative + infinitive expresses the prosecutors' perception of the facts. The implication is that they took advantage of those facts. The structure changes when the account becomes prospective. Double cretic clausula.

adfectum: not necessarily stronger than "suffering from" (as with a head-cold). The variant *afflictum* paints a more serious picture; but Deiotarus ought not appear so bowed and depressed by his rift with Caesar that he would contemplate assassination. Hence the understated words like *incommodis et detrimentis,* referring to some serious loss of estate in Caesar's resettlement after the battle of Zela (see 35).

incommodis et detrimentis: Both nouns have varying connotations from disadvantage or misfortunes to serious loss. Cf. *Caecil.* 8, *populus Romanus . . . tametsi multis incommodis difficultatibusque adfectus est*; *Balb.* 44, *quamquam nullo incommodo adficiantur,* "although they are in no way inconvenienced"; used together of personal loss at *Brut.* 4, *nostro incommodo detrimentoque, si necesse est, doleamus.*

offensionem animi: The genitive is objective. *Animi* treats the offense as a personal annoyance; see *Lig.* 35, *quam . . . animi.*

huic: deictic demonstrative, referring to Deiotarus, although not present; as to Q. Ligarius at *Lig.* 5, *hic,* and *Lig.* 11, *hunc.*

teque . . . cognoverant: The clause has been suspected as inconsistent with the implication of the tense of *iratum fuisse* above (not a problem; see note there) and because it assumes a friendship (unlikely, as critics believe) between Caesar and the prosecutors of this case. But Castor's family had been admirable (see 29); and the correlative establishes a link of suggestion that is alleged to have existed in Castor's mind: since Caesar was annoyed at Deiotarus, he would likely be better disposed toward Deiotarus' enemies. This is their idea, not Cicero's or Caesar's.

quodque: Manuscripts divide between *quodque* and *cumque*; both are causal. *Quod* + subjunctive for an alleged reason is appropriate, stressing the subjectivity of the logical process here described. For *-que* between independent predicates see *Marc.* 6, *easque detrahere.*

ipsum te: unusual word order for emphasis, as at *Lig.* 23.

de tuo periculo: See on 1.

exulcerato: strong, medical metaphor, used at *Dom.* 8, *ille tot suspicionibus . . . et scelere exulceratus,* and at *Scaur.* 35, modifying *animus.* Note that all the loaded words—*exulcerato, facile, fictum, insideret*—are attributed to the prosecutors.

fictum: as at *Lig.* 30.

insideret: continues the metaphor. If from *insido* (third conjugation), = "to take root in" (double cretic clausula), if from *insideo,* = "to be seated in" (dichoraeus clausula); either one partially explains the unusual position of *facile. Residere,* twice below, may argue for *insideo*; on the other hand, the second-conjugation form is stative, and *insido* strengthens the personification in the metaphor.

quam ob rem: rhetorical conclusion in sequential connective; see *Marc.* 19, *quare.*

primum: i.e., *antequam dico. Primum* is not sequential, though a listener might be expecting *deinde.*

per . . . tuam: Understand *te oro, te obtestor,* or the like. *Per* introduces what Cicero swears by when he makes his plea; so *per dexteram* below.

fidem: Caesar's long-standing relationship with Deiotarus. See on *Lig.* 6, *fide.*

ullam: in negative locutions is the adjective for the universal negative pronoun *quisquam.*

suspicemur: "subjective" for *ne resideat*; he emphasizes his own perception of the fact.

dexteram istam . . . istam . . . dexteram: chiastic arrangement in a phrase repeated to reflect heightened diction. The adjective–noun word order anticipates a modifying element. The listener expects a relative clause (*istam*

dexteram quae . . .), but paired adjectives are more emphatic and immediate than a second relative clause.

hospes hospiti: The word encompasses both principals in a relationship of
hospitality; the wordplay involving two cases of the same word in close
proximity is called *traductio* or *polyptoton*. Perhaps because it is so easy
to achieve in an inflected language, Cicero does not use it indiscriminately.
Given the reciprocal meanings of the word, it is significant that of the many
occurrences of *hospes,* this is Cicero's only use of the figure. Caesar's engagement in this relationship is treated as a point in Deiotarus' favor (see
at 39), although the latter is charged with abusing hospitality by attempting
to assassinate his guest.

non tam . . . quam: Linguists sometimes explain an anomaly by defining
it. This difficult expression is described as "double marking" of the comparative, by ending and by *non tam*. If it were a feature of Latin, however,
we should find it more often than here and once in Livy (28.39.12). If *tam*
is not deleted (as it was by an early editor, although it is in all the manuscripts and was known in the sixth century), emphasis falls on the correlatives and paired adverbial modifiers, and the comparative force of
firmiorem is downplayed: "By that right hand of yours, wonderfully strong
not so much in war and battle as in keeping promises and the faith."

tu . . . tu . . . te . . . te: heightened diction in insistent repetition of the
pronoun (cf. 5; paired between nominative and accusative in asyndeton),
the personifications of the sacred areas of Deiotarus' home, and the hendiadys *arae focique* (= "altar fires").

vetus hospitium: confirmed in *Bell. Alex.* 68. Caesar had been in Asia in
81–80 and 76–74. Deiotarus' active allegiance to Pompey, explained away
at 11, had intervened.

di penates: Roman names for household deities. Presumably Deiotarus had
his own, but association with Roman institutions is all to the good.

Deiotari regis: the only instance in the speech of the title following a name.

9

cum . . . tum: correlate the infinitives, simple and compound, of *orari,* the
latter meaning "to be prevailed upon by supplication"; cf. the harsh prin-

ciple of the Stoic Zeno at *Mur.* 61, *viri non esse neque exorari neque placari.*
As at *Deiot.* 39, *semel* = "once and for all." This compressed expression,
turned on the lexical distinction between the two forms of the verb and a
rare meaning of *semel,* is not at all typical of Cicero, but of the "pointed
style" of Silver Latin prose. On the other hand, Cicero is not always typical.
And most of the features associated with Silver Latin prose can be found
in Cicero.

soles: For the word in encomiastic language see *Lig.* 35.

nemo: a pronoun; *inimicus* is a predicate noun or adjective, strongly adversative. A weaker alternative: *nemo* adjectivally (but see at *Lig.* 11) with
inimicus as the noun.

ullas . . . reliquias: hyperbaton, striking for inclusion of the governing infinitive.

quamquam: a sentence fragment abruptly abandoning the previous argument, as at *Marc.* 27. It was prompted by his use of strong words like
inimicus and *simultatis.*

querelae: To reduce Deiotarus' culpability vis-à-vis Caesar to the level of
a personal quarrel is in itself an advantage, one Cicero also took at *Lig.*
23. He introduces, perhaps to anticipate, the stronger concept of *hostis,* a
state enemy, but ends with a euphemism.

quod . . . fuisset: subjunctive of alleged reason in a causal clause. It does
not insist that Cicero rejects it. But conflicts in *amicitiae* were common
during and in the years preceding the Civil War.

cui . . . daturum fuisse: future perfect infinitive for pluperfect subjunctive
in apodosis.

tamen: cannot be a sentence connective, since the sentence begins with a
semi-independent relative. Rather it makes the dative phrase in which it is
embedded concessive; see *Lig.* 12, *quae tamen.*

tum: found in one otherwise undistinguished manuscript; most have *cum,*
an early correction by someone who did not realize that the *si* clause is
compound in asyndeton.

vel . . . etiam: adds a second condition more generous to Deiotarus than
the first. Whether this represents what Caesar thought when Deiotarus ap-

peared in the camp of Pompey, or even at the time of the trial, is uncertain. Cicero speaks of the matter as a question more of form than of substance. This cannot be a blatant case of Cicero's putting ideas into Caesar's mind. Should the judge have a political or diplomatic interest in a disposition of this case favorable to Deiotarus, he might find it convenient to accept Cicero's interpretation; see the Introduction, section 3.3.

10

ita: as a sentence connective, sums up what has preceded; *itaque* (below) continues the run of the argument, narrative, etc.; so *Marc.* 12. The tense of *relinquebas* provides a temporal background for the four perfects that follow: "While you weren't entirely erasing the personal slight, you did not. . . ."

perparvam: vs. *maximis*; the diminutive force of the prefix is clearly heard in this infrequent word.

amicitiae culpam: a meaningfully compendious phrase; the genitive provides a definition or an appositive, as at 9, *aetatis excusatio*. Any modifier, such as *dissolutae,* would be too strong.

itaque: tricolon of the necessary conclusions of Caesar's decision, given in stark asyndeton, with insistent homoeoteleuton of disyllabic verb endings. *Non solum non* raises an expectation for the next predication stronger than *non . . . sed,* but different from *non solum . . . verum / sed etiam,* which tends to embellish or amplify the first item by the second, thus diminishing the first by comparison. Of the three verbs, the second two are more closely connected by content.

tui: objective genitive, as at 7.

errore communi lapsus: For the exculpatory language see *Marc.* 13, 20, and 30; *Lig.* 17; and *Phil.* 11.34, *quo in bello si fuit error, communis ei* [sc. *Deiotaro*] *fuit cum senatu.*

is rex: A weak demonstrative provides the only connective to this elaborate, embellished period. Note especially the superlatives and the emphasis on the reciprocal relationship between the Senate and Deiotarus. See 2, *eum regem quem,* and 15, *is . . . arguitur.*

quem . . . quique: two parallel relative clauses in different cases, here with conjunction (cf. 13 and 37, *eisque*), and with causal subjunctive; his behavior was to be expected.

isdem . . . quibus: The locution insists on exact identity of the cause of apprehension for Deiotarus and for Romans. Clear movement in hyperbaton to *nos* in antithesis. Cicero identifies himself with his client as he did at *Marc.* 2 and *Lig.* 6.

isdem rebus: Deiotarus had excused himself on the same grounds (see *Bell. Alex.* 67).

est perturbatus: stronger than at 1 or 3; idea of impaired judgment is in all three.

homo . . . alienigena: circumstantial and mitigating. *Homo* has function of setting off the appositive phrase; see 16, *homo . . . temerarius*; 11, *vir . . . amicissimus*; and *Lig.* 10, *homo . . . excellens*.

11

cum audiret: Two passive, complementary accusative + infinitive constructions divide the participants between Senate and responsible magistrates. Postponement in parallel constructions highlights intruded elements but also puts special emphasis on the second complement. Considerable suspense is created before the main predicate, bracketed by verbs, is reached.

senatus . . . auctoritate: On 7 January 49 the Senate had passed a decree, a *senatus consultum ultimum,* cited by Cicero in a letter of 13 January (*Fam.* 16.11), authorizing the consuls, praetors, tribunes, and proconsuls to see to it that the state not be harmed. Whenever invoked, the decree raised questions of legality. As an advisory body the Senate could not properly authorize a call to arms. It serves Cicero's purpose here merely to allude, by the phrase *senatus auctoritas,* to the fact that the decree was not passed. Rather it was vetoed by two tribunes, Antony and Q. Cassius, who then fled the constitutional chaos and joined Caesar. Caesar (*BC* 1.5.3–4) calls it a *senatus consultum.*

consentientis: probably not altogether accurate, although Caesar's quite different account (*BC* 1.2–5) is not disinterested. In discussing the place-

ment of the predicative participle, Laughton compares this passage with
two in the *Philippics* where the participle precedes the noun: *Phil.* 3.32,
magna vis est, magnum numen unum et idem sentientis senatus, and *Phil.*
5.32, *experietur consentientis senatus nervos atque vires* (see Laughton 2,
48). He argues that in the latter two passages, Cicero, addressing the Senate, is stressing their unanimity as an attribute; in our passage, an attempt
to justify Deiotarus' behavior to Caesar, the fact that the Senate took action
is paramount.

consulibus: (of 49), C. Claudius Marcellus (see *Marc.* 10) and L. Cornelius
Lentulus Crus, both Pompeians.

nobis imperatoribus: See at *Lig.* 7. The wording of *Fam.* 16.11.2 is *Senatus
consulibus, praetoribus, tribunis plebis et nobis, qui pro consulibus sumus,
negotium dederat, ut curaremus, ne quid res publica detrimenti caperet.*

rem publicam defendendam datam: The use of the gerundive phrase, ungoverned by a preposition, as the equivalent of a final clause seems to have
come out of common speech and suffered restrictions as time went on. In
Cicero and Caesar it is most frequently found with *curo*. Cicero uses the
gerundive with *dare* some seven times in the speeches, four in the *Philippics*
(5.7, 7.5, 8.15, 11.18), always with a transitive form of *do*. The construction, like all gerundive phrases, is highly predicative; hence "the defense
of the state," "the conduct of the war" (*Flacc.* 30, *cum illi bellum . . .
gerendum datum est*), except in the last instance, *Rosc. Com.* 74, *ipse per-
cussit an aliis occidendum dedit.* A molossus (three heavy syllables) before
the final cretic is a known substitution for double cretic, but the effect of
the sounds (*fen, den*; and *de, den, dam, da*) must have been startling.

animo: Latin tends to locate psychological responses in a part of the body;
e.g., *Brut.* 1, *maiorem animo cepi dolorem.* An adverb like "deeply" might
more idiomatically render the Latin, except where, as at *Caecil.* 41, *non
solum commoveor animo, sed etiam toto corpore perhorresco,* or *Verr.*
2.4.110, distinction is made between emotional and physical reactions. The
initial position of the first verb (the second brackets the clause) is emphatic.

vir . . . amicissimus: See on 10; the weighted subject, assured by appositival *homo*, is felt to be circumstantial to its predicate; see also 4, *tua . . .
natura.*

huic imperio: the legitimate *res publica perpetua* now represented by Caesar. If *huic* means "the one of which I have just been speaking," it would refer to Pompey's, as represented here by Cicero himself. Such an interpretation is neither necessary nor, to Deiotarus, useful.

in qua . . . suam: Cf. a similar play on the same word in different construction referring to different people at *Marc.* 22, *nihil . . . cogitans.* A suggestion of cause is felt in the indicative relative clause.

tamen: See on 9.

quiescendum: For the verb cf. *Lig.* 4, *conquievit.*

maxime . . . perturbatus est: Cf. 10, like *movebatur* above, which parallels the language Cicero used at 4 and 5 to describe his own confusion at the beginning of this trial.

(sic . . . nuntiabatur): a correcting parenthesis: see on *Marc.* 11. L. Volcatius Tullus and Ser. Sulpicius Rufus and, probably, P. Servilius Isauricus stayed. Nor did Cicero leave at Pompey's direction. So Lacey, 98, on *Phil.* 2.54, where Cicero more accurately says *qui per valitudinem* ("health permitting") *exsequi cladem illam fugamque potuissent.*

cunctum senatum: See Lacey, 98: "200 senators gathered at Thessalonica (Dio Cassius 41.43.2), only about half of the 370 who voted for disarmament in December 50 (App. *Bell. Civ.* 2.30)"; see, too, Shackleton Bailey 1.

effusam: The metaphor connotes a forceful, disorganized surge. See Nägelsbach, section 130.2.

talibus . . . rumoribus: datives: "the trek to the East was open to, prey to"; for the metaphor see *Font.* 24, *hanc patere inimicitiis viam,* and *Balb.* 54, *hanc Latinis . . . viam ad civitatem . . . patere* (where note the necessary alternation with *ad* + accusative). The position of *via* makes for a double cretic clausula.

nihil . . . audiebat: tricolon anaphorically introduced by *nihil*; the effect is pathetic.

condicionibus: which Caesar offered from Gaul in 50 (*Fam.* 16.12.3): *ut Pompeius eat in Hispaniam, dilectus . . . et praesidia nostra dimittantur; se ulteriorem Galliam Domitio, citeriorem Considio Noniano . . . tradi-*

turum; ad consulatus petitionem se venturum; . . . se praesentem trinum nundinum ("for a period of three eight-day weeks") *petiturum.*

conspiratione: here in our sense; in Latin it usually means a common effort in a good sense. Perhaps that is why the dependent genitive phrase is postponed until after *audiebat. De certorum hominum conspiratione audiebat contra tuam dignitatem suscepta* might have been neater but less emphatic. He ends with a double cretic.

certorum: including the consuls, Cato, Domitius Ahenobarbus, and others.

dignitatem: Caesar's public status; see on *Lig.* 18, *Marc.* 3, and, for the phrase *dignitatis contentio,* used already at *Mur.* 11 and 14, *Marc.* 30.

usque eo: precise antecedent to *quoad* in neat expository style.

litteraeque venerunt: The word order was chosen not solely to achieve a cretic + spondee clausula; *ad eum* might have preceded the compound and alliterative subject. The purpose is to separate Pompey's communication from the delegation and to highlight it. The effect is different from that of alliterative doublets like 28, *pudoris pudicitiaeque.*

12

ignosce: repetition without *inquam* as at 8, *per dexteram istam te oro . . . istam, inquam, dexteram; Marc.* 7, *totum hoc . . . , totum est, inquam tuum;* and *Marc.* 28, *illa, inquam, illa vita tua est.* In these cases there is a logical or rhetorical point made with insistence; Cicero here conveys only passionate entreaty in behalf of Pompey.

eius viri . . . quem: The antecedent–relative structure frames the antithesis of *rex* and *nos omnes* and contrasts *cessit* with *secuti sumus.*

cessit: some willingness involved, if only reluctant; see at *Lig.* 22.

ad quem: technically a second relative with the antecedent *eius viri;* see 37, *eisque.* Language becomes charged and construction tense: the two relative clauses distinguish *nos* and *tu,* although not symmetrically.

cum . . . tum: The correlative of the second, as at 1, involves a particular and special instance of a general adversative predication. On ellipsis to convey excitement see *Lig.* 28, *tum sero*.

plurima et maxima: Caesar's support of Pompey's extraordinary command over Mithridates in 67; his support, as consul, for settling Pompey's veterans at public expense; the marriage of his daughter, Julia, to Pompey; and other enhancements to Pompey's dignity.

idcirco: Cicero makes this point with insistent logic. At 32 *idcirco* anticipates an *ut* clause.

Cn. Pompei memoriam: Cicero certainly expressed doubts about Pompey in various private letters; but he never denigrated him in public, even when it might have been to his advantage. Caesar also treated the memory of Pompey with respect; see at *Lig.* 18.

in omni genere bellorum: no exaggeration. Beginning with combat in his father's private army during the Social War, he next sided with Sulla against Marius in the late 80s. He triumphed in 79 for victories over Marians, put down the rebellious consul M. Aemilius Lepidus, crushed the rebellion of Sertorius in Spain, and of Spartacus and the slaves in Sicily. He was by then about thirty-five. Victories over pirates and Mithridates earned him the extraordinary Eastern command, which brought him wealth beyond dreams and power beyond his capacity successfully to exploit it. See, too, 37. The death of Pompey and its manner worked on the imagination of the Romans. Almost thirty years later, describing the death of Priam, the model of Eastern wealth and power, Virgil alludes to Pompey at *Aen.* 2.557–58: *iacet ingens litore truncus / avolsumque humeris caput et sine nomine corpus.*

populi Romani: The genitives are more or less subjective; so *tui* ⟨*honores*⟩ are "the honors you bestow."

praestitisti: an epigrammatic closing, with correlatives balancing antithetical pronouns. In this conceit the balance of compliments falls rather to Pompey's favor, as Caesar's achievements, even though greater, are used for comparison.

itaque: The logic is not cogent. In this epigram the focus turns to Caesar.

numerabamus . . . enumerare: paronomasia based on simple and complex forms of the same word; see on 9.

13

igitur: resumes a narrative broken off at the beginning of 12. *Ad eum* picks up *ad quem*, above, and anticipates the relatives. Structure reflects the sad inevitability:

ad eum	*venit*	misero	fatalique	bello,	
quem antea		iustis	hostilibusque	bellis	adiuverat,
quocum					erat
		non	hospitio solum,		
		verum etiam	familiaritate		coniunctus,
et	*venit*	vel . . . ut . . .			
		vel . . . ut . . .			
		vel . . . ut . . . ;			
postremo	*venit*	ad . . . non ad . . .			
		ad . . . non ad			

quem . . . quocum: two relatives in asyndeton after *ad eum*; see 10, *quem . . . quique*, and 37, *eisque*.

iustis: "legitimate," as at *Lig.* 27, *iusto . . . imperio*, because against external enemies.

non hospitio solum: as he was with Caesar; see 39.

et venit: verb repeated to sustain the tricola of participles with anaphoric phrases; again repeated to govern the prepositional phrases, paired in antithesis; see on 3 and *Lig.* 24.

evocatus: as if, apparently, on special assignment.

is qui: *Qui* + subjunctive normally = *ut is* in purpose clauses. This construction, with the collocation of demonstrative and relative, has the force of strong identification and precise definition; perhaps: "the selfsame man who," "none other but him who"; so 2, *ei cuius*.

ad fugientem: For a positive characterization followed (more precisely defined) by its opposite, negatived, see *Marc.* 14. Pompey had left Italy for Greece on 17 March 49.

id est: This is a prosaic way to redefine a term. Madvig observed that *id est* presents a more conventional gloss on a novel or figurative locution that precedes (see Madvig 1, 261 [cf. 71–72). *Fugiens* and *insequens* describe the action in process more vividly than the gloss.

discessit: Cf. on *Lig.* 5, *discidio*. Note the brief sentences in asyndeton. The sequence of events is described with narrative brevity.

spem infinitam: with no defined goal.

vel … duxit: the only subjective sentence in the sequence, with a construction to reflect the thought process:

> vel officio   si debuerat
> vel errori   si nescierat

Alexandrinum bellum: Caesar followed Pompey to Egypt. In fall 48 some Egyptians and Romans staged an uprising and kept him besieged in the royal palace at Alexandria for some six months. Deiotarus' contribution is addressed in 24.

utilitatibus: The plural of this abstract noun is rare. Usually, since abstract plurals refer to particular instances, they are found with a plural genitive, as at 40, *eorum incolumitates*.

14

ille: begins the next four sentences enumerating Deiotarus' service to Caesar's interests.

Cn. Domiti (Calvini): whom Caesar had put in charge of his interests in Asia (*BC* 2.42, 3.34, 3.78; *Bell. Alex.* 34). This may be the same Cn. Domitius who is later found to be present at this trial (see 32). If so, it may seem odd that Cicero does not acknowledge that here.

ad eum quem: We do not know who this was, despite the specificity of identification; see 13, *is qui*.

omnibus: dative with *probatissimum*, rather than modifying *tuis* in a vast, awkward hyperbaton; *probatus* is usually associated with the dative.

pecuniam: alluded to at *Bell. Alex.* 31, from which it is clear that his contribution was not entirely voluntary; so too 13, *paruit,* for which see *Lig.* 22.

iterum . . . tertio: repetition of the pronoun to punctuate the adverbs.

corpus . . . obiecit: Cf. *Marc.* 32, *oppositus.* Latin prefers a physical object to the reflexive.

tecumque . . . fuit: the last two predicates without *ille.* It is tempting to conjecture *tuo* with *periculo* so that the last *ille* introduces a tricolon of predicates bound by forms of the second-person pronoun or adjective. For *tecum in acie* see on *Marc.* 14, *neque . . . illa nec ulla.*

Pharnacem: son of Mithridates, invaded eastern Anatolia after the death of Pompey. Deiotarus joined Domitius Calvinus in an unsuccessful attempt to stop him. When Caesar, sweeping up from Egypt through Syria and Anatolia, reached Pontus, where Pharnaces had ensconced himself, Deiotarus met him, wearing the dress of a suppliant. Caesar pardoned him, but with conditions. After his lightning victory over Pharnaces at Zela (see the Introduction, section 3.3), Caesar was entertained in Galatia by Deiotarus on the way back to Asia, where he redistributed the Asian kingdoms, substantially decreasing Deiotarus's holdings; see 36 and *Bell. Alex.* 66–78.

quidem: limits *quae* and implies a contrast with other behavior: "to mention no others." Deiotarus had already been called king of Lesser Armenia by the Senate; Caesar restored the title in his Eastern settlement.

eam: prompts the result clause; so 22, *eas copias.* The accusative prepositional phrase is peculiar with a verb that does not imply motion. But phrases like *in bonam partem* seem to exist independent of the predicate, to show the end toward which an understanding of something is moving: hence *Mur.* 64, *quod atrociter in senatu dixisti, aut non dixisses aut, si potuisses, mitiorem in partem interpretarere,* "What you said so severely in the Senate, you should either not have said or, if you had expressed yourself, you should have made your words understood in a gentler sense."

15

is igitur: In arguing the innocence of his client, Cicero shows first that facts make it unlikely that Deiotarus is guilty, second that his character makes it less so.

is . . . liberatus . . . ornatus: The participles of the weighted nominative phrase are adversative.

domi te suae: The word order reflects the meaning; see *Marc.* 6, *detrahere*.

quod . . . non potes: The noun clause refers to the infinitive phrase that is object of *arguitur*; for the construction see at *Lig.* 32, *quod soles*.

suspicari: See the distinction between suspecting and believing at 17.

profecto: See *Marc.* 3.

ut . . . omittam: Cicero mentions so many unmentionables in this extravagant *praeteritio* that he repeats this formula when he is ready to move on with his sentence. Note the anaphora and the dramatic language of colorful evocations.

cuius tanti sceleris: indirect questions, in the form of predicative genitives, as the objects of *omittam*. Whenever a pronominal adjective and a descriptive adjective modify a noun, the descriptive adjective must be qualified by *tam*. Thus *cuius tanti* (*tanti = tam magni*) is preferred to *quanti* or *cuius magni*; cf. *cuius tam inhumani*, below; 37, *quae tanta iniuria*; *Marc.* 19, *tuo isto tam excellenti bono*; and *Lig.* 15, *tanta tua fortuna*. So it might be tempting to read *cuius tantae ferocitatis*, below, with one manuscript. Still, in the next member Cicero switches to the related, but different *tam humani*; and in this *praeteritio*, especially with the repetition of *ut omittam*, the tricolon of *tanta(e)* might seem too predictable and smooth.

importunitatis: the opposite of *Marc.* 6, *opportunus*, and means "inconvenient," "ill-omened," hence "unnatural," "monstrous." *Portunus* was a native god of safe passage (cf. "portal") into port.

lumen exstinguere: For the metaphor see *Lig.* 6. *Lumen* can be a beacon, a bulwark, or an ornament. *Clarissimum* fits all three.

orbis terrae: about twice as frequent in the speeches as *orbis terrarum*.

in eo: Cf. 1, *in tuo . . . periculo*.

tyrannum: Even without a pejorative epithet this title is harsher than *rex*. The play on these words is framed by *in quo . . . in eo*. We are often told that the Romans hated the word "king," but there were statues of the kings on the Capitoline (see 33). *Rex* was a cognomen, and in foreign places the name "King" was reverenced (see on 40). Tarquinius Superbus had early given the title and institution a bad name.

furoris fuit: In such predicate expressions Latin used the indicative where English requires a conditional nuance; see 19, *magnum fuit*.

omnis, etc.: anaphora, leads to *unum*. Multiple usage of *omnis* and *multus* is a rhetorical device frequent in Latin writers of prose and poetry.

quonam . . . modo: "in what degree," not "in what way."

cum regno . . . distractus: not translated here by "along with," but taken closely with *distractus*; it has adversative force when used with compounds prefixed by *dis-*, as with *discrepare* ("differ with"), *dissentire* ("disagree with"), and *discordare* ("be at odds with"). The very contemplation of such a crime would have isolated him entirely. For the verb see *Marc.* 2 and *Lig.* 5.

tanto scelere . . . cogitato: For ablative absolute in last position see *Marc.* 2, *illo distracto*. Here it substitutes for the protasis of an unreal condition.

non modo . . . sed etiam: the lesser evil is stressed; so *Marc.* 32.

16

at: often introduces an objection the speaker is anticipating (whether or not his opponent ever thought of raising it). The figure is called *occupatio*.

credo: paratactic interjection, frequently sarcastic.

homo . . . temerarius: The adjective phrase is set off as circumstantial and, ironically, causal by *homo*; see 4, *tua . . . natura*, and 15, *is . . . ornatus*.

tectior: not *rectior*, assured by *Phil.* 13.6, *in posterum providet, est omni ratione tectior*. In *Bell. Alex.* 68 Deiotarus is called *homo tantae prudentiae ac diligentiae*.

quamquam: as at 9.

nota tibi . . . : brief anaphoric phrases, insistent without elevating rhetoric; cf. *Lig.* 12.

porro: in a rhetorical question, dismisses with a correction what precedes (private virtues).

qui modo: + indicative as at *Flacc.* 64, *qui modo umquam mediocriter res istas scire curavit*; see *Marc.* 32, *qui modo habent* (where there is a variant). Subjunctive is more frequent in Cicero's speeches (five instances), but the distinction may be purely between actual and characteristic circumstances and not one of syntactic convention.

integritas, etc.: These are core virtues, especially in the Roman sense of social virtues, as between client and patron or between allies. *Integritas* = honesty and incorruptibility; also being aboveboard and not scheming; so at *Lig.* 2.

quod . . . facinus: *Igitur* shows immediately that *quod* is not a semi-independent relative but will have an antecedent later in the sentence (here *id*); so at 18. Cogency of the *argumentum a fortiori* is implied by relative–antecendent word order.

igitur: as at 15, reveals the improbability of the consequence. The apostrophe to the accusers helps effect the movement of the speech to the refutation of particular charges.

in hominem . . . caderet: "happen to," "be suitable to"; *in* + accusative is as common as the dative. See 28, *in illam aetatem conveniret*.

propter . . . nisi: correspond rhetorically, *in . . . imprudentem* being parallel to *in facinerosum*, but with inconcinnity.

idem: See *Marc.* 1 and 24 and *Lig.* 20.

viro . . . homine: distinguishing, respectively, public and personal aspects of an individual; but the two nouns also serve to give equal weight to each adjective.

minime stulto: superlative of the negative. The figure is litotes.

cogitatum: Although passive in form, this is the polar opposite in sense of *caderet* above.

confingitis: The compound, a rarer variation on *fingere* (cf. *Lig.* 30, *fictum crimen*), "trump up some charge," secures the double cretic rhythm. The tense and number of the verb are effective: Deiotarus lacked the potentiality for such behavior; that it should be attached to him would strain the credulity even of his accusers.

17

at: here changes the direction of Cicero's argument, with some exasperation.

non credibiliter: Understand *confingitis* in an ellipsis conveying excitement, here outraged; cf. on 12, *cum . . . tum*. Cicero has countered the plausibility of the accusation. He will now attack the prosecutors' account of the assassination attempt, affecting to supply their narrative and commenting on it. Irony and wit informed his treatment of the wartime career of the Tuberones (*Lig.* 20–29); in the following he rises to travesty.

suspiciose: adverbial form, not unique in the speeches; used here to effect maximum terseness.

Blucium: Strabo (12.5.2) mentions two buildings in the capital of the Tolistobogi, Blucium and Peion, the first being a treasury, the second a palace. Two locales are described in the narrative; it is clear at 21 that Caesar goes to a new location. Manuscripts always read *Lucium*, a corruption of *Blucium*. Cicero may have used one name for the whole palace, and a dutiful scribe corrupted the unfamiliar word consistently. Otherwise, confronted with two unfamiliar words, a scribe must have taken it upon himself to reduce them to one.

locus erat: slightly illogical after the *cum* clause, where we should expect "he planned to direct you to a place." The simple, nominal predication marks topographical description in plain narrative style. This place should be the treasury (Blucium). Is it where Caesar was being entertained? Or did he come first to Peium (*domum regis*), whence he was escorted to this place?

munerari: the only occurrence in the speeches. Active is more frequently found in classical authors than the deponent form, although Gellius (*Att. Noct.* 18.12) claims that the older writers used the deponent of this and other verbs with collateral forms. Cicero uses the word once in the letters (*Att.* 7.2.3), as a deponent in conjunction with another rare word, *opipare* = "sumptuously." It should be remembered that in our passage Cicero puts the word in the mouth of the prosecutor in a listless narrative.

e balneo: The preprandial ablution would take place in the midafternoon.

priusquam accumberes: Romans ate recumbent. By using the subjunctive Cicero insists on defining the chronology, i.e., "before the time that you would," rather than the act.

erant enim ... qui: The (prosecutor's) narrative continues with an art-lessness deliberate on Cicero's part; so too *in eo ipso loco* after *locus*.

armati: substantive; *conlocati* is strictly descriptive.

en: dramatic expostulation, more vivid than 21 and *Lig.* 2, *habes,* inter-rupting the narrative.

dominum servus: follows *regem fugitivus,* in a more emphatic position, as a generic impiety.

mehercules: See *Lig.* 12 and cf. *Marc.* 10, *medius fidius.*

delata: not in the technical sense of presenting a case to the praetor in requesting a trial, but "related or reported," by someone sympathetic to Deiotarus.

ita: for *ista,* which seems to make no sense in address to Caesar; but cf. *isto adulescente* below. Mueller's emendation is almost universally ac-cepted, providing an antecedent to the accusative + infinitive (so *OLD* 193, section 15), as at *Flacc.* 49 and *Verr.* 2.1.64, both with *detulit.* But *causa* with an epexigetic or appositive noun clause (accusative + infini-tive) is not different from *crimen* so constructed at *Lig.* 1.

missus esset: a purely conventional subjunctive in a relative clause depen-dent on an accusative + infinitive, without intrinsic subjunctive nuance.

adulescente: Castor. *Iste,* second-person demonstrative, in trials usually refers to one's opponent. In the Caesarian speeches, however, the reference is more typically to Caesar. For *adulescens* see *Lig.* 8.

hac ... suspicione: By relating his thought process, Cicero tacitly appeals to Caesar's courtroom experience and a lawyer's cynicism; hence the direct speech that follows, representing his suspicion in terse parataxis. A charge is a strategy to be countered; hence "the usual practice of making accu-sations." *Hac* emphatic in hyperbaton; *sum* has the force of an enclitic, as at *Marc.* 13, *sumus ... compulsi.*

videlicet: = *videre licet* (cf. *scilicet*), usually labeled as ironic. If it is so here, it is self-irony, undercutting the cleverness and confidence of Cicero's mistaken deduction, vividly expressed in parataxis with change of tense.

etsi . . . longe: Cicero stresses by his articulation of the elliptical period the reasonable presumption of a false prosecution, not his own failure to read it correctly.

18

at: similar to the beginning of 17; here Cicero argues that it would be a more reasonable charge if Deiotarus had planned to assassinate Caesar by poisoning him.

fieri potuit: the thought compressed; a rapid statement, perhaps, of the obvious. The more prudent procedure, expressed in comparative adverbs, is carefully developed by *primum* and *deinde etiam*. But predicates are minimal, and the condition for them, "if by poisoning," suppressed. With *at*, Cicero seems to argue for the cogency of his deduction and the superiority of such a prosecution.

impunius: Cf. at *Lig.* 10, *impunitas*, and *occultius* below.

si palam te interemisset: no sentence connective; *palam* is in antithesis to *occultius*. Cicero is now discussing this fanciful plot with Caesar, judge and intended victim. The verb is brutally strong.

omnium in se gentium: The word order is effective. Position reflects thought; cf. 15, *domi te suae*. Cicero does not dilute the effect by adding a perfunctory but distracting *unum*.

odia . . . arma: zeugma, in which the two objects require a slightly different sense of their governing verb. Cicero is elevating the diction.

si veneno: Understand *te interemisset*; the two *si* clauses are parallel, but not antithetical.

quidem: independent clause made, in sense, dependent on the next; in two other places where demonstrative + *quidem* is so used (27 and *Marc.* 9), a strong *sed tamen* marks the next sentence as adversative. Here, where the argument is the reverse of an *a maiore ad minus* (if the gods could be deceived, men could), and the purely practical issue, however impious, is given prominence, *fortasse* balances *quidem* and suggests that he would have gotten away with it; see *Lig.* 1. It should be noted that *quidem* is not essential for bipartite antithesis in asyndeton, and Clark omits it with one manuscript. M. Lob, following Ernesti, reads *ille quidem*. But that suggests the wrong antithesis and creates a hyperbaton of *Iovis . . . hospitalis* the virtue of which is hard to discern. *Potuisset* is not a case of doubly marking the past potential, but rather is essential to the distinction being made.

cautius: variation on *impunius* above, after repetition of *occultius*.

tibi: Point of address shifts to the physician, no doubt in connection with some look or movement.

ut putabat: a gratuitous slur.

de armis: second part of an *argumentum a minore* in an independent sentence asyndetically linked to the first. There is already substantial material in the first half: the *quod . . . id* structure, the recapitulation of the two grounds for preference, the two-part identification and characterization of the man. To have put all that into the syntactically minor premise of an argument circumscribed by a single period would perhaps have been difficult. And it would have detracted from the force of a more directly stated main premise.

19

at: anticipating the prosecutors' characterization of the fabricated charge, which he then continues to narrate, again in their words; see 33.

contexitur: The metaphor is not like English "weaving tangled webs" but, rather, like "paying out (fishing) line." At *Cael.* 18, after quoting a line of Ennius, Cicero says: *Ac longius mihi quidem contexere hoc carmen liceret,* "I could quote this passage at even greater length"—and then quotes another line.

fortuna: a necessary attribute of a successful man; see at *Marc.* 6.

negavisti: verb in initial position in asyndeton; see *Marc.* 29, *vagabitur*.

quid postea? an . . . : forceful interrogatives in a cross-examination; cf. 21, *quid? . . . quid tum?* and 26, *quid deinde?* For *an,* assuming a suppressed first alternative like "Did Deiotarus adopt a new plan, or . . . ," see *Lig.* 5.

dimisit exercitum: a formal expression and grandiloquent (even to a double cretic clausula) when used for calling off a gang of thugs. Terence parodied the expression in *Eun.* 814, where a parasite speaks of his slaves.

at (eodem): Cicero himself counters the reason he offered to explain the failure of the plot.

itaque: The *-que* is a copula; *ita* goes closely with the verb. Parataxis here is essential; cf. the alternative, *te . . . rediturum sicut redidisti dixeras* (cf. *Lig.* 13, *sicuti est,* and 14, *quod et fecimus*).

magnum fuit: Latin idiom differs from English here. "The indicative (of certain verbs) is used to express positively [i.e., in the positive degree] the existence of power, possibility, duty, convenience, etc. in contrast to particular acts" (Roby, 2: section 1535, citing *Sest.* 12, *longum est ea dicere: sed hoc breve dicam.* So too *Clu.* 36, *longum est dicere . . . exitum cognoscite,* where we would render "It would take a long time" (or "It is too long"). See, too, *Planc.* 86, *decertare mihi ferro magnum fuit cum reliquis eorum* (followers of Catiline), *quos ego florentis atque integros sine ferro viceram?* "Would it have been a big thing for me . . . ?" See Lacey, sections 27 and 103. Ellendt and Seyffert, section 214 n. 1, analyze the phenomenon differently: "Adjectives which in themselves have some sense of reproof tend to be found in Latin in the positive, though we translate them as comparative with 'too,' or 'so very.' E.g., *angustos fines habere,* 'to have too narrow limits'; *lente agere,* 'to manage too slowly'; *longum est,* 'it would be too long'."

comiter et iucunde: Caesar was, apparently, good value as a dinner guest. See *Att.* 13.52.1, *fuit enim periucunde,* of the present affair; *ibid.* 2, *libenter fuit,* "Caesar had a good time." The use of the adverb with *est* is colloquial. See LH&S, 171.

ut dixeras: repeated; Caesar's movements were well advertised.

quo in loco: narrative specificity of commentary style; so *Lig.* 3, *qua in legatione.*

Attalus: Attalus II of Pergamon (died 133); not, apparently, the man Cicero remembers from the history books, or perhaps books of *exempla* for the use of orators. It was rather Antiochus VII of Syria who sent Scipio the lavish gifts which the general, with a fastidiousness unusual under such circumstances, caused to be displayed to his men.

usque ad: Numantia was a city in Spain pacified by Scipio Aemilianus in 134–133; the title Numanticus was awarded to him as a result. The preposition is used with the city to express direction of the predicate, not its goal. *Usque* emphasizes the distance.

inspectante exercitu: describes the point of comparison beyond its present relevance, except insofar as it sets up a compliment to Caesar. The account Cicero read probably concentrated on the integrity of Scipio Aemilianus as a paradigm.

praesens: in the sight of witnesses.

regio et animo et more: The word order is very ornate. For the collocation see on *Lig.* 35, *quam . . . animi.*

20

obsecro: emphatic appeal. Generally in paratactic constructions with imperatives the indicative word (like *quaeso*) follows, tempering the command (see at *Marc.* 25); it might have done so even with two following imperatives. *Obsecro* is used only twice with imperatives (*Lig.* 37, *noli, obsecro, dubitare*); the word is very ancient and very solemn (by ancient etymology, Paul. ex Fest. p. 207 L. = *opem a sacris petere*).

repete . . . pone . . . recordare: tricolon of asyndetic imperative clauses asking Caesar to remember three things with special attention to each. Each of them is structured with its own virtually synonymous verb and thus given equal prominence. See *Marc.* 13, *nam cum,* and *Marc.* 19, *a virtute . . . a fortuna.*

ante oculos: See *Marc.* 5.

intuentium . . . admirantium: hendiadys for "looked on you with admiration." The participles recall the action, rather than the fact, of what they did. For *intueor* see 5.

quae trepidatio: the only usage in the speeches. The expanding tricolon of *quid* is more ornamental than emotive; cf. 30, *parietes.* So too, with anaphoric *nisi,* two adverbs are linked to a weighted prepositional phrase. *Ad*

Her. 2.8 describes the rhetorical strategy of which this is a variation, *consecutio* (we might say "reaction"): "When it is asked with what indications of guilt or innocence they [the accused] react, the prosecutor will say, if he can, that when he approached his opponent, the man blushed." At *Milo.* 61 Cicero uses as a proof of his client's innocence Milo's demeanor when he returned to Rome after the death of Clodius. See also *Lig.* 9, *nimis urgeo.*

ex . . . disciplina: education of a (Roman) gentleman; prepositional phrase of derivation.

quid . . . causae: The partitive dissolves any possibility of a considered motive.

lautum . . . cenatum: There is sarcastic humor in the very terseness of this antithesis in asyndeton. *Lautus* is usually distinguished from *lavatus* as meaning "spruced up" and so "splendid" or "refined," not merely "washed."

21

inquit: Cicero's contrived "narrative" of the prosecution's account continues, replete with his acerbic commentary.

cum . . . ibi: a slight inconcinnity here, to be attributed to the "narrator." Cicero has created him and made him less than articulate and engaging.

Blucium: See on 17. By this account, Caesar returned to his room at fort Peion after viewing his gifts. The entourage is now returning to the treasury.

ventum esset: Impersonal passive offers a neutral kind of narrative, subject-free.

non video: an ironically self-effacing interruption of the account.

sed tamen: For the strong adversative see on 18; Cicero pretends to dismiss his own incomprehension and give the prosecutor the benefit of the doubt.

acta res criminose est: "but (never mind), the handling of the affair invited accusation." Interpretation of these words has exercised commentators, because of the lack of a named agent and the meaning of the adverb. Is the agent implied by the passive predicate Deiotarus (*res* = plot), or by the prosecutor (*res* = accusation, which is less likely)? If the former, the judgment may be that of the prosecutor or of Cicero, as an ironic, still disingenuous concession (so R&E, 97). The adverb appears in only one other speech, where it is paired with *suspiciose*; it is glossed in Merguet by "accusingly, maliciously, reproachfully." But it should mean precisely "in an indictable manner." Cicero lightly concedes that the change of locale, as arranged by Deiotarus, gave cause for suspicion of criminality—though he can not at all figure out why. This interpretation takes account of the unusual word order *acta res . . . est*; it is unwise to make too much of word order, but verb-first in the perfect passive is noticeably less frequent (so *Marc.* 31, *perfuncta res publica est*).

vomere: an expedient to allow further gorging (but see Seneca *Ad Helv.* 10.3, *vomunt ut edant, edunt ut vomant*), and a fairly common practice at a time when eating spoiled food was unavoidable. Cf. *Att.* 13.52: "He was anointed with oil, he took his place. He was practicing expurgation; and so he both ate and drank without fear or restraint."

ibi enim: no drama or suspense—bespeaks a not very competent storyteller; cf. 17, *erant enim*. What *Ad Her.* 4.16 describes as *aridum et exsangue genus orationis*.

at: The particle dramatically upsets the expected sequence of events.

perduint: an archaic present subjunctive (the form is actually optative), in this ancient imprecation, formed with the long -*i*- of the optative mood, found regularly in the perfect subjunctive and in the present subjunctive of *sum* and *volo*.

ita: formulaic, giving the reason for the curse. Its occurrence in Plautus bespeaks only its antiquity, rather than any special affinity to comic vocabulary; see on *Lig.* 12, *me hercule*.

nequam et: *Nihili es* is Clark's conjecture, cleverly derived from the singular reading of *D*, accepted by the most recent Teubner editor, although it imports a form otherwise not found in Cicero; *nihili* = "worthless," common in Plautus. More reliable manuscripts have only *non modo improbus*; the vulgarizers offer *nequam et* with the right sense. Clark may be right; *fatuus* appears only here in the speeches—of five sure instances in the letters, two come from correspondents. It practically falls off the scale of propriety in describing a fool; *nequam* is current.

signa aenea: contemptuous reference to the assassins as immovable objects. The force of passive *transferri* is similar, but the better manuscripts read *transire*.

habes: vividly presented; cf. *Lig.* 2, *habes*.

inquit: Phidippus claims to have been an eyewitness; his credibility must now be impugned.

quid tum: incredulous and impatient; see on 19.

ut . . . dimitteret . . . mitteret: compound clause in asyndeton. Echo of complex verb form in the simple form with *etiam* is more vivid than *non solum . . . sed etiam*. *Romam* is emphasized in hyperbaton.

```
ita ille demens          erat
ut eum
     quem conscium . . . habebat,
                    ab se           dimitteret, [end of unit]
                    Romam etiam   mitteret, [end of period]
```

Here Cicero appends (leading from *Romam*) a locative clause which is cast in the subjunctive mainly because it describes circumstances that make the supposition unlikely: i.e., "even though he knew that at Rome were . . .":

```
ubi et inimicissimum sciret esse nepotem suum
                    et C. Caesarem
                         cui  fecisset  insidias,
praesertim cum           is unus esset
                         qui posset . . . iudicare?
```

quem conscium . . . habebat: At this level of subordination the subjunctive could be used conventionally with no circumstantial nuance; see on 4, *arguare*. But the indicative treats as fact the one quality of the man that makes the other suppositions unbelievable. Cf. the sense of *cui fecisset insidias* and *qui posset* (on *posset* see 18). The sentence is highly complex, but not periodic. The points that make Phidippus' story incredible are just added on.

is . . . qui: normal characteristic or potential subjunctive.

22

"et fratres . . .": The physician continues his narrative, as if without interruption.

quod erant conscii: indicative in causal clause; Phidippus implicates his brothers without question.

cum igitur: The logical connective introduces Cicero's deduction of an absurd contention.

eos . . . quos: Specific antecedent and the repetition of *scire(s)* press the point.

solutum: both figuratively and literally; *solvere* vs. *vincire*.

reliqua pars . . . duplex . . . una . . . altera: After the charge of attempted assassination is treated separately and ridiculed by a burlesque of the narrative of the alleged events, Cicero appears to put under a single classification two remaining charges: Deiotarus' diplomatic and military opposition to Caesar. He begins with a straightforward statement of a *divisio*; cf. *Cael.* 30, *sunt autem duo crimina: auri et veneni.* It will therefore be with some surprise that the listener learns at 24 that there is still one charge outstanding.

speculis: a watchtower, a vantage point; so at *Verr.* 1.46, *nunc autem homines in speculis sunt; observant . . .* , "But now all men have their eyes upon us; they are looking to see. . . ." Here = "alert and poised for action, should the chance arise to cause trouble"; cf. *Mur.* 79, *in speculis atque insidiis relicti,* of the survivors of the Catilinarian conspiracy who still pose a threat. Examples of this activity are cited in 25 from the accusation.

animo . . . alieno: At *Lig.* 6 and 24 he uses *aliena voluntas* for hostility to Caesar. The word order is unusual, with *a te* separated from *alieno*. Cf. the articulation when repeated at 24. Cadence of the type *esse videatur* is achieved.

magnum: generally precedes its noun, and the usual order of a noun phrase in hyperbaton is adjective–noun. The postponed adjective often gets a more predicative force; see on *Lig.* 30. Here *exercitum* comes first as the subject word, and *eum* is in weak second position, following Wackernagel's law.

Contra te contrasts with *a te*. The adjective is postponed also, so that the prepositional phrase, which properly depends on the infinitive, can be heard closely with *exercitum*.

ut cetera: Unclear, perhaps intentionally so, whether the verb would have been *dixi* or *dicam*. Notice the lack of sentence connectives in cursory account.

eas: A weak demonstrative can be used, like *eius modi,* to prompt result clauses; see 14, *eam partem. Maiores* and *exiguas* in the next sentence limit the reference to size.

populo Romano: subtle and deliberate substitution of the Roman people for Caesar. Deiotarus' association with the Roman state is more clearly established, as is the notion that in fighting Caesar he would be fighting the Roman people.

imperatoribus: including Cicero himself when governor of Cilicia in 51 (*Fam.* 15.4.5).

quidem: contrasts *antea* to *nunc* as if the first were in an dependent adversative clause; see 18 and *Marc.* 9. In the years 51–50, when Deiotarus was supporting Cicero's command, he could be counted on for troops (*Att.* 6.1.14) and praised for generosity and loyalty (*benevolentia et fide*) to the Roman people (*Fam.* 15.4.5). His resources seem to have been diminished by the time of Caesar's Alexandrian campaign (see 14), and Cicero insists on mentioning again at 25 that the king had to hold auctions to raise money for Caesar.

23

misit: no object. Since we learn that no troops actually went, the meaning is probably that he made overtures to, or got in touch with, Caecilius through ambassadors.

nescioquem Caecilium: The indefinite is not necessarily deprecatory (cf. *Arch.* 15, *tum nescioquid praeclarum ac singulare solere existere,* or even 24, *ait . . . nescio quem . . . servum iudicatum*) but is an intentionally careless way of referring to people (e.g., *Dom.* 81, *Anagnino nescio cui Menullae; Sest.* 68, *Ligus iste nescioqui Sextus Aelius Ligus*; or *Phil.* 11.1, *praemisso Marso nescioquo Octavio,* all three in attributive position); so the choice of manuscript reading here (but see *Milo.* 65, *quin etiam fuit audiendus popa Licinius nescioqui*). Not that the person is unknown (Ligus was a tribune), but that he is of no account, at least for present purposes. *At* does not guarantee that the epithet was used by the accusers, although this is part of the prosecution's account; Cicero would here endorse it. This Caecilius was a knight who fought with Pompey at Pharsalus and then nominally switched to Caesar. Either as an appointee of Caesar after pardon or as a conspirator, he imposed himself on Roman troops in Syria and led them in mutiny against Caesar until, after Caesar's death, he turned them over to Cassius. He was from Caesar's point of view an adventurer; that Deiotarus allied himself to him would be taken as an anti-Caesarian gesture. A year earlier, in a letter to the governor of Syria, Cicero had referred to him as *iste nescioqui Caecilius Bassus* (*Fam.* 12.18.1), though in *Phil.* 11.32, after Caesar's death, he would call him *fortis et praeclari viri.* The sarcasm of the next reference, in 23, confirms the suspicion that Caecilius, *in situ,* was by no means of no account. Cassius was proud to take over Caecilius' troops (*Fam.* 12.11.1).

sed . . . coniecit: Note the brief, clearly defined cola; a similar intensity is felt in the clearly articulated sequence of relative clause followed by accusative + infinitive, thrice introduced by *aut.*

noluerunt: the troops. The prosecution endorses this reason; hence the indicative.

non quaero: *praeteritio;* Cicero casts doubt on all aspects of this contention without responding to them or to the reason for the insubordination of Deiotarus' men.

aut . . . aut . . . aut: The figure Cicero uses is *climax,* a progression of propositions in which a part of the first is repeated in the second (here as a relative), and so forth. The progression goes from lesser unlikelihood to greater, an absurd *argumentum a minore.* The first and third relative clauses, although entitled by conventions of syntax to be subjunctive because depending on noun clauses, also have a circumstantial nuance.

dicto audientes: the regular military expression (five times in *In Verrem,* here, and *Phil.* 7).

sed tamen: Granting the point for the sake of argument (as at 21, 18, and

Lig. 2) and leaving those questions moot, he goes on to the more important question, now asked directly.

cum: + imperfect indicative for contemporaneity, as at 3.

utrum . . . an: poses a minor dilemma (see on *Lig.* 23 and 29): Deiotarus either must have been unaware that Pompey's cause (note the discreet *illam*) had been lost or have imagined that Caecilius was far more powerful than Cicero acknowledges him to have been. Continuing the fiction of Caecilius' worthlessness, Cicero responds only to that half of the dilemma.

magnum hominem: a regular honorific; *istum* and context reflect Cicero's contempt.

novit: purely descriptive of Deiotarus as one well acquainted with people of importance in Rome. Yet the relative clause also gives the reason for the validity of his assessment.

vel . . . vel: nonexclusive alternatives. In either case Deiotarus would have held Caecilius in contempt. The art of verbal insult is well served by this epigrammatic dart.

quia non nosset: Deiotarus' grounds; with the apodosis *contemneret*, past potential, understand an ellipsis of ⟨*si non nosset*⟩ with *quia non nosset* and of ⟨*quia nosset*⟩ with *si nosset*. Caecilius' obscurity is the main point, but Cicero cannot resist the temptation to suggest his depravity.

24

addit . . . illud: appends another accusation and disposes of it with increased succinctness (initial verb position for *addit* and *ais*; terse bipartite asyndeton at *non arbitror, non audivi*). Already accused of wanting to give military aid to the renegade Caecilius, Deiotarus is also charged with giving only perfunctory support to Caesar in Africa. This time the words of the prosecutor are not quoted but expressed in an accusative + infinitive, anticipated by *illud*. Cf. 25, *addit . . . ait . . . inquit*.

veteres, credo, Caesar: Cicero plays on the intrinsic ambiguity of *optimos*: the best," or "his best"—the prosecution meaning the latter, strengthened by the potentiality for litotes. *Credo* might be parenthetical or govern *nihil* ⟨*esse*⟩, but has stronger pathetic sense as the former. In that case (rather than as governed by *misit*) *nihil* . . . *equitatum* is absolute in a terse elliptical construction that sets up one predication for comparison with another via *sed*; *est/sunt* is regularly omitted in the first half. See *Lig.* 11, *haec admirabilia, sed* . . . . R&E (ad loc.) cite *De Orat.* 2.25, *virum non illiteratum, sed nihil ad Persium.* The oldest manuscripts have *veteres,* which all editors, following two otherwise undistinguished manuscripts, delete. It can be read in predicate apposition to *nihil* . . . *equitatum*; that *veteres* [sc. *equites*] = "veteran" and by implication "his best" can be exampled from *Piso.* 11, *veterum Catilinae militum,* or *Pomp.* 26, *vetere exercitu pulso* (where the parallelism is not vitiated because it follows *bellum* . . . *novus imperator noster accepit*). *Veteres* and *electos* would frame the construction, focusing on the sense that is wanted. Without *veteres* it is more difficult to take *credo,* now in initial position, as parenthetical. For *ad* = "compared to" see *Verr.* 2.5.25, *non ad Q. Maximi sapientiam, neque ad illius superioris Africani in re gerunda celeritatem, neque ad huius qui postea fuit singulare consilium* . . . , in a sarcastic evaluation of Verres' virtues as *imperator.*

ex eo numero = *ex eorum numero,* as at *Marc.* 21.

servum iudicatum: a secondary charge (presumably a slight one), that his army included a slave. As Cicero says, Deiotarus would not be culpable; and although the penalty for a slave's being inscribed in a Roman army may have been death (*Dig.* 49.16.11, no doubt of the slave), Deiotarus' army was not Roman; and, even there precedent had been set for relaxing the prohibition. Servius, the fourth-century commentator on Virgil and our source for this prohibition, also lists exceptions at *Aen.* 9.546.

arbitrarer: A verb stating a belief may be attracted into unreal condition— remarkable even if found also in English. Cicero responds to this slight charge with a tricolon of predicates.

speravit, credo: The irony in *credo* is that as Deiotarus did not participate in Caesar's discomfiture, his crime must have been wishing it on him and minimizing his chances for escape. But this is a facetious jab at the prosecutor. The real response to *alieno a te animo* begins with *at,* now Cicero's own objection.

Alexandreae: locative. The siege of Caesar at Alexandria, begun in fall 48, was one of his most difficult encounters. Loyalists of Ptolemy XII, angry that Caesar was rejecting their king in favor of his sister Cleopatra, contained Caesar in the royal palace for about six months. The siege was only broken with the aid of Mithridates of Pergamon and local Jews and African tribesmen. Alexandria is bordered on three sides by water, which would impede a departure.

exitus: plural striking, elsewhere limited to various deaths or issues (i.e., of war).

dedit . . . aluit: absolute expressions of support in asyndeton. The bipartite construction (vs. tricolon) supports the raised tension of *at*. This is the lapidary style described in Fraenkel 5, perhaps even that of the "field report," identified in Fraenkel 1.

ei . . . defuit, tibi . . . praesto fuit: two recipients of Deiotarus' support, in asyndeton with balanced initial datives. *In nulla re defuit* and *praesto erat* involve a negative predicate restated by a positive, an example of *variatio*. For *ad hospitium . . . ad periculum* cf. 13, *fugiens . . . insequens*.

quem Asiae: Domitius Calvinus (cf. 14). Deiotarus had good reason to join him. Pharnaces, whose father ruled the Bosphorus, had invaded Cappadocia and Lesser Armenia. He then crushed their joint forces at Nicopolis, and it remained for Caesar to regain control at the battle of Zela.

tibi victori: The dative phrase is predicative; see similarly 11, *vir . . . amicissimus*.

etiam: postponed for collocation with *atque*. *Periculum* refers to general peril, *aciem* to a life and death struggle.

25

secutum bellum: For word order see 21, *acta res*, and *Lig.* 6, *suscepto bello*.

bellum . . . Africanum: The remnants of Pompey's forces and the conservative Senate had gathered in North Africa, in the area around Utica. Cato the Younger was there; so was Ligarius. To the surprise—and embarrassment—of Cicero, who believed the cause had died with Pompey and, thus withdrew, these anti-Caesarians put up a spirited resistance in which Caesar's lieutenant, Curio, was killed. Caesar joined battle in late 47 and achieved a significant victory at Thapsus in the next year.

graves . . . rumores: Cassius Dio (47.26) reports that in response to rumors of Caesar's losses and death in Africa, Caecilius Bassus announced that he was taking command of Syria. Underlying the special pleading of some of this narrative is the real problem of discovering the facts of a situation amidst attendant confusion; so 11. Add the uncertainty as to who was in charge, and the indecision of men like Deiotarus, Caecilius Bassus, and even Cicero becomes understandable. Historical perspective is a tyrant for the student.

qui . . . excitaverunt: Position of the relative after a nominal predicative clause makes it almost semi-independent (= *et ei* or even *ei enim*; see *Marc.* 18 and *Cael.* 20, *graves erunt homines* [men allegedly cuckolded by Caelius], *qui hoc iurati dicere audebunt*, "in that they will dare to say this under oath"). The movement is staccato. Cf. perhaps *ita graves erant . . . rumores, ut . . . excitarent* in a more connected style.

furiosum illum Caecilium: With this locution the man's instability becomes a permanent attribute; so *Sest.* 37, *C. Marium . . . sextum illum consulatum gerentem* (his famous sixth consulship). Except where they become part of a man's name, adjectives cannot be added attributively to a proper name; even with a generic noun, like "father," Cicero adds *vir* in apposition for the adjective to modify; so 23 and *Lig.* 2. Otherwise he must use *ille* in the phrase.

qui . . . maluerit: a circumstantial relative, giving grounds for an answer to the question. This is the second mention of auctions held in Caesar's behalf (see 14); it is a strong, pathetic point, although motives might be questioned. It also bears out Cicero's contention at 22 that Deiotarus was pressed for cash.

subministrare: The only other use of this compound in the speeches suggests something surreptitious, as if his support of Caesar involved danger. Cf. *Cael.* 20, *palam in eum tela iaciuntur, clam subministrantur* "weapons are hurled at him openly, but they are supplied surreptitiously."

at: as at 23, but here with *inquit*; the prosecutor's narrative. No prepositions because spies were (purportedly) sent into the cities (cf. 19, *ad Numantiam*)—Nicaea in Bithynia, Ephesus on the coast of Asia Minor. The object of *mittebat* is in the relative purpose clause.

perisse . . . circumsederi: The effect of asyndeton is to connect these two events as an appropriate motivation for the quotation. After a chaotic landing in North Africa, Caesar was hemmed in at Ruspina, between Hadrumetum and Leptis Minor, and sought the aid of Domitius Calvinus.

eadem sententia: Deiotarus would have said it in Greek (the original has not survived, although there are fairly close parallels for the commonplace; cited in R&E, 100). The Latin scans as an iambic senarius and sounds old because of the elisions. On the other hand, Cicero, himself a more than competent poet, knew how to translate verse into Latin. Caesar, of course, would have understood the original, but reciting Greek in a courtroom was not the habit of orators, even assuming that Cicero knew the original verbatim. Apparently Domitius did not die but was present (see 32) to speak to Deiotarus' character.

si: = *etsi* (here reinforced by *tamen*) as at *Marc.* 23.

immanis: See on *Lig.* 11. The word *immanis* derives from an old Italic root **mān-*, meaning "good," as in *Dis Manibus*. More fanciful etymology associates it with *mănus*, "hand"; there is paronomasia here with *man⟨u⟩suetus* = "used to the hand, tame, civilized."

autem: introduces a contrasting, though not antithetical or adversative argument; see on *Marc.* 11, *ceterae . . . huius autem*. After Caesar's settlement of Asia, with Domitius in charge, Deiotarus' relationship with Domitius may have been less warm. Cicero takes literally what may have been a less than accurate antithesis in the quoted verse.

porro: strong denial of the preceding, introducing its correction; so 16.

belli lege: See on *Marc.* 12.

26

quid deinde?: so 19, *quid postea?*

furcifer: Although a physician, he was yet a slave. For some minor infraction a slave might be forced to walk around with his arms tied to a fork-shaped pole behind his neck and recite his offense, "more as a degradation than a punishment" (Donatus [second cent.] on Ter. *Andr.* 618).

ait: Cicero claims to introduce this charge in the accuser's words. Readers should keep in mind that all speeches in Cicero's orations must be suspected of having been composed by Cicero.

se obruisse: a strong word (see 37) colorfully used to refer to alcoholic excess; so twice of Antony at *Phil.* 3.31 and *Phil.* 13.31.

nudum: stripped down to undergarments; see on Virg. *G.* 1.299.

saltavisse: Only the sternest Romans objected to dancing per se. Some dancing was ritual, and certain displays were countenanced at banquets when performed by hired dancers. But for guests to participate was considered undignified; so *Mur.* 13, *nemo fere saltat sobrius, nisi forte insanit, neque in solitudine neque in convivio moderato atque honesto.* Cicero accuses more than one opponent of public dancing (e.g., at *Piso.* 22) and indignantly excoriates Antony's performance during the Lupercalia of February 44 (*Phil.* 2.84–87).

quisquam ... umquam: A negative response is clearly expected, so *quisquam* (vs. *aliquis*) and *umquam*, strategically placed.

praecipue: an unanticipated antithesis with *omnes*. Note ellipsis of verb.

frugalitas: does not entail merely financial restraint, but control of all excesses. Cicero glosses it at *Tusc.* 3.16 with Socrates' word *sophrosyne*, self-restraint occasioned by a knowledge of one's limitations; so *modestiam et temperantiam* below.

etsi: *correctio* in a sentence fragment explained in next sentence; cf. *Lig.* 31, *quamquam*.

frugi: dative of *frux*, frozen as an indeclinable adjective. Effective word order: *frugi*, first as subject word; *dici* separated to avoid jingle; *non multum*, a litotes, emphasized by separation from its dependent genitive (it also makes a phrase of *laudis in rege*); *in rege* in emphatic position, a major qualification. *Hominem* is needed because the predicate substantive is not in accusative case (see on 16) but perhaps, too, to distinguish kings (and their virtues).

multum habet laudis: "to have scope for," "bring about," as at *Mur.* 89, *habere dolorem* = "be grievous" (vs. "be grieved"), and *Verr.* 2.5.182, *quid habent ... periculi?* = "what danger [does their enmity] present?" (vs. "to be in danger"); see Shackleton Bailey 1, 1:352 or 5:286.

fortem . . . liberalem: Accusative adjectives follow construction with *dici*; they are summed up by *hae* (so 30, *hoc est*; *Marc.* 8, *haec*), leading to *illa*. With their emphasis on generosity and benevolence, these were Caesar's virtues. *Liberalis* = "worthy of a freeborn man."

ut volet: (sc. *id quod dicam*) sounds like a common phrase but is not otherwise attested. Brief future condition has a somewhat dismissive sense; so *Marc.* 27.

maximam iudico: double cretic in two cretic words. Had Cicero reversed the word order, the rhythm would have been the same and *maximam* would have a different emphasis. Cicero takes *maxima virtus* as a concept, like *summum bonum*. The postposition of the adjective is striking.

haec . . . perspecta et cognita: a handsome, complimentary sentence with hyperbaton postponing the doublet predicate and careful phrasing of a *cum . . . tum* correlative. Anaphoric repetition and expansion in the first half is balanced in volume by the relative clause in the second.

ab ineunte aetate: For the ablative phrase see 2.

a cuncta Asia: personified (so *Lig.* 4, *Africa*). The perfect passive is in secondary sequence, truly past *and* passive, and so agency is expressed; cf. *Marc.* 3, *intellectum est . . . mihi.*

27

quidem: for constrast with *sed tamen* as at *Marc.* 9: Deiotarus as king and a (Roman) gentleman. So the contrast between perfect and imperfect: "Although already established he would . . . ."

quidquid (sc. *temporis*) **. . . vacabat:** accusative of extent of time, like *Lig.* 5, *quod . . . restitit.*

res rationesque: phrase embellished by alliteration; so 2, *tueri et tegere*; 28, *pudoris pudicitiaeque*; 30, *ingrate et impie*; *Lig.* 36, *tot ac talibus*; and *Marc.* 23, *perculsa atque prostrata.*

pater familias, etc.: a gentleman, and a Roman gentleman at that. Varro (*De Re Rustica* 1.1.10) reports that one Diophanes of Nicaea sent Deiotarus his translation of the six-volume work on agriculture by Mago of Carthage.

qui . . . is: compact, ornate (rhetorical question), epigrammatic conclusion to a refutation (*igitur*). It is unclear (perhaps unimportant) whether the clause is characteristic, causal, or concessive in this *argumentum a fortiori*.

ea . . . eaque: response to *adulescens* and *gloria praeditus*. The demonstrative, even *is,* can have a qualitative connotation, and so may trigger an *ut* clause as at 22; cf. 28, *eum virum unde.*

28

Castor: not mentioned by name since the exordium (2), now addressed for the first time. This is, in effect, an encomium to Deiotarus through a *vituperatio Castoris*. The logical place for *potius* would be before *imitari,* balanced by *quam maledicere*. But Cicero brackets the period with the infinitives; and *potius* is effective before *avi mores.*

disciplinamque: moral training, as well as education; so at *Lig.* 20.

quodsi . . . habuisses: Positive before negative description concedes the former.

pudoris pudicitiaeque: not a synonymous doublet; the first is a state of mind, the second refers to behavior.

in illam aetatem conveniret: Cf. at 16, *in hominem . . . caderet*; evokes a pathetic image, exploited in the next lines and contrasts with the youthful insensitivity of Castor.

quibus . . . ea: relative–antecedent order in expository style; so *Marc.* 15.

non saltandi, sed . . . ut: The directional sense of *studium* can be satisfied by a gerundive or by a final clause. Change from one to another between *non* and *sed* is striking; it sets in relief the relationship between the two actual goals, delineated by the degrees of the two adverbs.

tamen: as if the sentence had begun; *quibus quidem* like 27, *multis quidem,* but here concessive movement is not signaled.

itaque: visual images, noble but pathetic, presented dramatically: (1) the effort to get Deiotarus on his horse; (2) he kept a firm seat, though an old man and (by implicit contrast with *plures*) unaided; (3) the impression he left (subjective mode).

plures: = *complures,* which has no comparative force and so is more apt, but avoided because of *cum.*

haerere: The subjunctive leaves no doubt as to how remarkable this feat was perceived as being. It was not just a question of sitting, but of staying on; cf. Horace C. 3.24.55, *nescit equo rudis / haerere ingenuus puer.*

hic vero adulescens: strong contrast and vivid identification with deictic pronoun. He was with Cicero's forces in Cilicia in 51; in Greece with Pompey's troops, as was Cicero.

commilitio: Caesar so describes those with him in the common cause (Suet. *Div. Iul.* 67).

una: so used in *Marc.* 23, and alone in the verse quoted in 25.

pater: Tarcondarius Castor (Caesar *BC* 3.4).

quos concursus: that is, what a commotion he made.

in illa causa: The construction of the phrase is deliberately vague, placed between *nemini* and *studio*. Prepositional phrases do not usually modify nouns or pronouns; cf. *Lig.* 29, *de vestra in illa causa perseverantia.*

29

exercitu amisso: A compendious ablative absolute gets the narrative past the battle and to the point at which Cicero wants to begin.

ego . . . hunc: The *qui . . . abiciendorum* interrupts the predication with a long qualification. The prominence of *hunc* and delay of the main clause stress Castor's recalcitrance.

pacis semper auctor: as at *Lig.* 28.

post . . . proelium: cut out by some editors (such as R&E, 163) as a gloss on *exercitu amisso*; but it provides a good contrast to *semper.*

suasor: a rarer word than *auctor*; used here for variety with much the same meaning. Cicero expresses the new depth of his pacifism by a correction in echoing genitive plural gerundives. The jingle of these disyllabic endings is unmistakable and hence only selectively used; see *Marc.* 2, *studiorum ac laborum.*

non . . . sed: There was no longer any reason for anyone to pursue the Pompeian cause. This passage should be compared with *Marc.* 5 and *Lig.* 28 for differences in tone, attitude, and content. For example, at *Lig.* 28 Cicero admits to an enthusiasm close to *ardebat . . . belli* here. There his strategy was to suggest Tubero's enthusiasm; here he wants to isolate Castor's enthusiasm from the general feeling of defeat and resignation.

auctoritatem: Cf. *auctor . . . fuissem*, above.

patri: Context colors the commonplace: filial piety is never contemptible, but here by contrast it constitutes an attack on the elder Castor, Deiotarus' son-in-law. So *domus*, stressing the close relationship disgracefully violated. Deiotarus' loyalty to Pompey is more favorably described at 13. Cicero did not cavil with Cato for adhering to the cause not only after Pharsalus but after Pompey's death, although he himself thought the fight was over.

felix . . . calamitosus: antithetical exclamations in the nominative, the latter describing the losses involved in a legal conviction; so *Lig.* 16.

qui . . . accusetur: parallel in syntax to *quae adepta sit,* but less neat. The king is degraded in three ways. He is, like Ligarius, accused by fellow Pompeians; he is accused before (the aggrieved) Caesar, who had pardoned Castor; he is accused by his own relatives. Cicero divides it [A] + [*non modo* B, *sed etiam* C] to distinguish the degradation of the charge itself from the litigation it spawned.

vos vestra . . . fortuna: For the *interpretatio* see *Marc.* 6, *vos . . . non potestis . . . esse contenti* span the period.

30

sane: The intensive particle takes its color from context. At *Marc.* 22 it reinforces the exhortation; here it is concessive.

quae . . . debebant: After independent concessive subjunctive, movement of the statement becomes complicated. *Sint . . . inimicitiae* is countered by the independent clause *tamen inimicitias . . . gerere poteratis.* Concession is qualified first by a relative clause explained in a parenthetical sentence (note *enim* and see 11). Now a concessive clause, *quamvis . . . repudiaretis* (resuming with *sed* after the parenthesis), restates *quae esse non debebant* with more colorful language, providing a protasis for the main predicate.

e tenebris . . . evocavit: The most colorful language of the period falls in the parenthesis. This metaphor for obscurity of birth is found only here; and it is significant that Cicero does not qualify it; see *Marc.* 2, *quasi quodam.*

quis . . . audivit: a devastating locution introduced without a connective. The object of *audivit* is an indirect question compared with another indirect question in a temporal clause. The subject of both questions is the same; but it was drawn back into the main clause as an accusative. The construction is well established, but not frequent in prose. Its use here can hardly be avoided because of the double questions with predicate nominatives dependent on a question itself introduced by *quis.*

ingrate et impie: alliterative doublet; so 27, *res rationesque.*

necessitudinis nomen: kinship as a concept, where the genitive is appositional or explanatory. The figurative use of *nomen* extends from 40, *regium nomen in hac civitate sanctum fuit,* to *Phil.* 13.1, *dulce . . . est nomen pacis, res . . . cum iucunda, tum salutaris,* to *Balb.* 54, *genus ipsum accusationis et nomen.*

hominum more gerere: for whom family relationships are natural. For *more* with a genitive to produce a simile cf. *Verr.* 2.4.5, *sacra quae . . . more Atheniensium virginum reposita in capitibus sustinebant.* The locution is not frequent in Cicero and may be elevated: cf. Virg. *Aen.* 4.551, where Dido wishes she had lived out her widowhood free of marriage, like a wild animal (*more ferae*).

poteratis: governs both the positive infinitive that precedes and the three negative ones that follow in anaphora.

expetere vitam: Cf. *Lig.* 13, *sanguinem petere;* in earlier speeches Cicero generally used *sanguinem* and *vitam* as a phrase (e.g., *Quinct.* 39, *Rosc. Am.* 7), also *caput* and *vita* (see Landgraf, 26). This compound form of *petere* is used only here with *vitam,* and once with *sanguinem* (*Piso.* 99). The charge of malevolence interrupts two strictly judicial considerations. *Capitis* is genitive of the charge. With the negative infinitives *debebatis* would have been more accurate.

esto: a formula of concession, completely dropping an argument.

adeone: another concession, again qualified; a vivid ellipsis for *adeone concedendum est?*

omnia . . . iura: figuratively for the human contract, as only slightly less so for the civic contract at 32, *ut huius urbis iura et exempla corrumperes.* Cicero maintains that Castor fails to adhere to the lowest code of conduct for civilized men. The notion of *humanitatis iura* is commonplace, but not always noble. At *Balb.* 57, noting that his client's opponents slander him behind his back, Cicero says that they envy him *more hominum.*

abducere domum: verbal prefix separative, accusative directional.

omnibus familiis: the sanctity of the Roman household and of *pater familias* (an area in which Deiotarus distinguished himself). Cicero highlights the antithesis of *uni . . . omnibus.* He had raised this point at 3, *de fortunis communibus.* The whole natural domestic order is upset if slaves (who are counted among the *familiares*) can so act against their masters.

ista corruptela: Note the constructions: *esto,* a single word predicate expanded by a construction depending on *adeone*; then, without sentence connective, a list of infinitive phrases merely registered and then summed up by the definitional clause *hoc . . . est*; see 26, *fortem . . . liberalem.* Next an expansion is introduced by *nam.* The orator is turning his subject into a disquisition. The theme word is placed first, *si* postponed. The language and constructions are embellished and an *exemplum* will be introduced. The three other times that *corruptela* appears in the speeches, it is in the plural, "cases of corrupting," but not the abstract "corruption." Cicero wants a terse but loaded phrase: *servi* is objective, as if *corruptela* were a highly predicative verbal noun—to work with the *impunita . . . adprobata* balance.

auctoritate: abstraction for person, i.e., = Caesar = *Caesare auctore,* so introduced by *a.*

parietes: concrete for abstract.

leges . . . iura: If *leges* are strictly distinguished from *iura,* they refer to particular statutes. But *iura* are rules; and *leges* may be similar, as at *Mur.* 11, where *lex accusatoria* means the usual practice of prosecutors. The tricolon does not expand; see *Lig.* 5, *Uticae . . . maluisset?* and *Lig.* 33, *moveant . . . germanitas*, vs. *Lig.* 6, *o . . . decorandum.*

quod intus est: what goes on inside the walls; a part of the fabric of the *familia.*

evolare: a metaphor of slaves running away, applied to the countenancing of a slave's public revelation of what goes on within the walls of a *domus.*

fit in dominatu: This figure of reversal in neat collocation is called *commutatio.*

31

o tempora, o mores: It is surprising how rarely the great phrasemaker repeats himself. This locution, from *Cat.* 1.2, following *Verr.* 2.4.56, introduces a pointed comparison with older and better times.

Cn. Domitius ille: Romans were taught civic virtue by example (see on 19). Cn. Domitius Ahenobarbus hauled M. Aemilius Scaurus before the Comitia Tributa (*in iudicium populi*) on a charge of impiety in connection with the cult of the Penates at Lavinium, which was under Scaurus' charge (*In Scaur.* 18–19, Clarke). Motive was probably personal (so *inimico* below; Scaurus had failed to nominate Ahenobarbus to the college of augurs), which makes this *exemplum* more apropos. The construction of this single, anecdotal period presents all the relevant facts and circumstances before ending with the point of the story; cf. 25, *itaque . . . intercidant.*

quem . . . vidimus: Personal reminiscence sharpens historical perspective; cf. *Arch.* 16, *hunc . . . quem patres nostri viderunt, . . . Africanum.* Ahenobarbus was censor in 92, when Cicero was fourteen. For the collocation of demonstrative and relative see on 2, *ei cuius.*

principem civitatis: This was not, like *princeps senatus*, an official title, nor was it one when Octavian modestly permitted himself to be called *princeps* ⟨*civis*⟩.

ad eum clam domum: in effect three adverbs, the accusatives separated by *clam*; *domum* = "to his home."

hominem: *Homo* can substitute for a form of *is*; see *Marc.* 14. As such, it is especially at home in plain style, informal narrative.

vide quid intersit: presses Castor directly and vividly.

etsi: sentence fragment, as at 26; this is not addressed to Castor. At *Piso*. 8 Cicero also apologizes for a comparison between his opponent and a more worthy person, and then goes on with *sed tamen* to dismiss the apology and make the comparison.

sed tamen: With the strong particles, the comparison comes as an appendage to the correction, rather than as a consequence of *vide quid intersit*. *Tu* and *ille* alternate as in the famous comparison between a general and a jurisconsult at *Mur.* 22.

servum contra dominum: The prepositional phrase (adverbial) should modify the verbal aspect of *adiutorem*; see 28, *in illa causa*. Cicero places *adiutorem* first for antithesis with *accusatorem*, collocates the appositive nouns, and creates a concept *servum contra dominum*.

32

at: Cicero sarcastically adduces the accusers' contention that although they had bribed Phidippus at the outset, he had admitted it and recanted, and that his present testimony was freely given and untainted. It is unlikely that Castor would have made his point in just this way. The facts of this matter are recorded only here, and by an interested party. Phidippus apparently did admit to having been bribed and was still appearing against Deiotarus. Cicero's interpretation is that he was bought a second time.

semel: so at 9, *tum . . . cum*.

a vobis: by father and son at the outset, when Castor seduced him away from the embassy.

perductus: drawn to, by reason or other inducements. This is the reading of most manuscripts and describes a time before the trial. Some manuscripts and editors read *productus*, "introduced in court," and assume that Phidippus' change of position occurred once the trial had begun.

Cn. Domitium: with Servius Sulpicius Rufus and T. Torquatus, present (so the deictic demonstratives) to speak to this point as *advocati*, character witnesses, at Cicero's request. Cn. Domitius (if he is the Calvinus of 14 and 25) had survived rumors of his death and returned to Rome, where he was host at the dinner at which Sulpicius, the distinguished legal scholar and consul of 51 and Torquatus, otherwise unknown, were present. Sulpicius was an old and generally admired friend of Cicero. His *consolatio* on the death of Cicero's daughter is preserved as *Fam.* 4.5. *Phil.* 9 is a eulogy to him.

a te . . . tuis: The anaphora at the beginning of parallel phrases in asyndeton is forceful. Cicero is representing Castor's argument.

quae est ista: formula for outraged or pathetic questions; *est* = "means." See *Verr.* 5.58, *quae est ista tandem laudatio*; *Leg. Ag.* 2.79, *quae est ista superbia et contumelia*; *Phil.* 1.21, *quae est ista cupiditas legis eius ferendae*.

ista tam impotens . . . inhumanitas: anaphoric tricolon, perhaps corresponding to *nonne . . . nonne . . . nonne* (above), at once ornate and forceful, in the form of an outraged exclamation. For *tam* (impossible to translate literally) see 15, *tanti sceleris,* and *Marc.* 18, *bellum tantum et tam luctuosum.*

idcirco: The purpose clause is carefully anticipated in this neat (*idcirco . . . ut*) enthymeme.

huius urbis: echoes *in hanc urbem,* as if to say that Rome, by virtue of its superior civilization, gave Castor singular scope for his repugnant behavior. Cicero had done his best to make Deiotarus into a Roman gentleman (27; and note *di penates* at 8 and 25, *ipse enim mansuetus, versus immanis*); now he appeals to xenophobia to damn Castor; see *Lig.* 11, *immanium.*

iura et exempla: the social behavior of Romans, based on rules of conduct (extrapolated from the *mos maiorum* and the example, as at 31, of Romans past, like Domitius Ahenobarbus.

domesticaque: opposed to *nostrae,* and obviously much stronger than *vestra* would have been: "that you are pleased to practice in your home." See the citation of *Brut.* 258 at 37, *eisque.*

inmanitate . . . humanitatem: paronomasia of opposites, as at 8, *orari . . . exorari*; 20, *voluerit . . . noluerit*; 25, *amicus . . . inimicus*; and 31, *incorruptum . . . corrupisti.* At 25 *mansuetus . . . immanis* is keyed to a different relationship between the words (see note there).

inquinares: a very strong word for defilement; cf. *Cael.* 78, of Clodius: *hominem . . . ore, lingua, manu vita omni inquinatum.* Cognate with *caenus* = mud, slime, or what floated in the Cloaca Maxima.

33

at quam acute: As at 19, *quam festive,* Cicero makes an abrupt transition to another part of the accusation with an ironic appeal to Caesar's professional admiration. This is a return to the argument interrupted at 28 by his *vituperatio Castoris.* It is hard to imagine that Blesamius' letter, even with the criticisms of Caesar, would have played a large part in the charges; it is extraordinary that in this and the next section Cicero defends, not Blesamius against having made the charges, but Caesar against being guilty of them.

Blesamius: a member of Deiotarus' inner circle and part of his embassy to Rome (see 41), accused of having communicated to the king rumors about popular dissatisfaction with Caesar.

eius enim nomine: The public recitation of such scurrilities by the prosecution, Cicero suggests, was a disservice as much to the dictator as to Blesamius. The ample genitival phrase describing Blesamius is in effect a defense against his having vilified Caesar.

nec . . . ignota: Litotes strengthens the affirmative.

in invidia esse: provides a passive for *invidere,* much as *in odio* does for *odisse.*

tyrannum: strong negative sense, as at 15. Statues of Caesar were being installed on the Rostra in the Roman Forum—not a novel practice—by order of the Senate (also unsurprising). One in ivory, to which a chariot was later added, was also ordered set up in the Circus Maximus; another in the temple of Quirinus, inscribed DEO INVICTO; a third on the Capitoline, near those of kings of Rome. These may have fanned the rumors that Caesar aspired to monarchy. The suspicions persisted and did Caesar no good. All this seems to have sapped Cicero's newly found enthusiasm for Caesar (*Att.* 12.45.3, 13.17.3).

plaudi: true at the Ludi Circenses of 45, a fact Cicero reports with glee in *Att.* 13.44.1. Public reaction to public figures at theatrical performances and games was an expression of the *vox populi*. It was, of course, open to manipulation and to various interpretations, but it did matter, both to the great *patroni* of the Republic and later to emperors. The circuses may have been calculated to distract the Roman people, but they also provided the opportunity for politicians to be seen by constituents and to "press the flesh." Students of democratic politics will be interested in *Sest.* 115–27.

malevolorum sermunculis: The diminutive expresses Cicero's contempt for the true source of these slanders attributed to Blesamius.

Blesamius . . . scriberet: The subjunctive is deliberative, cast as a question.

multorum . . . multos . . . multas: sarcastic exaggeration supported by initial position and anaphora. There is a nervous lack of balance: *multorum* and *multas* are adjectives, *multos* is substantive; three adjectives (see below) modify *multos*; *multas* modifies a noun otherwise modified by a pair of passive participles; a fourth phrase object to *viderat* is added, also modified by a passive participle, but with a different phrasing and without a form of *multus*.

capita: The severed heads of the proscribed had been fixed on poles and displayed in the Forum in the time of Sulla. A similar fate awaited Cicero in December 43.

viderat: Pluperfect, even indicative, can convey unreality, especially after *enim,* and supplies a sarcastic explanation for something that never happened (*scriberet*). Blesamius must have been in Rome, but he could never have seen these things.

vexatos: functions as the passive to *persequi*. Alliteration pairs two adjectives, making them in feeling distinct from *necatos* in spite of the homoeoteleuton that binds them all. After the sensory verb, all the participles describe actions vividly observed.

adflictas et eversas: Both are strong verbs and have some overlap of meaning. The second describes more than physical destruction, extending to the posterity of the family.

refertum forum: practically, "filled to capacity." It had been teeming with Pompey's soldiers in 52 for the trial of Milo, but, more relevant, also in the 80s during the civil disturbances. The adjective is colorful but not necessarily pejorative; cf. *Pomp.* 44, *cum universus populus Romanus referto foro . . . Cn. Pompeium imperatorem depoposcit.*

quae semper: an abrupt return to reality in asyndeton. Cicero deliberately avoids summing up the envisioned horrors of war with a transitional *haec* or *ea* in initial position. In this highly epigrammatic period *quae* waits until the main clause for its antecedent, emphatically placed before *te victore.* In addition to antecedent–relative order the paronomasia of *victoria* and *victore,* the phrase *civili victoria,* and antithesis in the similarly placed verbs make this a handsome coda.

in civili victoria: for *belli civilis victoria*; a striking phrase, almost an oxymoron, fraught with pathos (cf. Luc. *Phar.* 1.1, *bella per Emathios plus quam civilia campos*).Position of adjective suggests it is predicative; so *Marc.* 18, *civile bellum.*

sensimus . . . non vidimus: At *Marc.* 17 he used *vidimus . . . non vidimus*; here all sources of knowledge are elicited.

34

inquam: affirms the entire statement, not just *solus*; see at *Marc.* 28, *illa, inquam.*

nemo nisi armatus: The same phrase occurs at *Lig.* 19, the same point at *Marc.* 17, *gladium vagina vacuum . . . non vidimus.* There is little evidence to refute the claim—but, then, Caesar won.

et quem . . . is: The *et* is a highly rhetorical conjunction; cf. *Lig.* 18, *aut tua.* It replaces one passionate outburst with another. See, too, *Phil.* 1.12, *quis . . . senatorem coegit? aut quid est ultra pignus aut multam.* For word order, reversing relative and antecedent and thus strongly marking the identification, see at 33, *quae . . . ea*; *Marc.* 8, *haec qui faciat . . . eum*; and *Marc.* 15, *qui . . . is.* Precise articulation of a perverted *argumentum a maiore,* i.e., "if we who were raised in liberty do not conceive of Caesar as a threat to liberty. . . ."

nos . . . Blesamio: inconcinnity in the balances: nominative pronoun against dative noun, nominative participial phrase against relative clause; compound accusative phrase (*tyrannum*) against predicate nominative (*tyrannus*). In the latter two the Roman side is amplified, first to establish the glory of Republican freedom, then to pay a special compliment to Caesar. Defending Caesar against a charge of aspiring to tyranny has its problems; the fact that he was merciful is not really cogent. Cicero opts for appealing to the more credible authority. *Liberi* is not just padding to reinforce the symmetry:

quem nos	liberi in . . . libertate nati non . . . tyrannum . . . vidimus
is Blesamio	
qui vivit	in regno tyrannus videri potest.

The orator invites the suggestion of a suitable parallel adjective to modify Blesamius.

non modo non: addition of *non* alters only the first half of the formula *non modo . . . sed etiam*; so at 38 with *verum*.

nam: The sentence connective is not logically consequential. It explains how unknowledgeable Blesamius is as a critic of Roman affairs. With this connective, like *nam si locus* below, Cicero enthusiastically introduces a point only to refute it (an *occupatio*: see 16, *at credo*).

queritur: indicative, not potential: "what Roman?"

una: separated from its noun so that it can be the point of an opposition with *multas* (thus *tam multas* vs. *tantas* or *tot*). The number is, of course, not the point.

praesertim: adds to a preceding element a specification of logical or rhetorical import. The most common construction is with a causal (*cum* clause, relative + subjunctive, or sometimes causal participles), but it can also introduce individual words, as here and in *Marc.* 9, and more rarely ablatives absolute (see on *Marc.* 3 and 20).

valde: vehement, but less subjective than *profecto* (see *Marc.* 3), which does not take first position in a period; here, ironic.

invidendum est: responds to 33, *in invidia est*.

non invidemus: Rhetoric calls for a strong adversative, but Cicero insists on a purely descriptive relative, focusing the syntax on *eius statuis cuius tropaeis,* bracketed by two forms of *invidere*.

locus: Again Cicero obfuscates; the Capitoline statue was criticized for the royal company it kept, not statues on the Rostra. He could hardly expect to have confused Caesar on this point.

nec . . . umquam . . . non numquam: a delicate explanation of an embarrassing situation. It is surprising that Cicero even mentioned it, especially considering his lack of sympathy; see *Att.* 13.44.1, where Cicero congratulates the people when, at the Ludi Victoriae Caesaris, a statue of Victory being carried in procession was not applauded *propter malum vicinum*, that is, because a statue of Caesar was being carried next to it (see Tyrrell and Purser, 5:159). The play on *nec . . . umquam . . . et non numquam* is perhaps meant as a distraction. For *qui = nam is* see 35, *quod abest*, and *Marc.* 18, *qui . . . excitaverunt*.

qui . . . desideratus: that is, a missed object of longing. The question is answered in a relative clause; less obviously rhetorical than *nempe* + demonstrative + relative at *Lig.* 7 and 9.

in te: more delicate than *a te*; not a question of Caesar's feeling the lack.

obstupefactis . . . admiratione: The ablative absolute is causal; *admiratione* is instrumental with the participle. Perhaps an example of the kind of adulatory reasoning that was far exceeded by imperial orators; but see Ellman, 49, describing how Ruskin's lectures were received by Oxford undergraduates in the 1870s: "His eloquence led them to clap for him as for no other professor, or even—greatest tribute of all—to forget to clap." Or did Ellman know his Cicero? Like so much in the *Caesarianae*, this might be understood as precisely the trained orator's answer to a question unceremoniously introduced: e.g., *de plausu quid respondeam?* Cicero could also interpret embarrassing silences, as when he says (*Cat.* 1.21) of the senators' failure to support him vocally, *cum tacent, clamant*.

35

praeteritum: As Cicero preceded his refutation of the charges with a discussion of the prosecutor's motivation, so after his refutation he insists on Deiotarus' lack of motivation for killing Caesar. The section begins with a prothesis; and the articulation of the problem is set out with almost excessive explicitness: *nihil . . . praeteritum, sed aliquid . . . reservatum. id . . .*

ad extremam partem: Three variants occur in the manuscripts, none impossible, but one is preferable. *Extremum* (= "the end") is used in his philosophical works, but not in the speeches, in a philosophical sense; and the dependent genitive would not be an obvious construction. Including the genitive in the accusative phrase is neater, and perhaps, given the plain style of the context, for that reason less preferable.

id . . . aliquid: as if in quotation marks; so *Lig.* 22.

reconciliet: At 8 Cicero insisted that the reconciliation had taken place.

illud vereor: Instead of *sed ne* Cicero uses fuller parataxis and provides a demonstrative *illud* (even in the vicinity of *illi* and *illum,* and not corresponding to a *hoc*) in order to state his concern with utmost clarity. The pronoun also provides an antecedent for *quod* in the next sentence; cf. 4, *perturbat me etiam illud . . . quod.*

quod abest: (sc. *a vero*). Semi-independent relative substitutes for demonstrative + sentence connective (here = *sed id,* as at 34, *qui = nam is*).

mihi crede: the almost invariable order of the two words in this expression, at least in the speeches. *Crede/credite mihi* occurs in the more colloquial letters (in *Att.*; only once in *Fam.*)

quid . . . retineat . . . non quid amiserit: Positive–negative articulation stresses both; cf. *neque . . . arbitratur, sed . . . non recusavit,* below. The position of the main verb helps balance the two. In Caesar's resettlement of Asia (see the Introduction, section 3.3), he lost everything outside of Galatia, including Armenia.

cum existimaret: generalized second-person, as at 4; not Caesar. The third-person reading in some manuscripts (*C* and *H*) is easier, but still attractive. Cicero cannot be expecting Caesar to believe Deiotarus' generous reconciliation to his privations. But if he does believe it, Cicero has an even more farfetched example of ungrudging resignation to tell below.

multis . . . multa: by contrast with *qui in altera parte fuisset,* referring to more loyal or effective Caesarians in Asia, like Mithridates of Pergamon. For similar paronomasia with *omnis* see 15; a form of *traductio,* for which see on 8, *hospes hospiti.*

ea (sumeres): nicely indefinite. The closest referent, *multa*, allows the implication that the losses were not great.

36

etenim: strong confirmatory connective: affirming by *et* and explaining by *enim*.

Antiochus Magnus ille: another complex anecdotal period (like the one on Ahenobarbus at 31), encompassing all relevant circumstances and the point at the end. Here, the anecdote and the period extend beyond the bon mot to end with a different instructive point. Antiochus Magnus III (223–187) had ruled the Seleucid kingdom from the Hellespont to the Indus. He was defeated by Scipio Asiaticus in 191 and ended up with only Syria.

> si Antiochus Magnus ille, rex Asiae,
>> cum
>>> postea quam a L. Scipione devictus Tauro tenus regnare iussus est,
>> omnem hanc Asiam
>>>> quae est nunc nostra provincia
>> amisisset,
> dicere est solitus
>>> benigne sibi a populo Romano esse factum,
>>>> quod . . . liberatus modicis . . . uteretur,
> potest multo facilius hoc se Deiotarus consolari.

After this extravagant period the constructions become decidedly less ornate; note the asyndeton.

tenus: the only example in the speeches of this usually postpositive preposition.

magna procuratione: Cicero cannot really be suggesting that this witty but mordant utterance will be Deiotarus' consolation. His point is that Deiotarus will not just live with the settlement, but will bear no hard feelings. There is also the suggestion, above, of an exceptional stoicism in his understanding of Caesar's need to strip him of his lands.

hoc: accusative of respect; leads to next sentence, with explanatory *enim*.

furoris . . . erroris: The lesson of the exemplum is expressed in a simple antithesis, unadorned by complex syntax; the commonplace is found in the correspondence between *errorem appellant* and *crimine furoris* in *Lig.* 17–18. Mistakes may be culpable, but are easily forgivable; see *Marc.* 13 and *Lig.* 1.

omnia: Cicero conveys his client's dignity and pathos through straightforward sentiments handsomely but simply expressed. *Omnia, magno,* and *multa* begin periods with no sentence connectives; Cicero deliberately avoids development of logical or emotional movement.

tu . . . Caesar: the words embrace *Deiotaro* as Caesar does Deiotarus.

cum . . . concessisti: temporally simultaneous, not (explicitly) causal, as at *Marc.* 13, *cum M. Marcellum . . . conservavit,* and *Lig.* 18, *cum pacem esse cupiebas.* By the order of clauses, the honored title outweighs all tangible gains—now, in any case, lost.

nomen . . . nomine: On repetition of an antecedent word in a relative clause see on *Lig.* 2, *legatione.*

hoc . . . nullum . . . nullum: effective restatement (*interpretatio*) of the preceding.

populi Romani . . . senatus: Caesar had maintained the republican legitimacy accorded him. Elements are set in antithesis by insistent, bipartite, anaphoric *nullum* in asyndeton.

ne fortunae quidem: as a more likely cause for losing heart. Cicero portrays him rather in this spirit at *Div.* 1.27: "But the best thing about him was this: he said he never regretted the auspices that showed favorable to him as he set out to meet Pompey. For the authority of the Senate and the liberty of the Roman people and the dignity of their rule had been defended by his arms. . . . He considered his glory something of longer standing for him than his possessions."

37

multa: in emphatic position, as opposed to what he has lost.

in animo atque virtute: perhaps similar to the collocation of *animus* and *ingenium* at *Lig.* 35. The preposition may be locative with *animo,* but goes less well with *virtute,* which is not located in the body. *Virtus* is a strong word, but essentially all-purpose in referring to a person's inner assets. See on *quid . . . dicam* below. Perhaps a hendiadys = "manly spirit." Deiotarus is forced to deal with tangibles and find solace in memories.

possit amittere: double cretic.

quae tanta . . . iniuria: The rhetorical question insists on the point. For *tanta* see *quae tanta delebit oblivio* below. The position of *possit* creates a double cretic cadence (the dactylic *iniuria possit* is thereby avoided) marking a clausula and assuring emphasis on *omnium* as the first word in a colon.

omnium . . . decreta: Word order continues to be striking. The unit, enclosing the prepositional phrase between modified genitive and its governing noun, has impressive volume. Cicero recalls Deiotarus' distinguished record of service to the Roman state at *Phil.* 11.33, mentioning Sulla, Murena, Lucullus, and Pompey, with all of whom he fought against Mithridates in Asia, Pontus, and Cappadocia, and Servilius Isauricus, whom he helped in Cilicia (78–75) as he did Cicero a quarter of a century later.

decreta delere: Awaited in hyperbaton since *possit* and held together by alliteration, they close the period with a cretic + spondee rhythm.

est . . . is ornatus: The word order is elaborate: the predicate, *est . . . ornatus,* is punctuated by *ab omnibus . . . eis . . . qui. Enim* is postponed, but not to establish *est* = "exists" (see *Marc.* 8). The temporal clause is deliberately made to modify, not the main predicate, but *gesserunt.*

per aetatem: found only half a dozen times in the speeches.

iudicia: Cf. 36, *iudicium de se senatus.* At *Phil.* 9.7 the authoritative judgment of the Senate took the form of a *consultum.*

tam multa: *Tot* would be usual, but consider 34, *tam multas,* and the wish for anaphora.

litteris monumentisque: The first are formal reports preserved in archives, the second are inscriptions on bronze or stone tablets, duplicated for exhibition both at the temple of Fides in Rome and in the relevant country abroad. Note the specific mention of the Roman people in the context of senatorial recognition; see at 36.

quae . . . vetustas . . . aut quae . . . oblivio: *interpretatio* as at 29, *vos vestra . . . fortuna; Marc.* 7; and *Lig.* 11. *Aut* introduces a second rhetorical question almost as a rhetorical alternative, as at *Lig.* 18; cf. *Deiot.* 34, *et quem.* The cadence is double cretic.

quid ... dicam?: Cf. word order of the same formula at 34, *de plausu quid respondeam,* to introduce a new topic. Arguments here are more general and expansive. The second prepositional phrase is a gloss on *virtus.*

quae ... sola: The Stoics called virtue the only good. This is not a deep, philosophic reflection, but a commonplace (inner virtues are the most important possessions) that is given a more scholarly and reflective expression by reference to a difference in emphasis between two philosophic schools. At *Marc.* 19 Cicero has a different reason when he distinguishes virtue from (external) good fortune: it is a greater benefit and joy; so it is irrelevant to dwell on philosophical controversy. Here, where virtue is the solace for a monarch deprived of much of his kingdom, reflection on the value of virtue alone makes acceptance more palatable, and the fact of acceptance more admirable.

bona sola: emphasizes the distinction; *sola bona* is the normal order. See 26, *virtutem maximam.*

eisque: When two relative clauses modify a single antecedent, they may be joined in one of the following ways:
1. Asyndetic repetition of the relative. Cf. 12 and 38 and *Rosc. Am.* 2, *si quis istorum dixisset, quos videtis adesse, in quibus summa auctoritas est atque amplitudo.* Usually the first is a purely essential attributive, the second "accidental"; so *Amicit.* 27, *ea caritate quae est inter natos et parentes, quae dirimi nisi detestabili scelere non potest.*
2. Joined through *et* or *-que,* with or without the repetition of the relative.
   a. Repetition is necessary:
      (1) when the case of the relative changes: *Phil.* 7.7, *qui semper pacis auctor cuique pax ... in primis optabilis,* "who was ... and to whom it was ...."
      (2) when the relatives designate different objects: *Fin.* 4.40, *omnia quae leget quaeque reiciet unam referentur ad summam.*
      (3) when the antecedent clause follows: *Fam.* 1.9.24, *quae ad me ... scribis quaeque mihi commendas, ea tantae mihi curae sunt. ...*

   b. Without repetition: *Marc.* 10, *quibus . . . dignitatem reddidisti nobilissimamque familiam . . . vindicasti.*

3. The second relative is replaced by a demonstrative. Cf. *Brut.* 258, *omnes tum fere, qui nec extra urbem hanc vixerant neque eos aliqua barbaries domestica infuscaverat, recte loquebantur.*

Of these, the repetition of the relative with a connective is most frequent in Cicero. In this instance, where the relative is semi-independent and = *et ea*, no alternative to the demonstrative is possible.

38

reputans et . . . cogitans: formulaic; cf. *Marc.* 22, *de te dies noctesque, ut debeo, cogitans.* Active, concomitant participles can set a reflective mood. So *De Orat.* 1.1, *cogitanti mihi saepe numero et memoria vetera repetenti. Reputo* occurs three times in the speeches. The following context suggests accountancy.

non modo . . . non: not followed by *verum etiam*, because the movement is not merely to a stronger case or statement, but rather to a different expression in which the first is no longer considered; so too *Marc.* 9 and 34.

esset enim . . . : parenthetical.

tranquillitatem . . . acceptam: "*ab urbe condita* construction," as at *Marc.* 3. The participle became closely attached to *refert* in the idiom of business: *acceptum referre* = "to credit the receipt of"; cf. *Phil.* 2.12, *ut esset nemo qui mihi non . . . vitam suam, fortunas, liberos, rem publicam referret acceptam.*

quo: = *et eo*, the gratitude Cicero has just ascribed to his client.

quidem: contrasts Deiotarus' state of mind before and after the embassy to Tarraco. Cicero insists on parataxis, as at *Marc.* 15.

cum . . . tum: correlation essentially temporal: "at a time when he was already . . . , he was lifted." It also correlates a general circumstance with a particular, in the kind of adversative in which A was good but B was better; see 1 and 12.

quarum . . . quas: On two relative clauses with one antecedent see 37, *eisque.*

exemplum: One might send copies of letters he wrote or received, either in toto or excerpted.

Tarracone: It appears that Deiotarus sent Blesamius, as his envoy, to Tarraco during Caesar's Spanish campaign against Pompey's son, Sextus, in 46–44. Ablative of source or origin.

iubes enim: present tense, because the letter is in Cicero's hands. The words of encouragement need not have been imperially expressed. At *Lig.* 7 (see note) Cicero cites his own letter from Caesar, of August 47, with the enjoinder in a jussive clause: *ut essem idem qui fuissem.*

scribere meque . . . iussum: change of tense: "I remember your writing and that I was urged. . . ."

39

laboro: See on *Lig.* 31.

equidem: The reinforced form of *quidem* has largely the same effect, here anticipating a contrast, which comes with *sed cum . . . laboro.* See at *Lig.* 30.

amicitiam . . . hospitium . . . familiaritatem . . . necessitudinem: a number of peculiarly Roman sociopolitical relationships, presumably in ascending order. *Necessitudo* involves the strongest ties of obligation stemming from a personal relationship, stronger even than the normal range of familial ones (recall that household slaves are among the *familiares*). *Hospitium*, a tie between Caesar and Deiotarus that Cicero exploited (see on 8), goes back to the relationship between host and foreign guest found in Homer. The Romans, with an eye to international affairs and economics, conducted much of their foreign policy along the same lines as they did their domestic affairs, basically through patron–client relationships. Cicero speaks elsewhere of his relationship with Deiotarus (*Fam.* 9.12.2, *hospes vetus et amicus*) and of his debt to him (e.g., *Fam.* 15.4.5 and *Phil.* 11.34). *Amicitiae*, though no doubt accompanied by outward displays of affection, were often practical relationships; see Rawson, 6).

res publica: Cicero's own public affairs, that is, his governorship of Cilicia.

hospitium: not properly a direct object; see 13, *hospitio . . . coniunctus*;

rather, an internal accusative: *coniungere coniunctum (quod est hospitium)*.

summam vero: Cicero deliberately breaks the symmetry of asyndetically connected predications with *vero*, which throws considerably more weight to the second part; see *Marc.* 7. He accentuates his effort to give prominence to the last member by switching to a plural verb and expanding with prepositional phrases. The repetition of *in* is not necessary but is rhetorically effective; see on *Lig.* 2, *in qua*.

cum (laboro): + indicative, not strictly temporal, but concomitant or (better, as at 1 and 38) adversative: "although I am doing X, I am also doing Y." As at 12 there is no verb in the second half, an indication, perhaps, that the correlatives might be better taken simply with the prepositional phrases in parataxis.

semel: as at 9 and 32 and below, of an action that will not be repeated; so Hor. *C.* 1.28.15–16, *sed omnis una manet nox et calcanda semel via leti*. Cicero is not so much talking about double jeopardy as suggesting that the security felt through being pardoned would be shattered if Caesar's pardon, once granted, were to be altered in Deiotarus' case.

ignotum . . . esse: impersonal passive. The expression is fairly colorless. Then diction becomes elevated: *haerere* (see 28); *sollicitudinem sempiternam*; the tension between *incipiat* and *semel* and between *timere* and *liberati timore*.

quisquam: for *aliquis* because of the negative cast.

40

The peroration is the time for unrestrained emotional appeals to the judge (note the full vocative; see on *Marc.* 2, *C. Caesar*). This practice Cicero claims to eschew, allowing the intrinsic elements of the case to affect Caesar spontaneously. He assumed the same attitude at *Lig.* 31. As elsewhere in *Pro Ligario* and *Pro Rege Deiotaro* he seems to be saying, "I will not insult your intelligence with shameless appeals to your emotions. I won't do that; but I expect that you will be moved just the same by the merits of the case" (similarly at 7). As one would expect, this is a *praeteritio*: the *maerentes amici* are waiting in the wings.

periculis: a technical term in the courts; as at 1.

ecquonam modo: = *num quonam modo*. *Ec-* is an infrequent prefix often corrupted to *et* in manuscripts (especially in minuscule manuscripts where *t* and *c* were frequently confused).

opus est: absolute; usually constructed with a dative of interest and a predicate nominative or instrumental ablative of what is needed, less frequently with an infinitive phrase. *Nihil* is, as at 35, *illud vereor*, an accusative of respect.

occurrere: The personification is striking, especially because the activity seems routine. Understand "when you are judge"; this does not, therefore, contradict *quod fieri solet*.

nullius: as at *Marc.* 4.

propone ... dabis: For imperative + future indicative in parataxis and asyndeton = *si proposueris, dabis* see *Lig.* 30 and *Sulla* 5, *recordare de ceteris ... intelleges* ("Consider those other things ... and you will realize ..."). On *propone* cf. *Marc.* 5, *ante oculos ponere*.

duos reges: Deiotarus and his son. As a matter of foreign policy, Deiotarus' successor might be of some interest. But that is not the issue here; cf. 41.

id ... quod: an explicit frame for the antithesis of *animo* and *oculis*.

dabis ... denegasti: another epigrammatic, almost self-standing sentiment, using the same *id ... quod* structure. In this, the verbs bracket the sentence.

multa ... sed maxima: Balance in the adjectives and an alliteration can be heard in these brief, independent clauses. *Clementiae* is probably dative. The position of *eorum* is determined primarily by a need to establish *maxima* as predicative in this deliberately lean construction.

incolumnitates: a term of the courts, vs. *periculum* and *calamitosi* above. For the plural see 13, *utilitatibus*. If thought about, this is a tough concept for Caesar to deal with. *Clementia* is a policy whose success depends on the endorsement of its recipients.

in privatis: For the preposition see 1, *in tuo ... periculo*, and 34, *in te*.

in regibus: The antithetical prepositional phrase brackets the sentence and achieves a double cretic rhythm.

regium nomen: As at 30, the concept or institution is stressed, not the title or individuals. See *Arch.* 19, *sit . . . sanctum apud vos . . . hoc poetae nomen*, and *Arch.* 18, where he glosses *sanctos*: "because they seem to have been commended to us as if by gift of the gods." Scipio Africanus makes an important distinction at Livy 27.19.4, *regium nomen, alibi magnum, Romae intolerabile esse.* Still, statues of Roman kings stood on the Capitoline; Caesar could claim a royal ancestor (Ancus Marcius; see Suet. *Iul.* 6). See 33, *tyrannum.*

As to the genitival adjective, Cicero uses it with *nomen* at 27, at 36, and at *Mur.* 34; with *potestas* and *dominatus* five times (four in the *Philippics*) and elsewhere in this speech: 19, *regio et animo et more*; 3, *regiam condicionem*; 26, *regiae laudes*; 41, *legati . . . regii*; and 17, *servum regium.* The basic sense is "that is associated with, belonging to, monarchy (rather than an individual king)."

41

quod nomen: not semi-independent; the entire clause, of which it is the direct object, is predicate to *retentum . . . et . . . confirmatum* as the object of *tradituros se esse.* A sentence connective might have been employed, so its omission is deliberate.

hi reges: observations on this aspect of Roman foreign policy, now related to Deiotarus and the question of succession (see on 40)—a concept as un-Roman as monarchy, but destined soon to change. For deictic pronoun and absent individuals see *Lig.* 5 and 11.

te victore: ablative absolute by placement, given temporal force and causal force.

Hieras . . . Dorylaus: Little is known of these ambassadors or how familiar they would have been to Caesar. This is the moment in a speech to exploit the friends of the accused for sympathy, as at *Lig.* 33; but, as in the case of Ligarius, Cicero does not have much to work with. Note that the insistence on their being "proven" was much in evidence in *Pro Ligario* as well. Caesar had had dealings with the first three at Tarraco (see 38) and with Hieras in the East as well, though Cicero can only hope that Caesar will remember them. Dorylaus is clearly a newcomer.

tibi . . . probati: The nominal list lies in apposition to *hi* in an artfully

unbalanced bipartite construction: the first three are described in a predicate phrase, then a fourth is added, characterized in a participial phrase
and described in a relative clause, before all are once more described in a
compound correlative predicate phrase, pointed by *cum . . . tum*, in which
a clause is added to lend weight to the second part and avoid concinnity;
cf. *Arch.* 3, *veniam accommodatam huic reo, vobis, quemadmodum spero,
non molestam.*

42

exquire de Blesamio: The denial might have been elicited at 33, but it
would have interrupted the series of arguments evoked to show the prima
facie weakness of the accusation. Perhaps, too, under the circumstances of
the trial, the calling of witnesses was inappropriate.

ad regem: A prepositional phrase is preferred to the dative for antithesis
with *contra*.

Hieras quidem: in contrast to Blesamius.

suscipit . . . supponit: an alliterative pair.

causam omnem suscipit: The meaning is not to undertake a case at law,
although that is not precluded, but to associate oneself with a cause, as at
Lig. 26, *de suscepta causa.*

criminibus: dative with *supponit*. At *Verr.* 2.5.75, Verres, having allowed
a pirate to bribe his way to freedom, substitutes (*suppositum a te*) someone
else for execution. There seems to be no basis in Roman law for such a
substitution.

qua . . . plurimum: See at *Lig.* 35. Position of the relative clause makes it
causal in feeling.

negat . . . dicit: The verbs bracket two statements; the positive one continues. There was no mention of this eyewitness in the narrative of the
alleged events; the argument would have had more force than the evidence
of a friendly witness without much *auctoritas*. In any case, an indication
of Cicero's defense strategy.

in primis finibus . . . usque ad ultimos (fines): inclusive; the *cum* clauses, with the powerful homoeoteleuton of the verbs, cover the critical periods. This insistence is not casual.

adsiduitatem: "persistent attendance." Quintus Cicero (*Pet.* 3) advises his candidate brother to practice *cottidianam amicorum adsiduitatem ac frequentiam.*

43

quam ob rem. . . . quocirca: first a summation of the Hieras account; immediately following, a summation of the entire speech.

eorum: Cicero might have identified them more closely with their source by using *istorum*; *eorum* makes the charges seem more remote; so *illorum* below.

cogitatum: "premeditated, designed, intended"; so *Lig.* 30, *"non fecit, non cogitavit."* Deiotarus might have been specified here, dative with *obiecta.*

quocirca: appears only three times in the speeches, but at *Dom.* 144 it introduces a very dramatic and moving prayer addressed to the Capitoline Hill.

velim existimes: Paratactic use of *volo* with the subjunctive is distributed almost equally between *velim* + present subjunctive (second-person seven times, third-person thrice) and *vellem* + imperfect (six times) or pluperfect subjunctive (six times), all third-person. In the imperfect the sense is of *utinam* for an unfulfilled wish. In the present it indicates a polite request.

hodierno die: more weighty and emphatic than *hodie*. See on *Marc.* 1.

cum . . . dedecore . . . pestem . . . famam cum salute: formally chiastic. *Cum* is frequently postponed in modified phrases; its neutral position is first. Here it plays off the second phrase.

importaturam: The metaphor, an elevated synonym for *adferre,* is as old as Pacuvius fr. 178R, *quantamque ex discorditate cladem importem familiae.* Its sphere is commerce, but it is not used literally by Cicero in the speeches. In its three other occurrences it governs *calamitatem.*

illorum: See *eorum* above.

crudelitatis . . . clementiae: Defining genitives qualified respectively by *illorum* and *tuae*. Recall 2, *crudelem Castorem*.

clementiae tuae: plain, definitional balance. The defense has directed itself as much towards leniency as equity. The closing words seem flat for this place in a speech, but they press Caesar in an effective way, raising again questions of the scope for emotional appeal and Caesar's status that Cicero dealt with earlier.

GLOSSARY

Boldface terms within entries indicate cross-references to other items in this glossary. Particulars are given as felt useful. Fuller references to many of the features in the commentary are given in the General Index.

ablative absolute: In later speeches Cicero extends the simple adverbial function of this construction. It may lie outside the syntactic limits of the period, following the predicate, and generate its own construction. This usage more closely approximates that of the historians, not least of all Caesar.

abstract nouns: Many abstract nouns were firmly embedded in the language by Cicero's time and were used without particular effect. Cicero's use of less common abstract nouns and coinage of new ones is usually determined by considerations of style and construction. Two particular usages for stylistic purposes may be remarked: he uses abstract nouns when he seeks an essentially plain diction with colorless words, or when he seeks concision. See *Marc.* 32, *sanitas*; *Lig.* 4, *profectio . . . remansio*; *Lig.* 36, *bonitas*.

"ab urbe condita construction": a phrasal complex (adjective + noun) in which focus shifts to a predication in the adjective, and the complex acquires a verbal or clausal nuance. Like an **ablative absolute**; see the Introduction, section 1.2. Examples at *Marc.* 3, *ex quo . . . gloria*; *Lig.* 25, *acceptae iniuriae*; *Deiot.* 2, *ineuntis aetatis*; *Deiot.* 38, *tranquillitatem . . . acceptam*.

accusative + infinitive: As a verbal noun, the infinitive treats the verb as a fact, rather than an act. With subject accusative (e.g., *Q. Ligarium in Africa fuisse*), the complex functions as a noun clause.

addressee (= **point of address**): Readers unaccustomed to the literary genre of oratory must pay close attention to the person or persons the orator is addressing at any moment, and especially to shifts in the point of address. See the Introduction, section 1.2, and notes at *Marc.* 1, *patres conscripti*; *Lig.* 2, *habes igitur*; *Lig.* 23, *vide . . . Caesar*; *Deiot.* 18, *tibi*; and on *Deiot.* 28. Cf. **vocative**.

alliteration: successive words beginning with the same sound. An early feature of style used with restraint by Cicero for special effect. See notes at *Marc.* 9, *litteris atque linguis*; *Marc.* 12, *victoriam vicisse*; *Marc.* 17, *dubitare debeat*; *Deiot.* 2, *tueri et tegere*; *Deiot.* 27, *res rationesque*; *Deiot.* 37, *decreta delere*. Cf. **doublet**. For alliterative prefixes see at *Marc.* 11, *conficiat et consumat*. Alliteration creates **hypallage** at *Marc.* 17, *vagina vacuum*.

anacoluthon: a deliberate deviation from the syntax established in a sentence to reflect excitement, confusion, colloquial informality, etc. See on *Marc.* 11, *quae quidem*; *Lig.*, 28, *an*.

anaphora: repetition of initial word of phrases or clauses to link successive units and support parallelism. It reinforces both **tricola** and **bipartite antithesis.**

antecedent: Use, absence, and placement of antecedents to a **relative clause** is a major technique for marking the progression of a period with desired emphases. Cicero often modifies the antecedent with a demonstrative pronoun or adjective as a means of anticipation to keep a following relative clause periodic. Occasionally the demonstrative modifying an antecedent will lead to an *ut* clause. In this kind of periodic expectation and resolution, other works that anticipate constructions— e.g., *ita* and *sic* for result clauses, *idcirco* causal clauses—function similarly. A neuter demonstrative pronoun and, occasionally, *sic* or *ita* may act as antecedent to prompt an accusative + infinitive.

anticipation: the numerous ways a periodic stylist has of signaling to the audience what to expect syntactically, rhetorically, or logically. See the Introduction, section 4. Taking advantage of syntactic expectations, for example, that an adjective expects a governing noun, the writer can create suspense. Such expectations may be disappointed by the author; the order noun–adjective can effect surprise. For the expectation of constructions with particular words see the Introduction, section 4. For the anticipation of an opponent's objection see **occupatio.**

antithesis: the generic word for balances both parallel and opposite. This **Gorgianic figure** is basic to **bipartite construction.** In the **periodic** style such balances usually occur at the level of clause; in the **pointed** style, generally associated with **Silver Latin,** they are more likely to turn on phrases or single words.

aporia: a figure of speech in which the speaker claims to be unable to proceed because of confusion or insurmountable odds against him. So *Lig.* 1, *quo me vertam nescio.*

aposiopesis: the dramatic halting of a syntactic unit to avoid the articulation of something frightening, threatening, or embarrassing. See notes at *Marc.* 17, *alterius vero parte*; *Lig.* 9, *nimis urgeo*; *Lig.* 28, *an*; *Lig.* 30, *taceo.*

apostrophe: dramatic direct address; see *addressee*. See *Lig.* 2, *habes igitur,* and note at *Marc.* 10, *C. Marcelli.*

appositive: Not merely one noun glossing another (see esp. *vir* or *homo* used in honorific appositive, *Lig.* 2, *qua virum*; 10, *homo*; *Deiot.* 10, *homo . . . alienigena*), but as a noun clause glossing another noun clause and explaining or characterizing it, as at *Marc.* 7, *quod . . . maximum est*; *Marc.* 18, *quod . . . verebamur*; *Lig.* 2, *quod . . . optandum*; *Lig.* 32, *quod soles*; *Deiot.* 17, *ita.*

argumenta:
a. **a fortiori**: from a stronger case to a weaker. So at *Marc.* 21, *quisnam est iste*;

34, *cum . . . praestiterim*; *Lig.* 5, *desideri*; 14, *si*; 15, *quam multi*; *Deiot.* 16, *quod . . . facinus*; 27, *qui . . . is.*

b. **a maiore**: from a greater instance to a lesser. So at *Marc.* 4, *non dicam . . . sed*; *Deiot.* 18, *quidem*; *Deiot.* 34, *et quem . . . is.*

c. **a minore**: from a lesser instance to a greater. So at *Marc.* 10, *vero.*

d. **ex contrariis**: from the unacceptability of the opposite; see *Lig.* 10, *quorum . . . eorum.*

e. **ex difficiliore**: from a more difficult proposition to an easier or more palatable one. So on *Lig.* 8, *qui . . . non dubitem*; 31, *sperandi . . . deprecandi.*

Asianism: a label, perhaps invented in the 40s, for a style of composition, purportedly fostered by Greek rhetoricians of Asia Minor and the islands, that concentrated on ornamentation more than style(see the Introduction, section 1.1). The other stylistic polarity in the controversy was **Atticism**, which claimed for itself a direct and **plain style** once exhibited by Lysias and Thucydides. The style finds its most complete description in the *Orator* and is criticized in the *Brutus*. It is uncritically identified with Cicero. The dichoraeus clausula is associated with it.

asyndeton: omission of a **sentence connective** or of connectives between members of a series. Because in narrative and expository style such connectivess are expected, their absence is usually remarkable, except when the new sentence begins a new thought, starts with a **semi-independent relative**, is deliberately artless (*Deiot.* 36, *Antiochus Magnus*), or consists of an **occupatio**. **Asyndeton** links two units thus joined particularly closely and often supports a **bipartite antithesis**, setting in initial position the same word—i.e., **anaphora**.

Atticism: stylists, real or imagined, of a restrained school vs. **Asianists**. Cicero's style in the *Caesariana*, so perceived, should be attributed not to literary polemics but to circumstances of the speeches; see the Introduction, section 4.

balance (structural): distribution of elements in one unit to correspond, though rarely symmetrically, with those of another unit; e.g., *Marc.* 19, *a virtute . . . a fortuna*; 20, *viris bonis.* Cf. **antithesis, isocolon**. Techniques of balance may be applied to **tricola** or to more limited phrases. The diagrams in this work attempt to present balances visually. For grammatical vs. syntactic balance see *Marc.* 1, *diuturni silenti*; 13, *ignoratione . . . crudelitate*; for antiphonal balance see *Marc.* 13, *nam cum.*

bipartite construction: the pairing of balanced **parallel** or **antithetical** units ranging from words and phrases to clauses and sentences. See *Marc.* 19, *tantus est enim.* It is antiphonal and insistent and plays against the more expansive rhythm of the **tricolon**; see *Marc.* 24, *tanto . . . tanto.* Often supported by **anaphora** and appearing in **asyndeton**, such constructions convey a tension, nervousness, or excitement; see *Lig.* 21, *ita . . . ita.*

bracketing: inclusion of dependent material between two words expected to go together, e.g., between demonstrative adjective and noun or between noun and descriptive adjective or participle. Other forms of bracketing occur, e.g., a verb at beginning and end of a compound sentence. See *Marc.* 7, *adversarium . . . praestantem*; 8, *extollere . . . iacentem*; 17, *vidimus . . . non vidimus*; 21, *huius . . . suae*; 23, *omnia*; 24, *omnia*; 25, *parum; istam* (hyperbaton makes attributive what it brackets); 26, *admirationis . . . gloriae* (antithesis of genitives); 29, *vagabitur . . . (habebit); erit . . . dissensio* (predicate brackets); *Lig.* 6, *voluntatis*; 25, *quae . . . querela* (adjective–noun); 30, *quaere* (imperatives bracket); 31, *sperandi . . . deprecandi* (gerund); 38, *longiorem . . . breviorem* (producing an epigram, bracketed by its key words); *Deiot.* 3, *etiam ab invito*; 5, *causam . . . dico*; 11, *cum audiret*; 28, *Castor*; 34, *non invidemus* (bracketed by two forms of *invidere*); 40, *dabis . . . denegasti*; 42, *negat . . . dicit* (verbs bracket two statements). See also **hyperbaton**.

brachylogy: brevity of diction attained by a compendious or elliptic use of grammar. *Marc.* 11, *hunc . . . diem.*

cadence: See **clausulae.**

chiasmus: a word order in which corresponding elements are disposed AB:B¹A¹. See *Marc.* 1, *diuterni silenti . . . finem, . . . initium . . . dicendi*; 7, *numquam enim*; *Lig.* 3, *partim . . . partim*; 25, *venissetis . . . venistis*; 35, *exterminandi*; 38, *illi absenti . . . ; Deiot.* 2, *ornare*; 8, *dexteram istam . . . ; 43, cum dedecore. . . .*

clausulae: use of patterns of heavy and light syllables at the ends of periods, clauses, and even phrases; see the Introduction, section 1.1. Kinds of clausulae and their frequency vary in speeches (and in other Ciceronian prose, from which clausulae are not absent). The ignorance of modern philologists on the subject is considerable; see on *Marc.* 3, *tanta gloria.* For an internal clausula see *Deiot.* 35, *quae tanta . . . iniuria,* and cf. **colon.** Rhythms found most frequently in the speeches include cretic + trochee, double cretic, double trochee, and *"Poenulum tuum"* (see further citations in the General Index).

climax: a progression of propositions in which a part of the first is repeated in the second, and so forth. See *Deiot.* 23, *aut . . . aut . . . aut.*

colloquial speech: affected, as a literary device, in the **plain style**; see *Lig.* 14, *cave.*

colon: technically the equivalent of Latin *membrum,* a unit of speech larger than a *comma* (Latin *incisum*), smaller than a period. Eduard Fraenkel attempted to identify it as a rhythmical unit of thought, bordered by other such units and separated by a natural breathing pause (see Fraenkel 3 and 4). See the Introduction, section 1.1; *Marc.* 7, *se . . . offert; Lig.* 1, *non auditum; Deiot.* 4, *tua . . . natura*; and **weighted phrase.**

commentary style: a plain, unornamented narrative style found, it is thought, in official reports to the Senate and, with much subtle and hidden art, in the *Commentaries* of Caesar. In this style it is not unusual for an antecedent word to be repeated in the relative clause; see *Lig.* 2, *qua in legatione.* See also **Curia style.**

commutatio: figure of reversal in neat collocation; see *Deiot.* 30, *fit . . . dominatu.*

conceit: the idea or handle on which turns the expression of a predication. It may be contextual, a metaphor or some other trope; it may be an attitude adopted by a figure of thought. It may also be grammatical or syntactic, a **balance, alliteration,** or **antithesis.** See *Marc.* 1, *diuturni silenti . . . finem*; 12, *detrahet . . . adfert* and *vereor*; 17, *quoniam . . . conservat*; 28, *quae miretur . . . quae laudet*; *Lig.* 10, *quorum . . . eorum*; *Deiot.* 12, *praestitisti.* See **epigram.**

concinnity: See **inconcinnity.**

congeries: a list of items without apparent limit or structure; see *Marc.* 6, *virtus . . . commeatus.*

consecutio: figure by which an orator imagines, describes, or predicts the reaction of another person, *Deiot.* 20, *quae trepidatio.* So Cicero on both Tuberones.

copula: The **sentence connectives** convey a variety of rhetorical relationships. See, particularly, for *-que*, *Marc.* 6, *easque detrahere*; 22, *doleoque*; and *Deiot.* 8, *quodque*; for *sed*, see *Lig.* 16, *sed tamen.* For *atque, at,* and *sed* see the General Index.

correctio: device by which a speaker insists on one thing by adducing and rejecting an alternative. So *Marc.* 4, *non dicam . . . sed*; *Lig.* 1, *non liberationem*, etc.; 19, *non modo . . . sed nimirum*; 22, *vel potius paruit*; 26, *nescio an melius*; *Deiot.* 2, *ne dicam*; 26, *etsi.* Cf. *Marc.* 12, *vereor*, where, however self-consciously, Cicero admits that his meaning may not be pellucid.

Curia style: a direct, bureaucratic style of reporting to the Senate; see *Marc.* 13–14, *bellum. . . . quo quidem in bello.*

deictic: the "pointing" demonstrative *hic/haec/hoc* has a dramatic function in oratory and theater that the contemporary reader must supply; see *Marc.* 7, *huius gloriae.* The orator might point to someone absent, as if present; see *Deiot.* 8, *huic.*

deprecatio: designates a judicial strategy by which the advocate throws his client on the mercy of the court; see *Lig.* 2, *confitentem reum.* Whether a whole defense could be so conducted before judges, as opposed to dictators, is in question; see *Lig.* 30, *ad iudicem sic. Pro Ligario* is said to be a *deprecatio,* but is in fact both more and less; see 10, *egimus*, and 14, *si.* Even as an argument in the larger defense it allows of various treatments, from irony at *Lig.* 1 to pathos at 25, *hi . . . tui.* See the Introduction, section 3.2, and *Lig.* 30, *tecum . . . te . . . tuorum.*

dilemma: a form of argument in which the speaker adduces alternative possibilities and argues that both are unacceptable. See *Lig.* 23, *vide Caesar.*

divisio: division of argument into kinds, classes, possibilities. See *Lig.* 3, *profectio . . . remansio*; *Deiot.* 2, *alterius . . . alterius (crudelem Castorem . . . fugitivi)*; 22, *reliqua pars*, etc.

doublet: a pair of terms that are either synonymous or used in a context where no distinction is emphasized. It is a form of padding (see *Marc.* 6, *mens aut cogitatio*) at home in a **middle,** decorative style; see **alliteration.** The second term of an apparent doublet sometimes develops and expands meaning; so *Marc.* 11, *conficiat et consumat*; *Deiot.* 5, at *ad motum animi*.

ellipsis: omission of an easily understood word. See *Marc.* 2, *eadem causa in qua ego*; 19, *cetera*; 33, *quodam modo* (ellipsis bespeaks informality, as at *Marc.* 15, *minus mirum*; *Lig.* 17, *quod nullo de alio quisquam*; 21, *magnum etiam vinclum*). For ellipsis of a construction see *Marc.* 20, *nullo modo*; of a notion, *Marc.* 12, *quae tamen*. Cf. **brachyology**.

enclitic: generally a particle, like *enim* or *autem,* found in second postion in a sentence; see **Wackernagel's law**. For forms of *esse* in enclitic position see *Marc.* 7, *quam . . . adeptus*; 23, *etiam*. Note too *Lig.* 2, *Q. enim Ligarius*. Elements that come second in their units, like weak pronouns, help to determine the beginning of a **colonn**. Enclitic *-que* is not generally attached to prepositions by Cicero; see *Lig.* 31, *ab eisque*.

encomium: a part of a speech devoted to formal praise of a person. Like its opposite, **vituperatio,** it can be treated in ways both ornamental and passionate. See the General Index.

enthymeme: a thought, perception, or point housed in a rhetorical form such as an **epigram,** abridged syllogism, aphorism, **argumentum,** or the like; a **conceit.** See *Lig.* 10, *quorum . . . eorum*; *Deiot.* 32, *idcirco*.

epigram: Pithy, balanced expressions, often forming codas to arguments, are a feature of the **middle style**; see, e.g., *Lig.* 16, *qua qui . . . utetur.* And see citations in the General Index. For conceits that turn on single words without much structure see **pointed style.**

exemplum: a figure by which a historical figure is evoked as an apposite and instructive instance of a point in an argument. See on *Deiot.* 31 and 36.

exordium: Opening section of a speech, usually in embellished **middle style** but with some exceptions. See *Lig.* 1, opening note.

expository style: conceived of as an unadorned, undramatic genre of prose writing for simple exposition of narrative and arguments in a two-tiered analysis of style; Cicero uses his **periodic** composition in complex sentences for clarity of movement; see the Introduction, sections 1.1, 1.4. It is more formal, somewhat more embellished than **plain style,** but without the more evocative devices associated with the **grand style.** Periodicity, particularly the structural order of relative clause + antecedent clause with explicit **antecedent** word, and **sentence connectives** are among the markers of the expository style. For use of indefinites see *Marc.* 7, *totum tuum est.* Elevates to more ornate style; see *Marc.* 30, *oblivio*. Uses **ellipsis**; see *Lig.* 21, *magnum etiam vinclum.* For other references see the General Index.

Gorgianic figures: predominantly aural figures of speech (**antithesis, isocolon, homoeoteleuton**) exploited by the sophist rhetorician Gorgias of Leontini, who impressed Athenian audiences and informed Athenian stylists beginning in 427 B.C.

Cicero, having trained his audiences to respond to more complex turns of language, makes limited use of these figures. See on *Lig.* 10, *genus hoc causae.*

grand (high) style: This term has undergone a confusing redefinition. Originally it was associated with oratory designed to arouse the emotions and move men's minds and was therefore appropriate to political and, selectively, to judicial speeches. The use of **periodic** sentence structure in such contexts would be limited by its obvious artificiality. Technical features that do distinguish it were avoided by austere stylists, which perhaps accounts—rather ironically—for its later association precisely with the ornateness of Ciceronian periodicity (an ornateness employed far more indiscriminately by Ciceronians than by Cicero himself).

hendiadys: a figure employing two parallel terms where one is, in sense, dependent on the other. So *Deiot.* 7, *usu atque exercitatione* = "habitual training," and *aliqua spe et cogitatione.* Further examples may be traced through the General Index.

homoeoteleuton: an aural, **Gorgianic figure** that insists on **parallelism** and creates an echoing effect by pairing words of similar ending. So at *Deiot.* 10, *animadvertisti . . . liberavisti . . . agnovisti . . . reliquisti.* For further examples see the General Index.

hypallage: transferral of attributive adjective from its proper noun to another in the context. So *Marc.* 17, *vagina vacuum*; *Lig.* 24, *huic victoriae.* . . .

hyperbaton: a figure which describes the forced separation of two words or units expected to be found in collocation. It is the chief means of **bracketing.** If the first term in hyperbaton implies the second (e.g., subject implies verb, or adjective implies noun), the figure produces **anticipation** and resolution and contributes to **periodicity.** See **interlocking word order.** Examples may be traced in the General Index.

hypotaxis (vs. **parataxis**): a composition employing essentially subordinate syntactic structures. Such complex sentence constructions may be by accretion (*lexis eiromene*) or interweaving of constituent members (periodic or *lexis katestrammene*). See *Marc.* 21, *non enim.*

inconcinnity: deliberate deviation from symmetrical balance. See at *Lig.* 14, *oppugnari . . . tollere.* It is a feature usually associated with Thucydides, Tacitus, and Sallust but not foreign to Cicero.

infinitives: neuter nouns that present actions as facts, as opposed to **participles,** which describe the action in process. For infinitives see at *Marc.* 8, *animum vincere,* and **accusative + infinitive.** For participles see *Marc.* 8, *iacentem*; *Marc.* 10, *praesentem*; and *Marc.* 16, *extimescentem.* Gerunds supply the oblique cases of infinitives.

interpretatio: restatement of a previous point. See *Marc.* 6, *quidquid . . . gestum*; 7, *numquam enim*; *Deiot.* 29, *vos vestra . . . fortuna*; 37, *hoc . . . nullum . . . nullum,* and *quae vetustas,* etc.

interlocking word order: a device related to **hyperbaton** and stylistic **interweaving.**
See on *Marc.* 2, *quasi quodam,* and 26, *pervagata magnorum . . . fama meritorum.*

interweaving: the *lexis katestrammene,* in which the constituent syntactic elements
of a complex sentence are interwoven into a **periodic** construction, rather than
merely added, one after another, as in the *lexis eiromene.* **Hyperbaton** often involves
interweaving, which can be of various types: a word from the second clause moved
up into the first; a dependent clause interrupted by its governing verb; a **relative
clause** between the accusative and infinitive of its governing structure. See, e.g.,
Marc. 4, *quam eam quam*; 13, *fato . . . funestoque*; 29, *stabilita*; Avoided at *Marc.*
15 and 29, *cum tum.*

isocolon: a **Gorgianic figure,** insists on correspondence of word order and grammatical forms in parallel or antithetical units. So at *Marc.* 30, *certamen . . . duces*;
Lig. 4, *non turpem.* Insistent at *Lig.* 8, *quid cupiebas.* Avoided at *Deiot.* 1, *quantum
. . . tantum.* See **symmetry.**

litotes: a not uncommon trope creating a strong affirmative statement by the ne-
gativing of its opposite. So *Deiot.* 8, *non erant nescii*; 33, *nec . . . ignota*; other
examples at *Marc.* 26, *parumne,* and *Lig.* 3, *non mediocri cupiditate.*

marking: any sign, rule, or technique of grammar, syntax, rhetoric, or vocabulary
by which the function of a unit of a sentence is communicated to the audience,
including, but not limited to, declensional and conjugational endings.

meiosis: Cf. **litotes.** See *Deiot.* 2, *ne dicam.*

metaphor: comparison made without the use of "as" or "like." The force of metaphors must be understood by their function in context, their intensity by their relationship to the general level of figurative elevation of their context. See references
in the General Index.

metonymy: substituting an attribute for its possessor (e.g., *Marc.* 10, *illa auctoritas*; 12, *haec . . . lenitas florescit*) or a proper name for one of the possessor's
qualities.

middle style: describes what is to Cicero a valid, functional oratorical style, as opposed to the epideictic literary style. The difference is that the artist of the middle
style must be at pains to disguise his art. Its use in oratory is, like that of other
levels of diction, determined by subject matter and the speaker's intention. Because
it is described as elegant, charming, brilliant, florid, colored, polished, it is associated with **Asianism.** See **expository style.**

narratio: Assigned by rhetoricians to follow the **exordium** of a speech, the narrative
can in fact appear in a variety of places and take a variety of forms. Narration of
Ligarius' activities in Africa (2–7) is intertwined with a precise logical argument;
the Tuberones' perigrinations to Pompey (22–27) drip with sarcasm and disbelief;
the account of the young Tubero at Pharsalus (9) is dramatic and libelous; Cicero's
adaptation of the prosecution's narrative of Deiotarus' plot against Caesar (17–

22) is burlesque. *Narratio* may begin with subject's name; see *Lig.* 2, *Q. enim Ligarius.* For *narratio* as a feature of Caesarian narrative see *Lig.* 2, *qui sic*; of **plain style,** informal narrative, see *Deiot.* 31, *hominem.*

occupatio: a rhetorical figure by which the speaker anticipates the objection of an opponent and responds to it. See *Deiot.* 16, *at*; 34, *nam.*

parallelism: See **antithesis.**

parataxis: coordinate sentence structure. Progression is marked by **sentence connectives** and other particles. Cicero uses parataxis while implying subordination; see the Introduction, section 4; see *Marc.* 15, *vero*; 20, *non enim*; *Lig.* 30, *itaque*; 31, *quidem*; *Deiot.* 37, *quidem.* Used to achieves vividness at *Deiot.* 17; informality and directness, at *Lig.* 30, *causas . . . multas,* and 31, *dic.* Parallel independent predicates: *Marc.* 28, *oportet*; *Deiot.* 25, *per me licet*; *Marc.* 25, *quaeso.* Construction, *Deiot.* 40, *propose . . . dabis*; cf. *Lig.* 30, *dic.* Rhetorically essential, *Deiot.* 19, *itaque.*

parenthesis: insertion of an independent syntactic unit within another. Clearly signaled in Latin by use of a **sentence connective** (*nam* first or *enim* second in unit). So *Marc.* 16, *non enim*; *Deiot.* 38, *esset enim.* Shows urgency, *Lig.* 14, *intellego quid loquar*; makes correction, *Deiot.* 11, *sic . . . nuntiabatur*; *dicam* parenthetic in correction, *Marc.* 5; in **anacoluthon, Marc.** 12, *quae quidem.* Predicates in parataxis, *Marc.* 28, *oportet*; *Deiot.* 30, *quae . . . debebant.* Further examples may be traced in the General Index.

paronomasia: including, but not limited to, punning; an aural technique, used selectively by Cicero. Examples may be traced in the General Index.

participles: The verbal aspect of these adjectives can govern constructions and therefore function in a way similar to fully articulated clauses. They may be considered as a concise stylistic alternative to **relative** and adverbial clauses. Active participle describes process (e.g., *Marc.* 16, *extimescentem*) vs. infinitive asserting fact. As adjectives, they may be attributive or predicative; see *Marc.* 12, *cogitans.* For **hyperbaton** of verb in perfect passive participle see *Marc.* 7, *quam . . . adeptus.* See **weighted phrase** and **ablative absolute.**

periodic: a **hypotactic** style in which the sense and syntax of a number of verbal units are resolved simultaneously at the end of the structure (usually the sentence). It is the feature of style most closely identified with Cicero, though not his only style of composition; he avoids it at *Marc.* 9, *ut eos,* and 12, *cotidie magis.* It is intrinsic to the **middle style,** but not limited to it. The period may be complex (see **interweaving**) or simple. The full Ciceronian period may reflect the compelling logic of its contents or obfuscate less than logical argumentation. See the Introduction, section 4.

personification: a figure by which human attributes are given to inanimate objects;

at home both in embellished expository and grand style. Examples may be traced in the General Index.

plain style: a literary style that professes colloquial straightforwardness and conceals embellishment. It can support a variety of tones, from factual to pathetic. Cicero (*Or.* 87–90) associates the style somewhat disparagingly with the **Atticists.** It is appropriate for **narrative** and **expository** passages and judicial oratory. He narrates anecdotes (see **exemplum**) in concise, involuted **periods.** See the Introduction, section 4.

point of address: Cf. **addressee.**

pointed (or **epigrammatic**) **style**: opposed to the **periodic** because dependent for effect on the relationship between words and brief phrases, rather than on syntactic units.

polyptoton: the same word used in different declensional endings; see *Deiot.* 8, *hospes hospiti.*

postponement: Certain words, particularly **sentence connectives,** prepositions, and clausal conjunctions, are expected to come first or second in the clause; see **enclitics.** A delay in appearance would be noted by listeners.

praeteritio: a figure by which the speaker claims he will omit to mention something even as he speaks of it. See *Deiot.* 23, *non quaero.*

predicative element: any one of a number of constructions that create or imply a full verbal predication. Adjectives: *Deiot.* 9, *inimicus* (adversative). Genitives: see at *Deiot.* 15, *cuius tanti sceleris* and *furoris fuit.* Neuter adjective + infinitive: see at *Lig.* 37, *nihil est tam populare.* Predicative apposition at *Deiot.* 24, *tibi victori.* For predicative placement of **participle** see *Deiot.* 10, *consentientis.* Further examples may be traced in the General Index.

prose rhythm: This salient and innovative feature of all prose style (see the Introduction, section 1.1), to which Cicero devotes much of his *Orator* (see Gotoff 2, 57–64 and Appendix II), contributes to the goal of preparing the listener for the end of a **period.** Among the techniques for making prose rhythmical (which include **antithesis** and **homoeoteleuton**) is the use of **clausulae.**

pro(s)thesis: The figure by which an orator announces his movement in an argument, stressing his organization. See *Marc.* 21, *nunc venio*; 33, *sed ut, unde est orsa, in eodem terminetur oratio*; *Lig.* 9, *ad me revertar.*

relative clause: adjectival subordination using the finite form of a verb and closely paralleled by the participle in attributive usage or even by an adjective. Clauses introduced by a relative but taking the subjunctive are usually adverbial in that they are circumstantial to the predicate. Indicative relative clauses, however, can have strong circumstantial nuances; so *Marc.* 13, *quorum et frequentiam*; 18, *qui . . . excitaverunt.* After a nominal predicative clause they are virtually characteristic:

see at *Deiot.* 25, *qui . . . excitaverunt*; *Lig.* 28, *qui . . . veneras*; *Deiot* 11, *in qua suam*. A relative clause may (1) precede its antecedent clause (e.g., *qui . . . is*), (2) follow it unperiodically, (3) follow it after the prompt of a demonstrative adjective modifying the antecedent noun, or (4) be embedded in the antecedent clause. A relative clause anterior to its governing clause is often picked up by an explicit antecedent pronoun in the ensuing clause for expository clarity and precision of balance. Sometimes the antecedent pronoun is the last word of the antecedent clause and comes directly before the relative pronoun, e.g., at *Deiot.* 2, *ei cuius*, and 13, *is qui*. For parallel relative clauses paired with the same antecedent see *Deiot.* 37, *eisque*.

semi-independent relative: A relative the antecedent of which is in the preceding sentence forms a smooth, tight connection between sentences. Where it is used, other **sentence connectives** are not permitted. For *qui = nam is* see *Marc.* 18, *qui . . . excitaverunt*; see also at *Deiot.* 34, *nec umquam*, etc.; 35, *quod abest = et ea*. *Quae omnes = nam ea omnes* at *Deiot.* 37. Almost parenthetical at *Marc.* 3, *ex quo . . . gloria*; 13, *quorum . . . frequentiam*; *Lig.* 1, *quae mea*; 27, *ut . . . cetera*; 32, *non dubito*. Not semi-independent at *Deiot.* 41, *quod nomen*. For referent in preceding sentence vs. semi-independent relative see *Lig.* 12, *quae tamen*. Subordinating conjunction competes with relative at *Deiot.* 1, *quod . . . etsi*. Further examples may be traced in the General Index.

sentence connectives: the expository style of Cicero expects particles suggesting the relationship of a sentence with the previous one. The relationships may be subtly expressed; readers should note the absence of sentence connectives in expository style. Note the distinction between *itaque* (sequential) at *Lig.* 2 and *ita* (consequential) at *Marc.* 6 and *Deiot.* 10. See **copula**.

sentence fragments: always noteworthy in periodic writers. To take *quamquam* and *etsi* as adverbial when the clause they introduce is not governed by an independent clause is to miss the nuance of informality and spontaneity. Examples may be traced in the General Index.

sermocinatio: a dramatic dialogue imagined by the speaker; so *Marc.* 26, *"parumne . . . relinquemus"*; *Lig.* 12, *"ego vero . . . postulo."*

Silver Latin: a modern term for Latin literature of the Empire. In general, authors demonstrated less restraint in the use of rhetorical tropes and figures. With political oratory less vital (see on *Deiot.* 9, *cum . . . tum*), mannered declamation superseded the orator's art. **Periodic** composition, mastered by Cicero, gave way to a **pointed style** in which conceits turned on smaller elements—the phrase rather than the clause—in precious **epigrammatic** expression.

symmetry: structural symmetry in balanced clauses (**isocolon**) with meticulous correspondence (*parison*) is identified with early rhetoric and the **Gorgianic figures**. Cicero uses symmetry selectively and for special purposes, generally substituting other techniques of construction in order to prepare audience for what will follow.

synecdoche: a figure using the part for the whole, as at *Lig.* 8, *mucro.*

tetracolon: the longest controlled multiunit construction, less frequent than either **bipartite** or tripartite (**tricolon**) constructions. See *Marc.* 1, *tantam . . . tam*; 28, *certe*; and **congeries.**

traductio (= **polyptoton**): wordplay involving two or more cases of the same word in close proximity. So *Deiot.* 8; *hospes hospiti,* and 35, *multis . . . multa.*

tricolon: tripartite structure at the level of word, phrase, clause, or period. A basic rhythm of Indo-European languages, it conveys a sense of resolution, especially when the members expand in length. By contrast, **bipartite constructions** convey tension; so *Marc.* 19, *tantus est enim.* Further examples may be traced in the General Index.

variatio: Any deviation from verbal, structural, or rhetorical correspondence and balance was noticed by the ancient audience. *Variatio* is thus a figure central to Cicero's goal of avoiding predictable balance and symmetry in his periodic style. See **inconcinnity.** The orator may use synonyms to articulate parallel constructions (so *Deiot.* 24, *ei . . . nulla in re defuit, tibi . . . praesto fuit,* as opposed to *et ei et tibi praesto fuit*); English style is generally less tolerant of casual repetitions than Latin.

vituperatio: condemnatory speech (vs. **encomium**). See on *Marc.* 10, *parietes . . . gestiunt; Deiot.* 28, *Castor.* Caesar's *Anti-Cato* (see the Introduction, section 2) was a *vituperatio.*

vocative: Cf. **addressee** and **apostrophe.** On punctuation see *Lig.* 7, *Caesar.*

volume: not an ancient term; indeed, I owe my awareness of the concept to my wife, a sculptor. The architecture of a periodic construction requires attention to the balance (or imbalance) of material, to structural "carrying" weight. "Padding" may be a stylistic necessity, even a virtue. See *Marc.* 1, *tantam . . . tam . . .* ; 10, *commemorabile*; 13, *nam cum.*

Wackernagel's law: from his observation that, after stressed initial position in an Indo-European sentence, a weak word is placed in the unemphatic second position.

weighted phrase: modified nouns become rhythmic units with breath pauses before and after, especially if the modifier is verbal (participle or verbal adjective) and governs or controls further circumstantial information. See on *Marc.* 7, *se . . . offert.* See **colon** and examples given in the General Index.

word order: The disposition of words for sound and emphasis is a concern at every level of style. Word order is not random in Latin; see **hyperbaton.** For word order in **periodic** constructions see **antithesis, bracketing,** and **postponement.** For references see the General Index.

zeugma: two objects that require a slightly different sense of their governing verb. So *Deiot.* 18, *odia . . . arma.*

BIBLIOGRAPHY

Adams, J. N. "A Type of Hyperbaton in Latin Prose." *PCPS* 17 (1971): 1–16.

Ahlberg, A. W. "De traiectionis figura ab antiquissimis prosae scriptoribus latinis adhibita." *Eranos* 11 (1909): 88–106.

Albrecht, M. V. [1] *Meister römischer Prosa von Cato bis Apuleius*. Heidelberg, 1971.

————. [2] "Rhetorik." *RE* Suppl. 13 (1973): 1237–1347.

André, J.-M. *L'otium dans la vie morale et intellectuelle romaine*. Paris, 1966.

Axelson, B. *Unpoetische Wörte*. Lund, 1945.

Axer, J. *The Style and Composition of Cicero's Speech "Pro Q. Roscio Comoedo."* Warsaw, 1980.

Bauman, R. A. *The Crimen Maiestatis in the Roman Republic*. Johannesburg, 1967.

Berger, A. *Encyclopedic Dictionary of Roman Law*. Philadelphia, 1953.

Berger, D. *Cicero als Erzähler europäischer Hochschulschriften*. Vol. 15. Frankfurt, 1978.

Bolzan, V. *Orazione pro Ligario*. Florence, 1955.

Bowersock, G. W. "Historical Problems in Late Republican and Augustan Classicism." *Entretiens Hardt* 25 (1979).

Bringmann, K. "Der Dictator Caesar als Richter." *Hermes* 114 (1986): 72–88.

Bush, A. C., and S. Cerutti. "A Use of the Term Frater in the *Pro Caelio*." *CJ* 82 (1986): 37–39.

Cameron, A. *Bread and Circuses*. Inaugural lecture, King's College. London, 1974.

Caplan, H. *Rhetorica ad Herennium*. Cambridge, 1968.

Castorini, E. *L'ultima oratoria di Cicerone*. Catania, 1975.

Chausserie-Laprée, J. P. *L'expression narrative chez les historiens latins*. Paris, 1969.

Clark, A. C. *The Descent of Manuscripts*. Oxford, 1918.

————, and W. Peterson. *M. Tulli Ciceronis Orationes*. 6 vols. Oxford, 1901–11. [Cited in commentary as "Clark"]

Classen, J. C. [1] "Cicero *Pro Cluentio* 1–11 im Licht der rhetorische Theorie und Praxis." *RhM* 108 (1965): 104–42.

————. [2] "Ciceros Rede für Caelius." *ANRW* I.3 (Berlin, 1973): 60–74.

Cortini, G. *L'orazione "Pro Marcello."* Turin, 1931.

Craig, C. [1] "The Central Argument of Cicero's Speech for Ligarius." *CJ* 77 (1984): 193–99.

———. [2] "Defining Cicero's Audience: Quo Usque Tandem." Typescript. 1984.

———. [3] "Dilemma in Cicero's *Div. in Caecil.*" *AJP* 106 (1985): 442–46.

Davies, J. C. [1] "Cicero's Plain Style." *Latomus* 29 (1970): 729–38.

———. [2] "Molon's Influence on Cicero." *CQ* 18 (1968): 303–14.

———. [3] "Phrasal *Abundantia* in Cicero's Speeches." *CQ* 18 (1968): 142–48.

———. [4] "Reditus ad rem." *Latomus* 27 (1968): 894–903.

Douglas, A. [1] "Bibliography of Cicero's Writing from the Year 1945." *ANRW* I.3 (Berlin, 1973): 132–38.

———. [2] *Cicero: Brutus.* Oxford, 1966.

Drumann, W., and P. Groebe. *Geschichte Roms.* 6 vols. Berlin and Leipzig, 1899–1929.

Ellendt, F., and M. Seyffert. *Lateinische Grammatik.* Berlin, 1880.

Ellman, R. *Oscar Wilde.* New York, 1988.

Ernout, A., and F. Thomas. *Syntaxe latine.* Paris, 1951.

Fausset, W. Y. *Cicero: Orationes Caesarianae.* Oxford, 1906.

Fraenkel, E. [1] "Eine Form römischer Kriegsbulletins." *Eranos* 54 (1956): 189–94 = *Kleine Beiträge,* 2:69–73.

———. [2] "Kolon und Satz." *Nachr. Gött. Ges. der Wiss., phil.-hist. Kl.* (1932): 197–213 = *Kleine Beiträge* (Rome, 1964), 1:73–92.

———. [3] "Kolon und Satz." Part 2. *Nachr. Gött. Ges. der Wiss., phil.-hist. Kl.* (1933): 319–54 = *Kleine Beiträge,* 1:92–130.

———. [4] *Leseproben aus Reden Ciceros und Cato.* Rome, 1968.

———. [5] "Vrbem quam statuo vestra est." *Glotta* 33 (1954): 157–59 = *Klein Beiträge,* 2:139–41.

Gelzer, M. *Caesar.* Translated by P. Needham. Cambridge, 1968.

Gotoff, H. [1] "Analyzing Cicero's Style from the Text of Cicero." *CP* 77 (1982): 336–39.

———. [2] *Cicero's Elegant Style.* Urbana, Ill., 1979.

———. [3] "Cicero's Style for Relating Memorable Sayings." *ICS* 6.2 (1981): 296–316.

———. [4] "Towards a Practical Criticism of Caesar's Prose Style." *ICS* 9.1 (1984): 1–18.

Greenidge, A. J. *The Legal Procedure of Cicero's Time.* Oxford, 1922.

Greenwood, L. H. G. *Verrine Orations.* 2 vols. Cambridge, Mass., 1948.

Guttmann, C. *De Caesarianarum orationum genere dicendi.* Dissertation. Greifswald, 1883.

Halm, K. [1] *Ciceros Reden für T. Annius Milo, Q. Ligarius, König Deiotarus.* Berlin, 1899.

———. [2] *Rhetores Latini Minores.* Leipzig, 1863.

Hands, A. "Humor and Vanity in Cicero." In *Studies in Cicero,* edited by J. Ferguson et al. Rome, 1962.

Heinze, R. "Ciceros Rede pro Caelio." *Hermes* 60 (1925): 193–258.

Hellmuth, H. *De sermonis proprietatibus in prioribus orationibus*. Dissertation. Erlangen, 1871.

Humbert, J. *Les plaidoyers écrits et les plaidoiries réelles de Cicéron*. Paris, 1926.

Johnson, W. R. *Luxuriance and Economy: Cicero and the Alien Style*. Berkeley and Los Angeles, 1971.

Kennedy, G. A. [1] *The Art of Rhetoric at Rome*. Princeton, 1972.

———. [2] "The Rhetoric of Advocacy in Greece and Rome." *AJP* 89 (1968): 419–36.

Klotz, A., and F. Schöll. *M. T. Ciceronis Orationes Caesarianae*. Vol. 8. Leipzig, 1914.

Klotz, R. *Ciceronis Orationes Selectae XIV*. New York, 1876.

Kroll, W. "Studien über Ciceros Schrift *De Oratore*." *RhM*, n.s. 58 (1903): 552–97.

Kühner, R., and C. Stegmann. *Grammatik der lateinischen Sprache*. 2 vols. Hannover, 1912–14.

Kumaniecki, K. "Der Prozess des Ligarius." *Hermes* 95 (1967): 434–57.

Lacey, W. K. *Cicero: Second Philippic Oration*. London, 1986.

Landgraf, G. *Kommentar zu Ciceros Rede Pro Sex. Roscio Amerino*. Berlin, 1914.

Laughton, E. [1] "Cicero and the Greek Orators." *AJP* 82 (1961): 27–49.

———. [2] *The Participle in Cicero*. Oxford, 1964.

———. [3] Review of E. Fraenkel's *Leseproben aus Reden Ciceros und Cato*. *JRS* 60 (1970): 188–94.

Laurand, L. *Etudes sur le style des discours de Cicéron*. 3d ed. 3 vols. Paris, 1928–31.

Lausberg, H. *Handbuch zu Rhetorik*. 2 vols. Munich, 1960.

Lebreton, Jules. *Etudes sur la langue et la grammaire de Cicéron*. Paris, 1901.

Leeman, A. D. *Orationis Ratio*. Amsterdam, 1963.

Leumann, J., B. Hofmann, and A. Szantyr. *Lateinische Syntax und Stilistik*. Munich, 1965.

Linde, P. "Die Stellung des Verbs in der lateinischen Prosa." *Glotta* 12 (1923): 153–78.

Lob, M. *Cicéron, Discours: Pour Marcellus, Ligarius, le Roi Dejotarus*. Paris, 1952.

Long, G. *M. Tulli Ciceronis Orationes*. Vol. 4. London, 1858.

McDermott, W. "In Ligarianam." *TAPA* 101 (1970): 317–47.

Mack, D. *Senatsreden und Volksreden bei Cicero*. Wurzburg, 1937.

Madvig, N. [1] *M. Tullii Ciceronis De Finibus Bonorum et Maiorum*. Copenhagen, 1876.

———. [2] *Opuscula Academica*. Reprinted. Hildesheim, 1977.

Malcovati, H. *Oratorum Romanorum Fragmenta*. Turin, 1955.

Merguet, H. *Lexicon zu Ciceros Reden*. 4 vols. Jena, 1877–84.

Mitchell, T. [1] *Cicero: The Ascending Years*. New Haven, Conn., 1979.

————. [2] *Cicero: The Senior Statesman.* New Haven, Conn., 1991.

————. [3] *Cicero: Verrines II.1.* London, 1987.

Mommsen, T. *Römische Geschichte.* Vol. 3. 9th ed. Berlin, 1904.

Müller, C. F. W. *Ciceronis Opera.* Vol. 3, part 2. Leipzig, 1878.

Nägelsbach, K. *Lateinische Syntax.* Nuremburg, 1905.

Neumeister, C. *Grundsätze der forensischen Rhetorik.* Munich, 1964.

Nicholas, B. *Introduction to Roman Law.* Oxford, 1962.

Norden, E. [1] *Die antike Kunstprosa.* 2 vols. Reprinted. Stuttgart, 1958.

————. [2] "Aus Ciceros Werkstatt." *Sitzungsberichte Deutsches Akad. Wissensch.* (Berlin, 1913): 13–31.

————. [3] *Vergilius Aeneis VI.* 5th ed. Darmstadt, 1957.

Olshausen, E. "Die Zielsetzung der Deiotariana Ciceros." *Monumentum Chiloniense* (Amsterdam, 1975): 109–23.

Orelli, I. C. M. *Tulli Ciceronis Opera Quae Supersunt Omnia.* Edited by J. G. Baiter and C. L. Kayser. Leipzig, 1860-69.

Palladino, A. *Orazione pro Rege Deiotaro.* Florence, 1958.

Parzinger, P. *Beiträge zur Kenntnis der Entwicklung des Ciceronisches Stils.* Dissertation. Landshut, 1910.

Paterson, J. *Cicero's Speeches for M. Marcellus and Q. Ligarius.* London, 1938.

Porten, B. *Untersuchungen über die Stellungsgezetze des Verbum finitum in Ciceros Reden, Briefen und philosophische Schriften.* Dissertation. Cologne, 1922.

Primmer, A. *Cicero numerosus.* Sitzungsberichte, Österreichische Akademie der Wissenschaft, Phil.-hist. Kl., 257. Vienna, 1968.

Puccione, J. M. *Tulli Ciceronis orationum deperditarum fragmenta.* Montadore, 1972.

Radermacher, L. *Quintiliani Institutio Oratoria.* 2 vols. Leipzig, 1959.

Rawson, B. *The Politics of Friendship.* Sidney, 1978.

Reeder, H. *De codicibus in Ciceronis orationibus recte aestimandis.* Dissertation. Jena, 1906.

Richter, F., and A. Eberhard. *Ciceros Reden für M. Marcellus, Q. Ligarius, König Deiotarus.* 4th ed. Leipzig, 1904.

Roby, H. *Latin Grammar.* 2 vols. London, 1874.

Ruch, M. *M. T. Ciceronis pro Marcello oratio.* Paris, 1965.

Settle, J. *The Publication of Cicero's Orations.* Dissertation. Chapel Hill, N.C., 1963.

Seyffert, M. *Laelius: De Amicitia Dialogus.* Breslau, 1876.

Skutsch, O. *The Annales of Q. Ennius.* Oxford, 1985.

Shackleton Bailey, D. R. [1] *Cicero: Epistulae ad Familiares.* 2 vols. Cambridge, 1977.

————. [2] *Cicero: Philippics.* Chapel Hill, N.C., 1986.

————. [3] *Cicero's Letters to Atticus.* 7 vols. Cambridge, 1965–70.

————. [4] "The Roman Nobility in the Second Civil War." *CQ* 54 (1960): 253–70.

Solmsen, F. "Cicero's First Speeches: A Rhetorical Analysis." *AJP* 69 (1938): 542–56.

Solodow, J. *The Latin Particle Quidem*. American Classical Studies, 4. Boulder, Colo., 1978.

Stroh, W. *Taxis und Taktik*. Stuttgart, 1975.

Tyrrell, R., and L. Purser. *The Correspondence of Cicero*. 7 vols. Dublin, 1904–33.

Vahlen, J. *Ennianae Poesis Reliquiae*. Leipzig, 1903.

Wackernagel. J. "Über ein Gesetz der indogermanischen Wortstellung." *Indg. Forsch.* 1 (1892): 33.

Walser, G. "Der Prozess gegen Q. Ligarius im Jahre 46 v. Chr." *Historia* 8 (1959): 90–96.

Weinstock, S. *Divus Julius*. Oxford, 1967.

Wiesthaler, F. *Die Oratio Obliqua als künstlisches Stilmittel in den Reden Ciceros*. Innsbruck, 1956.

Wilamowitz-Moellendorf, U. von. "Die Thucydideslegende." *Hermes* 12 (1877).

Wilson, J. P. "Three Non-uses of *Frater*." *CJ* 83 (1988): 207–11.

Wolf, F. A. *M. Tulli Ciceronis Quae Vulgo Fertur Oratio pro M. Marcello*. Berlin, 1802.

Woodcock, E. *A New Latin Syntax*. London, 1959.

Yavets, T. *Julius Caesar and His Public Image*. London, 1983.

Zielinski, T. *Das Klauselgesetz in Ciceros Reden*. Leipzig, 1904.

INDEX OF CITATIONS

Appian
Bell. Civ. 2.30: 219
Asconius
in Scaur. p. 18fCl.: 252
Caesar, Julius
B. Alex. 31: 223
  34: 223
  66–78: 224
  67: 217
  68: 214, 226
B. C. 1.2–5: 217
  1.5.3–4: 217
  1.6: 160
  1.9: 146
  1.31: xxxiv, 154
  1.32: 44
  2.42: 223
  3.4: 248
  3.34: 223
  3.78: 223
  3.82.3: 54
  3.82.4: 54
  3.91: 146
  3.98.2: 13
B. G. 2.20.1: 21
  7.19: 56
  7.27: 161
Catullus
  1: 156
  8.15–18: 127
  11: 20, 42
  36.16: 38
  64.117: 203
  64.177–81: 108
Cicero
Amicit. 27: 264
  82: 203
Arch. 1: 30

2: 119
3: 76, 208, 270
8: 175
15: 119, 238
16: 252
18: 269
19: 269
26: 78
28: 115
29: 77
30: 83
Att. 1.1.1: 151
2.1.6: xx
2.3.4: xx
2.19: xx
2.21: xxi
3.8.2: 38
4.5.1: xxii
4.6.2: xxii
6.1.14: 238
6.6: xxxii
7.2.3: 228
7.3.3: 164
7.3.5: 148
7.18.2: xxii
8.7: xxiii
8.11.3: 54
8.11D.6: 51
8.15A: xxiii
8.15.2: 117
9.1.4: xxxi, 48
9.6A.1: xxiv
9.7C.1: 15
9.10.2: xxiv
9.10.3: xxiv
9.10.6: 54
9.10.7: xxiv
9.10.9: xxiv

9.11A: xxiv
9.15: xxiii
9.18: xxiii
9.19.2: 51
10.4.5: 177
10.8.5: xxiv
10.8B: xxiv
10.9A.5: 51
11.6.2: 54
11.6.6: 57
11.7.5: xxv
11.16: xxv
11.16.1: 124
11.20: xxv
12.45.3: 255
13.2: 138
13.12.2: xxxvii
13.13.1: 151
13.17.3: 255
13.19.2: xxxvii
13.20.2: 107
13.44.1: 175, 255, 259
13.52: 235
13.52.1: 231
13.52.2: xxix
14.4.3: xxix
14.17.6: xxix
Balb. 7, 9: 32
13: 81
44: 212
51: 153
54: 219, 250
56: 138
57: 251
Br. 1.15.10: 15
Brut. 2: 20
4: 212
42: 142
45: 50
157: 12
250: 46
251: 166
251ff: 165
253ff: xxvi
258: 254, 265
278: 57, 178
Caecil. 1: 132
8: 212

24: 78
41: 198, 218
64: 143
Cael. 13: 30
18: 231
20: 243
30: 237
33: 56
69: 153
71: 67
74: 61
78: 255
79: 43
Cat. 1.1: 105, 156
1.2: 74, 252
1.21: 259
1.29: 126
2.2: 38
2.19: 37
2.20: 56
2.21: 61
2.29: 37
3.13: 89
3.18: 37
3.23: 211
3.26: 79
4.11: 153
4.22: 45
Clu. 10: 120
31: 181
36: 232
51: 198
73: 119
74: 91
138: 59
169: 116
Corn. 1 (fr. 3, P): 88
1 (fr. 38, 62 P): 172
De Orat. 1.1: 265
1.6, 8: 25
1.99: 156
1.120: 198
2.25: 241
2.55: 53
2.73: 152
3.52: 131
3.213: 210
3.214: 108

3.217: 108
Div. 1.27: 262
2.85: 33
Dom. 23: 117
40: 117
47, 83, 92: 39
81: 238
88: 62, 65
115: 61
144: 271
Fam. 1.9.8: xxi
1.9.19: xxii
1.9.22: 20
1.9.24: 264
3.33.1: xxvii
4.4: 122
4.4.2: 68
4.4.3: 22, 34, 62, 89
4.4.4: 12, 13, 14, 34, 77, 89
4.5: 254
4.7.3: 203
4.9.3: 44
4.9.4: 91
5.2.9: 89
5.10A: xxix
6.6: xxviii
6.6.6: 14, 49, 51
6.6.8: 170
6.12.2: 172
6.14: 137
6.14.2: 138
7.2.4: 12
7.3: xxv
7.17.1: 27
7.33.2: xxvii
9.2.5: xxvii
9.6.2: xxvii
9.16.2: xxvii, 53
9.12: xl
9.12.2: 266
9.16.3: 203
9.18.2: 50
11.8.2: 116
12.2.2: 132
12.11.1: 239
12.18.1: 239
12.30.3: 203
13.17.2: 91

14.23: 124
15.4.5: 205, 238, 266
15.5.2: xxvi
15.9: 19
16.11: 217
16.11.2: 218
16.12.3: 219
Fin. 2.45: 71
4.40: 264
5.22: 203
Flacc. 26: 62
30: 218
49: 229
64: 87
98: 49
Font. 2: 25
24: 219
49: 20
Har. Resp. 6: 19, 153
29: 201
42: 181
50: 39, 44, 47
Inv. 1.5: 16
Leg. 2.15: 16
Leg. Ag. 2.79: 254
Milo. 6: 111, 145
7: 211
10: 141
18: 27, 150
26, 65: 32
30: 153
58: 205
61: 234
65: 239
76, 87: 39
79: 56
91: 16, 56
92: 205
93: 47
100ff: 111
103: 27
Mur. 11: 251
13: 245
34: 269
61: 208
62: 112
64: 224
79: 237

88: 108
89: 245
Nat. Deor. 1.59: 203
 2.15: 16
 2.26: 68
 3.88: 60
Off. 1.4: 169
 1.22: 71
 1.80–81: 178
 2.44: 204
 2.46: 203
 2.49ff: 132
 2.67: 203
 3.10.42: 27
Orat. 56: 210
 157: 135
Parad. 3.25: 16
Phil. 1: 118
 1.7: 114, 135
 1.12: 257
 1.18: 167
 1.21: 254
 1.26: 110
 1.28: 151
 1.fin: 70
 2.10: 181
 2.12: 265
 2.25: 132
 2.29: 153
 2.23: 71
 2.32: 164
 2.44: 88
 2.54: 219
 2.67: 39
 2.84–87: 245
 2.86: 175
 2.116: 46
 3.4: 65
 3.31: 245
 3.32: 218
 5.7: 218
 5.13: 71
 5.32: 61, 218
 6.9: 153
 7.5: 218
 7.7: 264
 8.15: 218
 9.7: 263

 9.109: 82
 10.11: 16
 10.12: 120, 122
 11.1: 238
 11.18: 218
 11.31: 172
 11.32: 239
 11.33: 263
 11.34: 201, 216, 266
 12.9: 203
 12.24: 203
 12.30: 118
 13.1: 250
 13.6: 226
 13.12: 203
 13.31: 245
 13.48: 38
Piso. 6: xix
 8: 253
 11: 241
 21: 38
 22: 245
 33: 39, 131
 58: 110
 59: 79
 68: 53
 73: 50, 62
 99: 250
Planc. 1: 40
 5: 89
 11: 61, 177
 29: 47, 175
 52: 110
 59.90: 32
 86: 232
 87: 175
 93: xxii
 95: 39
 97: 153
Pomp. 26: 241
 35: 81
 42: 15
 44: 257
Prov. Cons. 24: 43
 25: xxii
 30: 67
 33: 28
 41: xx

Quinct. 8: 70
 39: 250
 42: 61
 97: 47
Q. Fr. 1.1.43: 82
 2.9.3: 178
 2.13.1: xxii
 3.5.4: xxii
Rab. Perd. 11: 181
Rep. 1.8: 71
Rosc. Am. 5: 200
 7: 250
 29: 88
 88: 207
 95: 39
 120: 205
 142: 50, 52
 150: 139
Rosc. Com. 74: 218
Scaur. c.1.4: 79
 21: 73
Sen. 85: 16
Sest. 12: 232
 26: 127
 30: 39
 37: 243
 39: 153
 40: 90
 68: 238
 73: 69
 82: 61
 93: 117
 115–127: 256
 121: xix
Sul. 72: 15
Top. 76: 67
Tusc. 1.12: 44
 1.16: 156
 3.16: 245
 5.12: 27
 5.73: 78
Verr. 1.158: 200
 2.1.64: 229
 2.1.74: 115
 2.1.144: 152
 2.2.8: 19
 2.2.40: 78
 2.2.86: 38

 2.2.158: 106, 132
 2.2.187: 19
 2.3.88: 128
 2.4.1: 152
 2.4.5: 250
 2.4.56: 252
 2.4.110: 218
 2.5.11: 156
 2.5.25: 241
 2.5.35: 19
 2.5.41: 16
 2.5.42: 113
 2.5.58: 254
 2.5.75: 270
 2.5.113: 182
 2.5.115: 15
 2.5.132: 38
 2.5.139: 20, 146
 2.5.174: 131
 2.5.175: 21
 2.5.182: 245
[Cicero]
 Ad Her. 1.5: 131
 2.8: 234
 4.11–16: 150
 4.16: 235
Digesta
 1.2.2.46: 127
 49.16.11: 241
Dio Cassius
 Rom. Hist. 38.14: 175
 41.43.2: 219
 42.20.1: xxxiii
 43.17: 145
 43.17.4: 46
 44.6.1: 88
 47.26: 243
 56.31: 175
Ennius
 Ann. 191 Sk.: 51
 513 Sk.: 45
 72V (69–71 Joc.): 122
 284–85V (217f Joc.): 108
Euripides
 Med. 502–5: 108
Gellius
 Att. Noct. 18.12: 228
Horace

Odes 1.27.1: 72
  1.28.15–16: 267
  3.11.35: 141
  3.24.55: 248
Livy
  9.24.13: 38
  22.45: 21
  27.19.4: 269
  28.39.12: 214
  39.15.11: 21
Lucan
  Phars. 1.1: 257
  1.128: 149
Lucretius
  De Rer. Nat. 4.14: 145
Nepos
  Thras. 1.4: 30
Pacuvius
  f. 178R: 271
Paulus
  ex Fest. p. 207L: 233
Plato
  Rep. 3.414: 141
Plautus
  Amphit. 1046: 169
  Ps. 1.3.131: 204
Pliny the Younger
  Ep. 6.16.17: 22
Plutarch
  Brut. 11: xxxvii
  38: 30
  39: 52
  39.6–7: xxxiv
  46, 48: 56
  Cic. 39: xxv
  Pomp. 61: xxiv
  Sulla 31: 134
Quintilian
  2.17.26–27: 142
  4.1.39: 106
  4.1.63–67: 111
  4.2.51: 117
  4.2.89–94: 142
  4.2.129: 113
  5.10.92: 125, 168
  5.11.42: 149
  5.13.5: xxxvii, 129
  5.13.20: 131

  6.3.108: 178
  7.4.17: xxxvi
  7.4.1718: 166
  8.3.85: 140
  8.4.26–27: 127
  8.5.10: 129
  8.5.13: 130
  8.6.11: 128
  8.6.12: 127
  9.2.6–7: 127
  9.2.28: xxviii, 123
  9.2.38: 127
  9.2.57: 128
  9.4.92: 106
  9.4.99: 129
  10.1.114: 165
  10.2.17: 142
  11.1.57: 132
  11.1.78: xxxiii, 127
  11.3.108: 106
Sallust
  Cat. 31: xvii
  51: 166
  51.14: 82
  51.20: 78
Seneca the Younger
  ad Helv. 10.3: 235
  Epist. 114: 179
Shakespeare
  Jul. Caes. 2.1.215ff.: xxxvii
  3.3.111ff.: xxxvii
Strabo
  12.5.2: 228
Suetonius
  Div. Iul. 6: 269
  40–44: 68
  41: 68
  42: 68
  67: 248
  71: 157, 166
  75: 57
  86: 70
Tacitus
  Ann. 1.1: 82
  Dial. 21.5: 165
  34.7: 165
  39.4: 208
Terence

Andr. 618: 244
Eun. 72: 51
  814: 232
  852: 166
Heaut. 976: 166
Hec. 516: 108
Phorm. 140: 166
Varro
  Re rust. 1.1.10: 246
Virgil
  Aen. 1.8–9: 23
  1.25ff: 157
  1.73: 33
  1.108: 177
  1.590: 203

2.281: 122
2.200: 145
2.557–58: 221
4.406: 128
4.551: 250
4.595: 146
4.667: 38
6.816: 180
8.1: 21
9.327: 33
9.546: 241
10.800: 203
11.5–11: 42
11.38: 38
Georg. 1.299: 245

GENERAL INDEX

Capitalized items are also in glossary; where citation is not followed by lemma, Latin word is in lemma.

ABLATIVE ABSOLUTE, xiii–xiv
dismissive, *Lig.* 1: *omissaque controversia*
expanded usage, *Marc.* 2: *a me . . . distracto, Marc.* 32: *salvo . . . salvi*
in final position, *Marc.* 2: *illo . . . distracto, Deiot.* 15: *tanto scelere . . . cogitato*
historical, *Lig.* 7: *suscepto bello*
with *praesertim, Marc.* 3: *commemoratis . . . offensionibus*
with predicate construction, *Marc.* 32: *te . . . manente, Lig.* 7: *C. Pansa . . . preferente*
with semi-independent relative, *Lig.* 3: *quo audito*
structural function, *Lig.* 19: *utrisque . . . aberrantibus, Lig.* 33: *illo . . . exulante*
cf. weighted substantive, *Marc.* 7: *se . . . offert*
abstract noun
for brevity in nominal sentences, *Lig.* 33: *germanitas, Lig.* 37: *bonitas*
infinitive as abstract verbal noun, *Lig.* 22: *voluisse*
for people described, *Marc.* 10: *auctoritas, Lig.* 33: *splendorem omnem*
in simplest narrative or expository style, *Lig.* 4. *profectio . . . remansio* (*Lig.* 2 *legatione*)
in *-tio, Lig.* 1: *ignoratione*
adjectives

descriptive, qualified by *tam, Marc.* 19: *tuo isto tam excellenti natura, Lig.* 15: *tanta tua fortuna*
similarly after interrogative, *Deiot.* 15: *cuius tanti sceleris,* 37: *quae tanta . . . iniuria*
ALLITERATION. *See* Glossary
an
ellipsis understood from, *Marc.* 21: *an, si nihil tui cogitant sceleris, cavendum est ne quid inimici*
hyperbaton emphasizes negative and perhaps reflects content by word order
introduces second of alternative questions, first suppressed, *Lig.* 5, *Lig.* 28, *Deiot.* 18: *quid postea? an, Marc.* 21: *an ex eo*
ANAPHORA. *See* Glossary
ANTICIPATION. *See* Glossary
ANTITHESIS. *See* Glossary
APORIA: see *Marc.* 33 *unde* for *dubitatio* or *aporia,* in which the speaker feigns utter confusion as to how to proceed; so *Lig.* 1 initial note and *quo me vertam nescio*
Aposiopesis: felt at *Marc.* 17: *alterius vero partis*
APOSTROPHE. *See* Glossary
ARGUMENTA. *See* Glossary
asseveration: *vero* "no, but" at *Marc.* 15 vs. adversative, *Marc.* 33: *sed.* See also *vero*
ASYNDETON. *See* Glossary

at
  counters concession, *Marc.* 25: *addo
    . . . at*
  embedded in clause, *Marc.* 13: *at . . .
    certe*
  introduces accuser's objection, *Deiot.*
    32
  something unexpected, *Marc.* 7: *at
    vero*
atque
  introduces new direction (vs. *at*),
    Marc. 13, *Marc.* 16: *atque huius
    quidem*
auctoritas
  abstract noun for person, *Marc.* 10:
    illa auctoritas
  of advocate, *Marc.* 2: *non illius
    solum, Deiot.* 6: *civis . . . regi, Lig.*
    30: *confugio . . . peto . . . oro,* cf.
    Lig. 19: *dignitas*
  as agent introduced by *a, Deiot.* 30:
    auctoritate
autem: introduces rhetorical contrast,
    Marc. 11: *ceterae . . . huius autem*

BALANCE. *See* Glossary
Brutus, xxvi–xxvii passim

Caesar
  birth, xvii
  career, xvii
  as orator, xxvi–xvii, *Lig.* 30
  relation to Cicero, xvii–xxix
  style of:
    ablative absolute, *Marc.* 2: *illo . . .
      distracto*
    narrative sentence connector, *Lig.* 3:
      interim
    repetition of antecedent in relative
      clause, *Marc* 13: *bellum* (13) *. . .
      quo quidem in bello, Lig.* 2: *qua in
      legatione*
    semi-independent relative as sen-
      tence connector, *Lig:* 2: *cui sic*
    semi-independent relative in ablative
      absolute, *Lig.* 3: *quo audito*
certe

at certe coordinates with negative
    conditional to mean "yet at least,"
    Marc. 13: *at . . . certe*
certe scio, Lig. 13
  marks first clause in parataxis con-
    cessive and so anticipates the next,
    Marc. 6: *nam . . . et certe . . . at
    vero, Marc.* 8: *quod . . . maximum
    est*
  shades of meaning, *Marc.* 13: *at . . .
    certe*
  tentative asseveration, *Marc.* 20:
    stulta fortasse, certe non improba
Cicero
  career, xvii–xxix
  dependence of phrase on clause,
    Marc. 9: *in iracundia . . . superba
    est*
  propaganda for Caesar, xxvsq
CLAUSULAE, xiv–xv. (int. = internal,
    res. = resolved)
  exception to *ac* and *nec* before conso-
    nants, *Marc.* 9: *atque*
  rhythm not only at end of clause,
    Lig. 1: *non auditum.*
  cretic + trochee (or spondee), *Marc.*
    2: *(vehe)menter angebar, Marc.* 12:
    visque devicta est, Lig. 6: *(monu-
    men)tisque decorandam, Marc.* 12:
    ipse vicisti, Marc. 13: *(funest)oque
    compulsi*
    res. at *Marc.* 8: *(ex)tollere . . . ia-
      centem, Lig.* 34: *esse voluisse, Lig.*
      38: *longiorem . . . breviorem,
      Deiot.* 11: *litteraeque venerunt,
      Deiot.* 19: *acta servari, Deiot.* 37:
      decreta delere
    see at *Lig.* 16: *aliud est*
  dactylic (rare), *Marc.* 12: *vicisse vi-
    deris* (int.)
    avoided, *Deiot.* 7: *actioque . . .
      loco, Deiot.* 37: *quae tanta . . .
      iniuria*
  double cretic, *Marc.* 2: *restitutam
    puto, Marc.* 3: *(grav)issimo et
    maximo* (cf. *Deiot.* 12: *plurima et
    maxima), Marc.* 4: *pace dicam tua*
    (int.), *Marc.* 6: *omne ducit suum,*

Marc. 12: *adferet laudibus, Marc.*
21: *anteponat suae, Marc.* 23: *insidiarumque . . . consensio* (two
int.), *Marc.* 24: *stabilitatis suae*
(int., res.); see *Marc.* 29: *stabilita,
Marc.* 29: *magna dissensio, Marc.*
34: *cederem nemini, Lig.* 27: *in
. . . venit . . . iniuria, Lig.* 31: *tui
necessarii*
avoided, *Marc.* 32: *fracta dissenio
est* ⟨*armis*⟩
res., *Marc.* 4: *genere praestantior.*
res. (‾˘˘˘˘˘), *Deiot.* 7: *actioque . . .
loco*
res. to molossus + cretic (‾‾‾‾˘‾),
Deiot. 11: *defendendam datam* (cf.
Deiot. 16: *defendendam puto*)
double spondee, *Marc.* 10: *complectemur, Lig.* 1: *non auditum, Lig.*
13: *ignoscatur, Lig.* 18: *propulsare, Lig.* 19: *adiuverunt*
double trochee (dichoreus), *Marc.* 8:
dignitatem (int.), *Marc.* 10: *intuemur* (int.), *Marc.* 10: *vindicasti*
(echoing int. *reddidisti*), *Lig.* 4:
conquievit, Lig. 18: *conveniret,
Lig.* 22: *occupatam, Lig.* 25: *detulistis, Lig.* 34: *iudicares fuisse,
Deiot.* 6: ⟨*testarer*⟩ *ipsum*; see
Deiot. 8: *insideret*
associated with Asianism, 275
Poenulum tuum, *Marc.* 3: *tanta gloria, Marc.* 21: *nostra cautio est,
Marc.* 22: *pendere omnium, Deiot.*
43: *clementiae tuae*
clementia
Caesar's use of, *Lig.* 29: *vel*
called insidious, xxiii
development of term, *Marc.* 1: *mansuetudinem*
as propaganda, xxv
CLIMAX. *See* Glossary
coda: achieved by clausula, word order, epigram; e.g. at *Marc.* 7:
numquam enim, Marc. 19: *a Virtute . . . a Fortuna, Marc.* 24: *vulnera . . . sananda . . . mederi,
Marc.* 26: *meritorum, Lig.* 10:

quorum . . . eorum, Lig. 23: *grata
. . . probata, Lig.* 33: *quem ad
modum cetera, Deiot.* 3: *etiam ab
invito, Deiot.* 33: *quae semper*
complex sentence
periodicity, xli
word order, xiii
CONCEIT. *See* Glossary
concession
in apposition, *Marc.* 7: *illa ipsa . . .
domina*
concessive subjunctive, *Marc.* 35: *sed
ierit*
implied by *tamen, Lig.* 34: *quos . . .
tamen*, so *Deiot.* 9
marked by *certe, Marc.* 6: *nam . . . et
certe . . . at vero*
marked by *modo, Marc.* 29: *vagabitur*
marked by *quidem, Lig.* 31
in predicate adjective, *Marc.* 10:
etiam mortuis
simple addition of a concession in indicative, *Marc.* 25: *addo . . . at*
cum . . . tum, Marc. 19, *Deiot.* 1
Curia style, *Marc. bellum* (13) *. . . quo
quidem in bello*

deictic pronoun/adjective
with expansive gesture, *Marc.* 27:
haec . . . hic . . . hoc
force after adversative, *Lig.* 2: *sed tamen hoc*
introduces accusative and infinitive:
see *Marc.* 5: *idque . . . usurpare*
referring to someone absent, *Lig.* 2:
hic, Lig. 11: *hunc, Deiot.* 41: *hi
reges*
vividness, *Marc.* 7: *huius gloriae,
Marc.* 11: *haec . . . res*
doublet
alliterative, *Marc.* 8: *litteris atque linguis, Deiot.* 2: *tueri et tegere*; see
at *Deiot.* 22: *litteraeque venerunt*
intensified by prefix, *Marc.* 1: *inusitatam inauditamque*

of literal and figurative terms, *Marc.*
14: *pacis et togae, Marc.* 11: *latebrae . . . recessus*

non-synonymous pairs, *Marc.* 8: *debilitari frangique, Marc.* 11: *conficiat et consumat*

synonymous or semi-synonymous
pairs: *Marc.* 1: *angebar, Marc.* 6:
mens aut cogitatio

dumtaxat: see at *Marc.* 22, *Deiot.* 1

ellipsis
with adverbial *tamen, Lig.* 12: *quae
tamen*

dramatic, at *Lig.* 28: *sed tum sero*
and *omnes inquam*

for epigrammatic effect, *Deiot.* 23:
quia non nosset

for pathos in rhetorical question, *Lig.*
14: *quanto hoc durius*

verb (with change of person) not repeated, *Marc.* 2: *in eadem causa in
qua ego*

of verb, in informal style, *Marc.* 15:
minus mirum, Marc. 33: *quodam
modo, Lig.* 30: *certe numquam*

enclitic position
between *cognomen* and *nomen, Lig.*
2: *Q. enim Ligarius*

copula found in, *Marc.* 7: *quam . . .
adeptus*

ego in, *Marc.* 8

etiam, Marc. 23

igitur in, *Marc.* 11: *hunc tu igitur*

-que regularly not attached to prepositions, *Lig.* 31: *ab iisque*

encomium
doublets, *Marc.* 13: *pacis et togae*

encomiastic conceit, *Lig.* 38: *homines . . . hominibus*

hyperbole in, *Marc.* 8: *deo*

language of, *Marc.* 1: *paene divinam,
Lig.* 35: *solere*

personification, *Marc.* 10: *parietes
. . . gestiunt*

praise by comparison, *Marc.* 17:
alterius vero partis, Deiot. 28
Castor

enim
in parentheses, *Marc.* 16: *non enim*

postponed, *Marc.* 8: *nulla est enim,
Marc.* 26: *quidquid est enim*

epigram: e.g. at *Marc.* 3: *ex quo . . .
gloria, Marc.* 7: *numquam enim,
Marc.* 19: *a virtute . . . a fortuna,
Lig.* 10: *quorum . . . eorum, Lig.*
11: *quae tamen, Lig.* 15: *si in
tanta . . . , Lig.* 16: *qua qui . . .
utetur, Lig.* 38: *longiorem . . . breviorem, Deiot.* 12: *praestitisti,
Deiot.* 23: *vel . . . vel, Deiot.* 27:
qui . . . is, Deiot. 30: *quae semper,
Deiot.* 40: *dabis . . . denegasti*

Erasmus, xl

etiam: position of, *Marc.* 23

EXPOSITORY PROSE, xli
abstract nouns in expository narrative style, *Marc.* 4: *profectio . . .
remansio*

clear, expository locution with antecedent emphatically placed, *Marc.*
8: *ea tamen . . . quae*

definitional articulation in expository
style, relative clause preceding antecedent, *Marc.* 15: *qui . . . is*

hoc explicitly anticipates accusative
+ infinitive, *Marc.* 4: *tamen hoc
adfirmo*

in narration, *Lig.* 2: *qua in legatione*

nominal defining sentence in simplest
style of philosophical exposition,
Marc. 26: *quidquid est enim*

orderly, syntactically marked progression, *Marc.* 6: *ego nisi ita . . . ut*

usque eo precise antecedent to
quoad, Deiot. 11

verb (form of *esse*) omitted in plain
exposition, *Marc.* 21: *magnum
etiam vinclum*

word order relative antecedent, *Marc.*
10: *quidquid . . . id*

future tense
future indicative + imperative in
asyndetic parataxis, *Deiot.* 30: *dic*

two meanings of, *Marc.* 12: *anteponis*

gerund(ive)

absolute and impersonal, *Marc.* 14: *audiendum*

for action as fact, *Marc.* 20: *conservandis*

as final clause, *Deiot.* 11: *rem publicam defendendam datam*

vs. gerund with object, *Lig.* 38: *dando*

in + ablative of gerund(ive) = "in the process of . . . ," *Lig.* 32: *in . . . conservando*

grand style, *Marc.* 4: *nullius . . . flumen ingeni*. *See also* Personification; *see* "expository prose" in Glossary

HENDIADYS: *Marc.* 1: *vocem et auctoritatem*, *Marc.* 8: *ferro et viribus*, *Marc.* 11: *opere et manu*, *Marc.* 23: *insidiarumque . . . consensio*, *Lig.* 5: *desideri*, *Deiot.* 5: *conventus*, *Deiot.* 7: *aliqua spe et cogitatione*, *Deiot.* 8: *tu . . . tu . . . te . . . te*, *Deiot.* 20: *intuentium . . . admirantium*

Hermagoras of Temnos: stasis theory at *Lig.* 10: *genus hoc causae*

homo

in informal narrative, *Deiot.* 31: *hominem*

neutral for person, *Marc.* 14: *hominem*

used in appositive phrases, *Lig.* 10, *Deiot.* 10

with *vir*, *Deiot.* 16: *niro . . . homine*

HOMOEOTELEUTON: e.g. at *Marc.* 10: *vindicasti*, *Marc.* 19: *cetera*, *Deiot.* 10: *itaque*, *Deiot.* 33: *vexatos*

HYPERBATON

bracketing the correlative clause, *Deiot.* 5: *causam . . . dico*

of compound predicate, *Marc.* 11: *adlatura . . . sit*, *Marc.* 13: *sumus . . . compulsi*, *Marc.* 29: *stabilita*, *Marc.* 30: *obscuratura . . . sit*

creates a heavily weighted nominative, *Deiot.* 4: *tua . . . natura*

inclusion of the governing infinitive, *Deiot.* 9: *ullas . . . reliquias*, *Marc.* 26: *illustris . . . meritorum*

makes attributive what it brackets, *Marc.* 25: *istam*, *Lig.* 9: *destrictus in acie Pharsalica gladius*

with *plus*, *Marc.* 26: *admirationis . . . gloriae*

postponed adjective often gets a more predicative force, *Lig.* 30: *multas*

predicative in hyperbaton, *Marc.* 31: *iustissimum*

word order in, *Deiot.* 22: *magnum*

imperative: + future indicative in asyndetic parataxis, *Deiot.* 30: *dic*

inceptive

imperfect, *Lig.* 24: *veniebatis*

infix, *Marc.* 12: *florescit*, *Marc.* 16: *extimescentem*

inconcinnity

between superlative and comparative, *Deiot.* 5: *quae . . . leviora*

phrase and clause, *Deiot.* 16: *propter . . . nisi*

possessive genitive and adjective, *Marc.* 2: *non illius solum sed etiam meam*

in several balances, *Deiot.* 34: *nos . . . Blesamio*

sloppy, *Deiot.* 21: *cum . . . ibi*

indicative

cum clauses temporal, *Marc.* 3: *cum . . . concessisti* (so 15)

concomitant actions, *Deiot.* 39: *cum (laboro)*

contemporaneous action, *Marc.* 13: *nam cum*

double marking allegation in *quod*-causal, *Lig.* 25: *a quo queramini*

with neuter adjective, *Deiot.* 19: *magnum fuit*, cf. at *Lig.* 23: *quid*

in periphrastic future apodoses, *Lig.* 23: *quid*

with predicate genitive for conditional, *Lig.* 28: *erat . . . amentis*,

Lig. 16: *hominis, Deiot.* 15: *fu-roris fuit*

predicates existence, *Marc.* 26: *quid-quid est enim*

in provisos, *Marc.* 32: *qui modo*

in *quod*-noun clause, replaced by subjunctive, *Lig.* 10: *quod . . . quod . . . viderit*

in relative clauses with circumstantial nuance, *Marc.* 18: *qui . . . exci-taverunt, Marc.*31: *eosdem, ibid.*: *ingratus . . . civis qui, Lig.* 23: *cuius interfuit*

verb of judging in implausible suppo-sition, *Marc.* 23: *credimus*

infinitive phrase

circumstances abstracted into general situation, *Deiot.* 4: *dicere*

with *opus est, Deiot.* 40

presents Caesar's supreme virtues as facts, *Marc.* 8: *animum vincere*

initial position

equidem, Marc. 22

negative, implies a following positive, *Lig.* 7: *nulla vi coactus*

participles in ablative absolute, *Lig.* 7: *suscepto bello*

pronoun, *Marc.* 10: *vero*

supports sarcastic exaggeration, *Deiot.* 33: *multorum . . . multos . . . multos*

tamen, Marc. 4: *tamen hoc affirmo*

theme of argument, *Lig.* 10: *in hac causa*

verb, *Marc.* 17: *vidimus . . . non vidi-mus, Marc.* 29: *vagabitur, Marc.* 31: *perfuncta, Deiot.* 19: *negavisti*

with *esse* predicating existence, *Marc.* 4: *est vero, Marc.* 29: *erit dissensio, Marc.* 30: *erat obscuritas*

of second-person verb, *Lig.* 2: *habes igitur*

inquam: with repetition of word or phrase, *Marc.* 28: *illa, inquam*

internal clausula: marking of, *Deiot.* 35: *quae tanta . . . iniuria*

ita: vs. *itaque* consequential vs. se-quential, *Marc.* 12

properly modal = *tam, Marc.* 6

me dius fidius, Marc. 10

mehercule, Lig. 12

METAPHOR, xiii

from accounting, *Marc.* 34: *magnus . . . cumulus*

for ambition, *Marc.* 27: *immortalita-tis amore flagravit*

of arming the spirit, unique, *Marc.* 31: *armorum . . . animum . . . armatum*

from augury, *Lig.* 5: *desideri*

from commerce, *Deiot.* 43: *importa-turum*

of conflagration extinguished, *Marc.* 31: *inflammaret . . . leniret*

of *curriculum, Marc.* 2: *nec mihi . . . ducebam*

of erosion or destruction, unique, *Marc.* 23: *dilapsa . . . diffluxerunt*

of flowing water for talent, *Marc.* 4: *nullius . . . flumen ingeni*

of growth, *Marc.* 12: *florescit*

from health, *Marc.* 29: *salute . . . restinxeris*

of hope rising with new dawn, *Lig.* 6: *lux . . . aboriatur* (cf. *Deiot.* 15: *lumen exstinguere*)

of kindling, *Marc.* 9: *incendimur*

from law, *Marc.* 6: *quasi suo iure*

from medicine, *Deiot.* 8: *exulcerato* and *insideret*

of paying out (fishing) line, *Deiot.* 19: *contexitur*

for obscurity of birth, *Deiot.* 30: *e tenebris . . . evocavit*

origin in doubt, *Marc.* 2: *consuetudi-nem . . . aperuisti, Marc.* 10: *pec-tus memoria obfudit*

qualified, *Marc.* 2: *quasi quodam socio*

by *quidam, Lig.* 5: *incredibilem quendam*

for Republic in shambles, *Marc.* 24: *quassata*

of rousing dead, *Marc.* 17: *si posset
... quos potest*
of runaway slaves, *Deiot.* 30: *evolare*
of sloughing skin, *Lig.* 14: *exuisses*
spatial, *Marc.* 25: *modum ...
definies*
from theater, *Marc.* 27: *haec ... hic
... hoc*
of welding bronze, *Deiot.* 34: *conspirantem ... conflatum*
of wounds of war, unique, *Marc.* 24:
vulnera ... sananda ... mederi
by *tamquam*, *Marc.* 14: *ruerem*
see also *Marc.* 29: *vagabitur*, *Lig.* 15:
redundaret, *Deiot.* 6: *consumptam*, *Deiot.* 7: *parietes*
Molon, xviii
multi: = "many [others]," *Marc.* 3: *in
multis*

names: adjectives not added attributively with, *Deiot.* 25: *furiosum illum Caecilium*
nemo: nominal and predicative, *Marc.*
17: *socium habes neminem*, *Lig.*
11: *civis ... nemo*
nescioquis: of unknown or despised
person, *Deiot.* 23: *nescioquem
Caecilium*
noun clause
anticipating ensuing item, *Marc.* 17:
quod ... verebamur, *Marc.* 33:
quod ... potuisti
in apposition to predicate, *Marc.* 7:
quod ... maximum est

opinio: construction with, *Marc.* 20
oportet: constructions with, *Marc.* 28

PARENTHESIS
a correcting parenthesis, *Deiot.* 11:
(*sic ... nuntiabatur*)
credo, *Deiot.* 24: *veteres, credo,
Caesar*
epigrammatical, *Marc.* 11: *nihil est
enim*
non dicam ... sed parenthetical,
Marc. 5, cf. *Deiot.* 2: *ne dicam*

oportet, *Marc.* 28
parenthetical clause, *Lig.* 35: *etiam te*
parenthetical sentence, *Marc.* 16: *non
enim*, *Deiot.* 38: *esset enim ...*
semi-independent relative clause as,
Marc. 3: *ex quo ... gloria*, *Marc.*
13: *quorum ... frequentiam*,
Marc. 24: *quae mea*, *Lig.* 27: *ut
... cetera*, *Lig.* 32: *non dubito
ut fit*, *Lig.* 28
PARONOMASIA: *Marc.* 4: *cuius ex salute* (*ventura sit* and *pervenerit*),
Marc. 6: *maiora* (after *magna*),
Marc. 12: *victoriam vicisse*, *Marc.*
22: *augeamus ... augebimus*,
Marc. 22: *immortalis ... mortalis*,
Marc. 34: *unum innumerabilia*,
Lig. 20: *atque* (of *parere*), *Lig.* 22:
una ... una, *Lig.* 23: *Caesarine
... Caesarem*, *Lig.* 25: *tulistis ...
detulistis*, *Lig.* 30: *non fecit* (*falsi*
and *fictum*), *Deiot.* 12: *numerabi-
mus ... enumerari*, *Deiot.* 25: *immanis* (with *man⟨u⟩suetus*), *Deiot.*
32: *immanitate ... civitatis* (of
opposites), *Deiot.* 33: *quae semper*
(of *victoria-victore*), *Deiot.* 35:
multis ... multa (see *Deiot.* 15:
omnis)
participles
absence of, for *esse*, *Lig.* 10: *homo*
adversative in weighted nominative
phrase, *Deiot.* 15: *is ... liberatus
... ornatus*
provisional apodosis, *Marc.* 18: *vel
placati ... vel satiati*
construction with *natam*, *Lig.* 22:
natum ad bellum ... gerendum
explanatory (*lapsis*), *Marc.* 20: *viris
bonis*
motivational nominative participle
(*coactus*), *Lig.* 7: *suscepto bello*
perfect passive emphatic by position,
Lig. 3: *suscepto bello*, 19: *cognita
... clementia*
in *ab urbe condita* construction,
Marc. 3: *ex quo ... gloria*, *Lig.*
25: *acceptae iniuriae*

attributive, *Lig.* 26: *de suscepta causa*

predicative, *Lig.* 22: *iam occupatam*

placement of, *Deiot.* 11: *consentientis*

present active

adversative, *Lig.* 2: *itaque*

attributive, *Marc.* 22: *nihil . . . cogitans*

concomitant set reflective mood, *Deiot.* 38: *reputans et . . . cogitans*

with constructions, *Lig.* 19: *utrisque . . . aberrantibus*

describes action rather than fact, *Deiot.* 20: *intuentium . . . admirantium*

in genitive with object, *Marc.* 14: *civium . . . flagitantium*

position, *Marc.* 8: *extollere . . . iacentem*

predicative, *Marc.* 22: *cogitans*, *Lig.* 2: *recusans*

represents conative imperfect (?), *Lig.* 2: *decedens*

after sensory verb, *Marc.* 16: *extimescentem*

substantive, *Marc.* 25: *quamvis sis sapiens*

separation of verb and participle in perfect passive, *Marc.* 7: *quam . . . adeptus*, *Marc.* 30: *obscuratura . . . sit*

passive: to omit blame, *Marc.* 30: *erat obscuritas*

perfect passive

primary with dative, *Marc.* 3: *intellectum est . . . mihi*

secondary with ablative of agent, *Deiot.* 26: *a cuncta Asia*

PERSONIFICATION, *Marc.* 1: *hodiernus dies, Marc.* 6: *mens aut cogitatio, Marc.* 7: *cedit, Marc.* 10: *parietes . . . gestiunt, Marc.* 11: *conficiat et consumat, Marc.* 12. *florescit, Lig.* 9: *mucro* and *qui sensus erat armorum?, Lig.* 26: *quibus . . . eas ipsas, Deiot.* 8: *tu*

. . . tu . . . te . . . te, Deiot. 40: *occurrere*

pluperfect: with implication of lack of fulfillment, *Lig.* 1: *veneram*

political terms: *cupiditate* (cf. *studium*), *Marc.* 13, *alii . . . Lig.* 17.

possessive adjective

abnormal position, to achieve clausula, *Marc.* 21: *huius . . . suae*

normal position, *Marc.* 16: *quasi suo iure*

preferred to genitive pronoun, *Marc.* 10: *his sedibus, Marc.* 22: *nihil . . . cogitans, Deiot.* 7: *tuum est*

postpositive, *Marc.* 2: *ergo, Marc.* 29: *servi igitur, Deiot.* 36: *tenus*

igitur in third position, *Marc.* 11: *hunc tu igitur*

praesertim, Deiot. 34

predicative

ablative descriptive with noun, *Lig.* 1: *praestanti . . . ingenio, Lig.* 10: *homo*

adjectives with adverbial force, *Marc.* 1: *idemque*

ab urbe condita construction, *Marc.* 3: *ex quo . . . gloria*

neuter adjective for predicate genitive, *Deiot.* 7: *tuum est*

position, *Lig.* 15: *si in tanta*

position of *quidem, Marc.* 24: *omnia*, of *certe Lig.* 19

stressed by hyperbaton, *Marc.* 19: *tantus est enim*

word order, *Lig.* 25: *res tuae gestae, Deiot.* 33: *civilis victoria, Lig.* 28: *nec haec . . . illa*

genitive, *Marc.* 34: *summae benevolentiae, Lig.* 16: *hominis*

generalizes, *Lig.* 16: *hominis*

indicative preferred even when unfulfillment is implied, *Lig.* 28: *erat . . . amentis*

as indirect question, *Deiot.* 15: *cuius tanti sceleris*

gerundive phrases, *Deiot.* 11: *rem publicam defendendam datam* initial position of *sum*, *Marc.* 29: *erit . . . dissensio*

Nemo as predicate noun, *Marc.* 17: *socium habes neminem*, *Lig.* 11: *civis . . . nemo*

participle pres. concomitant, *Marc.* 22: *tam nihil . . . cogitans*

placement of, *Deiot.* 11: *consentientis*

profecto, 63

-que

adversative *Marc.* 20: *contraque*

consecutive *Marc.* 27: *constituas . . . fruare*

= "rather," *Marc.* 14: *semper*

force between independent predicates, *Marc.* 6: *easque detrahere*, *Marc.* 10: *nobilissimamque*

with resumptive pronoun, *Marc.* 30: *idque . . . usurpare*, *Lig.* 1: *idque*, *Lig.* 31: *ab eisdem*

quendam (see *Marc.* 13: *fato . . . funestoque*)

pronoun for person identifiable, but not named, *Marc.* 18: *quidam* (*Marc.* 2 above)

quidam

modifying adjectives, *Lig.* 5: *incredibilem*

modifying nouns, *Marc.* 2: *quasi quidam*

quidem

anticipating contrast, *Marc.* 3: *quidem*, *Marc.* 3: *ille*

attaches to pronouns without specifically qualifying them, *Marc.* 8: *quidem*

effectively subordinates first paratactic sentence to next, *Marc.* 28: *quae miretur . . . quae laudet*, *Deiot.* 18: *quidem*

expands proposition with strong endorsement, *Marc.* 12: *et . . . quidem*

following resumptive pronoun or *et*, creates framework for elaboration, *Marc.* 29: *et quidem*

introduces amplification of preceding, *Marc.* 11: *quae quidem*

prospective, *Marc.* 4: *quod quidem*

sums up, *Marc.* 6: *quae quidem*

quod: + subjunctive for alleged cause, see *Lig.* 25: *a quo queramini*

RELATIVE CLAUSES

conditional with indicative. *See* indicative

definitional, *Marc.* 12: *recte igitur*

follows its antecedent at distance with no anticipating element and is felt as practically circumstantial, *Marc.* 18: *qui . . . excitaverunt*

repetition of antecedent in, *Lig.* 2: *legatus . . . qua in legatione. See* "commentary style" in Glossary

semi-independent relative, a neutral sentence-connective, *Marc.* 3: *ex quo . . . gloria*

in ablative absolute, *Lig.* 3: *quo audito*

feature of Caesar's style, *Lig.* 2: *cui sic*

moves without pause for breath, *Marc.* 25: *cuius*, *Lig.* 8: *cuius . . . industriae*

substitutes for demonstrative + sentence connective, *Deiot.* 35: *quid abest* (*sed id*, 34: *qui = nam is*); see *Lig.* 12: *quae tamen*

strictly co-ordinating (= *et ea*) and almost parenthetical, *Marc.* 34: *quae mea*; see *Marc.* 13: *quorum et frequentiam*

two modifying a single antecedent, *Deiot.* 37: *eisque*

virtually parenthetical, *Lig.* 27: *ut . . . cetera*, *Lig.* 32: *non dubito*

repetition, *Marc.* 14: *semperque dolui*, *Lig.* 24: *prohibiti estis . . . et prohibiti*, *Lig.* 17: *vidimus . . . non vidimus*, *Lig.* 6: *vide . . . vide*, *Lig.* 14: *quam multi*, *Deiot.* 5: *dico . . . dico*, *Deiot.* 12: *ignosce*

of antecedent in relative clauses. *See* RELATIVE CLAUSES

of deictic, *Marc.* 27: *haec . . . hic . . . hoc*

with *inquam.* See *inquam*

of prepositions, *Marc.* 9: *gestis rebus, Lig.* 2: *inque*

of relative in parallel relative clauses, *Deiot.* 37: *eisque.* See *"anaphora"* in Glossary

for strong rhetorical balance, *Deiot.* 7: *pro multis saepe*

rerum: used as filler at *Marc.* 15, *Marc.* 22

result clauses: unanticipated by *ita, tam, sic* semi-independent, *Marc.* 9: *ut eos, Marc.* 17: *ut . . . debeat*

Roman Comedy, *Lig.* 30: *ignoscite, dic*

sane: intensive particle takes its color from context, *Deiot.* 30

sed tamen: a strong adversative, *Marc.* 11

SENTENCE FRAGMENTS

answers to vigorous question, *Lig.* 7: *apud quem*

etsi, Deiot. 26

in interrogation, *Marc.* 21: *de tuisne? . . . an . . . qui una tecum fuerunt?, Lig.* 4: *certe*

quamquam, Marc. 27

tametsi, Marc. 21

sole judge, xxxiii–xxxiv, *Lig.* 6: *populus Romanus, Lig.* 31: *in eorum studiis*

stasis theory, see *Lig.* 10: *genus hoc causae*

subjective mode: speaker insists on introduction of personal aspect to narrative or expository objectivity, e.g. *Marc.* 13: *credimus, Marc.* 23: *sentis, Lig.* 31: *vidi, video, Deiot.* 6: *meminisset,* at *Deiot.* 28: *itaque*

subordinating conjunctions: where semi-independent relative and the subordinating conjunction compete for first position, the former prevails, *Deiot.* 1: *quod . . . etsi*

suspense. *See* "anticipation" in Glossary

for affirmative after negative, *Lig.* 11: *non habet*

lost in bad style, *Deiot.* 21: *ibi enim*

by neutral participle, *Lig.* 3: *spectans . . . cupiens*

by structural postponement, *Marc.* 17: *alterius vero partis, Lig.* 31: *vidi, Deiot.* 11: *cum audiret*

vs. surprise in hyperbaton, *Marc.* 3: *fructum . . . maximum, Lig.* 30: *multas*

TRICOLON

of asyndetic imperative clauses, *Deiot.* 20: *repete . . . pone . . . recordare*

or complex bi-partite, *Marc.* 7: *non offert . . . . cedit . . . fatetur*

avoided for drama, *Marc.* 11: *cave*

complex third member, *Lig.* 6: *litteris monumentisque*

of deictic pronouns, *Marc.* 27: *haec . . . hic . . . hoc*

distinguished from bi-partite, *Marc.* 19: *tantus est enim, Marc.* 22: *nihil . . . cogitans*

of exclamatory clauses, *Marc.* 10: *quibus studiis*

ornamental, *Deiot.* 30: *quae trepidatio*

redundant, *Marc.* 22: *casus . . . eventus . . . fragilitatem*

of weighted genitive plurals introduced anaphorically, *Marc.* 5: *omnes nostrorum . . . posse conferri*

verbs

ellipsis of. *See* ellipsis

initial position of. *See* initial

mood, intrinsic vs. conventional, *Lig.* 10: *quod . . . quod . . . viderit, Deiot.* 17: *missus esset*

vero

dismissed in favor of strong affirmation, *Marc.* 3: *illi, Marc.* 4: *est*

vero, Marc. 6: *maximam vero partem*
vs. sed. See *sed tamen*
volume
  increasing in tetracolon, *Marc.* 1: *tantam ... tam ... tantam ... tam*
  in multisyllabic word, *Marc.* 10: *commemorabili.* See *Deiot.* 37: *omnium ... decreta*

Wackernagel's law: see *Marc.* 7: *se ... offert, Marc.* 10: *quibus tu, Marc.* 11: *hunc tu igitur, Deiot.* 22: *magnum*
WEIGHTED PHRASE, xv, *Marc.* 7: *se ... offert, Marc.* 9: *non ... quidem*
concessive, *Marc.* 7: *illa ipsa ... domina*
dative, *Marc.* 23: *omnia*
genitive plural, *Marc.* 4: *omnes nostrorum ... posse conferri*
honorific, *Lig.* 1: *praestanti ... ingenio*
with interlocking order, *Marc.* 32: *omnis fracta dissenio est*
objective clause determines colon, *Marc.* 25: *invitus*
prepositional phrase, *Deiot.* 1: *cogor*
vocative, *Deiot.* 6: *hanc ... causam*
WORD ORDER, xiii
  determined by polarities, *Marc.* 26: *admirationis ... gloriae*
  effective at, *Marc.* 16: *causas ... victoriae, Lig.* 36: *quam ... cum ... dederis, Deiot.* 18: *omnium ... in se gentium*; see *Marc.* 14: *prudens et sciens*
  hyperbaton of compound predicate, *Marc.* 13: *sumus ... compulsi*
  in hyperbaton for surprise, *Marc.* 3: *fructum ... maximum*
  interlocking, *Marc.* 2: *distracto, Marc.* 16: *quotiens ego eum et*

quanto cum dolore vidi and *non ... causae inter se sed victoriae comparandae, Marc.* 32: *... excubias et ... laterum oppositus et corporum, Marc.* 26: *illustris ... meritorum, Marc.* 29: *obscuratura ... sit, Marc.* 32: *omnis fracta dissensio est, Lig.* 7: *eam nullis spoliatam ornamentis.*
  intricate in conceit, *Marc.* 12: *detrahet ... adferet*
  normal reversed for antithesis, *Marc.* 9: *gestis rebus* (with *fictis*), *Marc.* 18: *civile bellum*
  ornate, *Deiot.* 19: *regio et animo et more*
  participle before noun, *Deiot.* 25: *secutum bellum*; see also *Deiot.* 1: *acta res, Lig.* 6: *suscepto bello*
  relative-antecedent in expository construction, *Marc.* 10: *quidquid ... id,* so *Marc.* 6: *quidquid ... gestum, Deiot.* 16: *quod ... facinus, Deiot.* 35: *et quem ... is*; see *Deiot.* 33: *quae ... ea, Marc.* 8: *haec qui faciat ... eum, Marc.* 15: *qui ... is*
  reversed, *Marc.* 2: *virum talem*
  with rhythms supports movement, *Marc.* 1: *tacitus praeterire ... possum*
  two adverbs follow verb, *Marc.* 12: *cotidie magis*
  unusual, *Marc.* 24: *multa perderet* et for emphasis, *Deiot.* 8: *ipsum te ut ea vix,* for *vix ut, Marc.* 6
  variety, *Marc.* 1: *tantam ... tam ... tantam ... tam*
word position
  reflects meaning, *Marc.* 6: *detrahere, Lig.* 3: *nullo ... negotio, Lig.* 4: *belli discidio, Lig.* 6: *voluntatis, Deiot.* 15: *domi tu suae, Deiot.* 18: *omnium ... in se gentium*